T0317685

Distant Tyranny

THE PRINCETON ECONOMIC HISTORY
OF THE WESTERN WORLD

Joel Mokyr, Series Editor

A list of titles in this series appears at the back of the book

Distant Tyranny

MARKETS, POWER, AND BACKWARDNESS
IN SPAIN, 1650–1800

Regina Grafe

PRINCETON UNIVERSITY PRESS ✦ PRINCETON AND OXFORD

Published by Princeton University Press, 41 William Street,
Princeton, New Jersey 08540

In the United Kingdom: Princeton University Press, 6 Oxford Street,
Woodstock, Oxfordshire OX20 1TW

press.princeton.edu

Library of Congress Cataloging-in-Publication Data

Grafe, Regina.
  Distant tyranny : markets, power, and backwardness in Spain, 1650–1800 /
Regina Grafe.
      p. cm.
  Includes bibliographical references and index.
  ISBN 978-0-691-14484-9 (hardcover)
  1. Spain—Commerce—History—17th century. 2. Spain—Commerce—History—
18th century. 3. Spain—Economic conditions.   I. Title.
  HF3685.G73 2012
  381.0946—dc23

                                                        2011037110

British Library Cataloging-in-Publication Data is available

This book has been composed in Sabon LT Std

Printed on acid-free paper. ∞

Printed in the United States of America

10 9 8 7 6 5 4 3 2 1

Contents

Acknowledgments

THIS BOOK WAS CONCEIVED AT THE LONDON SCHOOL OF ECONOMICS and in Oxford and, after research in Bilbao and Madrid, reluctantly brought to this world in Chicago, Princeton, and Buenos Aires. I wish to extend my warmest thanks to the staff at the Archivo Histórico Nacional and the Biblioteca Nacional in Madrid, as well as at the Archivo Foral de Bizkaia and the Archivo Provincial de Vizcaya in Bilbao. Librarians at the Institute for Advanced Study (IAS), Princeton, and Northwestern University found sources in some of the least obvious places and patiently borrowed books from around the world on my behalf. Without their unfailing support my research would have been impossible.

A Prize Fellowship at Nuffield College, Oxford, and a Mellon Fellowship at the IAS afforded me with the luxuries of time, scholarly resources, and—most important—debate and critique. I have benefited from the comments and criticisms of a great many people, who countered my doubts and my certainties in equal measure. Jordi Domenech, Avner Greif, Jonathan Israel, Michael Martoccio, Deirdre McCloskey, David Moon, Hamish Scott, Tuanhwee Sng, Joachim Voth, and Bartolomé Yun read the full manuscript or substantial chunks of it. They inspired me with new ideas and saved me from many embarrassments. Joel Mokyr plowed through more versions and learned more about *bacalao* than any person should. He placed his trust in this project and its author at a stage when the former was at best a crude sketch of unsure contours and the latter an unproven academic migrant. *Vorschußlorbeeren* are such a rarity that they will entail everlasting gratitude. In all, most of the merits of this book, such as they may be, are shared among many; all of the errors are exclusively mine.

An early version of some of the ideas developed here was presented as the first S.R. Epstein Memorial Lecture at the London School of Economics in 2008, and I am grateful to all those who helped create that lecture series and those who commented on my presentation. Other parts of the book benefited significantly from discussions with participants at a conference on mercantilism organized in 2009 by Carl Wennerlind and Philip Stern at Barnard and in seminars at Caltech, the IAS, and Northwestern. Oscar Gelderblom, Joost Jonkers, Leandro Prados de la Escosura, and Michael Kwass let me learn from as yet unpublished research. Enrique Llopis Agelán and his research group and Pedro María Legarreta Iragorri shared that most precious commodity of the economic historian, unpublished data, with me. I am deeply in their debt and I can only hope they feel that I made good use of their contribution. I also thank Xavier Lamikiz for making me aware of some of these unpublished sources. Without the enormous generosity of my Spanish colleagues, work would have been incomparably harder and life much duller.

Chieko Maene of Northwestern did much of the mapping while graciously pretending that she was in fact teaching me how to do it. In the end, I am indebted to her for both the maps and teaching me how to use GIS software. Eva Zehelein and Mareike Schomerus proofread chapters on such short notice that it is a miracle friendship survived. Ed Campos wielded the ax in equal measure on the excesses of my German subordinate clauses, a Spanish love for adjectives, and a few acquired, typically British errors of grammar, all of it with admirable speed, skill, and patience. When the going got rough friends and colleagues in Argentina, Germany, Norway, Spain, the United Kingdom, and the United States kept me going. They know who they are and how much I owe them. Behind everything, however, stood Ale, always. The better half of my research, my thinking about the workings of early modern Spain, and my writing has evolved out of hers and ours. She has struggled through every sentence with me and made sure common sense prevailed over stubbornness most of the time. And whenever it did not, she helped pick up the pieces.

Throughout the writing one absence has been impossible to fill. This book and I owe a lot to Larry (S.R.) Epstein, and it would have been a smarter and better book had he been able to put me through my paces. His incomparably incisive questions would linger on in my mind for weeks until one fine day their full implications would dawn on me. Grudgingly, I would then accept that an argument had to be rewritten, a research question had to be asked in an entirely different way. I miss that. I would like to think that this book carries in it just a little bit of his belief in academic endeavor, his dedication to economic history, and whatever might have rubbed off from his exceptional mind and humanity.

Preface

"SPAIN IS DIFFERENT." Many Spaniards and quite a few non-Spaniards over the age of forty remember this slogan. It appeared on brochures and posters distributed by the Franco regime to entice tourists to spend their valuable hard currency on Spain's beautiful beaches. They came in the millions. The advertising campaign was so successful because it basically affirmed what in the 1960s Spaniards and non-Spaniards alike thought of as an obvious truth: Spain was not really a European country at all.[1] When in 1975 at the start of the transition to democracy the new Spanish king Juan Carlos I declared that the "The idea of Europe would be incomplete without reference to the presence of the Spaniard . . . and we Spaniards are Europeans," it was for his audience a bold statement of ambition rather than an obvious fact.[2]

This book is an attempt to return the history of Spain in the long eighteenth century to where I think it belongs: at the very heart of European history. Its objective is twofold: first, to explain the painful slowness and regional diversity in the development of Spain toward a nation-state and toward a domestically integrated economy within a European context; and second, to explore what the history of nation-state building and market-building in Spain can teach us about our established models of European states and markets. The argument is simple. If we stop thinking about Spain as somehow outside the European norm, we can first of all understand Spain better. Second we can revisit whether there was a European norm, and if so, what kind of norm historians should consider more generally.

The main focus of this book is the historical political economy of Spain. At the core of European political-economic development in the seventeenth to nineteenth centuries are the twin processes of the emergence of the nation-state and the creation of nationally unified markets. The chapters that follow offer a revisionist view of how these processes proceeded in Spain. They are underpinned by an approach that integrates social and political history into the economic analysis in order to understand the complexities of historical development more fully. Methodologically the research thus consciously straddles the boundaries of academic disciplines in the social sciences and the humanities.

At the same time, this interdisciplinary examination of Spanish history challenges the currently dominant model world within which political economy and historical sociology analyze nation-state building and market integration in general. Some of the fundamental assumptions of our existing models are patently inapplicable to Spain. This book hence also offers an

[1] Wattley Ames, *Spain Is Different.*
[2] Cited in Preston and Smyth, *Spain, the EEC and NATO*, 24. Cf. Hontanilla, "Images," 136.

alternative model of European state and market building that is constructed from the bottom up.

The underlying method pursued is therefore comparative, even if this book is primarily about Spain. It is written in the perhaps old-fashioned conviction that careful comparison across shared interpretive categories is still one of the most exciting and enlightening ways to go about history writing. But it insists that this process ought to be a two-way street: As useful as the European models of state- and market-building are in understanding these key processes in Spain, we will also see that the Spanish case challenges the European models in significant ways. Thus this book should be of interest not only to economic historians of Spain and Europe as well as those interested in political economy but also to social and political historians of early modern Europe.

The notion of Spanish distinctiveness runs deep in the historiography. Some historical subfields, especially cultural and social history, have done much in recent years to question Spanish exceptionalism while others, notably economic history, have found it harder to overcome this. Reflecting on perceptions of Spanish identity, the new social and cultural history goes a long way to explain the peculiar longevity of ideas of Spain as a European "other." Erasmus of Rotterdam, that hero of European humanism, famously declined to accept invitations to travel to Spain because in his view it was a country "without Christians."[3] Like other northern Europeans of the sixteenth century, he thought Spain suspect because of its long Jewish and Muslim history. In the minds of northern European contemporaries, seven centuries of Christian, Jewish, Muslim *convivencia* meant Iberians could be halfway reliably Christians at best. This theme could, and was, exploited far beyond the religious realm. In the propaganda wars of the sixteenth century that pitted the Dutch against Spain, the Count of Orange's calling the Duke of Alba a "Moorish tiger-beast" helped establish the association of Spain with "oriental cruelty" and otherness.[4]

It is not a little ironic, therefore, that the same place considered too ethnically and religiously heterogeneous to be civilized and European in the sixteenth and seventeenth centuries was by the eighteenth century thought to be uncivilized and un-European because it failed to adapt to the new enlightened ideas of tolerance of heterogeneity. Now Catholic fanaticism was constructed as a new means of establishing that Spain was different. The light bearers of the French Enlightenment quipped that "Spain is a country, with which we are no better acquainted than with the most savage parts of Africa, and which does not deserve the trouble of being known."[5] In Europeans' view, Spain was now home to the *auto de fe* and censorship, a country opposed

---

[3] Fuchs, *Exotic Nation*, 116–20.
[4] Ibid.
[5] Voltaire, *Oeuvres complètes*, 1:390–91, cited in de Salvio, "Voltaire and Spain." See also Hontanilla, "Images," 127.

to new science, technology, and the freedom of the individual. Spaniards were lazy, oppressed, and backward.[6] In a nutshell, Spain stood for obscurantism and against the Enlightenment. There was really no point in trying to understand it.

In the realm of economic history the corresponding notion that stuck was that of *backwardness*. It is a contested term in Spanish historiography, and its inclusion in the title of this book warrants comment. The perception that Spain, at least from the eighteenth century onward and possibly earlier, was backward in social, political, cultural, and intellectual terms has provoked a counterreaction among historians of Spain who have questioned the comparator: backward compared to what or to whom?[7] There is little doubt that much of the discussion of Spanish history has suffered from a fundamental flaw that collapsed a questionable notion of Spanish difference into an even more problematic one of Spanish backwardness. Indeed, I will argue in this book that most of our political economy and historical sociology models of European nation-state and market-making resorted to declaring Spain the odd one out precisely because their assumptions of near linear development across time are mistaken. Simplistic modernization paradigms, which assume that European nations emerged out of a number of intellectual, social, and political changes that each country had to complete in checklist fashion, are unhelpful.

At the same time, we should be careful not to let a rejection of such deterministic narratives tempt us into rejecting comparison altogether, as social and cultural historians have tended to do. From the economic history perspective, it is paramount to do away with the notion of a stagnant, entirely rural, extractive, old regime political economy in Spain and I will try my best to help in this task. There was "growth in a traditional society," as Phil Hoffman's wonderful book on ancien régime France has shown; and Spain's political economy was neither particularly extractive nor totally stagnant.[8] Yet when all is told and counted, we will see that growth in Spain over the seventeenth to early nineteenth centuries was slow, haphazard, regionally diverse, and intermittent by European standards. At the end of the period under consideration here, Spain appeared economically backward because economic transformations had occurred faster elsewhere in Europe. Doing away with the term "backwardness" just means taking away the mirror that reflects what Spaniards at the time knew only too well: they lived in a place where local food shortages still occasionally occurred, where markets were poorly integrated, where new consumer goods penetrated at a turtle's pace, and where finding work might mean long days on poor roads.

Integrating Spanish early modern history into the narrative of the genesis of the western European nation-states is a serious challenge. Spain does not fit into most of the stylized facts we teach our students about how European

---

[6] Kagan, "Prescott's Paradigm"; MacKay, *Myth and Reality*.

[7] Burguera and Schmidt-Nowara, "Backwardness and Its Discontents."

[8] Hoffman, *Growth in a Traditional Society*.

nation-states came into being. To begin with, there were supposedly two kinds of European countries: the early nation-states, such as England, France, and Spain, and the nineteenth-century latecomers, like Italy and Germany. Spain is counted among the former because its origins go back to the unification of Castile and Aragon in the late fifteenth century. Yet by the early nineteenth century Spain did not look anything like France or England and rather a lot like Germany or Italy in terms of its economic, social, linguistic, cultural, or political integration—or the lack thereof.

Historical sociologists, social historians, and economic historians generally argue that the consolidation of European nation-states and the creation of integrated "domestic" markets were the inevitable results of fiscal-military competition in Europe. In this view, most strongly associated with the work of Charles Tilly, the inescapable logic of the fiscal-military arms race required states to increase their administrative capability and overcome the shared sovereignties of late medieval and early modern polities.[9] From this process emerged the nation-state with a common territory, a people, and a unified source of state power; and it slowly but surely turned people with diverse linguistic, cultural, and social backgrounds into citizens of a nation-state. However, in Spain on the whole it did not, in spite of the fact that the constituent reigns had been unified under one crown so early and that it remained engaged in military competition in Europe, the Americas, and Asia.

Instinctively, social science–based historians have tended to look at this Spanish *Sonderweg* in the way in which model-based disciplines are prone to react: in the face of an incompatibility between models of the genesis of the nation-state and Spanish history, they have opted for arguing that there was something wrong with Spain. Nation-states were meant to be successful, and Spain was not; this makes for an uncomfortable case. In much of the comparative historiography on pre-twentieth-century nationalism Spain is not even mentioned; rare index entries on "Spain" are usually followed by "see Basques," "see Catalans," or "see Spanish America" with apparently no irony intended.[10]

Thus both economic and political historians of the creation of the nation-state struggle equally to account for Spain's double "failure": it failed as an emerging nation-state, and it failed to conform to the available model.[11] The divergence is explained by a number of factors alternatively or as a combination thereof. The usual cast include Spain's Moorish heritage, its status as an imperial power, mercantilist follies, religious intolerance, an

[9] Tilly, *Coercion*.

[10] See, e.g., Gellner, *Nations and Nationalism*; Anderson, *Imagined Communities*; and Greenfeld, *Nationalism*. Hobsbawm comments on the late arrival in 1884/1925 of the word *nación* in its modern meaning in the standard Spanish dictionary but explains that away by arguing that this was not unusual since "nineteenth-century Spain was not exactly in the vanguard of ideological progress." Hobsbawm, *Nations and Nationalism*, 15–17.

[11] See, e.g., Anderson, *Lineages*, chapter 3; Ertman, *Leviathan*, chapters 2 and 3; Mann, *Sources I*, chapters 13–15; and Glete, *War and the State*, chapter 3.

anti-Enlightenment elite, and its military overstretch as a result of a money illusion caused by American silver. Others interpret Spain as a semi-exploited European economic periphery with a bourgeoisie engaged in "Braudelian" treason, that is, a rentier class that shunned productive investment thereby stifling economic and social development.[12] The challenge of making sense of Spanish history in the standard framework built around such concepts as "absolutism," "mercantilism," and "bourgeoisie" can be illustrated by taking a look at one recent attempt:

> Just as we have implied the existence of a deformed or *pseudo* mercantilism [in Spain] through the agency of a dependent *pseudo*-bourgeoisie, we posit a *pseudo* absolutism–a barely concealed consensus of aristocratic, bureaucratic, and merchant elites sanctioned by the ecclesiastical establishment.[13]

In Spain nothing was what it was supposed to be, we are told. This convoluted assessment is neither unusual nor entirely nonsensical. However, it suffers the consequences of trying to press the Spanish case into a set of ill-suited theoretical concepts and heuristic devices. There is an uncanny feeling that if model and history diverge, history must have been wrong. Does it not seem more reasonable to conclude that something is wrong with the way the structure of governance in Spain has been traditionally modeled? At present, Spain remains essentially unreconciled with sociological and political economy models of European state-building, not because "Spain is different," as Franco's tourism advertisers claimed, but because the current models desperately need revision. Indeed, Spain is an unwelcome, but useful, spanner in the works of explaining how European states emerged and became relatively strong autonomous organizations.

Equipped with plenty of theory, political, social, and cultural historians have in the meantime chipped away at the sorts of assumptions about European state-building that were once accepted. Gone are absolute Absolutists that controlled the mercantilist economy, punished their subjects for social and religious "crimes," and unified their territories through linguistic and religious impositions and service in the standing army for king and country rather than for a mercenary's pay. Gone is also the notion that the genesis of modern society was a class struggle that led to modern capitalist nations. Instead, it is being argued that nation-states were a construct of the historical imagination and hence subject to reinterpretation. Consequentially, cultural historians affirm that there was no common path toward the nation-state, just an idiosyncratic combination of outcomes largely due to contingent developments that were reconstructed in the public consciousness to reflect a nineteenth-century ideal of state and society.

The rich account that this literature has given us has unfortunately also refused to provide an alternative model of state formation or market-making.

---

[12] Braudel, *The Mediterranean*, 729.
[13] Stein and Stein, *Silver*, 103. Emphasis added.

If there was no clear path toward fiscal-military competition along the lines suggested by Charles Tilly or Eric Jones, why did the European system of warring medieval political units continue to develop into competing, but more unified, nation-states in the way it did?[14] Why did it not become an extended empire like China or the Ottoman Empire, or a system of states with much weaker territoriality as was the case in much of Africa? Indeed, the important methodological turn in history has arguably been better at demolishing the existing edifice than rebuilding one with which to replace the canon of the social science–oriented historiography. There is now a denser narrative available to qualify the development of society as well as religious and linguistic expression in many would-be European nation-states. But we still need to explain why, by the nineteenth century, European political constructs had evolved into administratively much more complex structures that gave more autonomy to the state and why this process occurred at a very different pace across Europe and along different paths. After all, what was understood as the European nation-state became the model of sociopolitical organization that has dominated human history ever since and has proven apt at surviving into an age of globalization.

The immodest challenge I have set out for this book is to offer an analysis that integrates the study of market integration in all of its quantitative and qualitative dimensions with one of the political economy that takes as its point of departure an equally careful analysis of the fundamental structures of Spanish governance. We need to replace the dominant normative historical economics model of the political economy of the Spanish monarchy in the early modern period. In spite of a large historical literature that has shown that Spain surely was not on a path to "orderly despotism" in the sixteenth to nineteenth centuries as North and Thomas once claimed, the myth of the predatory early modern Spanish state still dominates in the assessment of comparative European development.[15] The almost exclusive focus on states as predators that stifle growth through a diversion of individual incentives toward rent-seeking rather than productive investment does not fit the political economy of early modern Spain.

At the same time, we currently do not have a convincing narrative of the pattern of market integration in Spain either. Existing quantitative studies have done a lot to provide some benchmarks of various degrees of integration. Historians have suggested that an early integration of central Castile was followed by the disintegration of the internal market in the seventeenth century and a slow resurgence led by the coastal regions in the eighteenth. However, the regional differences are puzzling and astonishingly large and there are methodological problems in trying to explain them. The classic method in studying market integration uses grain price differentials and movements. Yet when markets are very poorly integrated as a consequence of

---

[14] Tilly, *The Formation of National States*; Jones, *Growth Recurring*; Jones, *The European Miracle*; Tilly, *Coercion*.

[15] North and Thomas, *Rise of the Western World*, 89.

political intervention and the "moral economy" of the old regime that placed a high priority on supplying town populations with bread, these quantitative analyses of market integration via wheat prices face serious identification problems. We will see, for example, that the narrative of the breaking apart of the internal market in Spain in the seventeenth century is just one chapter in a larger declension story that sees the roots of the problem in an interventionist powerful state. The interpretation of the economic geography of Spanish market integration thus followed the narrative of political economy—a narrative that is deeply flawed.

This book will revisit the link between market integration and the creation of the European nation-state from an entirely different vantage point. In some ways it returns to the question that set off new institutional economics once upon a time: Why did some European states become more autonomous, stronger units much earlier than others, and in which way was this driving, or driven by, the increasing integration of domestic markets? The empirical path chosen will be to try to explain why both processes were so slow and intermittent in Spain. My view looks from the European periphery toward the center. The quantitative and qualitative analysis of market integration relies on commodity prices, following an established literature in economic history. However, it diverges in one crucial aspect: the commodity in question. In order to overcome some of the problems associated with historical grain prices in Spain, this book relies throughout on an original dataset for one of the new transatlantic commodities turned staple food in the seventeenth century: dried and salted codfish, also known as *bacalao*.

In his 2000 book entitled *Freedom and Growth,* Epstein reminds economic historians that they ought to pay more attention to the jurisdictional fragmentation that characterized early modern European monarchies.[16] In corporate ancien régime societies sovereignty was fragmented and overlapping. The "freedoms" (Sp: *fueros*) of estates, guilds, towns, territories, or the Church were special rights that entitled them to make decisions about taxes, economic regulations, currencies, weights and measures, and forms of social and political organization. European monarchies typically struggled with the effects of fragmented authority, not with excessive power at the center.

Corporate "freedoms" often also implied separate *foral* jurisdiction, at least at lower levels of the court system.[17] Economic theory predicts that as a consequence contract enforcement would have been poor and property rights endangered. Most economic historians have thus focused on potential infringements of private property rights in trying to trace the sources of slow market development in Spain and other European monarchies.[18] Special

---

[16] Epstein, *Freedom and Growth.*

[17] There is no translation for the adjective use of *foral* institutions, that is, institutions that legally emanated from the freedoms (*fueros*) of towns, territories, estates, or corporations. Throughout the text I will therefore use the Spanish term *foral*.

[18] In Spain this goes back to Hamilton, "Spanish Mercantilism"; Klein, *The Mesta*; and Smith, *Spanish Guild Merchant.* See also Acemoglu, Johnson, and Robinson, "The Colonial Origins"; Hoffman and Norberg, *Fiscal Crises*; and Rosenthal, "Political Economy."

rights supposedly resulted in a severe distortion of economic incentives: the private rate of return moved further and further away from the social rate of return and the expansion of functioning private markets was hindered. In Elliott's famous phrase, the "nature of the economic system [in seventeenth-century Spain] was such that one became a student or a monk, a beggar or a bureaucrat. There was nothing else to be."[19]

However, while Spaniards like all Europeans in the society of orders of the old regime were not equal before the law, they did have remarkably equal access to the law and famously used it incessantly. I will argue that Spaniards of all walks of life were relatively well represented, and they defended their rights vigorously and quite successfully. Historians have shown for instance that appellate courts often upheld the rights of socioeconomically weak claimants against their social betters.[20] The argument developed here is precisely that hierarchies of power were extremely flat in Spain, necessitating constant processes of renegotiation of rights. It was not the infringement of property rights that was the problem in Spain. Rather, fragmented jurisdiction created sharply different rights and duties along territorial lines with regard to fiscal contributions, which in turn hindered market integration. Spain solved the problem of representation and legitimacy of rule quite successfully. But in the process it created serious limits to economic growth.

Strong local and territorial representation stymied market integration in two ways. Local control over revenue and expenditure imposed massive transaction costs on economic activity. At the same time, multiple and competing entities endowed with sovereign rights struggled to provide important public goods from infrastructure to less cumbersome economic regulation. Both of these effects were essentially coordination failures. The political powers failed in their important role as agents of integration. This revisionist interpretation of the origins of poor market integration and slow nation-state building in Spain resets our model of the relation between state and market. It suggests that economists and economic historians should take the question of how states became independent actors in the first place much more seriously. In doing so, it clears the way for a new, potentially rewarding reinterpretation of the twin developments of integrated "national" markets and European nation-states freed from the ideological, rather than empirical, ex-ante assumption of a fully antagonistic relationship between markets and states.

While the empirical part of this book draws most strongly on a set of price data for the *bacalao* market, the book's purpose is to embed this case study in the larger context of the Spanish and European political economy of the early modern period. So, like all history writing, this book stands on the shoulders of giants, and it acknowledges the inspiration and insights gained from recent historical political economy and historical sociology even where it tries to redress what it sees as some important shortcomings. But this study

---

[19] Elliott, "Decline of Spain."
[20] Cf. Kagan, *Law Suits and Litigants*, and Windler, *Lokale Eliten*.

also stands on a very large number of less well-known but sturdy shoulders. The attempt to synthesize and understand the political economy of taxation and the pattern of market integration in Spain in all its complexity would have been impossible without an astonishing number of local, regional, and some excellent "national" studies of these issues undertaken in Spain in the past thirty years. They have been an invaluable inspiration and source of data for the following analysis, even if some (perhaps many) of the authors of these studies might not agree with my conclusions.

Distant Tyranny

Chapter 1 _____

Markets and States

HISTORIANS OF EARLY MODERN EUROPE have to explain at least two exceedingly far-reaching phenomena. The first one turned people who had thought
about themselves as the citizens of a town or the subjects of an estate or
village—be it seigneurial or royal—slowly but surely into subjects and
eventually citizens of a nation-state. The second one, less often appreciated
but equally important, was that Europeans' livelihoods became subject to
changes in markets that were a long way out of their local or regional reach.
By the eighteenth century almost all people in Europe, even in relatively
remote areas, had become subject to the risks and opportunities of "national"
markets, "international" competition, and intercontinental trade.[1] These twin
developments and the cultural and social transformations they embodied are
the theme of national historiographies under such titles as "The Making of
Modern Country X," be it France, England, or even the more controversial
cases of Germany or Italy. It is a sign of the difficulties in accounting for these
twin processes in Spain that there is no "The Making of Modern Spain" to
the best of my knowledge.

The nation-state with a domestic, nationwide market has proven surprisingly long-lived even in today's global age. However, historiographical
scholarship has reached a consensus that this national focus has its limitations and pitfalls; this book is written in that spirit. Any sense of the national
complemented rather than substituted for local and regional allegiances,
while at the same time it was shaped by new global interactions.[2] The outlook
on life of fishermen in a Basque village remained shaped by local factors,
even if conflicts between the Spanish Crown and European competitors in
far-flung Atlantic waters might threaten their livelihood. Language, rituals,
religiosity, and traditions continued to be locally determined in most places.
This is probably truer in Spain than elsewhere in western Europe. Yet there
is a danger of getting lost in the marvelous idiosyncrasies of the local and
losing sight of the fundamental changes that were taking place at the same

---

[1] Debates about formal attempts to date the onset of the age of globalization are hardly
of any importance in this context. See Osterhammel, *Geschichte der Globalisierung* versus
O'Rourke and Williamson, "Once More." The mechanistic search for a "breaking point"
somewhere in the early modern period from which onward global rather than local, national,
or European markets existed seems largely ahistorical given that intercontinental contact
developed in typical slow and piecemeal fashion.

[2] For a fascinating study of this process on the Spanish-French borders, see Sahlins,
Boundaries.

time. By the early nineteenth century the European nation-state was a well-articulated bureaucratized apparatus that was more powerful than all of its predecessors. It was also governing over a territory that was considerably more economically integrated in the interior and often more integrated on the outside with neighboring countries, colonial offshoots, and faraway consumers and producers.[3]

Economic development was largely "Smithian" in the premodern era: it depended on the process of market expansion and deepening so aptly described by Adam Smith in the late eighteenth century.[4] This is not to downplay the importance of the contribution of intellectual developments, as well as science and technology. Yet even into the early phases of the Industrial Revolution economic growth derived predominantly from the benefits of increased division of labor made feasible through specialization and exchange.[5] Exchange fostered specialization; specialization improved skills; skills underpinned innovation.[6] Innovation led to new and cheaper consumer goods; new and cheaper consumer goods were an incentive to increase income; increased income raised demand; demand fostered further exchange.[7] The process is almost trivial and could be declined up and down in slightly altered sequences. Nonetheless, it was remarkably powerful. Integrated markets were no guarantee for economic growth. But without them, technological change, human capital improvements, and other potential sources of productivity gains were less likely to occur, and where they did happen, their impact on economic growth was seriously circumscribed.

Without integrated markets the fiscal base of the state was hard to establish and expand, too. Thus the relationship between emerging states and integrating markets worked both ways. For its survival and military protection the modernizing state depended increasingly on its subjects' economic well-being and its own ability to tax. The rise of the nation-state and the rise of nationally integrated markets was a dual but simultaneous process. It has attracted a lot of attention from various quarters including historical economics, sociology, and the study of nationalism, identity, language, and social habitus.

This chapter, however, concentrates on the dominant political economy models that try to explain the relation between markets and states in Europe's early modern economies. Placed into the context of Spanish history, some of the main assumptions of the model turn out to be highly problematic

---

[3] The creation of nation-states had, however, two contradictory economic effects on international integration. On the one hand, larger domestic markets often gave an impetus for international integration. On the other hand, increased consolidation of the nation-state increased border effects. See, for example, Engel and Rogers, "How Wide Is the Border?"

[4] Smith, *Wealth of Nations.*

[5] Epstein, *Freedom and Growth.*

[6] North and Thomas, *Rise of the Western World*, 93.

[7] For the role of demand in Europe's economics development, see de Vries, *The Industrious Revolution.*

and in urgent need of revision. A lopsided focus on the state as predator has distracted economists and economic historians from trying to understand better how states became jurisdictionally and economically integrated units in the first place. The void has been filled by a number of poorly historicized references to concepts borrowed from historians and historical sociologists such as "absolutism" and "patrimonialism." These concepts were supposed to delineate the development of European states from fragmented sovereignty to unified nation-states. Thus a particular kind of modernization theory was applied that could conveniently latch onto the idea of the "early modern period" as an era in which political and economic institution-building passed through a number of transformations that paved the way from a "premodern" to a "modern" world. Polities that failed to take the prescribed route hence became "failed" states. These terms, whether premodern or modern or failed, are all highly suggestive, but they are also per se perfectly empty of meaning.

Political Economy: What Sort of State Is Needed for Growth?

Historical political economy approaches the relationship between states and markets from a normative perspective by asking what kind of state and governance was conducive to the growth of private markets. Since the 1970s, institutional economics (often referred to as "new institutional economics," or NIE) has integrated the role of the state explicitly into neoclassical economics and has radically altered the way economists think about the state. Unlike Marxist or neo-Marxist theories, institutional economics does not see the state as an embodiment of power and class relations, and thus as the origin of markets. Instead NIE holds that markets largely (though not exclusively) emerge spontaneously out of Adam Smith's famous "propensity to truck and barter and exchange."[8] Exchanges of goods in the market are beneficial but not costless. They are subject to transaction costs associated with getting goods to and from the market, information gathering, protection against cheating, changing currencies or measures, and a whole litany of other costs.[9]

From the NIE point of view, economic growth depends on low transaction costs or, put another way, on efficient economic organization. In 1973 North and Thomas expressed in one succinct sentence what has become a credo for economists ever since: "Efficient economic organization entails the establishment of institutional arrangements and property rights that create an incentive to channel individual economic effort into activities that bring

---

[8] See Polanyi, *The Great Transformation* as opposed to North, "Markets and Other Allocative Systems."

[9] The importance of transaction costs was first discussed by Ronald Coase, who asked why firms used internally non-market allocation mechanisms. See his "Nature of the Firm."

the private rate of return close to the social rate of return."[10] Put simply, Adam Smith's invisible hand only develops to its full potential if institutions support secure property rights.[11] Greif more recently reformulated the link between institutions and markets as the "fundamental problem of exchange": for transactions to occur and the market to function, those involved need to commit ex ante and comply ex post. In plain English: economic agents need to trust their business partners before making a deal and be forced if necessary to fulfill their side of the bargain by some higher authority after they have agreed on a transaction.[12]

In many cases private order institutions can provide trust and enforcement based on common religious or ethnic backgrounds, or contractual agreements among their members.[13] Merchant guilds, like the Castilian, Basque, and Catalan *consulados*, were a case in point. Through social pressure and sometimes commercial tribunals, they kept members on the straight and narrow.[14] Yet the single most important "third party enforcers" were, and are, political rulers, be they town councils or kings.[15] The problem is that from a political economy point of view the role of power and the ruler is highly ambiguous. As the protector of individuals' lives and property, the ruler needs to be strong and have a monopoly of violence.[16] But as a strong actor with a monopoly of violence the state itself can become a predator that endangers personal property and safety.[17] Thus for states to be conducive to growth they need to protect subjects' or citizens' private property rights from threats at the hand of their fellow subjects or citizens without in turn becoming a threat to those very same property rights.

The specter of the predatory state has led historical political economy to produce an extraordinarily large corpus of research on the question of how to "tame" the state in its role as a potential threat to property rights. By contrast, the discipline has spent much less time trying to understand how states became autonomous, powerful actors that were able to extend protection in the first place. It has done so at its peril. What had begun as the important

[10] North and Thomas, *Rise of the Western World*, 1.

[11] North's view on this issue is not accepted by everyone. See, e.g., Grossman, "The Creation of Effective Property Rights."

[12] Greif, "Fundamental Problem," 254.

[13] The definition of "institution" is a vexed issue in this literature. For the purpose of this debate I will define them as socially determined conditional incentives and consequences to actions. Since they are parametrically given to every individual they create the structure of incentives in a given society. For a formal definition, see Aoki, *Toward a Comparative Institutional Analysis*, 26.

[14] For a discussion, see Gelderblom and Grafe, "Merchant Guilds."

[15] North and Thomas, *Rise of the Western World*. North initially distinguished between "institutions," essentially sets of social norms, and "organizations" such as the state but later relaxed that distinction.

[16] This part of Weberian thinking about the state is largely unquestioned. Weber, *Wirtschaft und Gesellschaft*.

[17] Greif, *The Path to the Modern Economy*, 91.

realization that markets needed states quickly became a study of how the state as the enemy of the market could be constrained.[18]

The Early Modern State as a Predator

Economists and economic historians have sidelined the question of state-building by referring to a set of assumptions derived from historical sociology that provide a parsimonious and supposedly uncorrelated, but problematic, prime mover for European state-building. The argument is that military competition between European rulers created a binding exogenous constraint on fiscal decision making in the early modern period. A "military revolution" necessitated the creation of a "fiscal-military state."[19] Competition between rulers for territory and subjects was undoubtedly a central feature of European political development in the Middle Ages. When exogenous changes to military technology, especially firearms and artillery, began to shift the advantage from defense to offense, this in turn necessitated large new investments in urban defense and other costly strategic changes.[20]

The increased size of European armies in the early modern period bears witness to some of these changes. Castile had 20,000 soldiers under arms in 1470; the "Spanish" army had 150,000 in 1550, 200,000 in 1590, and 300,000 in the 1630s at its peak.[21] Large numbers of mercenaries had to be paid with some regularity lest they join the enemy. Alternatively soldiers might choose to pay themselves and embark on looting campaigns that civilian populations in Italy, the Germanies, and the Netherlands came to fear more than anything else.[22] While Habsburg Spain built up the largest infantry seen in Europe since the Roman Empire, the Netherlands and Britain began to expand professionalized navies, substituting the earlier strategy of impressing merchant vessels into service.[23]

---

[18] Empirically it is not obvious at all that the fear of the predatory state was the single most important driving force of institutional development as is often assumed. For an attempt to place this fear in the context of several other possible factors, see Gelderblom and Grafe, "Merchant Guilds."

[19] See, e.g., Bonney, *The Rise of the Fiscal State*; Brewer, *Sinews of Power*; Braddick, *The Nerves of the State*; Braddick, *State Formation*; Tilly, *Coercion*; and Crouzet, *La guerre économique*. For a recent very perceptive account of the term's evolution, see Torres Sánchez, "Triumph," 14–21, and Storrs, *The Fiscal Military State*.

[20] Parker stresses in particular the *trace italienne,* an extremely costly structure for urban defense that converted military conflicts even more from open-field battles into siege warfare. Parker, *Military Revolution.*

[21] Yun Casalilla, *Marte Contra Minerva*, 44.

[22] The Spanish Habsburgs repeatedly suffered the political backlash from such mutinies, for instance, after Carlos V's German protestant troops sacked Rome in 1527 or Philipp II's *tercios* looted Antwerp in 1576.

[23] The Spanish Armada of 1588 was still largely comprised of impressed merchant vessels, but Spain also changed policy soon thereafter. Grafe, "Spanish Shipping"; Rodríguez-Salgado, "The Spanish Story."

Political economists have thus argued that a change in military technology and strategy and the impetus it gave to European state formation created an inescapable constraint on early modern rulers. Since military activity is subject to indivisibilities—larger armies are cheaper per capita—the optimum size of the state increased, and this fostered a territorial consolidation process.[24] In this phase of "mergers and acquisitions," roughly from the mid-fifteenth to the early nineteenth century, mere survival as a minor state was not an option most of the time.[25] Instead, states had to consolidate into larger units with larger fiscal potential to survive. Size alone, however, was no guarantee of success. The external constraint imposed by military contest also implied that rulers in any given polity had to push hard for fiscal resources.[26] That required a strong state. The ultimate winner of this contest was England, but there were second prizes. France, Sweden, Denmark, Spain, the Netherlands, and a number of smaller territories managed to hang on to independent statehood, something lost by most small territories, principalities, and city-states.

Military competition and the need for a strong state that it created, however, also meant that the state had a strong incentive to increase its revenue through predation.[27] Rulers were of course aware that expropriating their subjects and lenders through taxes or debt defaults was damaging to their reputation as borrowers in the longer run. But, faced with a threat to the survival of their rule, any concern about the future was supposedly heavily discounted.[28] States could thus become in Olson's famous phrase "stationary bandits."[29] Unless one argues that long-term economic development is ultimately the outcome of a cruel geographical lottery that favored some regions and limited others, institutions, chief among them the state, are the most likely source of differential growth paths across countries.[30] Having accepted (often implicitly) the supposedly overwhelming pressure for revenue, the question became how polities could maximize revenue while minimizing the threat to property rights domestically. With this the focus immediately shifted to domestic constraints on rulers' revenue raising and rules for spending.

---

[24] Bean, "War"; Parker, *Military Revolution*; Roberts, *The Military Revolution*.

[25] Mann, *Sources I*, 490ff.

[26] Brewer, *Sinews of Power*; O'Brien and Hunt, "Rise."

[27] It should be noted that some have argued that military campaigns sometimes could feed "off the land." Also, in some cases war stimulated taxable economic activity. For a case study of Dutch frontier towns, see Vermeesch, *Oorlog*.

[28] North and Weingast, "Constitutions and Commitment," 807.

[29] For the concept of the "stationary versus roving bandit" and an attempt to show formally that an autocrat will extract higher rents than will a majority coalition, see McGuire and Olson, "Economics of Autocracy," especially 93–96.

[30] Geography might have an impact through a variety of channels, such as resource endowments, climatic conditions, or disease environment. See, e.g., Easterly and Levine, "Tropics"; Diamond, *Guns, Germs and Steel*; and Engerman and Sokoloff, "Colonialism, Inequality, and Long-Run Path." On the burden imposed by disaster control and welfare, see Jones, *Growth Recurring*, 133–34, 144, and passim.

Political economy has argued that the existence or absence of "parliamentary representation," a political regime that tied rulers' decisions to the approval of a larger group of subjects or citizens, was the single most important variable in explaining long-term economic performance. The distinction between rulers, kings, princes, or modern autocrats who were not constitutionally constrained and those who were became the central causal element believed to explain the growth potential of early modern states.[31] In a seminal 1989 article, North and Weingast argued that the way in which the English Glorious Revolution improved the state's ability to finance itself demonstrated empirically the virtuous effects of such representation. Before the Civil War, Parliament's refusal to vote taxes for the Tudor monarchy had limited the Crown's foreign policy. Its credit was poor, and sovereign interest rates were high. Exactions, defaults, and forced loans provided a stopgap, but by expropriating its subjects and lenders, the Crown ruined its reputation among potential financiers even further.[32] By contrast, after Parliament's victory over the Crown, the government was able to borrow much larger amounts at significantly lower interest rates. Using sovereign interest rates as their indicator, North and Weingast concluded that investors evidently felt that the risk of the new (Dutch) rulers of England not honoring their commitments was considerably lower now that they were constrained by Parliament's "power of the purse."

A state that could finance itself more easily had less need to resort to tax hikes, defaults, monopolies, or other ways of reaching into its subjects' pockets. This benefited private investment. North and Weingast also argued that lower interest rates paid by the new Crown and Parliament and improved capital markets for public debt helped lower interest rates elsewhere in society and thus fostered investment and growth. Alas, there is little historical evidence that public and private interest rates were in fact integrated in the way North and Weingast assumed.[33] In addition, the authors argued that the new unwritten constitution of England, in which the Crown committed to respecting Parliament's rights to grant taxes and control expenditures, had created a system in which taxation was predictable and Parliament guaranteed

[31] De Long and Shleifer, "Princes or Merchants"; North and Weingast, "Constitutions and Commitment."

[32] Braddick, *The Nerves of the State*; Schofield, "Taxation and the Political Limits"; North and Weingast, "Constitutions and Commitment."

[33] Clark has shown that investors in early modern England knew to distinguish between private property rights, which were secured by a functioning legal system since the Middle Ages, and public property rights to taxation, which were not until the consolidation of the nation-state. Clark, "The Political Foundations"; Stasavage, *Public Debt*; and for Europe generally, Epstein, *Freedom and Growth*, 60. We will see in chapter 7 that Spanish private interest rates would support that argument. Note also that others have argued that the survival of usury laws was the main reason why private interest rates were kept low despite rulers' fiscal improbity. Hence credit rationing, rather than higher interest rates, restricted private investment but could direct more capital into public debt. See Temin and Voth, "Credit Rationing and Crowding Out."

that random expropriations would not occur. As a consequence, from the late seventeenth century through the eighteenth century, resistance to taxation decreased, and government's income became more predictable, providing a secure foundation for debt financing. Taxation levels could remain lower because taxation was more equitable and efficient.

The argument put forward by North and Weingast has become a paradigm that centers on the dichotomy between "absolutist" and "parliamentary" political regimes. The former are identified with extractive institutions and predatory states that hinder the optimum development of markets through exploitation of subjects' property or labor in forced labor regimes.[34] Political entities (medieval city-states, early modern parliamentary systems, modern democracies) that developed an institutional setup that restrained rulers from preying on their own people took part in the accelerating economic development; the others (medieval princes, early modern absolutist monarchies, modern dictatorships) were left behind.

The Ability to Tax of Early Modern European States

North and Weingast's formulation of the divide between "absolutist" and "constitutionally constrained" rulers simply suggests that the former were not encumbered in their ability to appropriate; when faced with military necessity, they infringed on their subjects' private property rights at will. Thus, "absolutist" regimes were supposed to be large but inefficient states. Here the lack of a theory of state-building, or power more generally, soon became apparent. The early NIE model was predicated upon an assumption that the state—in this case the early modern one—already *had* power that it abused to prey on its subjects. Hence, it could only be kept in check by parliament.[35]

Research on early modern fiscal systems, however, quickly demonstrated that the advantage of parliamentary regimes was not that they appropriated a *smaller* share of the national product in the form of taxes but that they were able to appropriate a *larger* share. Modern economists measure this burden as the ratio of the national income (GDP) that is being paid to the government in taxes. For historians national income is an elusive concept and should be handled with care even for the later eighteenth century.[36] English estimates

[34] Levi, *Of Rule and Revenue*; McGuire and Olson, "Economics of Autocracy"; North, Weingast, and Summerhill, "Order, Disorder and Economic Change"; Knack and Keefer, "Institutions and Economic Performance"; Rodrik, Subramanian, and Trebbi, "Institutions Rule"; Acemoglu, Johnson, and Robinson, "The Colonial Origins"; Acemoglu, Johnson, and Robinson, "Reversal of Fortune."
[35] See also Epstein, "Rise of the West," 234.
[36] See an interesting attempt to approximate something approaching a Castilian national income as early as the sixteenth and seventeenth centuries through urbanization rates and back extrapolation undertaken by Alvarez Nogal and Prados de la Escosura, "La decadenza spagnola."

are probably the best because England was politically, administratively, and fiscally far more centralized than its continental neighbors. The English state of the late eighteenth century took about 12 percent of national income in peace time, closer to 18 percent in war, according to O'Brien. Corresponding estimates for France are 11.5 percent, and for Spain I have elsewhere estimated a share of around 10.5 percent.[37] The latter figure meant a lower share than a century earlier (1660 = 12 percent) but a slightly higher one than in the late sixteenth century (1580 = 8 percent).[38] These estimates suggest that *overall* Peninsular Spanish subjects were not particularly hard-pressed, quite contrary to what a Northian view of "absolutist" governance would have suggested. England's state was able, and willing, to extract a much larger share of the "national product" than the French or Spanish states.

The focus thus shifted from the "protection against predation" side of the North and Weingast argument to the "reliability of taxation" feature also contained in it: where elites were represented in parliament, and thus involved in decision making over taxation, they were willing to pay more on a more equitable basis.[39] In this way of reading the constitutional divide, the problem with "absolutists" was not that they ruined the economy through extraction but that they were faced with corporatist power that severely restricted their ability to raise taxes. They engendered a weak state not because their greed cut short economic growth, as North and Weingast claimed, but because their subjects distrusted them and hence evaded and avoided taxation. The problem was jurisdictional fragmentation. "Absolutists" were anything but absolute; in fact, they shared sovereignty with elites represented in corporate bodies, and this undermined their ability to raise revenue. In Epstein's words, "Jurisdictional fragmentation . . . gave rise to multiple coordination failure. [This coordination failure] rather than autocratic rule was the main source of institutional inefficiency of 'absolutism' before the 19th century."[40]

The ability to tax of early modern European monarchical states has been studied most thoroughly for the case of France, and the French mirror has been extrapolated to view other European "absolutists." Velde and Weir have pointed out that the inability of eighteenth-century French finance ministers to bring down the cost of borrowing reflected investors' expectations and inbuilt constraints, not poor management. The fundamental problem was "a political system that completely separated the privilege of spending from

---

[37] O'Brien, "Political Economy"; Weir, "Tontines"; Daudin, *Commerce et prospérité*; Merino Navarro, *Las cuentas*. See also Grafe and Irigoin, "Stakeholder Empire," table 1.

[38] Thompson, "Castile: Polity," 176. Thompson cautions against over-interpreting these figures. Notwithstanding the large margin of error, however, the trends of increasing burdens toward the later seventeenth century and some relief for taxpayers in the eighteenth seem to coincide with other evidence. The relatively moderate share of GDP taken as taxes relativizes the notion of a more predatory state in the early modern period.

[39] O'Brien and Hunt, "Rise." See also Stasavage, *Public Debt*, 57.

[40] Epstein, *Freedom and Growth*, 15.

the obligation to pay taxes."[41] The Crown had full sovereignty over only a limited set of taxes, sharing jurisdictional control over all others with various corporate players invested with their own authority. These could only be raised in negotiation with the Church, or some of the provincial *états*, or the noble estate, or the mighty cartels of French tax farmers. The French Crown was thus far from absolute on the revenue side of the public accounts. By contrast, it had full executive decision over expenditure, that is, to start a war. The lack of a central budget added to the lack of transparency; the French kings (like their Spanish cousins) rarely knew what their disposable resources were or how much they had spent.[42]

The fundamental incongruence between decision making over revenues and expenditure created a dynamic that led to both lower revenue and higher risks of default. As Rosenthal has shown, negotiation between the elites and the Crown over taxation resulted paradoxically in the lowest revenue whenever the power to tax was shared almost evenly between elite and king.[43] The underlying logic of this insight is that of a prisoner's dilemma.[44] Crown and elite could have maximized their returns (the total taxes extracted) if they had cooperated. Alas, depending on how much power each side had, either one or both had an incentive to defect and free-ride on taxation raised by the other party. The outcome was a suboptimal lower overall payoff: less revenue.

The French Crown attacked the problem in two different ways but was eventually unable to overcome it. Before 1720 the Crown tried to expand its control over taxation at the expense of the elite and at the same time predated on economic activities by manipulating currencies, changing tariff rates, and selling offices and titles. After the 1720s, however, it increasingly tried to align elite interests and Crown policy by selling its debt to the general public rather than corporate bodies, which "brought to the Crown a clientele of lenders who were largely disenfranchised."[45] In addition, the Crown began to use those of the provincial estates (*états*, such as Provence or Languedoc) that had retained tax-raising abilities as intermediaries that raised debt for the Crown based on their better reputation as creditors. However, reform was incremental at best because the Crown was unwilling to negotiate its total control over foreign policy–related expenditure with the "elite."

Thus the increasingly desperate search for revenue pushed the Crown to levy prohibitive taxes on the few areas where it faced less organized opposi-

---

[41] Velde and Weir, "Financial Market," 6, 36.

[42] Storrs, *Resilience*, 108.

[43] Rosenthal, "Political Economy," 73–74.

[44] Rosenthal's model is more sophisticated, however, in that it can account for varying shares of power being given to elite and Crown.

[45] Rosenthal, "Political Economy," 68, 82. Michael Kwass has argued that the Crown alienated landowners in the *pays d'elections* and officeholders everywhere especially through the tighter application of the *taille* and the introduction of the *dixieme* and *vingtieme*, a process that might explain the anti-absolutist stance of a surprisingly large share of the French elites in the run-up to the revolution. Kwass, *Privilege*.

tion and to raise loans of the more expensive kind, such as life annuities. This aggravated the economic consequences of such a relatively weak political regime; though the extraction of resources from the economy was not excessive, marginal rates in some fiscal areas led to huge distortions.[46] The argument advanced by O'Brien that "absolutist" states suffered from poor tax compliance is thus pushed one explanatory step further. The inconsistency between the power to spend and the power to raise revenue in "absolutist" states ultimately forced the Crown into giving up more power to the elites whom it had to co-opt in a patrimonial way by offering offices and sinecures.[47] Jurisdictions that were shared and fragmented between Crown and "elite" made sudden tax increases (like those after 1635) or particularly large tax hikes extremely difficult to accomplish without threatening the cooperation between Crown and elites. This in turn undermined the long-term viability of the system. It limited France's ability to increase taxation quickly when war loomed and creditors demanded to know how their up-front loans would be serviced in the short and medium run, thereby handing a decisive advantage to its main contender, England. At least some historians would also still (or maybe again) argue that it contributed to the revolutionary challenge against the monarchy.[48]

Spain in the French Mirror

From the beginnings of NIE, attempts to identify what sort of state institutions supported or thwarted market growth in early modern Europe assumed that the French case could be extrapolated to construct a model of the political economy of early modern "absolutists." North, for example, states that the "similarities between the French and the Spanish political developments [in the early modern period] are striking."[49] Yet even a cursory look reveals a number of difficulties with this comparison, which result mainly from the lack of a proper historicization of the system of governance. Where power was located in Spain (in contrast with France), how it was legitimized, and how it was exercised shaped the relationship between subjects and Crown, corporate bodies and Crown, territories and towns, and so on. A central argument of this book is that these differences, rather than a simplistic distinction between "absolutist" and "parliamentary" political regimes, determined the complex outcome of state- and market-building.

---

[46] Hoffman and Rosenthal, "Political Economy." See also Weir, "Tontines."

[47] Hoffman, "France."

[48] Although socioeconomic explanations for the French Revolution have been out of vogue, a number of historians have begun to reconsider their impact within a larger sociocultural context. See, e.g., Kwass, *Privilege*.

[49] North and Thomas, *Rise of the Western World*, 127. See also North, *Structure and Change*, 152.

Military Necessity and Revenue Pressure

The first problem arises from the underlying assumption that military necessity created an exogenous constraint that forced all rulers to push for maximum revenue extraction. For political economists this is a convenient deus ex machina that identifies a prime mover of state institution-building that is an exogenous rather than an endogenous variable. But this view of the origins of the European nation-state is contested. To begin with, it is not clear that military technology was really an independent variable and the exogenous trigger of this development, as most economists and sociologists imply.[50] Military pressure pushed rulers to improve state institutions, but at the same time the increased technical and political capacity of states to raise taxes drove the scale and scope of war. Early modern philosophers and modern economists and sociologists alike have seen the creation of nation-states as a means of ending "the war of all against all," or at least of noble bully against noble bully. However, the process escalated the level of violence against individuals and certain populations, at least in the short run, with detrimental consequences, for example, for those engaged in long-distance trades.[51] Institution-building was as much a source of violence as a consequence of violence; and war and market integration were almost certainly negatively related in the short and medium term.[52] Yet, without question, once a European competitive state system had come into existence, military might was needed to guarantee survival, and the fiscal well-being of the state was a necessary if not sufficient condition for a functioning army and navy. Military expenditure everywhere was—as has often been pointed out—the single largest rubric of early modern state spending. Direct and time-deferred exenditure (that is, paying off the war loans) always exceeded two-thirds of the budget, rising to 90 percent during campaigns.[53]

Still, the case of Spain shows clearly that the fiscal imperative has been overdrawn in comparative studies of European fiscality, in large part because the French mirror has distorted the picture.[54] The general argument is that the recurrent defaults and/or failures to service the debt of the Spanish Crown, especially in the Habsburg period (1557, 1560, 1575–76, 1607, 1627, 1647, 1652, 1660, 1662, 1688) but also under the Bourbons (1727, 1739/1748), were obvious signs of the incompatibility of revenue and expenditure policies in Spain in ways that were comparable to what happened in France.[55]

---

[50] See Mann, *Sources I*, as opposed to Epstein, "Rise of the West," 247–49.

[51] Gelderblom, "Violence and Growth."

[52] O'Rourke, "Napoleonic Wars."

[53] Grafe and Irigoin, "Stakeholder Empire."

[54] See, e.g., the large comparative effort in Bonney, *Economic Systems*.

[55] See Artola, *La hacienda*, 219, 314, for the 1688 partial renegotiation and the claim that changes to the debt payments in 1729 equaled a partial default. See González Enciso, "Moderate Absolutism," 123–24, for the unilateral lowering of the interest rate in 1727 and the 1739/48 suspension of *juros* servicing that lasted till the reign of Carlos III.

As in all "absolutist" regimes, without constraints on spending the Crown was said to pursue a foreign and imperial policy it could ill afford and that wrecked its finances.[56]

But the evidence is not as straightforward as it once appeared. It is now widely accepted that the Castilian *cortes* (estates), which consisted of delegates from the most important towns, were far from powerless.[57] Throughout the sixteenth and early seventeenth centuries, they constrained the Crown fairly effectively.[58] Though they had no formal legislative initiative, they exerted increasing control. The share of royal revenue subject to grants by the *cortes* increased from a quarter in the 1560s to 70 percent in the mid-seventeenth century; and around 1600, empowered by the votes of a very important new tax, the *millones*, they acquired de facto legislative initiative.[59] This increase in the power of the estates in Castile was mirrored in some of the other territories of the Spanish monarchy, notably Navarre and the Basque Provinces.[60] The Crown stopped calling the Castilian *cortes* in 1665 out of its own weakness rather than strength.[61] Even so, the consent of the towns represented in the *cortes* was still required for regular prorogations of taxes, and the Crown shifted toward bargaining with individual towns rather than exerting central revenue-raising powers. The *cortes*-voting towns renewed the *millones* in 1667, 1673, 1679, 1685, 1691, and 1697 but only after negotiations with the *sala de millones*.[62]

Though historians have argued that the Crown under Carlos II (1665–1700) had effectively locked in the fiscal system by refusing to call the *cortes* so that no new taxes could be voted, it is now also clear that it not only renegotiated existing taxes but also agreed upon new taxes with the *cortes*-towns on several occasions.[63] Similarly, the towns were still powerful enough to reject fiscal changes. As late as 1712 the new Bourbon monarch Philip V called the deputies of the principal towns of Castile and Leon for their views on a radical shifting of the fiscal burden from local trade and consumption taxes to customs as suggested by the Count of Bergwyck.

[56] For the most eloquent statement, see Yun Casalilla, *Marte Contra Minerva*.

[57] Towns represented were in Old Castile (Leon, Burgos, Salamanca, Valladolid, Madrid, Guadalajara, Zamora, Toro, Soria, Segovia, Avila), in New Castile (Toledo, Cuenca), in the southeast (Murcia), and in Andalusia (Cordoba, Jaen, Seville, Granada).

[58] Thompson, "Absolutism in Castile"; Thompson, "Crown and Cortes"; Thompson, *War and Government*.

[59] For the *millones*, see Lovett, "Millones," and MacKay, *Limits of Royal Authority*, 45–46. See also Thompson, "Castile: Polity," 171.

[60] In Navarra the Cortes increased their power with the introduction of the *servicio extraordinario* in the 1650s. Solbes Ferri, *Rentas Reales de Navarra*, 81. For the Basque Country, see Bilbao, "Provincias exentas," 75–77.

[61] Fernández Albaladejo, "Monarquía"; Thompson, "Castile: Absolutism," 191.

[62] Storrs, *Resilience*, 175–82; Fernández Albaladejo, "Cities and State," 178–79; Fernández Albaladejo, "Monarquía"; Thompson, "Absolutism in Castile," 82.

[63] For the revision, see Storrs, *Resilience*. For an earlier view on the freezing of the tax structure, see Artola, *La hacienda*, 209–10. Cremades Griñán, *Borbones*, 101–3.

The towns could not agree on a common position and effectively blocked the plan.[64]

The fiscal situation of the Spanish Crown, at least in the sixteenth and eighteenth centuries (though not in the seventeenth), was also less dramatic than is often assumed. Twenty years ago Rodríguez-Salgado showed that the 1557 "default" was essentially a renegotiation.[65] Thompson has suggested that "defaults" in the sixteenth century should largely be interpreted as a rescheduling of debts within the existing contracts, which implied a consolidation of the public debt by converting loans from large banking houses into negotiable undated bonds, essentially a rights issue. In his view the restructuring brought the hacienda back onto a sustainable path. Drelichman and Voth go further by showing that up to the last decade of the sixteenth century the Crown's debt was in fact sustainable. Even after defaults the terms and conditions of new loans did not change significantly, illustrating that "defaults" were an anticipated part of the contract that was managed thanks to short-term lending.[66] Renegotiations continued in the seventeenth and eighteenth centuries as mentioned above, and not just in Castile. For instance, Catalonia had to renegotiate with its debtors in 1670.[67] But these measures were not unilateral defaults in the strict sense. Instead they were bi- or multilaterally sought solutions to recurring but fundamentally manageable fiscal problems. The sharp modern distinctions drawn between sovereign defaults caused by either insolvencies or debt repudiations on the one hand and renegotiations on the other are unhelpful in understanding how early modern monarchs and their creditors dealt with short-term liquidity issues in order to preserve medium- and long-term solvency.

Indeed, most of the time the Crown's creditors did not consider the situation too dramatic. The standard measure to gauge their concern is of course the interest rates the central hacienda had to pay on its debt. Figure 1.1 offers a first attempt to chart public rates in the sixteenth through eighteenth centuries. The Crown successively lowered the nominal interest rate (the "cupon rate") for its most important consolidated debt instruments, the *juros*, from 10 percent in the 1550s to 2.5 percent after 1728.[68] Yields are harder to come by; it is much more difficult to find information on the actual return investors realized from the *juros*, which reflected both the market price of the

[64] Matilla Tascon, *La única contribución.*

[65] Rodríguez-Salgado, *Changing Face of Empire.*

[66] Thompson, "Castile: Polity," 160–61; Drelichman and Voth, "Sustainable Debts"; Drelichman and Voth "Serial Defaults."

[67] In the process the interest rate was cut in half. Thus renegotiations were obviously not costless for the debtors. But they were still different from defaults, and Fernández de Pinedo argues that in the Catalan case at least capital holders were chasing few investment opportunities, thus enabling the Catalan *Corts* to lower the interest rate. Fernández de Pinedo, "Hacienda catalana."

[68] For the official rates, see *Novissima recopilación.* Legal changes implied that the rate was lowered to 3 percent in 1705, but the new rate was not applied until 1727. See Artola, *La hacienda,* 314, and Toboso Sanchez, *Deuda,* chapter 7.

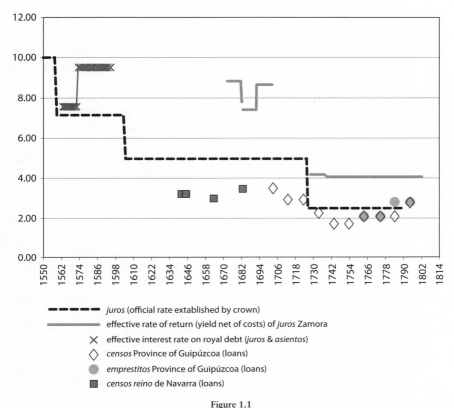

Figure 1.1

Public interest rates (1550–1830). *Source*: My own elaboration based on Alvarez Vázquez, *Rentas*; Drelichman and Voth, "Borrower"; Toboso Sanchez, *Deuda*; Solbes Ferri, *Rentas reales de Navarra*; and Mugartegui Eguía, *Hacienda*.

bond (as opposed to its face value) and the nominal interest rate paid on the face value. For the sixteenth century, some published data are available. The principal of the *juros* increased from about 2.3 million *ducados* in 1504 to 80 million in 1598, and the Crown defaulted (read renegotiated) three times in this period. Yet, in contrast to the NIE model, Drelichman and Voth's data suggest only a modest rise of the interest rate of the royal debt from about 7.6 to 9.5 percent for *juros* and *asientos* (loans from large banking houses) (see figure 1.1). An earlier alternative estimate by Ruiz Martín (not included in figure 1.1) argued that the effective interest rate actually fell from 10 percent to 5.8 percent over the same period.[69]

[69] Ruiz Martín, "Credito y banca"; Drelichman and Voth, "Sustainable Debts." In fact the rise in the rate is largely a composition effect caused by a change in the amount of long- and short-term debt in the portfolio, not by rate rises. I would like to thank Joachim Voth for making me aware of this. For a recent account of the surprising fiscal efficiency in the sixteenth century, see Yun Casalilla and Comín, "Spain."

Either figure is well within the range of rates paid by most European polities in the sixteenth century if we leave out the exception of Italian city-states that reaped the benefits of much more developed financial markets and therefore paid less, as Epstein has pointed out.[70] Spain's supposed early turn to "absolutism" and "orderly despotism" apparently had only a small effect on the Crown's "credit rating."[71] In light of recent research by Sussman and Yafeh showing that institutional reforms had only limited impact on sovereign interest rates in England and elsewhere, this is probably less surprising than once thought.[72]

No data on yields are available for the early seventeenth century. But figure 1.1 presents a first series for the later seventeenth century and much of the eighteenth using the returns on royal debt (*juros*) reported in Alvarez Vázquez's work on the Cathedral Chapter of Zamora (Extremadura). Like most sizable ecclesiastical institutions, the chapter engaged in large-scale financial transactions. Though its income depended mostly on the agricultural economy, the chapter's dealings illustrate the increasingly large role of ecclesiastical institutions in Spain in providing banking services; this is something that financial historians have paid too little attention to but it is reflected in a great many studies that focus on monastic communities.[73] Over time the ledgers reflect "the transformation of the money loan (or, acquisition of perpetual rents) to mortgages and modern credits for a fixed term; the change from a bond as a feudal rent of the twelve and thirteen centuries to the redeemable mortgage bond in the sixteenth and the fixed term credit of the nineteenth."[74] Thus, the Chapter of Zamora, not a particularly rich institution, managed, on average, loans and credits of 500,000 to 800,000 *reales* at any one time.

The data presented here reflect the yields the chapter realized from the *juros* net of all collection costs, taxes, and discounts that were imposed on them. *Juros* came in all kinds and shapes; they generally stipulated against what (local) revenue they were to be charged and thus the rates presented here are an average of a number of locally traded instruments. In that they reflect much of the Spanish public debt. Most historians agree that from the 1630s onward public finances were indeed on an unsustainable path and the dire straits of the Spanish Crown in the late seventeenth century are clearly visible. Yield rose to between 7.4 and 8.6 percent, twice the nominal interest rate. Since the interest on face value was fixed, the high net yield thus implies that the paper traded at a massive discount in the very active secondary

---

[70] The other exception was England, which paid very high rates in the sixteenth century and most of the seventeenth because it was fiscally backward. Epstein, *Freedom and Growth*, table 2.1, 16ff.

[71] North and Thomas, *Rise of the Western World*, chapter 10.

[72] Sussman and Yafeh, "Institutional Reform."

[73] See, e.g., Izquierdo Martín et al., "Corte." There is also some very good work on the Spanish Americas; see, e.g., Lavrín, "Nunneries," and Quiroz, "Credit."

[74] Alvarez Vázquez, *Rentas*, 24.

markets, an observation that is entirely consistent with most of the historiography.[75] These rates are lower than those estimated by some historians who have suggested on the basis of more scattered data that the real interest rate on the *juros* occasionally reached 14 percent in this period.[76] In any case, the lenders were getting nervous.

Surprisingly, however, no new *juros* were issued from the later seventeenth century onward.[77] In 1727 the Crown and its Councils brought down the legal interest rate on annuities from 5 to 3 percent.[78] González Enciso argues that this unilateral lowering of interest rates constituted an "aggressive [policy] against the financiers," essentially an expropriation.[79] Throughout the eighteenth century the Crown repeatedly changed the terms of the remaining *juros*, lowering their return. Yet it also retired substantial amounts through redemptions of its legacy debt.[80] This apparently did wonders for the secondary market value of annuities over which the Crown had little control. Thus, in the absence of new debt issues and after a monetary stabilization in the 1680s that ended the rampant inflation affecting small coin (*vellon*), the yield realized on the old *juros* of the Chapter of Zamora hovered around 4 percent in the eighteenth century. The rate had stabilized and the annuities were now trading much closer to face value, exceeding the legal interest rate by only 1 to 1.5 percent. Meanwhile, new central treasury debt largely took the form of short-term credit from suppliers that was available at low interest rates and apparently without constraints, suggesting that the Crown's "credit rating" was actually rather good.[81] As several fiscal historians have pointed out, the Crown's reluctance to raise debt either domestically or internationally was not a consequence of investors' unwillingness to lend.[82]

After the 1770s Crown finances worsened and moderate amounts of debt were issued again. Spain raised some capital for canal building in the Amsterdam market.[83] In the 1780s the hacienda gave out new domestic debt instruments for the first time in almost a century. The *vales reales*, a monetized bond issued via the Banco de San Carlos, drove up indebtedness dramatically by earlier standards.[84] The financial position then deteriorated quickly in the

[75] See, e.g., Garzón Pareja, "Carlos II."

[76] González Enciso, "Moderate Absolutism," 123. That *juros* were paid out of specific revenues means that it is perfectly possible that the range of yields for nominally identical paper increased when finances became more strained in the seventeenth century.

[77] The Council of the Indies in Madrid also stopped the sale of *juros* to the American possessions. Andrien, "The Sale of Juros."

[78] See footnote 68 above.

[79] González Enciso, "Moderate Absolutism," 123.

[80] For a detailed account, see Toboso Sanchez, *Deuda*, chapter 7.

[81] González Enciso, "Moderate Absolutism," 124.

[82] Ibid.; Torres Sánchez, "Possibilities."

[83] Riley, *International Government Finance*, 165–74. I would like to thank Christiaan van Bochove for making me aware of this.

[84] Tedde de Lorca, "San Carlos."

1790s and early 1800s when debt issues increased by a factor of five between 1782 and 1794. Yet even on the eve of the French war in 1793, Spanish "national" debt per capita was barely 5 percent of British debt per capita.[85] In 1800 investors in Amsterdam still trusted Spain's ability to raise revenue sufficiently to lend at 4.5 to 5 percent, the same rate paid by Britain in these years.[86] By 1800 Spain's financial position was without a doubt critical after continuous wars with first France and then Britain. A last massive issue of *vales* in 1799 doubled the outstanding debt and the paper depreciated drastically.[87] However, at this point Spain was hardly alone in this predicament among European states.

The point is not to paint too rosy a picture of the finances of the Spanish monarchy. In fact, its credit rating was worse than that of some of the Spanish historic territories, such as Guipúzcoa and Navarra, which ran independent fiscalities. This, too, is shown in figure 1.1. They were able to borrow at lower rates than the Crown, never paying more than 4 percent and at times less than 2 percent. Yet this comparison sets a challenging standard; these provincial interest rates were below the best rates enjoyed by the republican-minded Dutch Provinces in the seventeenth and eighteenth centuries.[88]

The surprising probity of the royal hacienda in the face of the low interest rates paid for much of the century on sovereign and provincial debt sets Spain apart in eighteenth-century fiscal history in Europe. Spain's central treasury hardly spent on sovereign debt after the 1710s and the crisis of the War of the Spanish Succession (1701–14, known in North America as Queen Anne's War). During a century in which the likes of Britain and France were spending about one-third to half of the annual budget on servicing their state debt, and the Netherlands between 40 and 70 percent, the expenditure of the Spanish central treasury on debt service was a mere 7 percent on average, and only reached 12 percent during the 1780s, when the issues of *vales* multiplied.[89] The French Crown's increasingly desperate and ultimately failed attempts to finance its gigantic debt in the eighteenth century could not have been more different from what happened across the Pyrenees.[90] Here, the

[85] Torres Sánchez, "Triumph," 44.

[86] Stein and Stein, *Edge of Crisis*, 337. Overall, Spain's borrowing abroad was very modest until the nineteenth century.

[87] Tedde de Lorca, "San Carlos," 515, appendix 511.

[88] I would like to thank Joost Jonkers and Oscar Gelderblom for sharing their unpublished data on the Dutch Provinces with me.

[89] British expenditure on interest and principal was around 30 percent in wartime and 56 percent in peace in the late eighteenth century. In France interest and capital consumed just under 50 percent. Grafe and Irigoin, "Stakeholder Empire," table 5. For the Netherlands, see Fritschy, "West European Trajectory," graph 4. Spain's estimate based on data by Jurado Sánchez, *El gasto*, table V.1. Though Spain stopped servicing its debt between 1748 and the 1760s, rates remained low when it restarted payments. Estimating the total debt is almost impossible. It should be noted that the American colonies had even lower levels of debt in the late eighteenth century. Grafe and Irigoin, "Stakeholder Empire," table 5.

[90] Rosenthal, "Political Economy"; White, "Financial Dilemma."

Spanish Bourbons almost balanced their budgets even in war years, at least before the last decade of the eighteenth century. Evidently all "absolutists" did not behave in the same way. Nor was the military fiscal imperative quite as dramatic as political economists have suggested.

Empire: Outsourcing the Problem?

The strongest argument of the accusation in the case of "NIE v. early modern Spain" has always been that Spain's system of governance was one that infringed more or less sytematically on its subjects' property rights in the Castilian heartland and even more so in the other territories of the composite monarchy. The one thing that set Spain apart from "absolutist" France in the minds of economists, economic historians, and sociologists was the empire, or at least the size of the imperial possessions. The Castilian Crown, on the one hand, supposedly had the power to extract revenue from the Netherlands, the Italian possessions, and of course the Spanish territories in America and, on the other, was intent on maximizing its revenue under (almost) any circumstance.[91]

The historiography, however, has clearly shown the limits of such revenue transfers from European possessions in the sixteenth and seventeenth centuries, when the European empire was at its height. Indeed, it is generally acknowledged that more often than not Castile cross-subsidized military and administrative activities elsewhere in Europe. Tracy has shown that the Netherlandish Estates at no point consented to vote revenue that was not to be spent within the Netherlands. When Charles V needed to raise troops for conflicts between the Dutch Provinces and one of their eastern neighbors, the Duchy of Guelders, money was voted for this strictly local purpose.[92] Beyond that, the Estates were unyielding. The ill-advised attempt of the Duke of Alba to create the infamous "tenth-penny" sales tax in 1569 and enforce it in 1571 in all of the Netherlands served as a rallying cry for the advocates of confrontation with Spain, as is well-known. It was resisted precisely because the Netherlands had never conceded any contribution to what Philip II considered the "common expenses" of the Habsburg monarchy.[93]

Even after the successful Dutch Revolt, the Army of Flanders to the south, like the Army of Catalonia and various armies in Italy, was subsidized by Castile until the end of the seventeenth century.[94] A Catalan document from the second half of the seventeenth century claimed that in Catalonia "there would not be a *doblon* [i.e., money,] if it was not for what the troops spend in

---

[91] North and Thomas, *Rise of the Western World*, 127–28; North, *Structure and Change*, 151.
[92] Tracy, *Holland under Habsburg Rule*.
[93] Ibid.
[94] Storrs, *Resilience*, 113.

Catalonia, exhausting all of Spain in their keep."[95] The situation was slightly easier for the Crown in Naples, but here, too, the resources that the Parlamento was willing to procure for non-local purposes were limited.[96]

In the Iberian Peninsula the three Basque Provinces of Guipúzcoa, Vizcaya, and Alava, the Kingdom of Aragon (comprising Catalonia, Aragon, Valencia, and Mallorca), the Kingdom of Navarra, Portugal (between 1580 and 1640), and even Galicia were all subject to separate processes of granting money to the Crown, which had negotiated with each of them on a case-by-case basis. Historians and economists have often singled out strong "republican" traditions in Catalonia as the counterpart to supposed Castilian "despotism."[97] We will return to this issue time and again. In terms of its constitutional structure, the Kingdom of Aragon was one of the European territories with the strongest parliamentary representation until 1707/14.[98] Extracting revenue from Aragon for military campaigns outside the *reino* proved next to impossible during the Habsburg period and difficult thereafter. Although Aragon's constitutional position changed radically after 1707/14, the Crown still found it quite impossible to tax the territory throughout the eighteenth century beyond a short-lived initial tax hike.[99]

More than in its Peninsular and European territories, however, the Crown supposedly extracted resources and disrespected the property rights of its subjects in the overseas empire. Commentators from the sixteenth to the nineteenth centuries were convinced that the Spanish Crown and its hacienda extracted fabulous riches from the Americas in particular.[100] Adam Smith famously thought that Spain alone had derived substantial benefits from its colonies, while the colonies of all other European nations were "a cause of expense and not of revenue for their respective mother countries."[101] For nineteenth-century historians and state-builders in Latin America, colonial exploitation served as an important device to explain the abysmal developmental trajectory of their countries.[102] Meanwhile, historians of Spain liked to interpret the alleged windfall from the Americas as another sign of how a corrupt and incompetent monarchy had quite literally squandered the family silver.[103] However, Prados's groundbreaking study of the impact on Spain

---

[95] Cited in Fernández de Pinedo, "Hacienda catalana," 219.

[96] Tracy, *Emperor Charles*. However, Naples contributed to wars fought in Lombardy and campaigns to recover Messina in the later seventeenth century. Cf. Storrs, *Resilience*, 114–15.

[97] North and Thomas, *Rise of the Western World*, 85–86.

[98] Elliott, *Catalans*.

[99] See chapter 5.

[100] It is generally accepted that the Asian possessions were unprofitable for the Crown, leading, in the case of the Philippines, to a somewhat peculiar notion that here colonization was completely focused on Christianization. See Bauzon, *Deficit Government*; Alonso, "Financing the Empire"; and Phelan, *Hispanization of the Philippines*.

[101] Smith, *Wealth of Nations*, 90.

[102] Adelman, "Imperial Revolutions."

[103] This is the theme of much of the "decline of Spain" historiography. See Elliott, "Decline of Spain"; Kagan, "Prescott's Paradigm"; and Kamen, "The Decline of Spain."

of the loss of the American territories between 1811 and 1825 suggests that the shock was regionally concentrated and severe in the short run but hardly devastating in terms of the national product.[104] This casts doubts on the importance of the American territories before this date.

From a strictly fiscal point of view, the direct extraction of resources from the Spanish Americas is easily overestimated. In the second half of the sixteenth century, the fabulous riches of first Upper Peruvian and then Mexican silver deposits were already systematically mined, and commerce with an increasing but still dependent immigrant population in Spanish America flourished. At this point in time, the Americas contributed on average 18 percent to the revenue of the Spanish central treasury, though the year-to-year fluctuations were huge. That was to remain the highest average ever; according to Yun, the American contribution to the Madrid hacienda was less than 10 percent in the seventeenth century. For much of the eighteenth century it accounted, according to my estimates, for about 5 percent before reaching 12 percent again in a few of the dire years of the late eighteenth century and after much effort of the Crown to increase income from the Americas.[105]

This was not a negligible share, especially in the early colonial period. But considering the size of the Spanish American economy, it was far from the extractive capacity that foreigners imagined. The foremost Spanish American fiscal historians TePaske and Klein have repeatedly pointed out that the overwhelming share of American revenues was spent in the colonies.[106] Indeed, Irigoin and I have calculated that by the late eighteenth century transfers to the metropolis made up only just over 5 percent of Spanish American revenue. Or to put it another way: 95 percent of taxes raised in the Spanish Americas were spent in the Spanish Americas.[107]

These figures suggest that the idea of the Spanish Empire as a centralizing and/or extractive machine needs to be revised, even if it is still widespread among social scientists and Latin Americanists. It has recently been argued that Spanish Peninsular finances were only saved from an even earlier collapse in the late eighteenth-century wars by a massive increase in revenue extraction and borrowing from New Spain (colonial Mexico).[108] American income clearly became more important for the Spanish treasury in the war periods; when revenue from the Peninsula collapsed after the French invasion

---

[104] Prados estimates that the loss shaved off about 6 percent of Spain's GDP. Prados de la Escosura, *De imperio a nación*, 67–94, 242.

[105] The sixteenth-century estimate is the arithmetic mean of annual shares during 1555–96 reported by Drelichman and Voth, "Borrower," table A1. For a slightly lower estimate, see Yun Casalilla, *Marte Contra Minerva*, 337. Seventeenth-century estimates are from Yun Casalilla, "The American Empire." The eighteenth-century estimates are based on Merino Navarro, *Las cuentas*, Cargos al Tesorero General. High percentages in some years in the last decade were in part explained by the complete interruption of transfers in others.

[106] Klein, *The American Finances*, 103–10.

[107] Grafe and Irigoin, "Stakeholder Empire."

[108] Marichal, *Bankruptcy of Empire*; Stein and Stein, *Edge of Crisis*.

of 1808, it turned into the only lifeline for independent Spain.[109] But the implicit assumption that the situation in the 1780s to 1810s reflected the fiscally extractive nature of Spanish governance in the Americas over several centuries is misleading.[110]

Spain's colonial fiscal apparatus was based on an expanding network of regional treasury districts, the emergence of which accompanied the imperial expansion until there were around eighty of them in the late eighteenth century.[111] The administration of revenue and expenditure was largely locally based and subject to local decision making and negotiation among local, colonial, and metropolitan authorities. By the eighteenth century about one-quarter to one-third of revenues collected in American treasury districts were fed into a system of intracolonial, interregional redistribution via the so-called *situados*.[112] These transfers in turn were largely privately managed, and they articulated the commercial links between the large Atlantic and Pacific ports and the hinterland. Spanish American colonial rule left plenty of room for local initiative.

The way Spanish imperial rule was organized on the ground was not compatible with the objective implied by economists and many Latin American historians, namely a simple maximization of revenue extraction. Instead, local involvement was used to organize the rolling out and maintenance of the empire, supported by regionally administered interregional transfers of revenues within the Americas (and to the Spanish Philippines). Widespread local control naturally led to a reinvestment of revenues in some of the colonies' key export sectors: commercial agriculture (tobacco, sugar, cocoa, and hides) and mining.[113]

Even in the sixteenth and seventeenth centuries, the impact of revenue from the Americas on policymaking in Spain was largely indirect. Spain's expansionist foreign policy during these centuries was not financed through actual income from the Indies but owed to credit. When debt secured against Peninsular revenue was insufficient to keep the sixteenth-century war machinery going, the large bankers who were called in demanded their loans to be secured against future colonial receipts.[114] The Crown could leverage future liquid income from Spanish America in financial transactions with its financiers. But its capital-raising capacity seems to have benefited at least as much from the myth of American riches as from actual remittances.[115] In

[109] Merino Navarro, *Las cuentas*.

[110] Spain, like any other European country, was increasing its fiscal share across all its territories, not just in the Americas. The treasury also increased collection across all sources of income, including, for example, monies taken in from the Church.

[111] Klein, *The American Finances*; Grafe and Irigoin, "Legacy"; Irigoin and Grafe, "Bargaining for Absolutism"; Grafe and Irigoin, "Stakeholder Empire."

[112] On the *situados*, see, e.g., Grafe and Irigoin, "Legacy"; Irigoin and Grafe, "Bargaining for Absolutism"; and Marichal and Souto Mantecón, "Silver and Situados."

[113] Grafe and Irigoin, "Legacy," 255.

[114] The standard reference is still Ehrenberg, *Das Zeitalter der Fugger*.

[115] Drelichman and Voth, "Sustainable Debts"; Elliott, *Imperial Spain*; Yun Casalilla, *Marte Contra Minerva*.

the same way, the really devastating fiscal situation of the mid-seventeenth century was aggravated by the fall of American income that could be used as collateral to appease the Genoese lenders to the Crown. Hence, as the century progressed, the Crown regularly demanded extra payments from the corporations involved in the Indies trade under various pretexts, all of which translated into extraordinary taxation.[116]

During much of the eighteenth century, however, the moderate overall transfers of colonial monies to Spain, together with the Spanish treasury's refusal to use its potential lines of credit despite fairly low interest rates, suggest again that the Crown applied restraint. This is inexplicable in the standard neoclassical political economy model that relies on the supposedly inescapable logic of military-fiscal competition. The modest rate of transfers from the Americas could probably be explained away by "soft" constraints that were embedded in the jurisdictional fragmentation of the empire, even though they were not the kinds of "constitutional commitment" that early NIE stressed. Yet there is no evidence that the Crown was subject to any constraints, formal or informal, that kept it from raising debt. It had done so before the 1670s and returned to the markets in order to borrow again after the 1780s. In the interim, however, it kept well below its ability to borrow, relying instead on credit mainly to smooth over the unavoidable temporal differences in revenue collection and expenditures.

Evidently, revenue maximization was not the only game in town for early modern emerging nation-states, even if it was undoubtedly a very important one.[117] The central conclusion has to be that the exogenous constraint imposed by military competition, the bottomless pit of sovereign treasuries through the ages, was far less binding than commonly asserted. That is especially true if we consider that Spain did not match its newfound financial prudence with a successful strategy to stay out of military engagements. Though Spain had ceased to be a serious contender on the European military stage in the mid-seventeenth century, it was at war for as many years in the eighteenth century as France and England, and built up a respectable navy in the mid-eighteenth century almost from scratch.[118] It also kept its huge transoceanic empire intact in the face of obsessive attacks from its European competitors, not a small feat in itself.[119] However, while England clearly pushed revenue raising to the limits of what was economically, politically, and socially possible, and France famously pushed beyond that boundary, relatively low interest rates in combination with a strategy to reduce the public debt suggest that the Spanish Crown applied deliberate restraint for most of the century.

This in turn reveals a degree of agency and choice within European fiscal-military states that has often been overlooked. Within the current NIE

[116] Storrs, *Resilience*, 137–43; Bernal, *Proyecto inacabado*, 187.

[117] The same conclusion emanates from the fiscal system in Spanish America. Irigoin and Grafe, "Response," 243.

[118] Britain was at war 46 years between 1700 and 1814, France 45, and Spain 51. For Britain and France, see Mathias and O'Brien, "Taxation," 603n601.

[119] Grafe and Irigoin, "Stakeholder Empire."

paradigm a constitutionally unconstrained, increasingly "absolutist" monarchy would have been expected to spend freely and then figure out whom to expropriate to recover revenue, or simply refuse to pay for the debt and expropriate its creditors.[120] Spain's eighteenth-century trajectory contradicts the one assumption that underlies NIE models of the need for governments' constitutionally anchored credible commitment to property rights, namely that rulers had no choice but to maximize revenue collection. Indeed, Spain chose not to in the eighteenth century.

This raises two questions: First, what explains Spanish rulers' apparent (self-)restraint in the absence of formal constitutional rules of the type that much of the NIE literature has stressed? Second, what does it mean for our understanding of the links between the process of nation- and market-building in early modern Europe more generally if we considerably relax the assumption that the early modern European fiscal-military state had little choice but to press its subjects fiscally as much as possible? In Spain, the Crown was apparently susceptible to much "softer" commitment devices. A continuous process of bargaining with the corporate holders of sovereignty evidently kept it on the straight and narrow in fiscal terms for much of the eighteenth century without the need for "formal" constitutional commitments à la North and Weingast, while it also successfully precluded the descent into fiscal chaos.

Recently Greif and his coauthors have explored one way to conceptualize an alternative path toward explaining how "coercion-constraining institutions" could evolve and under what conditions they could become self-sustaining.[121] They suggest that powerful administrators rather than parliamentary control over the state's finances made "constitutions" in medieval and early modern Europe self-enforcing. In this view, rulers who had to compete with overlapping jurisdictions could be effectively stopped from infringing on their subjects' rights. In other words, a distribution of administrative capacity could restrict abuse. Greif, González de Lara, and Jha point out, however, that a full model of such an alternative path toward self-enforcing constraints on the ruler is hard to develop at the moment. Institutional economics, political science, and sociology do not provide adequate models for the power relation between administrators and rulers or, for that matter, how an equilibrium between these two parties would affect economic growth.[122]

Nevertheless they provide some empirical consideration as to why in certain polities a self-enforcing equilibrium was achieved while elsewhere it was not. The path chosen here follows this strategy through in much more depth. It aims at constructing an alternative model from the bottom up through empirical analysis. Spanish history offers empirical evidence that should lead

[120] Rosenthal, "Political Economy."

[121] González de Lara, Greif, and Jha, "Administrative Foundations"; Greif, "Commitment, Coercion, and Markets."

[122] González de Lara, Greif, and Jha, "Administrative Foundations," 108–9.

us to reject the notion of the binding external constraint imposed by military competition. In fact, there is no theoretical reason why a monopolist—and the early modern state did largely succeed in capturing the monopoly of violence—should necessarily raise its price, that is, maximize taxation. As Hirschman has argued, most political monopolists would probably adjust the quality of their output downward rather than the price upward.[123] This is a possibility that neither historical sociology nor political economy have seriously explored thus far.

Instead, scholars have armed themselves with a whole array of apparently incontestable quotations attesting to the supposed inevitability of military-induced revenue maximization. The Milanese Gian Giacomo Trivulzio allegedly told Louis XII of France in 1499 that in wars "three things are necessary: money; more money; and still more money"; Edmund Burke quipped that "Revenue is the principal preoccupation of the State. Nay more it is the State." The Conde Duque de Olivares, the powerful *valido* of Philip IV, evinced a more sophisticated understanding when he argued in 1637 that war required "men, money, order and obedience."[124]

Revenue was a necessary but not sufficient condition for the survival of rule; by the seventeenth century, rulers did not *buy* an army any longer, states had to be able to *mobilize* resources. Alas, in a vector that also included men, order, and obedience, in addition to money, those three might only be available if the state were willing to forego some revenue (read money). Olivares famously lost his position when attempting to square this particular circle. But he had understood the constraints on his government more clearly than do most present-day political economists. What is missing from the theories so far is a more appropriate concept of governance that goes beyond the simplistic notions of predation and constitutional regimes. It has to be able to capture a variety of organizational and institutional solutions to the problems of rule, representation, and commitment to public and private property rights within the context of the premodern European state, which was not on a linear trajectory to more state autonomy everywhere, as it turns out.

Jurisdictional Fragmentation and Market Integration

Political economy has today, by and large, moved beyond the North and Weingast notion of the all-powerful, centralizing, expropriating early modern monarchs. Instead, it acknowledges that "absolutist" rulers were bound at every turn by the traditional freedoms and liberties that corporate entities and historic territories enjoyed. Epstein demonstrated the negative effects of

---

[123] Hirschman, *Exit, Voice, and Loyalty.*
[124] Trivulzio and Olivares are quoted in Glete, *War and the State*, 126–27. Burke is quoted in O'Brien, "Nature and Historical Evolution."

jurisdictional fragmentation in the case of the Italian city-states and came to the conclusion that political freedom was either unconnected or possibly negatively related to economic growth.[125] Hoffman and others have discussed the limits imposed on the French Crown. Winkelbauer has made the same case for Austria-Hungary.[126] Dincecco has shown that in a cross-country growth comparison jurisdictional unification was far more important for growth than political regimes before 1789.[127] However, substituting "jurisdictional fragmentation" for "political regime" as the main potential force thwarting the development of markets—and thus economic growth—in the early modern period just replaces one one-size-fits-all approach with another. Jurisdictional fragmentation is clearly now a more promising concept to explain what determined early modern European comparative economic development than a supposed dichotomy between political regimes. Yet it has so far largely remained a black box.

What forms of jurisdictional fragmentation obtained in European societies? National and regional historiographies have tended to stress both challenges to centralizing authorities and cooperation with the center almost everywhere. However, historians have said little about how and to what extent either development affected the exercise of power in a comparative trans-"national" perspective. The remarkable differences across Europe in the degree, form, and foundations of jurisdictional fragmentation, or how they were overcome, have barely been historicized in a comparative context, especially in terms of the economic consequences that resulted from these differences.[128]

The historical political economy literature has treated all types of jurisdictional fragmentation as essentially the same, that is, as an obstacle to rulers' control over currencies and taxes, measures and languages, legal systems, and military levies. This is obviously correct, but it leaves half of the story untold. What forms of jurisdictional fragmentation obtained made a crucial difference. Different forms of jurisdictional fragmentation—or to put it another way, where power was located, how it was legitimized, and how it was exercised—shaped economic development in the long run and most specifically patterns of market integration. The argument is simple: the historical context has to be taken much more seriously than most economists are willing to do.

It might be a forgivable simplification to argue that there were two main sources of persistent jurisdictional fragmentation in the emerging early modern European nation-states. On the one hand, corporate groups, the estates (as a social group, not necessarily as a representative institution), guilds, and

[125] Epstein, *Freedom and Growth*, 34; Epstein, "Cities."
[126] Hoffman, "France"; Winkelbauer, *Ständefreiheit*.
[127] Dincecco, "Fiscal Centralization."
[128] The best comparative account of the political and social variations across polities is undoubtedly Reinhard, *Staatsgewalt*. However, the author is not concerned with the economic consequences.

the Church held sovereign power. On the other, such rights and duties could be located in territorial units, historic territories that became part of the emerging nation-states or towns that held sovereign rights. In the former the struggle took place fundamentally between groups of social actors defined by status. In the latter it was defined by location.

In practical terms the question is: Was sovereignty contested between the Crown and a somehow-defined social group, let us call it "elite" or estates (as a social group)? Or was it mostly defined across territorial units? The most simplified version of this argument can be conceptualized through Hirschman's concept of *exit* and *voice*. Where the contest over sovereignty developed more along the lines of an elite or aristocracy versus Crown conflict the only viable option of protest against an encroaching Crown was, to use Hirschman's terms, *voice*. Hence, strategies of co-optation, enlargement of the nobility, and a little court-based power play were likely to render reasonable results for the Crown. Territorial conflicts, by contrast, always included an *exit* option of territories breaking away. Therefore, they shaped and delimited the exercise of power in very different ways.

Jurisdictional Fragmentation and Patrimonialism

Jurisdictional fragmentation is often identified with another important but ill-defined -*ism*: patrimonialism.[129] In the classic two-by-two matrices favored by political scientists, Ertman complements the economists' one-dimensional space of political regime from "constitutionally constrained" to "absolutist" with a second vector representing the character of their state infrastructure. Some polities, such as Britain, Sweden, Denmark, and the German territorial states, developed a technology of governance that was tending toward a bureaucratic state. Others, like Poland, Hungary, France, Spain, and much of Italy, employed a patrimonial structure.[130] But does this Weberian concept of the "patrimonial" state resolve the problem of the different paths of state-building, and in particular, does it adequately capture the problem of jurisdictional fragmentation?[131]

Again the influence of economic historians of France and their focus on the role of political and bureaucratic elites in strengthening or undermining the power of the monarchy has been decisive. In the absence of a proper theory of where power was located, how it was legitimized, and how it was exercised in early modern European societies, economists once again looked to historical sociology and political history for clues. In the French literature, implicitly or explicitly, the "elite" who were supposed to be the Crown's

---

[129] The classic sociological definition of patrimonial rule is the absence of an administrative body that is directly controlled by the ruler, who therefore has to rely on the willingness of his "associates" to obey. See Weber, *Wirtschaft und Gesellschaft*, section 7a.

[130] Ertman, *Leviathan*.

[131] Weber, *Wirtschaft und Gesellschaft*, 130–39.

counterpart are often equated with the aristocracy or with landed interests against capital holders.[132] This argument is underpinned by a notion that the rise of the modern nation-state implied the suppression of aristocratic power, either through an authoritative absolute rule of one, that is, an absolutist monarchy, or through a parliamentary regime.[133] According to Ertman, Spain, like much of Latin Europe, became patrimonial rather than bureaucratic because its *cortes* were allegedly "structurally weaker, status-based Estates which ultimately proved unable to resist the steady advance of royal power."[134] The monarchy pushed the "estates" (read the nobility) out of the way and undertook an increasing "irrationalisation" (Ertman's term) of governance through an alienation of state functions, which in turn limited royal prerogative. Ironically, neoclassical economists and historical sociologists alike formulate the problem in essentially Marxist terms.

Yet the traditional story of the creation of the modern state as dependent on the demise of the aristocracy is problematic to say the least.[135] Conflict between the Crown and the aristocracy was always the exception, not the rule.[136] The aristocracy placed important investments in the state and had become entrepreneurs in their own right. As states became more complex organizations, investment opportunities multiplied from military service, to lender, to officeholder, to tax farmer. The relative success of state-building in early modern Europe depended crucially on states' ability to co-opt their elites while defending their own autonomy, as historical research on the nature of absolutism has shown. The advantages of co-optation were obvious.

> A state that could co-ordinate its own interests with the authority and patronage that traditional local elites enjoyed among the common people had easier access to local resources. It could raise taxes or conscript soldiers and seamen with greater efficiency and less local resistance. The elite group might trade their local authority for increased influence over the central state, or they might use this authority in the interest of the state in exchange for even more local power guaranteed by the fiscal-military state.[137]

Spain is referred to as a quintessentially patrimonial state, that is, a state that loses domestic authority to elite groups within society in return for their

---

[132] This is, e.g., the formulation by Stasavage, *Public Debt*.

[133] In the English case this refers to the historiographical debate about the Whig-Tory competition, especially in the late seventeenth and early eighteenth centuries, which traditionally saw Tories as a threat to the credible commitment of the government. Alas, it should be noted that England did not default in 1710/11 and arguably the Tories established a sound fiscal basis for decades to come.

[134] Ertman, *Leviathan*, 155.

[135] For France, see Beik, "Absolutism." For a European overview, see Scott, "Consolidation."

[136] Glete, *War and the State*, 3–5.

[137] Ibid., 3.

allegiance and fiscal contributions.[138] Elites were brought into the new, larger state through the sale of civil, ecclesiastical, and military offices, sinecures, and participation in the fiscal system as tax farmers.[139] This alienation of functional parts of sovereignty checked the contravening efforts at central-ization of the monopoly of power embodied in the Crown's push against seigneurial rights. Driven by the need to increase income, the Crown perma-nently alienated important offices and rights to privileges and monopolies. In a patrimonial polity the pursuit of private interest was incompatible with "collectively positive outcomes in the political sphere."[140] In economic terms, private and social rates of return were poorly aligned. Public and private, the office and the officeholder, state and private finances were indistinguishable.

How, then, were some states able to create a bureaucracy and co-opt the elites without being co-opted in turn? If the suppression of early modern estates was not pushed through by the Crown against the elites but with their cooperation and participation in return for a new kind of contractual relationship that offered elite members a share of the new and larger pie, why did local elites not become "accomplices" of the state everywhere?[141] The prime piece of evidence cited for a move toward patrimonial structures is the sale of offices and sinecures on the one hand and the alienation of power to corporatist bodies with monopolistic economic rights, such as guilds, on the other. Yet again, a juxtaposition of the French and Spanish cases illustrates that the latter is hardly the mirror image of the former.[142]

The French institutionalization of the fiscal charges on the sale of offices through the *paulette*, an annual tax on officeholders worth around one-sixtieth of the offices' income, infamously removed restrictions on the inheritance of offices and thus strengthened the property rights of the officeholder vis-à-vis the state.[143] In Castile, by contrast, there was never a legal basis for the sale of offices, and receipts from the *media anata secular*, a one-off payment for offices, were never of fiscal importance.[144] The sale *por juro de heredad* (as hereditary property) was outlawed at the Cortes de Toledo of 1480, and the prohibition was reiterated in the two most important legal collections, the Recopilaciones of 1567 and 1805.[145] Castilians and their kings found ways around this, to be sure. The price for an office was labeled officially "a dona-tion" (*donativo*), and the transfer, which became common, was disguised as

---

[138] For a recent example, see Stein and Stein, *Silver*, 102–5. The authors argue that silver imports were the driving force behind patrimonialization.

[139] For the states' attempt to redistribute via salaries and offices in Spain, see Solbes Ferri, *Rentas Reales de Navarra*, 53, and Kamen, *Succession*, 37–38.

[140] Ertman, *Leviathan*, 154.

[141] Glete, *War and the State*, 7.

[142] For France, see Doyle, *Venality*.

[143] Mousnier, *Institutions*, 2:27–77.

[144] Ecclesiastical offices were subject to a similar due, the *media anata eclesiastica*.

[145] The following draws strongly on Tomás y Valiente, "Ventas," and Tomás y Valiente, *Gobierno*, 152–76.

a resignation in favor of someone else (*resignatio in favorem*). However, the prohibition helped limit the role of the sale of offices in some key positions.

As a consequence, very different rules applied to the distinct types of offices. It is important to dig a little deeper into this ill-researched field of Spanish history in order to understand the way it differed from the better-known French case. Tómas y Valiente suggests thinking about three categories: offices of the "quill," of "power," and of "money."[146] The first describes offices of notary publics and scriveners, who were generally subject to sale against a fixed fee but also to quality control, that is, the owner of the office had to demonstrate that the officeholder (not always the same person) had the necessary qualification. The most important offices in the second group of "power offices" were at no point subject to sale in the Peninsula. The highest royal offices in each district, the *corregidor* and the *intendencias* created in the eighteenth century, were never for sale in Castile, nor were judicial positions. Likewise, military posts were very rarely sold.[147] The legal heritage ring-fenced all judicial and the highest royal positions in the Peninsula in stark contrast to French practice.

Holders of these offices received a salary and had to fulfill minimum conditions of training. The relative importance of training, personal connections, having passed through the Colegios Mayores of the main universities, and other socioeconomic factors in determining access to posts in the administration changed.[148] The bureaucracy was obviously not a meritocratic, professional force; salaries were often inadequate, and there is evidence that indirect payments were made for offices that could not be legally sold.[149] Only in the later eighteenth century do we see the emergence of a clearer career path that stressed education beyond the formal degree and favored experience over socioeconomic factors.[150]

Yet the system was corrupt and an insider game rather than venal in the classic sense. Using Root's juxtaposition of nepotism and corruption, we can see that it was closer to a corrupt system that was open to market forces like Britain's than to a French-style nepotistic (that is, non-market) one.[151] The Francophone traveler Antoine de Brunel was puzzled by what he witnessed in Spain in the late seventeenth century. He was at pains to point out that the French system of venality was preferable since it guarded against the unhealthy Spanish habit of promoting social inferiors.

[146] Tomás y Valiente, *Gobierno*, 158.

[147] The intendent system was fashioned on French precedents. However, its introduction was haphazard and the officeholders never became remotely as powerful and important as their French counterparts. See also chapter 5.

[148] Kagan, "Universities in Castile"; Windler, *Lokale Eliten*, 23.

[149] Sánchez Belén, *Política fiscal*, 292. See also Storrs, *Resilience*, 123–24.

[150] Scholz, "Amt als Belohnung."

[151] Root argues that a corrupt system, such as the English, is economically preferable to a nepotistic one, such as the French, because it is receptive to economic incentives and thus more efficient in allocative terms. Root, "Redistributive Role."

Neither Governments, nor Military, nor Civil Charges are here [in Spain] sold, which is not altogether so commendable as it seems at first sight; for unworthy persons (if well looked on by Favorites) may more easily attain them than if they paid for them, and several of antient [*sic*] extraction and great abilities are willing to lay out their money to put themselves in a condition to serve their King with honour: neither in Countreys where Charges are most vendible, are they so to all Chapmen; but to Gentlemen only, and such as are qualified for them.[152]

Among "power offices," the only important ones that were subject to sale were the *regimientos* (aldermanships) and other municipal offices, especially in the second half of the seventeenth century.[153] Town councils were very powerful and aldermanships a sought-after prize in large towns where the town itself, and not the Crown, possessed in principle the right to suggest the officeholder. Yet even here the Crown could, and sometimes did, refuse the *resignatio in favorem,* and it also expanded their numbers to increase income, thus lowering their value. Contrary to French officeholders who had agreed to pay the *paulette* in return for guarantees of venality and the creation of fewer new offices, Castilian officeholders had at best the somewhat shaky right to the usufruct of an office but never full alienable property rights.[154] Spanish officeholders also obtained fewer benefits from their status. Tax exemptions, a major attraction of offices in France, were limited and often meaningless. The Spanish tax system relied heavily on indirect consumption taxes rather than direct land or wealth taxes. Thus exemptions were often unenforceable. By the eighteenth century, the municipal market for "power offices" was stagnating.

"Money offices," mostly related to tax and customs farms, were regularly sold, but holders generally had to post sureties for their office. Thanks to the need for upfront investments, the market for these became the most competitive and was entirely driven by supply and demand. Offices such as scriveners were sold against a fee to trained lawyers but this hardly constituted an alienation of fundamental functions of the state. Similarly, Spanish tax farms were essentially an agreement between a local, regional, or central authority and an individual investor, what we would call a public-private-partnership (PPP) today. Economists are unlikely to consider that a prejudice against state autonomy, though sociologists are more sensitive in this regard.

From a historical economics point of view, we might wonder if tax farming was the most efficient economic solution to tax collection. Yet, given the state of administrative technology, even in the eighteenth century it is likely

---

[152] Brunel and Aerssen, *Journey,* 29–30. The French edition was first published in Amsterdam or Cologne in 1655 and the text has been attributed by some to the Fleming François Van Aerssen or his grandson of the same name.

[153] The sale of town offices started in earnest as part of the negotiations between the Crown and its Genoese financiers, who were given blocs of offices to be sold off to the candidates of the towns. Drelichman has started to work on pricing these loan agreements properly. Drelichman and Voth, "Borrower," 12n11.

[154] Mousnier, *Institutions.*

that a fiscal system based mostly on local trade and consumption taxes, as in Spain, would have been impossible to administer directly.[155] The literature often refers to tax farming and the advance payments to the Crown it entailed as dangerous methods of non-market "inside finance" that empowered the lenders.[156] Yet in Spain they were largely a result of urban autonomy. Urban power and its impact upon the prevalence of indirect taxation, something we will return to in some detail, rather than the alleged patrimonialism of the governance system determined administrative structures. Even in the Americas, where the sale of offices had been legal since 1606 and widespread, the overall outcome was closer to a PPP than a classic patrimonial pattern, as Irigoin and I have argued elsewhere.[157]

All of this underlines that while sales of offices existed in Castile and the other Spanish territories, as in most other European states, important nuances in the practice reveal the problematic use of the concept of patrimonialism as a catchall phrase for bureaucratic failure or even jurisdictional fragmentation in Spain. The Spain of the seventeenth to late eighteenth century was never subject to conflicts between venal officeholders and the Crown in the same way as France was to that of the *noblesse de robe* and the monarchy, a fact ignored by much of the comparative literature on European state-building. The inevitable conclusion is that jurisdictional fragmentation should not simply be equated with patrimonialism and the implied creation of powerful elite groups with common interests.

Power and Markets

There are two main problems in the existing historical political economy model of the relationship between the creation of the nation-state on the one hand and market development on the other hand in early modern Europe, and they are intimately linked. First, systems and exercise of governance are poorly historicized. Second, the recourse to the supposedly inescapable exogenous constraint imposed on rulers by the "military revolution" (i.e., revenue maximization at almost any cost) is an elegant way of avoiding the problem of having to endogenize the impetus to state-building in the model. However, it is neither empirically nor theoretically convincing.

The key to providing a more accurate model of early modern state formation and its impact on market integration is to understand how different forms of jurisdictional fragmentation interacted with the exercise of power and thus through which channels the impact on market development occurred. The central hypothesis of this book is that the seeming self-restraint

[155] Hoffman makes this point for France even though indirect taxation was much less important there. Hoffman, "France," 232.

[156] On internal or inside finance, see Stasavage, *Public Debt*, 65–66.

[157] Grafe and Irigoin, "Stakeholder Empire," challenges the classic interpretation by Burkholder and Chandler, *Impotence to Authority*.

exercised by Spanish rulers was rooted in a system of governance that implied that most of the devolved power that limited the Spanish monarchy was territorial rather than a cleavage between the estates or an "elite" and the Crown. At least in the Castilian heartlands, the aristocracy (as an estate, not as individuals) was a relatively minor player in the development of political organization.

To be certain, there was conflict between the Crown and the aristocracy, and between towns and their seigneur, or their often noble oligarchies. Marxist historians of the 1970s argued that Spain had become particularly absolutist early on because the Crown had beaten the aristocracy into submission by the sixteenth century, especially in Castile. Compared to a much more powerful aristocracy in France or England the *grandes de España* were undoubtedly little more than a select group of royal servants, often placated with non-political positions at the court.[158] Even in high Church positions they were not favored in Spain, and the only sphere where they were systematically privileged was high military office.[159] The conflict over a reassignment of political and economic power in Spain, however, was never predominantly a conflict between the aristocracy, or even a more widely defined elite, and the Crown in the first place. Nor did the aristocracy exercise the same economic power as elsewhere. Like those of the officeholders—and officeholding and nobility often went hand in hand—their fiscal privileges were worthless in many areas of economic activity. In Castile, both nobility and clerics likely ended up paying more taxes than their peers elsewhere in Europe—possibly the best indicator that as a group neither nobility nor officeholders as a corporate order were the main bargaining partner of the Crown.

By contrast, territorially based jurisdictional fragmentation survived in Spain to an unusual degree. That early modern Spain never overcame its heritage of a composite state of historic territories is a well-known fact and has been stressed by historians from Elliott to Nader.[160] Spanish monarchs faced the possible "exit" option in much stronger forms than did their peers in other large European states. Governance thus remained about negotiation between the *reinos* and the monarchy long after a consolidation of territorial power into a more hierarchical centralized structure occurred elsewhere. Spanish history illustrates this vividly. Portugal was de facto lost in the 1640s (*de iure* 1668); the price for reintegrating Catalonia into the Spanish composite monarchy after an uprising and short interlude as a French satellite in the 1650s was half a century in which the Crown largely refrained from meddling in regional affairs, even after the territory had been used openly as a power base to challenge the Spanish succession in the late seventeenth-century

---

[158] Windler, *Lokale Eliten*, 24.

[159] Fraser, *Napoleon's Cursed War*.

[160] See Elliott, "A Europe of Composite Monarchies"; Nader, *Liberty*; but also Fernández Albaladejo, "Cities and State," and Yun Casalilla and Comín, "Spain," as well as a large literature on individual territories and towns.

crisis of the Habsburg monarchy.[161] There were important reasons for the survival of strong elements of sovereignty in the historic territories rooted in the constitution, in the German sense of *Verfasstheit*, not *Verfassung* (i.e., the way, in which society is constituted rather than the Anglophone written or unwritten constitution), as we will see.

Spain continued to grapple not only with the strong historic territories but also with a very large number of powerful semi-autonomous municipalities especially in Castile, as many historians have shown. This feature was rooted at least in part in two peculiarities of the political organization of Castile when seen in a European comparative context. First, Castile had no medieval tradition of feudal serfdom to speak of; personal freedom was a given, and labor services were largely unknown by the high Middle Ages, with the notable but limited exception of Galicia in the northwest.[162] Thompson has called Castile in the Middle Ages "the freest society in Europe"; lordship was generally separated from landownership and "primarily a matter of jurisdiction."[163]

Second, the basic unit of political and fiscal organization since the *reconquista* was the town, not the lordly demesne.[164] There were certainly large estates belonging to the aristocracy, especially in Andalusia, but these were not comparable to the rural demesnes with strong noble rights found in many parts of Europe.[165] Instead, Castile had royal towns, ecclesiastically controlled towns, and towns under jurisdiction of the nobility. Villages, hamlets and rural areas in turn were under the administration of towns. Nor did Castile have a noble representation in its estates, the *cortes*. The noble and ecclesiastical representations were sidelined early on and last participated at all in the *cortes* in 1538.[166] For all practical purposes the Castilian *cortes* represented the large cities of the realm; they were a thoroughly urban affair. There were late sixteenth- and early seventeenth-century attempts to alter the relation between *rey* (king) and *reino* (kingdom) toward one where the latter was represented by the Castilian *cortes*. Notwithstanding by the 1660s Castile had firmly returned to the model of a "community of communities," and the relation between municipalities and Crown would change little during the next century, as we will see.[167]

---

[161] Carlos II's half brother Juan José marched from Catalonia against the Madrid regency government running affairs on behalf of the disabled king. Kamen, *Spain, 1665–1700*.

[162] Whether Spain simply lacked the basic conditions for the establishment of a feudal order for demographic reasons or in fact was feudal in character but within a structure of *señorio colectivo*, i.e., one where town councils effectively controlled access to resources in their jurisdiction, seems to be an ongoing debate. See, e.g., Sánchez-Albornoz, *Despoblación*, and the interesting discussion in Sánchez León, *Absolutismo y comunidad*, 7–17.

[163] Thompson, "Castile: Polity," 142.

[164] Nader, *Liberty*.

[165] On the legal limitations of aristocratic power in Castile, see Atienza Hernández, *Aristocracia, poder y riqueza*, chapter 3.

[166] Ertman, *Leviathan*, 113.

[167] Thompson, "Absolutism in Castile."

The location of power therefore continued to reside to a large degree in the historic territories and towns because it guaranteed a form of "representation," for lack of a better and less anachronistic term, that legitimized the rule of the Crown.[168] The historically surprising fact is that the Spanish composite monarchy survived in its core territories and its huge American domains for so long without either centralization or total dismemberment. Since power was to a larger extent located in territorial units and the exit option existed, the Crown was time and again forced to negotiate on almost equal terms. But here, too, more than one outcome was possible. Austria-Hungary shared many of Spain's features of enduring territorial jurisdictional fragmentation, but a stronger increasingly pan-Austro-Hungarian nobility was likely the binding element in a "monarchical union of corporative states (*Ständestaaten*)," turning one group of players in the corporate structure into the key ally of the Crown.[169]

In Spain, by contrast, the Crown remained the only binding element. Spain had a reasonably national but weak high aristocracy, a large but entirely locally bound nobility, and no trans-territorial estates or other corporate institutions of any kind. Hence, the Spanish Crown became the ultimate arbiter of a very complex network of regional and local corporate entities with shifting overlapping hierarchies. This institutional structure was underpinned by an ideological notion of "representation" in the institutions of towns and historic territories that established relatively narrow boundaries for negotiation.

The path toward the nation-state in European monarchies was thus not necessarily primarily a prisoner's dilemma that pitched Crown against elites. In Spain it was instead a complex coordination game that required constant realignment and continuous negotiation. Like all coordination games, it resulted in many equilibria rather than a clear-cut outcome. Unification of power was one possible outcome, but decentralization was just as possible and most likely cheaper in political and fiscal terms. We need to relax the excessively restrictive ex ante assumption of maximization of fiscal resources, leading necessarily to a hierarchical ordering of revenue control (or revolution) if we want to understand the longevity of political entities in Europe (and elsewhere) that survived largely by minimizing violent opposition at the expense of lower revenues. In Spain this often implied a protracted delegation of power to all kinds of corporate bodies, the territories, and the towns. The important fact is, however, that contrary to the current political economy models, fragmented power effectively limited predation rather than increased it. Fragmented power was also devolved power that could protect rights often more effectively.

If we conceive of the creation of stronger, more autonomous national states and nationalities as a diachronic process, it can hardly surprise us

---

[168] The Spanish *representación* is a wider concept than the English translation, which tends to narrow the term down to mean popular representation.

[169] Winkelbauer, *Ständefreiheit*, 197.

that a synchronic snapshot at any point in time reveals significant differences between these would-be nation-states exhibiting different degrees of centralization and bureaucratization. It is important to remember, however, that this was not a linear modernization story toward the nation-state that simply started earlier or later in different polities. Global history reminds us that the European-style nation-state was not the only possible outcome to the struggle over a reassignment of rights and power between various corporate entities and players in early modern society. Throughout this book we will encounter time and again the successful resistance to a more unified autonomous nation-state in Spain that in turn shows that the historical sociology model of the fiscal-military state and its deterministic predictions is problematic to say the least.

The assumption of a more or less linear process from a decentralized feudal organization to one where monarchical power (or parliament) asserted a clear hierarchical precedent over the aristocracy, on the one hand, and corporate bodies, such as towns or guilds (and eventually the Church), on the other, is unhelpful. Yet teleology still reigns supreme in many otherwise highly insightful contributions to the debate about the link between the creation of "national" fiscal-military states and the development of markets. To quote one example:

> The fiscal military state . . . will mobilise more resources as it moves towards full sovereignty on a national scale, until which time it will have to assume the cost and inefficiency caused by coordinating a contending host of political and economic claims and sovereignties. . . . [All earlier institutional arrangements,] guilds, feudalism, moral economy, subsidised prices, bills of exchange, regulation of supplies or networking between co-religionist merchants [were] makeshift solutions that were not conducive to any growth policy.[170]

To put it another way: all states were supposedly on a trajectory that allowed them to achieve a state where military necessity had overcome corporate jurisdictional fragmentation and only then could markets fostering "national" policies be implemented. Thus, for Torres Sánchez, "national" policies of the mercantilist type were not the outcome of a voracious predatory state as NIE wisdom would claim. Instead, they were a necessary measure of a "national" policy for growth. The problem is of course that none of this explains why the fiscal-military state apparently failed to create the conditions that would foster a "national" market in Spain. Spain does not fit into the straightjacket of the neoclassical modernization story.[171]

As we will see, from a Spanish perspective the persistently non-hierarchical nature of corporate early modern society is what stands out. This was a

[170] Torres Sánchez, "Triumph," 27–28.
[171] Nor does it fit into the Marxist variety: Castile (and to a lesser extent Aragon) was never feudal; the aristocracy was not the main competitor of the Crown, and the corporate bodies were never tamed.

stakeholder polity where individuals were invested in the preservation of the political status quo through their socioeconomic investment in corporate bodies, first and foremost at the municipal level. The concept of patrimonialism that poses a conflict between a (noble) officeholder "class" empowered by a central monarchy and the monarchy itself is of little help in understanding the preferences and interests of Spanish stakeholders. However, Spanish history shows that the path toward the nation-state taken in more centralized, hierarchical polities like France or England was not an unavoidable outcome either. This needs explaining, too.

The central question for this book remains what the economic outcome of this coordination game was. Its effects were visible in all areas of state activity, the legal and monetary systems, the political process, social cleavages, and cultural and linguistic developments. But the clearest aggregate indicator of how the location and exercise of power affected and interacted with the economic development in Spain is how it affected market integration. The most important Achilles heel of Spanish political economy in the early modern period was not a predatory absolutist state, an overextended empire, the exploitation of Spain as part of the semi-periphery of a capitalist world system, or a bourgeoisie that chose a rentier's life. It was the fragmentation of the internal markets that resulted paradoxically from the very strength of a system of governance that allowed the Spanish Crown to rule by negotiation and compromise.

The empirical evidence presented in the following pages thus draws mainly on a study of market integration that aims to understand why it was so slow, haphazard, and regionally diverse in Spain and what this implied for Spanish economic development in general. The view from the consumer's perspective allows us to better understand what jurisdictional fragmentation really meant, why it persisted or even increased, and how it functioned. It can also illuminate why early modern European history was more complicated than the supposed trajectory from the fiscal-military to the unified nation-state allows for. This will become apparent when we get closer to the answers to a number of empirical questions about Spanish markets such as: how important was the impact of sovereign power of historic territories vis-à-vis that of the towns? The analysis of the market of one particular staple consumer good across the Spanish possessions in the Iberian Peninsula can give us a first idea of how exactly jurisdictional fragmentation shaped market-building.

Chapter 2

Tracing the Market

The Empirical Challenge

Measuring Market Integration

Historians and economists have quite distinct working definitions of market integration. On the one hand, historians of the early modern period tend to think about market integration as a process in which agriculture and manufacturing directed largely at guaranteeing subsistence were increasingly replaced by specialized production that had to be sold on the market in return for other goods. This was accompanied by a similar increase in labor allocation that was fully monetized. Hence, market integration was intimately linked to changes not only in the commercialization of agricultural and manufacturing goods but also in their production and consumption patterns.

On the other hand, economists tend to define market integration more narrowly through the "law of one price": if markets are fully integrated between two locations then the price of tradable goods should be identical in both places. If the price of grain, to choose just one popular example, in Seville diverged from that in Cadiz, and the markets between these two places were integrated, one would expect merchants to immediately take advantage of the difference and make it disappear through trade.[1] The following analysis will reflect both of these approaches. It integrates a study of changing production and consumption patterns (chapter 3) with a quantitative analysis that takes as its point of departure the "law of one price" (chapters 4–7).

The notion of arbitrage toward one price is obviously just a theoretical construct; like all social science models it is no "law" at all. In reality, at least transport costs had to be added. Hence, a wedge between prices could persist. Still, the possibility to measure how far from the "ideal state" markets were at a particular point in time is a powerful tool. It enables economic historians to trace change over time and across regions and to provide initial answers to a whole range of empirical questions such as the following: Did the absolute size of price differentials between various places change over time? Did a rise or decline in prices in one town translate into a similar rise or decline in another town quickly or slowly? Did the direction and size of movements of prices in one location coincide with those in another? The measurement of geographical, temporal, and structural market integration a priori tells us

---

[1] O'Rourke and Williamson, *Globalization and History*; Persson, *Grain Markets*.

nothing about the reasons why markets might have been more or less integrated. Yet it provides an invaluable yardstick for a comparative discussion.

The obvious but not trivial question is, of course, why markets were not already highly integrated in the early modern period. Marxists and some historical anthropologists used to argue that the agrarian populations of late medieval and early modern Europe were concentrating their efforts on guaranteeing little more than basic survival. They had a culturally determined absolute risk aversion and hence little propensity to engage voluntarily with the market.[2] However, there is now plenty of evidence that production for the market was a part of even the remotest agrarian settings in Europe and elsewhere early on.[3] People were not voluntarily refraining from buying and selling on the market. Instead, markets were simply not integrated enough to serve the needs of producers and consumers far into the early modern and modern periods in many parts of Europe. Hence, we need to return to our point of departure to answer the questions of how the process of market integration proceeded empirically in Spain and what impact the pattern of jurisdictional fragmentation had on this process. We need to ask, just how poorly were markets integrated?

For a quantitative analysis we need a common standard for market integration, a particular good that can be studied across time and space to see if Spanish markets moved closer to or further away from the "law of one price." For prices to serve as the basis of a study of market integration, however, the commodity in question must be a staple that is consumed everywhere. It also needs to be a homogeneous good; differences in prices should not reflect distinct qualities but instead how efficiently the market mediates supply and demand. With these requirements in mind, economic historians have generally looked at grain prices for evidence, arguing that grain was (a) the single most important item in most families' consumption basket; (b) the single largest item in local and regional trade, and (c) an item that varied little in quality. This is undoubtedly the case. However, the evident advantages of grain prices are outweighed by their disadvantages for the purpose of the current study. I therefore suggest going in an entirely new direction. The remainder of this book will use a different commodity that became a staple in Spain in the early modern period: dried and salted codfish, *bacalao*.

The Trouble with Grain

To see why cod prices are better suited than grain prices when trying to understand the link between Spain's political economy and its market integration, it is worth considering in more detail what determined prices and thus what information they can offer. Price differences between markets were

[2] Brenner, "Social Basis."
[3] Epstein, *Freedom and Growth*, 4–6.

caused very broadly by four variables. The first one was obviously freight, as well as a number of other transaction costs such as those arising from finding information about markets, potential customers, and so on. Let us denominate these as (F). The cost of transport and information gathering depended to a large extent on technology, for example, the state of roads, vehicles, and networks of postal communication. The second variable was uncorrelated supply shocks (S). These might be caused by sudden production changes, a shortfall or an increase caused by weather conditions, animal disease, or warfare, all of which could seriously raise or lower prices. The third variable to consider is uncorrelated demand shocks (D). These might be seasonal or they might be caused by changes in customer preferences or a sudden change in income. Finally, price differentials could also be the result of political economy intervention in the market in the form of taxes, buying and selling restrictions, or maximum and minimum prices (T).

Studying market integration through price comparisons hence faces the challenge of having to distinguish those sources of price variability and differences across locations that are directly linked to market integration, such as transport (F) and taxes (T), from those that mainly reflect production or consumption conditions, here (S) and (D). Ideally, the contribution of each of these variables to price variances would be clearly identifiable econometrically so as to discount (S) and (D) and be able to assess quantitatively the impact of (F) and (T) on market integration.

Empirical research is of course more complex. There are three ways of analyzing market integration quantitatively: the volatility of prices in a given location, the co-movement of prices between two locations, and the price differential between two locations. Depending on the commodity, it is easier to interpret price volatility, co-movements, or differences in order to disentangle (S), (D), (F), and (T). In addition, in different markets at specific times some commodities are more suited than others. Most important, the objective of the analysis should guide the choice of commodity. A study that focuses primarily on tracing the process of market integration as such, that is, how the degree of market integration changed over time and across space, will mainly be concerned with separating supply and demand shocks in the aggregate (D + S) from the sum of transaction costs (F + T). But for the present study it is crucial that one also be able to distinguish the effects of transport costs (F) from those of political economy interventions (T), since the latter are what tell us about the impact and shape of jurisdictional fragmentation in the territories and towns of the Spanish Crown.

The advantages of using grain prices are well-known thanks to a long tradition in the literature.[4] First, Grain was undoubtedly the main food staple

---

[4] This research goes back to a major project initiated by William Beveridge (LSE) and Francis Gay (Harvard) in the 1930s. Data published by contributors in a number of countries still form the backbone of a lot of research even today. Posthumus, *Nederlandsche Prijsgeschiedenis*; Beveridge, *Prices and Wages in England*; Hauser and International Scientific Committee on Price History, *Recherches et documents;* Pribram, Geyer, and Koran, *Geschichte der Preise und Löhne.*

and thus traded widely. Demand for grain was not constant; there is evidence that it was an inferior good. In hard times people increased their consumption of bread at the expense of almost any other product, thus affecting (D). Income effects, however, were probably more at work in the long run. Grain demand was reasonably inelastic in the short run, meaning that shortages and oversupply translated indeed into measurable price changes.[5] The second advantage is that grain prices can sometimes reflect discrete changes in transport technology (F) quite well. A bulky good meant that improvements in roads, for example, or the opening of canals can often be traced neatly in grain prices. Third, it helps that historians in fact know a lot about grain markets and their regulation. Grain's position as a very important staple meant that political authorities as well as contemporary commentators devoted much ink to documenting the grain trade.

The weaknesses of grain price studies in general are equally well-known. One problem is identifying how supply side changes (S) actually affected prices. Grain production was subject to idiosyncratic production shocks caused mostly by weather conditions. The infamous hailstorm just before the harvest in a single village has proven to be a tremendous problem for econometric analysis because the relationship between local production shortfalls on the one hand and price levels and volatility on the other is not stable. Lower degrees of market integration mean obviously a higher level of dependence on local harvest outcomes and should thus be associated with more volatility, that is, price hikes in times of shortage and large falls in the case of bumper harvests.[6] At the same time, if previously more or less self-sufficient producing regions become integrated into a larger market economy, this might for a time increase volatility in a local market because "national" demand swings could lead to local scarcity or oversupply where there were none before.[7] Thus, economic historians have tried to complement the analysis by estimating production conditions. However, with the exception of extreme years of good or bad weather, most of the supply shocks were precisely local, and they are almost impossible to identify econometrically.[8] As a consequence, grain price volatility proves to be an indicator that is hard to interpret because more market integration could increase volatility at least in the short and medium run as long as all regions were at the same time consuming and producing.[9]

A second problem is that longer-term changes in transport and related costs (as opposed to discrete shocks) are hard to identify in grain price studies

---

[5] Most existing estimates of the own-price-elasticity of grain suggest a value around −0.6. See Barquín Gil, "Elasticity of Demand," and Persson, *Grain Markets*, 54–63. Fogel has claimed that the own-price-elasticity of grain was much lower in nineteenth-century England. Fogel, "Second Thoughts." However, Barquín has shown conclusively that this estimate included an error.

[6] Reher, "Producción, precios e integración."

[7] See Yun Casalilla, *Sobre la transición* versus Llopis Agelán, "Almacenamientos."

[8] Persson, *Grain Markets*, 94.

[9] Yun Casalilla, *Sobre la transición*; Barquín Gil, "Transporte y precio."

because the most basic measure of price divergence, the price wedge between different locations, has no direct interpretation.[10] The reason is yet again that the commodity was both locally produced and regionally and interregionally traded. The direction and pattern of trade was ever-changing depending on regional weather conditions, storage, and other local short-term supply shocks. With the exception of international trade, which was generally registered at customs, the short-term fluctuations between surplus and deficit regions are rarely known, even if we have a fair idea as to which regions tended to be short of grain or grain abundant in the long run. Thus the idiosyncratic shocks to (S) also complicate the identification of longer-term trends in (F), which will have an impact on the aggregate outcome but are hard to separate out.

Besides these general problems, there are a number of issues that applied to Spanish grain markets in particular. To begin with, "grain" was in Spain a less homogenous good than in many northern European markets because different regions used different kinds of grains such as wheat, maize, and rice as basic cereal staples. Regional analyses are largely unaffected. However, interregional ones are made more complicated not only because supply shocks would be influenced by local weather conditions and such but also because these conditions affected different grains in distinct ways; the (S) of wheat differed from the (S) of rice or the (S) of maize. An exceptionally wet year might be bad news for peasants who were growing wheat, while those engaged in rice cultivation enjoyed excellent harvests. Integrating the analysis of Spanish domestic grain markets into changes in the international economy is even harder, especially before the nineteenth century.[11]

Most important, however, the grain market in early modern Spain was ruled by an exceptional set of political measures such as taxes, quantity interventions, and set prices. Grain's advantage as an indicator was that it was such an important staple. But this is also its biggest downside because grain prices were a prime concern of political authorities. It was the *only* staple commodity in Spain that was, at least in principle, subject to national rather than local and regional political economy interventions. Paradoxically, it was a special case in terms of the market interventions imposed, but it was also special because market interventions applied to other staples were not applied to grain. As a consequence, trends and fluctuations in grain price integration are not representative of what happened in the majority of Spanish markets at all in terms of their political economy (T).

[10] Persson, *Grain Markets*. Recently, Uebele has offered an interesting analysis of grain prices, attempting an identification of the local, national, or international share of divergences from price co-movements based on techniques borrowed from international business cycle research. However, they place very high demands on data quality and therefore are hard to use in analyzing pre-nineteenth-century grain markets. See Uebele, "International and National Wheat Market Integration."

[11] Northern Spain became a wheat exporter in the nineteenth century, which helps the international analysis, but it does not solve the interregional issue.

The "moral economy" of grain markets in early modern Spain complicates efforts to use grain prices in two ways that are hard to separate. Wheat markets were subject to Crown-set maximum prices, the *tasa*, that were implemented locally—or not—and abolished through a *pragmática* in 1765, which was locally implemented—or not.[12] Indeed, one of the main historical sources for late eighteenth-century grain prices, urban *mercuriales* or price lists, were compiled as a means for municipal authorities to monitor and, if necessary, intervene in the market.[13] Historians disagree on how much impact these interventions had. There is evidence that the market rate did not hit the price ceiling too often, which would imply that they had minor consequences.[14] Yet the pattern of market adjustments over time suggests that institutional intervention smoothed price shocks over a number of years.[15] In the period of 1764–66 alone the first minister of Carlos III, the Marqués de Esquilache, had more than 860,000 *fanegas* (46,000 tons) of wheat imported to remedy the impact of several years of bad harvests, substantially more than the total amounts that passed through the *posito*, the public granary, of Madrid in those years.[16] In other words, political intervention was positively correlated with scarcity and probably reduced volatility in difficult years.

In crisis years, local authorities began to interfere more aggressively to keep the social peace as well. In her *Travels into Spain* (1691), the maverick French traveler Madame d'Aulnoy relates how her party was told that no bread was to be had anywhere in the Duero valley. The river had frozen and had stopped all mills. In the face of famine, "the *Alcaide Mayor* of the town (who is he that orders everything and who is both governor and judge) had sent for all the bread and meal which was at the bakers and had brought it into his house to make an equal distribution of it, proportionable [*sic*] to the necessities of each particular person."[17] D'Aulnoy and her companions contacted the honorable mayor and were promptly sent more bread than they needed. The Frenchwoman was evidently quick to pick up how much power the town representatives had and how she could use it. But for historians idiosyncratic interventions by local authorities in the grain market on the back of the "national" royal *tasa* pose insurmountable problems in quantitative analyses.[18] To make matters worse, these interventions continued after the liberalization of the grain trade.[19]

---

[12] Palop Ramos, *Fluctuaciones*, 145–57. The *tasa* applied in Castile as well as in Navarra and in the Crown of Aragon after 1714. For Navarra, see Solbes Ferri, *Rentas Reales de Navarra*, 64.

[13] Palop Ramos, *Fluctuaciones*, 14.

[14] Llopis Agelán and Jerez Méndez, "Castilla y León," 47.

[15] Reher, "Producción, precios e integración," 563.

[16] Palop Ramos, *Fluctuaciones*, 60; de Castro, *El pan de Madrid*, 214–15.

[17] Aulnoy and Foulché-Delbosc, *Travels into Spain*, 136.

[18] See the excellent discussion in Llopis Agelán and Jerez Méndez, "Castilla y León," 39ff.

[19] Ağir, "From Welfare to Wealth."

Direct intervention in grain prices and quantities combined with the absence of *indirect* interventions that did affect almost all other commodities in Spain. Grain production was subject to taxation at the production end in the form of agricultural tithes and other levies, as were other agricultural products. Bread, however, was explicitly excluded from local consumption and trade taxes. The Castilian *cortes* had passed the exemption in the fifteenth century, and it was upheld until the nineteenth.[20] This excluded bread from indirect taxes, the chief form of taxation in early modern Spain. The exception applied initially only in Castile but was extended to the realms of the former Crown of Aragon with the Nueva Planta decrees of the early 1700s. Interestingly, the exempt status of bread has gone largely unnoticed in the literature.

Any analysis of the market based on a single commodity suffers from problems of extrapolation. The argument is hence one of representativeness, and the peculiar political economy of grain turns it into a poor proxy. For the purpose of the present study this outweighs the advantage derived from grain's role as the single most important staple. Indeed, the quantitative importance of grain or bread as part of all market transactions should be contextualized as well. Historians' estimates of the share of household expenditure (excluding housing) spent on grain/bread vary significantly from 25 percent to almost 40 percent for the poorest consumers.[21] These figures tend to be based on the expenditure of large households or charitable institutions. The only contemporary estimate by a seventeenth-century *arbitrista* (projector) puts the share below 15 percent. It was so low because all other staple products were taxed while bread was not. Spaniards were quite aware that the relative price of bread was low vis-à-vis other consumption goods.[22]

The political economy of grain was fundamentally different from what happened in the markets for most staple foods, salt, wine, oil, meat, fish, and so forth. Thus, even if grain (including wheat, rice, and maize) accounted by the crudest of estimates for anything between one-sixth and one-third of the domestic retail market, any estimate of the (T) component of the analysis based on grain does not reflect the (T) for the other two-thirds to five-sixths of market transactions at all. Indeed, the traditional focus on grain prices in market integration studies meant that economic historians focused on the single product that was exempted from the most important form of taxation in Spain. In doing so they inadvertently ex ante excluded the possibility of analyzing how and to what extent the political economy of taxation in

[20] Andrés Ucendo, "Herencia"; *Novisima Recopilación*, Libro X, titulo 20 (1805), http://fama2.us.es/fde//ocr/2006/novisimaRecopilacionT5.pdf. Palop; Ramos, *Fluctuaciones*, 142.

[21] Drelichman, "Curse of Moctezuma"; Llopis et al., "Indices de precios de la zona noroccidental."

[22] Sureda Carrión, *La hacienda castellana*. The overall consumption basket looks sensible and the estimates of income provided by the author match those of modern studies. It seems that the author in fact drew on "interviews" with workers about their income and expenditures, an interesting methodological approach at the time.

Spain, with its local and regional control over large parts of the fiscal system, affected the degree of market integration.

The Beauty of Cod

There are alternatives to using grain prices. The one that has proven particularly apt for the current study is *bacalao*. Dried and salted cod was first introduced into Spain in the sixteenth century and quickly became a staple foodstuff imported from the new British colonies in North America. As it turns out, compared to grain it provides an exceptionally good basis for a quantitative as well as qualitative analysis of market development in Spain for a number of reasons.

First, *bacalao* is actually a more homogeneous good, at least as it was sold in Spain. Throughout the early modern period there were two main cod fishing and processing regions, Newfoundland and New England, and each of them produced two qualities of fish. Low-grade "refuse" cod referred to poorly processed, broken, or oversalted "black" fish or to unpalatable quantities that had been exposed to humidity after drying. It was sold exclusively in the British, French, and (to a lesser extent) Spanish West Indies to planters in search of slave rations.[23] High-quality "merchantable" dried and salted cod (known as *marchante* in Spain) was sold in southern Europe, with Spain consuming the largest share. Anecdotal evidence from merchants in North America and Spanish ports, as well as public reports, confirm time and again that only *marchante* fish could be sold in Spain.[24] Spanish merchants scoffed that the bad or rotten fish that occasionally hit European shores could only be sold to the English navy, which strove hard to justify its reputation for mistreating its sailors. The evidence from Spanish buyers confirms this: on the few occasions that second-grade (though never third-grade) cod was bought it was usually explicitly acknowledged in the bookkeeping to explain the low price.[25] In other words, the prices paid for first-grade cod reflect prices for a very similar product over time and between places, and they can be easily identified in the sources.

Second, *bacalao* was definitely a staple food by the seventeenth century as the discussion of its consumption and market development in the following chapters will illustrate. Its demand was subject to an own-price-elasticity that was quite similar to that of grain. Some historians have argued that its

[23] Magra, *The Fisherman's Cause*, 27.

[24] Grafe, "Popish Habits"; Vickers, " 'a Knowen and Staple Commoditie,'" 190.

[25] For instance, in 1767 the Franciscan mendicants de Nra Sra de los Llanos in Albacete bought *segunda suerte* at 17.5 rs and *primera suerte* at 37 rs per @; in 1784 they bought *segunda* for 32.1 rs and *primera* for 35.5 per @. The premium was unstable and driven largely by the relative quality of the second-rate fish. On average it was about 50 percent. See Archivo Histórico Nacional (AHN), Clero, Libro 39 (Albacete), AHN, Clero, Libro 5330 (Sahagún), and Archivo Foral Bizkaia (AFB), Ecclesiastico, Zenarruza, Libro 32 (Bilbao).

consumption was heavily influenced by religious fasting.[26] It will be shown, however, that the main reason why increasing numbers of consumers in the Iberian Peninsula ate rising amounts of *bacalao* was that it was cheap protein. Hence, uncorrelated demand shocks do not pose a major problem; *bacalao*'s demand-side properties (D) were similar to those of grain.

The supply side, by contrast, looks quite different. *Bacalao* was primarily the product of North American fisheries. It was shipped from Newfoundland and New England ports to Spain's major coastal centers and traveled inland from there. Thus, most supply side shocks in fact applied to practically the entire catch in certain years. Whether supplies were scarce because of a poor fishing season or because wars interrupted trade between North America and Spain, all Spanish towns were probably affected in similar ways. This would suggest that volatility introduced by uncorrelated supply side shocks (S) was more uniform across locations than in the grain trade, though not necessarily smaller. Fewer localized idiosyncratic supply side shocks might have translated into stronger co-movement across Spanish towns. At the same time, fish is generally considered one of the most price-volatile commodities owing to patterns of migration, water temperature, and a host of ill-understood biological forces.[27]

In any case, the volatility and co-movement of cod prices represent market integration forces (F + T) much more directly than those of grain prices because the (S) component tended to be more uniform, and the most important source of shocks, wartime disturbances, are much easier to identify than production shocks in grain markets. This is an important advantage. It should also be remembered that the purpose of the present analysis is primarily to understand *trends* and *cycles* in market integration across Spain and between Spain and the rest of the world, that is, the process of price arbitration between North American ports and Spanish ports, on the one hand, and between Spanish ports and inland towns, on the other. The absolute *level* of market (dis-) integration as measured by volatility can only be interpreted through a contextualization, no matter the commodity in question. Hence, a direct comparison of grain and *bacalao* markets will be discussed whenever possible.

That *bacalao* was an imported foodstuff has other advantages. Cod always had a clear origin and destination.[28] The final price of cod in Madrid was the sum of the cost of fishing and processing in the North American Atlantic, marketing in New England or Newfoundland, transshipping to a Spanish port, and overland transport to Madrid, including customs, taxes, and road tolls of any kind. Consequentially, price differentials between locations, the

[26] See chapter 3 for an in-depth discussion.

[27] This holds true historically as shown by Jacks, O'Rourke, and Williamson, "Commodity Price Volatility."

[28] A small amount of cod probably entered western Spain, especially Extremadura via Portugal. But even the English consul in Lisbon in 1714 thought these quantities were modest. See Magra, *The Fisherman's Cause*.

price wedge, can be used in a quantitative analysis of market integration in a much more straightforward way than those of grain. In the case of the latter, we saw that it is practically impossible to analyze price differentials (as opposed to volatility and co-movement) in any meaningful way since most regions produced at least some grain, and cereals could flow in any direction.

By contrast, the correlation between distances traveled and *bacalao* prices can be obtained directly in a regression analysis since one can estimate the distance traveled from point of origin or point of entry into the Peninsula. Given the scarcity of direct data on freight costs, this is an invaluable advantage when trying to understand how transport costs developed in the long run (F). Again, it is likely that the absolute level of transport costs differed between cod and grain. There is no reason to assume, however, that longer-term trends and cycles in transport costs were different for cod than for those that applied to other commodities. The reason is simple: packaging technology in cod did not change over this period and thus changes in the (F) component of the final price should mirror the rise or fall of transport and related costs quite well.[29]

The most important characteristic of the *bacalao* market for the purpose of this study is, however, that it reflects the fundamental features of the political economy of Spanish market governance much more directly than grain. Cod was actually subjected to the fiscal system in much the same way as other important foodstuffs such as oil, wine, and vinegar (but not bread). Towns and territories applied trade and consumption taxes to cod in their attempts to finance the local public purse. The argument is not that the *rate* of taxation was in any way representative of the rates on all these products. On the contrary, *bacalao* is representative of the market precisely because it reflects the diversity of local and territorial taxation that governed between two-thirds and five-sixths of the Spanish markets, that is, everything but the grain trade. It thus allows us to estimate the effect of these local trade and consumption taxes on the price wedge and co-movements of prices between towns, and on price volatility; or to put it another way, the impact of (T). Cod prices are a better mirror of the degree of market integration from the point of view of the consumer, who for most products paid local consumption taxes, and thus of the impact of Spain's political economy on market integration.

In sum, cod prices allow us to study the pattern of market integration in a more comprehensive way than grain price studies could. Most important, they allow for a much closer examination of the impact of the political economy of Spain on market integration, and thus of the interactions between state-building and market integration, and of the longer-term development of transport costs. Indeed, the combination of two unique advantages of cod, that it was an imported commodity and that it was not subject to as many

---

[29] For the bias on market integration analysis that can result from changes to packaging technology, see Harley, "Ocean Freight Rates."

idiosyncratic shocks in (S), means not only that cod price differentials have a direct interpretation (that is, they reflect the transactions costs between town A and town B) but also that they can be "decomposed" into their various elements in ways that grain prices cannot. It is therefore possible to identify and compare the contribution of transport costs (F) and other costs caused by taxes and dues (T) to the differences between prices in each location. In other words, the *relative* impact of various kinds of obstacles to market integration, political and otherwise, can be assessed for the very first time.

Historians have stressed that territorially based jurisdictional fragmentation persisted in Spain for a long time both in the shape of the historic territories as well as in that of urban power. Yet the historical narrative has so far been unable to assess the size of its effect on the developments of markets in Spain. The fragmentation of the multitude of local and territorial taxes and other quantity and price interventions in the market means that their impact is very hard to measure directly. As a consequence, it has also been impossible to distinguish the relative contribution of transport costs versus political economy factors on the pattern of market integration, or the relative contribution of jurisdictional fragmentation between territories versus that between towns. The new approach pursued here opens up entirely new possibilities to test and analyze in much more detail the main hypothesis of this book, namely that territorially based jurisdictional fragmentation was the main Achilles' heel of Spain's early modern economy.

The Data Set

Everything hinges, however, on good price series, which are notoriously hard to come by. For periods before the regular appearance of price currents and other financial information, historians have traditionally relied on account books of religious and charitable institutions. For Spain this approach was most notably implemented by Earl J. Hamilton in his impressively large price and wage studies that have been employed by many economic historians since. Hamilton's data have been attractive for historians because he created series for a large number of products and various regions: Old Castile, New Castile, Valencia, and Andalusia.

However, some of Hamilton's data turn out to be a problematic base for the study of regional integration even though quite a few historians have insisted on using them for such purposes.[30] To begin with, Hamilton's data are sometimes not what the label suggests. O'Rourke and Williamson undertook the first attempt to use *bacalao* prices to analyze transatlantic integration but fell for one of the many traps in Hamilton's data: part of their series

---

[30] See, e.g., Reher, "Producción, precios e integración"; O'Rourke and Williamson, "Did Vasco Da Gama Matter"; Allen, "The Great Divergence." See, most recently, Allen, *The British Industrial Revolution in Global Perspective*.

consisted of prices of European pilchards rather than North American cod.[31] Hamilton's supposedly regional indices are subject to another set of problems. Given the difficulty of finding sources, Hamilton and his collaborators collated their series out of data obtained from a number of towns within a given area, which they aggregated. That was a perfectly understandable strategy in the 1930s and 1940s, but as a consequence, his 1650–1800 published Old Castile series are based on primary data from Valladolid, Palencia, Avila, Leon, Logroño, Salamanca, Santander, Castro-Urdiales, and Segovia; Andalusian prices are a mix of Seville and Cadiz prices.[32] In other words, Hamilton assumed ex ante that there were integrated Spanish regions; or to put it another way, he thought that the political economy of towns did not matter. This was a strong and indefensible prior as we will see below. Not surprisingly, his series sometimes exhibit sudden step changes that are the result of splicing the data from different towns together rather than a reflection of price movements.[33] Hence, the present analysis only uses those data compiled by Hamilton that identifiably relate to just one town based on the excellent reworking of some of his data by a group of scholars led by Enrique Llopis.[34]

The cod prices used in the analysis that follows are derived from a variety of Spanish ecclesiastical sources for single towns or cities or their immediate environs, a crucial step in a direction of accounting for local and regional factors. The series cover North America (Essex County, Massachusetts), the northern, southern, and Mediterranean coasts (Bilbao, Cadiz, Malaga, Barcelona), Old Castile (Sahagún), Navarra (Pamplona/Irache), New Castile (Madrid, Toledo), La Mancha (Albacete), and Andalusia (Seville). The series labeled "Bilbao" stems from Villaro/Areatza, a hamlet about 20 kilometers from Bilbao and probably overstates the cost of cod in the port itself marginally. It has been cross-checked for part of the second half of the eighteenth century with an alternative series from Zenarruza, another village at a similar distance.

The biggest omissions are Galicia in the northwest and Valencia on the Mediterranean coast, where sufficiently long series of monastic or other account books proved elusive. Fortunately, the latter might not be too problematic as we will see. The price series are of different lengths but internally fairly consistent. The data for the North American cod price series were

---

[31] O'Rourke and Williamson, "Globalisation," use Hamilton, *American Treasure*. Hamilton used the prices of locally caught pilchards up to the 1560s for his "cod" series since regular cod imports did not begin in the regions he looked at until the mid-sixteenth century. This did not matter for Hamilton, who was interested in estimating consumption baskets.

[32] Hamilton, *War and Prices*, xxiv–xxvi. The exception is his Valencia series, which contains prices only from the town. Here, however, the main series generally used for comparison, grain prices, consists of different grains, complicating its use even more. Palop Ramos, *Fluctuaciones*, 9.

[33] See the analysis performed by Reher, "Producción, precios e integración."

[34] For full references, see Note on the Sources. The complete data set and documentation are available via http://press.princeton.edu/titles/9625.html.

Figure 2.1
Spain: historical territories and towns represented in the data set.

compiled using Daniel Vickers's series from the Quarterly Courts of Essex
County 1640-1775. For the earlier years these were complemented with
prices provided by Peter Pope and Gillian Cell for Newfoundland, which
spliced together almost perfectly as Pope has shown; New England and Newfoundland cod prices were strongly integrated even in the 1640s.[35]

In the volatility and co-movement analyses nominal prices are used. The
only exception is the series for Albacete, a town in southeastern La Mancha
that used a mix of Castilian and Valencian monies. This made it necessary
to standardize prices to Castilian currency using silver equivalents.[36] Volatility is measured as the standard deviation of a price series that reflects the
variability of prices around their mean. A lower standard deviation means
less volatility and more market integration. However, in order to compare
the variability across different towns with distinct mean prices, one needs

[35] Vickers, "'a Knowen and Staple Commoditie,'" table 1; Cell, "English in Newfoundland"; Pope, *Fish into Wine*, 38.
[36] Conversion rates were taken from Feliu, "Monedes de Compte."

to look at the relative or percentage change of prices from year to year and de-trend the series. The standard transformation is to use the first difference of the natural logarithm of the nominal price.[37] This makes the results for each town directly comparable. Price co-movements are studied through the correlation coefficient for pairs of towns, the standard measure of association between prices in two places, again using the de-trended nominal series. In the price convergence analysis prices are converted into grams of silver in order to allow for comparisons of price quotes in English and Catalan pounds/shillings/pence and Castilian *reales/maravedies*, as well as occasional Valencian currency and sundry units of account or gold coins.

A few general caveats apply to this kind of source. First, hospitals, convents, and monasteries were wholesale rather than retail consumers. They would often buy *bacalao* for several months in considerable quantities up to a metric ton at a time, though most purchases were more modest. This feature presents a problem when trying to understand the retail market or domestic consumption. However, in terms of market integration it is rather convenient in that it provides a "standardized" consumer in all of the markets we look at. Second, cod was a relatively durable good, especially if it was of good quality; it was thought to be quite palatable for at least six months.[38] This had an impact on the purchasing habits of larger institutions, which naturally would have tried to minimize the purchasing cost. Hence, the prices paid by convents and monasteries were at the lower end of annual average prices because monasteries could easily wait for cheaper supplies if they thought these were forthcoming. Indeed, only in years of extreme price volatility would many institutions switch to regular purchases of lower quantities, presumably in the hope of lower prices. For this reason the price series offered here are also presented as annual observations rather than higher frequency monthly data, even where that was available.

[37] The first step, the conversion into logarithms, creates a series with a (nearly) constant variance, or homoscedastic series. The second step, differencing, then removes the trend, creating a stationary series. The remaining variation is white noise. In series that were subject to very strong trend growth, e.g., during twentieth-century episodes of hyperinflation, this procedure will not be sufficient. However, given the moderate inflation and deflation trends in this period, this is the accepted methodology for this kind of data.

[38] Fagan claimed it could be stored for up to five years (*Fish on Friday*, 66). But its quality declined over time and choosy Spanish consumers felt it should not be stored for more than half a year. Bernardos Sanz, "Abastecimiento," 15.

Chapter 3

Bacalao

A New Consumer Good Takes on the Peninsula

A New Atlantic Staple: *Bacalao*

> *Abadejo*, sea fish, well known, and of admirable fertility, fished in Newfoundland, and which is the great savior [*socorro*] of the poor, at the same time very much appreciated by the rich. . . . In some parts of Spain known as *Bacallao*, and in others as *Truchuela*.

THIS IS HOW THE GREAT SPANISH encyclopedia of Esteban de Terreros y Pando defined dried, salted codfish in the 1780s.[1] Quite a lot has been written about the rise of the cod trade as one of the first transatlantic commodities; indeed, cod might be the only fish that has had its (collective?) biography written.[2] Yet less is known about its introduction into southern European markets and next to nothing about how the transatlantic end of the trade interacted with markets within southern Europe. Since this book breaks new ground in using *bacalao* instead of grain in understanding market integration and its link with the political economy, we need to take one step back to analyze the emerging cod trade in more detail and contextualize the cod market within the frame of the new Atlantic trades. These were transoceanic in origin, and they brought about a new, global economy; but they also transformed in their course the domestic economies and societies of Europe.

The rise of these transoceanic goods to staple commodities in European countries has offered historians a unique opportunity to investigate the emergence of the early stages of a "consumer culture" in Europe and the expansion of markets that accompanied it. That is particularly true for a widely affordable good like cod. Spaniards were the first Europeans to indulge on a large scale in the sometimes exciting, sometimes simply nutritious novel commodities of the New World in what has become known as the "Atlantic Exchange." Enticing new foods and other consumption products, such as cocoa and tobacco, were widely known in the Peninsula from the mid-sixteenth century onward; by the early seventeenth century they were consumed outside elite circles and became part of Peninsular sociability and consumer pleasure.[3] Other products were less glamorous but not less useful. Maize cultivation

---

[1] Terreros y Pando, *Diccionario castellano*, 1:2.
[2] Kurlansky, *Cod*.
[3] Norton, *Sacred Gifts*.

on the poor soils of the northern Spanish Cantabrian coast turned a chronically grain-deficient region into a nearly self-sufficient one after the 1620s, changing century-old patterns of intra-European trade.[4] Equally *bacalao* would become a crucial part of southern Europeans' diet, remedying at least partially the constant lack of protein-rich foods on their plates.

Spanish *arbitristas*, writers concerned with the state of the commonwealth, were of two minds about this. In Spain, and elsewhere in Europe, the new imports regularly became the object of tracts and treatises against the "excessive consumption of unnecessary or luxury goods." Critical voices fused two distinct elements in their attacks. The warnings against "excessive consumption" emanated from a long tradition of moral arguments about abstinence and the desirability of a simple life. The label "unnecessary goods" reflected mercantilists' constant fretting over the balance of trade. "Unnecessary" here meant imported rather than homegrown or home-produced commodities, which would cause an excess of import over export values and thus an outflow of bullion in order to finance the realm's balance of trade deficit.

By the later eighteenth century, however, the intellectual tide had turned. Fewer and fewer contemporaries thought that limiting any kind of consumption was either desirable or economically beneficial.[5] Luxury was a necessary evil, argued Juan Sempere y Guarinos in his famous *Historia del luxo y de las leyes suntuarias* (1788) and not a sin to be prosecuted by the state. After all, Spain was "a state, in which all men were equal by nature, but where their constitution makes them very unequal, and where generally the means of moving into a superior class are not moderation and virtue, but riches or employment." In such a state the many without access to land necessarily had to be employed in the trades and crafts that produced, sold, or traded "unnecessary things." Moral disapproval was thus misplaced. Incidentally, these influential comments also suggest that eighteenth-century Spaniards were rather more comfortable with a shopkeeper mentality than economic historians usually allow for.

Sempere y Guarinos was, however, quite aware that one argument was more powerful than any other when trying to convince the politically influential in Spain of the usefulness of conspicuous consumption and its twin, trade. So he hastened to add that in addition to its beneficial impact on employment, consumption was a necessity for the state as the *only* way to increase revenue. What was the alternative? Sempere y Guarinos invited his readers to imagine that Spaniards were to stop using tobacco, "which is one of the commodities of least necessity." The result would be a fiscal disaster of frightening proportions.[6]

In a polity that relied more than other European states on trade and consumption taxes, it can hardly surprise that wherever consumers led the

---

[4] Grafe, *Mundo ibérico*, 129–30.
[5] Sarrailh, *España ilustrada*, 244–45.
[6] Sempere y Guarinos, *Historia del luxo*, 2:199–203. My translation.

way, the haciendas of Spain were not far behind. By 1636 the Cortes de
Castilla had established the first tobacco monopoly, "the precious jewel"
among Spanish taxes copied in many European polities thereafter. Thanks to
it, a Real Cedula exclaimed in 1684, "there is no monarch in the world who
derives a comparable treasure."[7] Cocoa and chocolate were taxed in many
towns, too.[8] In the northern regions discussions about the inclusion of maize
in the tithe payments promptly emerged in the early seventeenth century.[9]
New World commodities became an almost instant success with consumers
and tax collectors alike.[10]

Just as moral condemnation of "unnecessary consumption" of commodities of Atlantic origin gave way to enlightened praise of its benefits for traders,
consumers, and the taxman, *bacalao* became anathema to Spanish statesmen
and commentators. It seemed an unlikely target of public outrage; after all,
dried and salted codfish was about as innocuous a product as any. It was not
addictive like some of the New World goods. In fact, even today many people
consider it an acquired taste. Nor did *bacalao* carry any notion of syncretism
like cacao or tobacco, products that had made Peninsular Spaniards a little
more American. Yet Gerónimo de Uztáriz, the internationally best known
Spanish mercantilist, dedicated about twelve pages of his famous *Theorica y
práctica de comercio y marina* to what he saw as the "great damage" Spain
suffered as a consequence of this habit of eating salt fish.[11] He used his proto-
statistical skills to explain the pernicious nature of *bacalao*, arguing that
Spaniards in the early eighteenth century were consuming 497,500 quintals
of the stuff every year, about 22,400 tons.[12]

Uztáriz was not the only one who despised *bacalao* wholeheartedly. In
1784 Antonio Sañez Reguart, the author of the *Diccionario histórico de los
artes de la pesca nacional*, the foremost Spanish collection on anything to do
with fishing, dedicated a lengthy "Discourse against the use of *bacalao*" to the
question.[13] Blaming religion for *bacalao*'s popularity, he presented calculations concerning the cod trade that were even more devastating. Only one-
fourth of the population observed proper religious abstinence, he assumed;

[7] Escobedo Romero, *Tabaco*, 17. My translation. Revenue from the tobacco monopoly was
initially part of the taxes used to pay the *millones,* falling under the same administration and
forming part of the body of consumption taxes.

[8] See, for instance, Martínez Ruiz, *Finanzas municipales*, 300, 311.

[9] Casado Soto, "La implantación del maíz"; Grafe, *Mundo ibérico*, 130.

[10] Remarkably, Sánchez de Moncada commented as early as 1619 on the different elasticity
of demand of luxuries and necessities and the fiscal implications of that insight. Sureda Carrión, *La hacienda castellana*, 31–32.

[11] Uztáriz, *Theorica*, 67–69, 271–80. The tract was first circulated in Spain in 1724 and
published posthumously in 1742.

[12] A quintal contained four arrobas of 25 pounds each, essentially a hundredweight. It thus
varied slightly with the pound measure used. A Castilian quintal was about 46 kilograms.
Grafe, *Mundo ibérico*, 127.

[13] Sañez Reguart, *Diccionario histórico*. Emphasis added. He was particularly worried
about the impact cod imports had on Galician fishing.

the others were too young, too old, had dietary restrictions, or simply did not care. But at half a pound of fish per day and person on each day of a vigil, 1.25 million pounds of *bacalao* were consumed; that resulted in 65 million pounds on Fridays only. Adding forty days of Lent and another twenty fast days throughout the year, he estimated total consumption at a mind-boggling 64,000 tons.[14]

Though Sañez Reguart exaggerated cod consumption, cod clearly made a dent in Spain's balance of trade: by 1792 it accounted for more than 5 percent of the value of all Spanish imports and was the second largest food item after grain.[15] Therefore, concern was widespread: Antonio Valladares y Sotomayor's famous *Seminario erudito* collection published a fictitious dialogue between two Calvinists (!) ascribed to Melchor de Macanaz, an early Bourbon reformer who fell from grace.[16] They discuss the beauties and virtues of Spain after one of them has returned from a trip thereto but also its ills, among them the "great damage" done to Spain through the import of English *bacalao*, worth, they claimed, in excess of two million pesos a year.[17] The estimate, equivalent to twenty million *reales*, appeared again in Joseph de Olmeida's famous writings on public law, and he was equally disparaging about the strategic advantage the trade supposedly gave to the English.[18] For comparison, Prados de la Escosura has estimated that Spain's balance of trade deficit in the 1780s–1790s was just below sixty million *reales*.[19] *Bacalao* imports would thus account for one-third of the deficit.

No wonder, then, that mercantilists despised *bacalao* in spite of the fiscal potential that the sheer size of cod imports offered, and they recommended all kinds of cures for this particular threat to economic well-being. The eighteenth-century Spanish proto-economist Bernardo de Ulloa (1682–1740) insisted that there were other fish that could be cured and claimed they were even nicer than *bacalao* (*que hacen ventaja*) and not more expensive.[20] Uztáriz reminded his readers again and again that the fish was caught in American waters by the English, who—he was convinced—obtained huge benefits from the fishing, shipping, and trade. His suggested cure came right out of the toolbox employed by Spanish treasuries up and down the country: slap every conceivable tax on these imports at the highest possible rates. Customs, *millones, alcabalas, cientos, derechos de puertas*—the full armory of trade and consumption taxes was to be aimed at *bacalao* in order to reduce consumption. In addition, Uztáriz recommended, Spanish fishing should be promoted as a substitute and be free of all taxes. Alas, he had to admit that

---

[14] Calculation contained in a pamphlet preserved at AHN, Estado, leg. 3012 and reproduced in Meijide Pardo, *Comercio*, 19.

[15] Prados de la Escosura, *De imperio a nación*, 90.

[16] On Macanaz, see Kamen, "Melchor de Macanaz."

[17] Rafael Macanaz, "Noticias particulares," 156, 167.

[18] Olmeida y León, *Derecho*, 233.

[19] Prados de la Escosura, *De imperio a nación*, 75.

[20] Ulloa, *Restablicimiento*, 54.

the Basques, known to have engaged in the cod fisheries in the sixteenth century, were already tax exempt and would thus have to be offered monetary incentives and low-interest loans to entice them back into the fisheries. Spain's addiction to cod had no easy remedy.

Mercantilist considerations, however, were not the only reason why the mass consumption of *bacalao* upset eighteenth-century Spaniards. Uztáriz, like Sañez Reguart and many others, held religious fasting responsible for the foul habit of eating dried and salted cod. While mercantilists worried about Spain's balance of trade, Spanish Enlightenment writers blamed most of Spain's ills on what they saw as unproductive hordes of priests and regular clerics. Cod consumption and meat abstinence were just another nefarious conspiracy of the ecclesiastical estate against progress. A large number of idle, fish-eating monks and their religious followers became an enlightened mercantilist's nightmare. They had to be stopped. If Spanish supplies of fish could not be increased, demand had to be cut. Writers were forthright in their advice to Crown and Councils: lean heavily on the papacy and local bishops and get them to reduce the number of fast days or allow consumption of more alternative foods. If they proved obstinate there was still prohibition; after all, Spaniards had done just fine "for a thousand years" without salted cod and had been good Catholics all the same, Uztáriz exclaimed.

One fact no one disputed by the eighteenth century: *bacalao* was a staple everywhere. Foreign travelers to Spain observed the ubiquity of the commodity. Though most of them would have been familiar with varieties of *bacalao*, such as green fish (*morue*) consumed in France, *Stockfisch* in the Germanies, "poor John" in England, or *klippfisk* in the Nordic countries, the massive amounts consumed in Spain, as well as Portugal and Italy, were perceived as noteworthy and even made it into Samuel Johnson's *Modern Traveller*.[21] More sober Spanish reformers eventually pointed out the obvious: the cod trade was bad for Spain's balance of trade, but *bacalao* was a staple foodstuff without which ordinary Spaniards could not live any longer. In his famous *Proyecto económico*, Bernardo Ward (d. c. 1763) demanded that *bacalao*, like other foods that served basic needs such as meat, oil, and ham, should be free of any taxation, turning Uztáriz's argument on its head.[22]

The Origins of the Bacalao *Trade*

The cod trade from Newfoundland and New England was one of the first transatlantic staple trades, and some of its aspects have found increasing attention from professional and popular historians in recent years. Daniel Vickers's marvelous work on the fishing communities in seventeenth- and

[21] Johnson drew on Edward Clarke's 1763 note that Spaniards' "chief supply of fish is sent by the English . . . , the salt fish or what they call bacalao." Clarke, *Letters*, 291.

[22] Ward, *Proyecto económico*, 153, 202, 210, 269.

eighteenth-century Massachusetts brought to the fore the settlements of hardworking, hard-drinking, and generally quite ungodly fishermen immigrants into early New England, challenging the persistent narrative of the Puritan origins of Anglo-America with the rough economic realities of early settlement. Peter Pope, Mark Kurlansky, and Brian Fagan have traced the Anglophone end of cod fisheries and trade.[23] Chris Magra has argued that conflicts over New England fishing interests played an important role in stoking dissatisfaction with British colonial rule in the eighteenth century.[24] In short, the crucial significance of the early commodity trades in *bacalao* for the distinct Anglo-American settlements has been demonstrated beyond doubt.

Yet the historiography has said very little about the consumer end of the trade, which reached far beyond the Anglophone world.[25] The interpretative picture of an English Atlantic as a world of its own is both anachronistic and seriously misleading: the fish trade, for one, crossed the boundaries between the allegedly closed English and Iberian Atlantic trades from its earliest days. In Europe, cod partially displaced, and then hugely expanded, the preexisting commerce in dried and salted fish. Its success from its introduction in the sixteenth century onward was mostly due to its advantages over traditional salt fish, especially in the very warm climates of southern Europe. Herring and pilchards contain more oil and therefore spoil more easily—they had to be salted very quickly and often became foul-tasting.[26] Nevertheless, consumers took a while to catch on. *Bacalao* was still marginal in Iberian markets compared to traditional Dutch herring or locally produced pilchards and eels in the first decades of the sixteenth century.

The unfailing sign that *bacalao* had become a regularly consumed foodstuff was when treasuries turned it into a new source of revenue. In the mid-sixteenth century the town of Bilbao, the main Spanish Basque port, chose to buy a royal privilege that would give it more independence. So it did what Iberian towns usually did when they needed money: it turned to local trade and consumption taxes, *sisas*, on a number of staple foodstuffs to finance the outlay. On September 3, 1552, *bacalao* became for the first time the object of a consumption tax in Spain (to the best of my knowledge), at a rate of five *maravedies* (*mrs*) per *arroba* (@). The council scrivener quite literally added it as an afterthought to the list of food staples typically taxed: in the original document the item *vacallao* appears interpolated and squeezed in between more traditional staples.[27]

[23] See Vickers, *Farmers & Fishermen*; Kurlansky, *Cod*; Pope, *Fish into Wine*; and Fagan, *Fish on Friday*. See also earlier work by Innis, *The Cod Fisheries*, and Cell, "English in Newfoundland."

[24] Magra, *The Fisherman's Cause*.

[25] The notable exception is Abreu-Ferreira, "The Cod Trade."

[26] Fagan, *Fish on Friday*, 49.

[27] At this stage *bacalao* was evidently less appreciated than the more traditional herrings, which paid eight *mrs* per @ (25 pounds). AFB, Bilbao Antigua, 0014/001/018/f255r. and 256v.

Yet, unbeknownst to the scrivener, a pattern had been established: Bilbao would become the main port of import for dried-salted cod and remain so for centuries to come; moreover, cod would become one of the staple foodstuffs that financed Spanish municipalities and thus a share of the Spanish hacienda for almost as long. By 1561 *bacalao* had become sufficiently important for the local food supply that the aldermen of Bilbao worried about its price in a moment of market upheaval.[28] Around 1560 dried-salted cod paid 34 *mrs* per quintal for the *diezmos de la mar* (external customs) in the northern historic territories of Vizcaya and Guipúzcoa.[29] At this point the 400 tons of *bacalao* taxed accounted already for the largest share of the total amount of fish taken from the Basque Country to Castile via one of the main customs points.[30] In the late sixteenth century the fish appears regularly in the Mediterranean ports, too.[31]

By the turn of the seventeenth century the fish was a staple in Iberian port towns and their hinterlands, though not yet in the interior of the Peninsula. Miguel de Cervantes's famous novel *Don Quixote* is indicative of cod's relative penetration of Spanish markets at the time of its publication in 1605. On the one hand, Don Quixote, the heroic fool of the novel, reveals his ingenuity when he assumes that the *truchuela* offered for dinner in the Castilian Mancha is a small *trucha*, or trout. On the other hand, Cervantes still had to offer some explanation to his readers: "It was Friday and in the inn there was nothing to be had but a few portions of a fish, which in Castile they call *abadexo*, and in Andalusia *bacallao*, and in other places *curadillo*, and elsewhere *truchuela*."[32] Cervantes's readers could be expected to understand that the foolish hero had mistaken plain *bacalao* for precious trout. But the writer did have to make sure that everyone knew about the various regional names for dried cod, which would persist for centuries as Terreros y Pando's encyclopedia confirmed in the late eighteenth century.

Until the 1580s Spanish Basque fishermen participated in the Newfoundland fisheries alongside French Basques, Portuguese, and English. But just as Spanish consumers were getting hooked on *bacalao, abadejo, curadillo,* and *truchuela*, Basque fishermen lost control over the supply of cod from the North American fishing grounds to northern Spain. The Basque Country and neighboring Navarra were split between the Crowns of Spain and

[28] They set fixed retail prices at 10 *mrs* per pound. AFB, Municipales, Bilbao-Actas, Libro 006 (1560–61) f86v.–87r.

[29] Lapeyre, *El comercio exterior*, 118. Even though it was charged it did not appear yet in the formal list of taxable goods, the *arancel de los diezmos de la mar* of 1564. See Lapeyre, "El arancel."

[30] Lapeyre, "Algunos datos," 189.

[31] Ruiz Ibáñez and Montojo Montojo, *Entre el lucro y la defensa*, 90; Ling, "Long-Term Movements," 242ff.

[32] Cervantes Saavedra, *Don Qvixote*, book 1, chapter 2, p. 5. My translation. Strictly speaking, cod/*bacalao*/*curadillo* (*gadus morhua*) and pollock/*abadejo* (*gadus pollachius*) are not the same fish, while *truchuela* is cod but today tends to refer to a slimmer fish. Historically, however, all terms were used interchangeably for cod and differed by region rather than variety. See Cubillo de la Puente, *El pescado*.

France. The three northern provinces (Iparralde), consisting of the two Basque territories of Labourd (Lapurdi) and Soule (Zuberoa) as well as Basse-Navarre (Nafarroa-Beherea), belonged to France; the four southern territories (Hegoalde), consisting of the three Basque provinces of Guipúzcoa (Gipuzkoa), Vizcaya (Bizkaia), and Alava (Araba) as well as Navarra (Nafarroa), were part of the Spanish monarchy.[33] Yet in the first decade of the seventeenth century this distinction mattered little and fishing ventures were often undertaken collaboratively by Vizcayan and Guipúzcoan investors using Labourd vessels. Up to the 1610s, practically all vessels entering the northern Spanish port of Bilbao from Newfoundland were French Basque, financed at least in part by Spanish Basques.[34] And for the time being, the trade was successful and the number of ships involved increased quickly from four or five in 1598 to about thirty in 1613.[35]

Then, in the autumn of 1612, a convoy of nine English vessels laden with *bacalao* arrived in Bilbao without having first passed through an English port. This was the first time English traders and fishermen broke directly into the Spanish market. Legally they had been allowed to trade with Spanish ports since the peace of 1604.[36] The trade was apparently not an instant success even after 1612; direct voyages from Newfoundland by English vessels were rare in subsequent years.[37] But the tide began to turn. In the Newfoundland fisheries English and French interests had won out over Spanish and Portuguese by the early seventeenth century.

The reasons were complex. Most historians have blamed the decline of Basque fishing on scuffles with English or French fishermen in Newfoundland.[38] But the collapse of Basque fishing and shipbuilding was a result of developments closer to home, especially the atomized structure of northern Spanish shipbuilding, which had strong links with the fishing sector. A large number of small investors in spatially restricted local markets moved out of shipbuilding and fishing during the wars and war-related embargoes with England (1585–1604) and the Netherlands (1568–1609, 1621–48). When legal trade became possible again, skills had been lost and capital dissipated.[39]

Once the Spaniards and Portuguese had disappeared from the scene, English tentative settlement at Newfoundland from the 1620s also seriously restricted French activities, and by the 1620s French Basque participation in

[33] Presently, the inclusion or otherwise of Navarra within the term Basque Country, or Euskal Herria, is a heavily contested political issue in Spain. Historically, Navarra was an independent territory; the three Spanish Basque Provinces were independent but organized into a loose federation.

[34] Barkham, "French Basque 'New Found Land' Entrepreneurs."

[35] Guiard Larrauri, *Historia del consulado*, 1:165; AFB, Varios, Instituciones, Consulado de Bilbao (CB), Libro 208, números (núm) 3, 5, 6, 11, 13, 16 (Cuentas de averías Terranoba y Nantes).

[36] Grafe, *Der spanische Seehandel.*

[37] AFB, CB, Libro 210, núm 13.

[38] Cell, "English in Newfoundland"; Guiard Larrauri, *Historia del consulado.*

[39] Grafe, "Spanish Shipping."

the Newfoundland fisheries had declined. Cod processing required a presence on the beach where the daily catch would be cut, cleaned, salted, and placed on stacks to dry.[40] With a small year-round settlement, English fishermen could reserve the best landing places and reuse some of the wooden facilities year after year. The French retreated to western Newfoundland, where they continued to fish and process cod. Over time, their fishing rights were further restricted by the Treaty of Utrecht in 1713 and the loss of all Canadian territory in 1763. In addition, French fishermen concentrated on "green" or "wet" fishery that was unsuitable for the southern European climate as it was strongly salted but hardly cured.

Meanwhile, the English also controlled the New England coast, and with it its fishing, from the outset. Not surprisingly, there was a huge upturn in cod shipments delivered by English West Country merchants with close connections to the English settlements in North America. From the 1630s, Spanish sources began to refer to these supplies increasingly as *bacalao de la Birginia,* cod from New England, rather than Newfoundland. By the early 1640s, eighty to one hundred ships per annum carried cod into Bilbao, and practically all of them were English shippers.[41] They had, in effect, a monopoly on the kind of fish that could be sold in Spain, Portugal, and Italy from the 1620s onward.

North American and British historians have always argued that the transatlantic cod trade was highly profitable from the start because it was driven by a combination of high demand for cod in southern Europe and the privileged fishing conditions for the English and Anglo-Americans in Atlantic waters. The only point of debate has been how much these profits contributed to the early colonies' escape from initial economic hardship.[42] While most historians of Massachusetts see fish-export-led growth in the colony from the 1640s, others like McWilliams have argued that the economic stimulus from cod exports has been exaggerated given that "numbers required to support a quantitative, export-led interpretation do not exist."[43] But everyone so far has assumed that the trade was extremely profitable from the very beginning.

The evidence for cod prices in Spain collected for this study shows, however, that the early North American cod exports to Spain were far from profitable. The thesis of high profits was anchored in a comparison of Newfoundland or New England cod prices with those from the Spanish interior. However, these prices included the cost of overland trading from the coast to the Castilian hinterland. They were hence much higher than those that English or North American merchants could hope to obtain in Spanish ports. Peter Pope, for example, estimated that a Newfoundland "sack" ship,

[40] Pope, *Fish into Wine*, chapters 1 and 2.

[41] AFB, CB, Libro 212. Grafe, *Mundo ibérico*, 135–59, illustrates the typical triangular circuit undertaken by West Country vessels.

[42] Bailyn, *New England Merchants*, 5ff; Vickers, *Farmers & Fishermen*, 98ff; McCusker and Menard, *The Economy of British America*, chapter 5.

[43] McWilliams, "First Depression," 4.

a transport vessel that picked up *bacalao* in Newfoundland for sale in Spain, could realize a return for the freighter on the journey from Newfoundland to Spain of about 14 percent.[44] However, if we repeat Pope's own calculation with the prices English merchants could charge in Spanish ports for high-grade "merchantable" cod, the journey from North America to Spain alone would have resulted in a *loss* on investment of 37 percent.[45] Exporting cod was better than sending ships back in ballast when faced with the need to offer something in return for urgently needed English manufactures. Yet the English merchants engaged in the cod trade did not earn their money with cod initially, as we will see.

One reason why cod alone was not profitable in the early phases was that the English were still price takers in Spanish ports in spite of their de facto monopoly of supply. In the 1640s, cod was not yet important enough a staple in Iberian markets, and local substitutes like fresh fish, herring, or salted pilchards kept sale prices down. The early shipments of cod into northern Spain were losing ventures rather than a business that "brings in great store of bullion from Spain," as a member of the English Parliament boasted in the 1620s.[46] Anglophone historians have been misled by English West Country fishing and trading interests who lobbied Parliament for extensions of their rights and control over the fisheries vis-à-vis foreigners and sometimes Newfoundland settlers.[47] Bullion extracted from Spain was a favorite topos used in each and every debate on trade with Spain, in favor of or against any commercial measure proposed anywhere in Europe and at any time between the mid-sixteenth and the late eighteenth century. Yet care should be exercised when such topoi were invoked; in this particular case it was used in defense of West Country commercial interests that had little opportunity to earn ready money in Spain. They simply knew what Parliament wanted to hear. The notion of "fish for gold" repeated time and again was wishful thinking in the early decades.[48]

---

[44] Pope, *Fish into Wine*, 116. This estimate does not include the opportunity cost of having capital employed for at least four months.

[45] Pope (like all other authors) uses Earl Hamilton's cod prices for New Castile. See Vickers, "a Knowen and Staple Commoditie," and Pope, "Adventures in the Sack Trade." Most recently Magra, *The Fisherman's Cause*, 85–86. Pope thus uses 30 *rs* per quintal for a 1630s comparison, when the price on the Spanish coast was about 17 *rs*, as can be seen in figure 4a). He assumes total costs of £3,405 against returns from the sale of fish of £3,780, and another £575 net income on the leg from Spain to England for a total profit of £900, or an impressive 26 percent. At 17 *reales* per quintal the sale of fish would, however, have resulted in £2,142, an overall loss on the triangular trip of £688, or 20 percent on investment.

[46] Cited in Magra, *The Fisherman's Cause*, 109.

[47] Magra offers a fascinating discussion of the opposition of West Country merchants to permanent settlement in Newfoundland, which they saw as competition that undermined their dominant position in the cod trade. Ibid., 30ff.

[48] Lydon, "Fish and Flour." Strictly speaking the hope was of course for silver not for gold.

The Structure and Consolidation of the Bacalao *Trade*

Nevertheless, the trade did expand quickly. McWilliams is wrong to claim that there is no material evidence for the fast quantitative expansion of New England cod exports. It just happens to lie in Spanish archives.[49] From the Spanish end the emergence of the transatlantic cod trade looks rather different. Large amounts of New England cod began to arrive in southern Europe by the 1630s, not during the English Civil War as Anglophone historians claim.[50] The trade was organized by a sizable English merchant colony in the port of Bilbao with strong connections to New England. More than forty resident merchants were supported by cape merchants and partners in the West Country and New England. It was surely no accident that shortly after the 1632 establishment of Robert Trelawny's fishing station in Richmond Island (the nucleus of Portland, Maine), a John Trelawny took up residence in Bilbao where he traded in fish and wool for at least fifteen years and where he probably lived until his death.[51]

What, if not profits, drove the expansion and why did the trade become a strongly defended mainstay of West Country interests in the English Parliament? As it turns out, the fish trade came into its own in the 1630s when merchants like the Trelawnys began to combine two apparently unrelated exchanges. On the New World side of the Atlantic, early New England settlers struggled to pay for vital supplies of merchandise from England and recognized fish as their only exportable commodity.[52] Yet demand for dried and salted cod in England was very modest. On the Old World side of the Atlantic, English textile producers shifted into the so-called New Draperies, or lighter cloths. The growth of this industry especially in the West Country, however, resulted in strongly rising demand for wool in general, and for high-quality Spanish merino in particular. The latter became a vital input in the new types of textiles, such as the aptly named "Spanish Cloths."[53]

Though England is commonly thought of as a wool-exporting country, by the mid-sixteenth century Castile exported about eight to fourteen times more wool than did England. Indeed, the latter finally prohibited exports of raw wool in 1619.[54] Industrial growth in England had outstripped the agri-

---

[49] McWilliams discusses why there was little demand for cod in the British West Indies in the 1640s, but he completely misunderstands the cod market and manages not to mention Spain, the main trading partner, once. McWilliams, "First Depression."

[50] Most historians of New England argue that exports to Spain only began when the Civil War interrupted the West Country–controlled Newfoundland trade. See, e.g., Magra, *The Fisherman's Cause*, 31, 78–79.

[51] For John Trelawny, see Archivo Histórico Provincial de Vizcaya (AHPV), legajo (leg), 4730/s.f., 2556/f.472-3, 4331/f.283, AFB, CB, 066, núm. 74, leg. 2674/016, 0321/017, 0172/021, and 2195/0113. For the Trelawny colony, see Baker, "Formerly Machegonne," 7. On the English merchant community in Bilbao, see Grafe, *Mundo ibérico*, chapter 7.

[52] See Hosmer, *Winthrop's Journal*.

[53] Mann, *Cloth Industry*; Supple, *Commercial Crisis*.

[54] For the following, see Grafe, "Globalisation of Codfish and Wool."

cultural basis, and relative scarcity was reflected in prices: the real price of wool in England rose throughout the sixteenth century and up to the 1660s.[55] Consequentially, in the 1630s West Country merchants began to import large amounts of very high-quality merino wool. The trade expanded rapidly. The lack of port books from the English outports as well as smuggling in the poorly policed provincial ports mean that these imports are well documented only in Spanish sources. Often wool that paid duties in northern Spain had miraculously disappeared from board when the same vessel moored in the West Country.[56] Yet by the 1630s and 1640s exports of Spanish wool to West Country ports were equal to about 10 percent of the entire domestic production of England and Wales.[57] The problem for English merchants was that demand for English products, such as cloth, was at an all-time low in northern and central Spain after a long period of economic hardship from about 1580 to the 1620s.[58] Thus wool imports could not be financed with English exports.

Enter North American cod. The demand for wool for the New Draperies in the English West Country could be supplied by merchants who combined wool imports from Spain with a new multilateral trade in manufactures and other necessities to the early North American colonies. Ships returned to Europe with the only export staple New England could produce, *bacalao*, which was taken directly to northern Spain. Profits from the Spain-England and England–North America legs compensated the losses from the North America–Spain leg. English and North American merchants were willing to use cod as a loss leader until at least the mid-seventeenth century because the shipments enabled them to sustain a profitable return trade in wool from Spain. In the meantime, they actually subsidized Spanish consumers who were able to purchase *bacalao* at prices that did not even cover the cost of fishing, processing, and delivering the fish to Spain. Contrary to the boastful advocates of West Country interests in the English Parliament, the lack of English goods that could sell in northern Spain meant that bilateral trade for Spanish wool would have had to be paid for with English bullion *exports* to Spain or by means of bills of exchange. Given this balance of trade and the extreme shortage of bullion in England, neither was an option. Only the export of *bacalao* from North America to Spain relaxed both constraints, even if in the early stages it was a loss leader. The trade expanded in this way even though it was loss making in bilateral terms.

Hence, supply side forces—rather than an insatiable Spanish demand and high cod prices in the Peninsula—determined the basic structure of this new intercontinental trade well before the mid-seventeenth century. The foundations

[55] Overton, *Agricultural Revolution*, 64, table 3.3.

[56] Grafe, *Mundo ibérico*. The notoriously poor performance of English Customs before the late seventeenth century has made it almost impossible to study these trades from English sources, as shown by Evan Jones in "Illicit Bias."

[57] Grafe, *Mundo ibérico*, 145.

[58] Priotti, *Bilbao*.

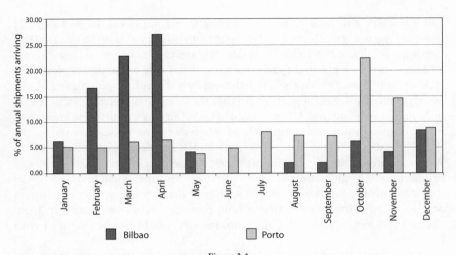

Figure 3.1
Seasonality of cod import shipments: Bilbao, 1635–36 and Porto, 1639–79. *Source*:
Bilbao: AFB, CB, Libro 212, núm. 36; Porto: Abreu-Ferreira, "The Cod Trade."

were a number of triangular interconnected exchanges. Since the trade was profitable only as a multilateral venture rather than a bilateral one, North American
trades had to be linked with intra-European ones and seasonality turned out to
be the defining feature. Northern Spain received by far the largest share of its
bacalao from New England. The seasonality of northern Spain's wool exports
over the summer (after early summer shearing, washing, and transport to the
coast) coincided rather well with the delivery of New England cod of the highest
quality after the spring fishing season, though New England could deliver some
regular supplies throughout the year. Merchants aiming to import wine from
Portugal and later from southern Spain would by contrast ship Newfoundland
fish, which was available after the very short and hectic summer fishing season
in the far north. This pattern is visible in the seasonality of vessels entering the
ports of Porto and Bilbao seen in figure 3.1. In the northern Spanish port, fish
arrived during the spring from mainland North America. Newfoundland supplies in turn went in October and November to northern Portugal.

The triangular trade to northern Spain in the early to mid-seventeenth
century involved a late autumn journey from the English West Country to
North America with a load of manufactures and other supplies. Ships would
spend the winter in the colonies, possibly engaging in coastal trade or even
a trip to the Caribbean or in the fisheries. In the spring they would travel
with a cargo of fish to northern Spain, whence they would return to the West
Country with a precious lading of Spanish merino. The triangular structure
allowed merchants, shippers, and fishermen to overcome the two crucial
limitations of early modern "international" trade: the difficulty of financing
bilateral trades that forced vessels to make one journey in ballast; and bal-

ance of payments constraints caused by poor financial integration and the widespread prohibition of bullion exports.[59]

It is almost impossible to determine when the cod trade itself began to turn a profit. Scale mattered, and the quantitative development of the wool trade suggests a stabilization on a high level after the 1650s. Real prices of wool in England also began to level off and even decline around 1660. Meanwhile *bacalao* imports continued to expand rapidly. Wool and cod trade were starting to move apart, and the cod business turned profitable in its own right at some point between 1650 and 1670. Since cod prices were not rising in Spain, it is likely that productivity gains in fishing, and possibly shipping, made New World cod more competitive. In other words, margins improved because production and trade costs had fallen, not because the sale price had gone up in Spain. Improved fishing techniques would have reduced the price of fish in North America; better shipping lowered the price of transport to Europe.[60] In both cases the increased scale of the trade was likely to have resulted in economies being made. Either way, the export of cod from North America to Spain eventually became profitable.

Exports to northern Spain, which are the best documented, expanded rapidly. From 1632 to 1638 total imports averaged about 11,000 quintals per annum; by 1640 to 1644 they had risen to 14,500 quintals. In 1686, 11,000 quintals were imported from New England alone, rising to 25,000 in 1700 and to 60,000 in 1713 after the War of the Spanish Succession.[61] New England was the most important source of cod in Spain, and northern Spain was the most important recipient of New England cod. Seventy-five percent of dried cod exported from Boston went to the port of Bilbao in 1699.[62]

Bilbao's imports, displayed in figure 3.2, can serve as a guide to the trends in Spanish overall imports over the eighteenth century. Anglophone historians have long argued that Newfoundland supplies dominated the southern European markets in general. That was true for Portugal and Italy and possibly for part of Mediterranean Spain.[63] However, northern Spanish import statistics tell a different story even in the eighteenth century. New England supplies dominated as late as 1775 until the English Parliament passed the New England Trade and Fishery Prohibition Act, better known as the Restraining Act, in order to subdue the increasingly unruly colonies. With the 1764 Sugar Act, New England fishermen and merchants had already lost the right

---

[59] Wilson, "Treasury and Trade Balances"; Grafe, "Atlantic Trade."

[60] For the early decades of the trade neither of these two is easy to document, though Magra has recently shown that from 1675 to 1775 productivity in fishing increased by 75 percent, and we will see that transatlantic trade also became cheaper in the long run. Magra, *The Fisherman's Cause*, 63.

[61] Imports into Alicante, the main Mediterranean port, started later but mirrored Bilbao's quantitative development in the seventeenth century. Ling, "Long-Term Movements," 256.

[62] Magra, *The Fisherman's Cause*, 83.

[63] Ling, "Long-Term Movements."

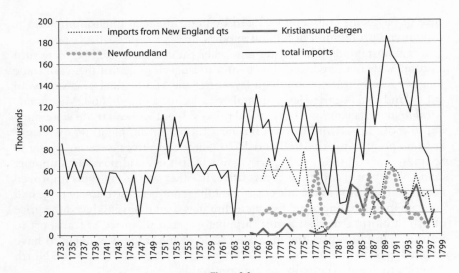

Figure 3.2
Bacalao imports into Bilbao by origin, 1733–1800 (qtls).
Source: Zabala Uriarte, *Mundo urbano*, 793.

to sell refuse fish to the French Caribbean, where they traded it for very competitively priced French sugar. Parliament had given in to British Caribbean sugar lobbies, which complained about higher prices for refuse fish and slaves caused by competition from the more efficient French sugar producers.[64] On top of these restrictions the general measure of 1775 now excluded New Englanders from the fisheries altogether and from trading with any place other than Britain and the British West Indies. Consequentially, the export trade in "merchantable" cod to Spain collapsed too, as shown in figure 3.2. Magra credits both acts with contributing considerably to the willingness of New England fishermen and traders to put their knowledge and resources at the disposal of the anti-colonial struggle—not least by sourcing war supplies from their established contacts in northern Spain in a trade that was now illegal anyway.[65]

The outcome of that particular historical episode is well-known. What concerns us here was its impact on cod exports to Spain. These would not resume until 1783 since the Massachusetts Provincial Congress in turn prohibited exports of high-grade fish, allowing only the trade in refuse fish to the West Indies, and Spain prohibited imports from England between 1779 and

[64] Magra, *The Fisherman's Cause*, 99ff. Already in 1699 Parliament had upset New England fishing interests with the Act to Encourage the Trade to Newfoundland, which tried to keep them out of the Newfoundland fisheries to the benefit of English West Country merchants.

[65] Calderón Cuadrado, *Empresarios españoles*.

1783.[66] A report prepared by Thomas Jefferson for the third session of the first U.S. Congress in 1791 claimed that the New England cod fisheries were still producing only about two-thirds of their prewar catch.[67] U.S. export statistics for the 1790s would suggest a similar cycle, though they tend to underestimate the total volume of trade significantly.[68] But even when New England supplies were so limited, Newfoundland fish could pick up only some of the market.

Instead, the prohibitions of the Massachusetts Provincial Congress allowed an entirely new competitor to intrude in its previously faithful Spanish market after 1776. Norway would expand its exports to Spain throughout the nineteenth century, a period known as Spansketiden (Age of the Spaniard) in Norwegian historiography.[69] In the fish trade at least, the commercial policy of the yet to be founded United States was off to an unpromising start. Nevertheless, interruptions were always temporary and the trend toward increased imports was unstoppable even if the overall imports of cod into Bilbao fluctuated especially with wars like the War of Jenkins' Ear, the Seven Years' War, the American colonial conflict, and the 1793 English French War. Shipments of cod from North America to Bilbao had increased by a factor of ten from 580 tons in 1630 to 5,600 tons by the time Jefferson was sitting down to write his reports to Congress.

Spain imported a total of about 32,000 tons of *bacalao* by 1785. The largest quantities were still imported by Bilbao, which received about 7,987 tons, a quarter of the total.[70] The remainder of the northern coast comprising Santander, Asturias, and Galicia imported 2,714 tons, and Andalusian ports imported approximately 2,323 tons.[71] On the Mediterranean, Barcelona was the most important port, importing 4,894 tons in 1789. But less well-known Alicante had imported 2,652 tons in 1751, most of it probably for trans-shipment to the larger city of Valencia, which lacked a deep seaport, and to

---

[66] Magra, *The Fisherman's Cause*, 200–202; Cubillo de la Puente, *El pescado*, 127.

[67] First Congress of the United States, 3rd Session, *Fisheries: Communicated to the House of Representatives, February 4, 1791 by Th Jefferson.*

[68] Pitkin, *A Statistical View*, 85, reports total exports of first class dried from the United States to Spain of about 72,300 qtls (3220 tons) from August 1789 to September 1790, when Bilbao alone imported 3,240 tons annually as seen in figure 3.2. Similarly low figures based on U.S. statistics have been reported by Lydon, "Fish for Gold," 552–55; and Richards, *Unending Frontier*, chapter 15. A source of 1852 seems more accurate, alleging that the territories of the later United States exported a total of 25,650 tons (560,000 qtls) in 1675, 30,933 tons (670,000 qtls) in 1795, and 74,947 tons (1.6 Mio qtls) 1828. See De Bow, *Encyclopaedia of the Trade and Commerce of the United States*, 463.

[69] Scheel, *Østersjøfart*, 198. For Norwegian exports, see Brautaset, "Norsk Eksport," chapters 6 and 7.

[70] A Bilbao qtl was about 107 "good pounds" according to Arriquibar, which refers to Vizacayan pounds of 488 grams rather than a Castilian of 460. Arriquibar and País, *Recreación política.* Zabala Uriarte speculates that Bilbao qtls might have been *quintales macho*, which would have been 55 percent larger, but there is little evidence to support this claim. Zabala Uriarte, *Mundo urbano*, 207.

[71] Meijide Pardo, *Comercio*.

the Castilian interior.[72] Cartagena was said to be a very important port for *bacalao*, most likely exceeding Alicante.[73] At 1780s prices of *bacalao* at the coast of Bilbao, the total import value amounted to 12,720,000 *reales*. Given the cost in the interior, Macanaz's warnings about 20 million *reales* spent on cod were probably not alarmist at all.[74]

That all cod was imported allows us to assess its availability in the Spanish market much more precisely than what would be possible in the case of any domestically produced foods. Taking the estimate of 32,000 tons of cod imported in 1785, and a population of about 10.8 million in 1800, per capita consumption reached about 3 kilograms in the late eighteenth century.[75] Excluding the population under the age of four, the estimate rises to about 3.3 kilograms per annum.[76] No reliable estimates for total imports exist for earlier dates. Yet the rate of growth of imports since the mid-seventeenth century in the most important port of Bilbao can serve as a yardstick. This proxy would suggest that imports rose at an annual rate of about 1.4 percent over the second half of the seventeenth century and the first half of the eighteenth, notwithstanding the violent fluctuations shown in figure 3.2.[77]

Over the same period the Spanish population grew much more slowly. During the seventeenth century the highest reasonable estimate does not exceed about 0.11 percent per annum, while in the eighteenth, population growth might have reached about 0.52 percent.[78] Based on these growth rates, per capita consumption was at most 0.7 kilograms of *bacalao* in 1650.[79] In other words, the amount of cod offered per person in 1785 was

[72] This was at least the pattern in the seventeenth century, for which we have more information. Ling, "Long-Term Movements."

[73] Uztáriz's estimate from the 1720s had not been far off; Sañez Reguart had overestimated the real number by 100 percent. For Alicante, see Figueras Pacheco, *El consulado marítimo*, 30; Laborde, *Itinerario*, 57, 294. The author also confirmed that Bilbao still received about 160,000 qtls in peacetime.

[74] Using an average of 3.18 *rs* per kilogram, the average price in the late eighteenth century from the database of this book.

[75] Population figure based on *Floridablanca Census* of 1787 including adjustments suggested by Plaza Prieto, *Estructura económica*, 131.

[76] Estimate for population under the age of five based on 1787 census figure of 18.24 percent under the age of seven and linear interpolation, which underestimates the number of small infants who were subject to higher mortality rates. It thus biases the estimate downward. For census age structure, see ibid., 119.

[77] Estimate based on imports of 580 tons in 1630 and 5,600 tons in 1791; see this chapter. It is likely that this biases the growth rate downward, since Bilbao's dominance probably declined slightly over time as more and more ports began to receive *bacalao* shipments.

[78] Seventeenth-century estimate from Comín, Hernández, and Llopis Agelán, *Historia económica*, 123. Eighteenth-century estimates based on Plaza Prieto, *Estructura económica*, 131. Comín, Hernández, and Llopis Agelán argue that eighteenth-century population growth did not exceed 0.38 percent.

[79] Estimate based on back extrapolation of total imports using estimated growth rate for 1650–1785, a population of 7.5 million, and the same share of infants as in 1787.

almost five times that available 135 years before. As we saw, supply side forces explain that the trade initially emerged not because of huge profit margins but as a means of solving typical balance of payments problems. But by the mid-seventeenth century it had come into its own, and the increase in supplies in the long run was unbroken. By the late eighteenth century it is easy to see why *bacalao* had achieved such prominence in the writings of contemporary "economists."

Consumption

The dent cod evidently made in the balance of trade and the estimates of average consumption levels do not tell us anything, however, about who bought *bacalao* and where and why it was consumed. Nor do they help us understand how the market for this imported product grew so large. Understanding consumption is crucial for several reasons. On the one hand, I have claimed that demand conditions were stable enough to use *bacalao* prices for a study of the impact of transport costs and jurisdictional fragmentation. Social and cultural historians rightly remind economic historians that consumers made choices based on a number of variables that included their household economy as well as entirely unrelated social and cultural factors. Thus, we need to look in more detail into consumption patterns in order to be certain what prices and price movements actually meant. On the other hand, market integration was precisely about increasing consumer choices. New goods altered consumption patterns. Understanding what motivated these choices is thus central to understanding how they in turn shaped the market.

The Spanish historiography has offered two competing hypotheses that would explain the success of cod in Spain (and elsewhere in southern Europe). The first one is cultural. It takes as its point of departure eighteenth-century commentators who blamed the much-maligned expansion of this trade on the fasting habits of Catholic Spaniards. The second, by contrast, stresses an economic rationale to increasing consumption. Terreros y Pando's definition, quoted above, suggested that the consumption of cod was driven exclusively by the need of the poor (and the tastes of the rich). In other words, *bacalao* was a cheap staple food. Yet was the order of magnitude of cod consumption sufficient at all to have a real impact on the overall consumption possibilities of the average Spaniard? After all, even 3.3 kilograms a year does not sound like much.

The impression is deceptive, however, because dried cod is not only calorie rich, it also added to the diet one ingredient that was in chronically short supply: animal protein. In Spain, as elsewhere in Europe, meat consumption provided the bulk of animal protein. However, is seems likely that the availability of meat had continuously fallen since the Middle Ages even if few consumption estimates are available. In the 1780s Madrileños probably had on average as much as 33–41 kilograms of all kinds of meats per person and year; in 1826 the first statistics counted 30 kilograms per person.[80] Meanwhile, in small, bourgeois Leon, meat consumption might have been over 50 kilograms, but most estimates for the early modern period fall between 20 and 30 kilograms.[81] In early modern Europe meat consumption was generally much higher in towns. With this in mind and given the admittedly very sketchy urban estimates that are available, it is unlikely that overall consumption in early modern Spain exceeded 25 kilograms per person and year.[82] This estimate would still compare favorably with a French estimate of about 19 kilograms in the same decade and constitutes an upper-bound estimate that is biased against giving too much importance to cod.[83] Indeed, biasing the calculation at every turn in favor of the highest reasonable estimate of meat-based protein suggests that the average supply would have covered the need of an adult male for about 120 days a year.[84] Meanwhile, the average supply of *bacalao* would have added 33 days of protein intake per year to the diet of a male manual laborer, more in the case of women and children.[85]

The Mediterranean diet provided a larger share of protein through grain and leguminous vegetables than was available in northern Europe. Notwithstanding, animal sources accounted for about 150 days' worth of protein, and by the later eighteenth century more than 20 percent of that came from *bacalao*. The cod consumption of the average person helps establish on the one hand the true expansion of the market and on the other the impact on overall consumption possibilities. Yet it also confirms a wide variety of studies on the seventeenth and eighteenth centuries that suggest higher consumption levels in Spanish society than once assumed possible.[86]

[80] The most important kinds of meat were beef and ham. Notably, the account books of religious institutions reviewed for this study reveal only limited amounts of mutton consumption.

[81] For Madrid, see Gutiérez Alonso, *Estudio sobre la decadencia*, 281–85, cited in Cubillo de la Puente, *El pescado*, 283–84, who also cites estimates for Valladolid, Oviedo, and Murcia. For Leon, see Cubillo de la Puente, "Carne y pescado."

[82] Baics, "Feeding Gotham," 204. Baics points out that differences between town and country were extreme in the French case; Parisians consumed about four times the average amount.

[83] Ibid.

[84] Historians of nutrition suggest that an adult male needed a minimum of protein of about 56–69 grams per day. Livi-Bacci, *Population and Nutrition*, 29. Beef was the predominant meat in Spain. However, even high-quality beef contains only about half as much protein per weight as *bacalao*. Hence the uppermost estimate for annual beef consumption, 25 kilograms, could at best provide the protein need of 120 days.

[85] I would like to thank Rick Steckel and the late John Richards for pointing me to http://www.ars.usda.gov/main/site_main.htm?modecode=12-35-45-00 (accessed February 2, 2010) for the protein content of various foodstuffs. Cod contains about 63 grams of protein and 290 kilocalories per 100 grams. A relatively high-quality piece of beef (chuck steak) provides about 29 grams of protein and 189 kilocalories for the same serving.

[86] Cf. Llopis Agelán and García Montero, "Cost of Living."

The Case for Popish Habits

The Catholic Church saw fasting as an important expression of religiosity throughout the premodern period. However, one should carefully avoid the cultural determinism implied in many references to Spain's Catholic heritage. The importance attributed to fasting was not a constant factor over time, nor should we assume a priori that the population's adherence to such rules was uniform over time and space. The very insistence of Church authorities on fasting suggests otherwise. The number of "fish days" changed significantly over time and also differed between regions due to local festivities.

Historians of religion have argued that in the Counter-Reformation climate of the early seventeenth century, fasting was observed more strictly than either before or after. Religious authorities sometimes imposed fines on those who failed to observe Friday or Lenten fasting.[87] A Guipúzcoan source from 1631 stated that during "half of the year less a seventh one fasts"; that makes for around 130 days of fasting.[88] Uztáriz thought that 120 days were observed in Castile and 160 in Aragon in the 1720s.[89] In Inquisition trials of the late sixteenth and seventeenth centuries, testimonies claiming that an accused had not observed fasting days were considered an important indicator of heterodoxy.[90] All of this anecdotal evidence would suggest that the social pressure to strictly adhere to the rules was strong. Yet it did not apply to all faithful in the same way. In the case of "Old Christians," the Church often looked the other way. In the case of "New Christians," the large segment of the Iberian population whose ancestors had converted from Judaism or Islam sometime before 1614, it paid extra attention to any sign of relaxed observance.[91]

There is other anecdotal evidence that religion mattered in shaping the demand for *bacalao*. Town councils worried about the steady supply of dried and salted cod during Lent, partly because at the same time the council-run slaughterhouses would be officially closed in many towns.[92] Before 1619 the municipal fish stalls of Jaén opened only during Lent, on Fridays, and on other days of abstinence. Later, opening hours were extended allegedly because "many religions [religious orders] eat fish on weekdays." Those devoted to the Virgin of the Carmen were singled out as particularly inclined to fish eating.[93]

---

[87] Cubillo de la Puente, *El pescado*, 113.

[88] Fernández Albaladejo, *Guipúzcoa*, 68n139. See also Cubillo de la Puente, *El pescado*, 115–16, for similarly high estimates for Castile.

[89] Uztáriz, *Theorica*, 272ff.

[90] See the discussion of reasons for the Inquisition to take action in Thomas, *In de Klauwen*.

[91] Cubillo de la Puente, *El pescado*, 113. With the expulsion decrees of 1492 (in the case of Jews) and 1609–14 (in the case of Muslims), the descendants of Jewish or Muslim families remaining in Castile and Aragon were forced to convert and thus became subject to the jurisdiction of the Holy Office.

[92] For Madrid, see Fernández García, *Madrid*, 97.

[93] Coronas Tejada, "Abastecimiento de pescado," 35–36.

Toward the late eighteenth century the number of fast days fell slowly, a trend that accelerated in the nineteenth century. Ernesto López Losa found that the Seminary of Bergara (Guipúzcoa), formerly a Jesuit school that became a nucleus of the Enlightenment after their expulsion in 1767, still observed on average eighty-nine days of abstinence in the period 1784–98.[94] Yet a new indulgence was sold that allowed the consumption of meat on some days during Lent and on other days of abstinence after the publication of Pope Pius VI's "Meat Bull" of 1778.[95] Likely as a consequence, the seminary reduced the number of days of abstinence to fifteen by 1822–31.[96] It is, however, unclear how the ability of the few to buy an indulgence affected the consumption habits of the many who had little money to spare. It seems in fact probable that the "Meat Bull" of 1778 was a response to the extraordinary shortage of *bacalao* in the Spanish markets caused by the wars of independence in North America in those years. Its purchase hardly made sense for anyone other than large institutions. Thus it did not dramatically change religious observance in Spain for the population at large.

Days of abstinence were unequally distributed throughout the year, and many historians have argued that seasonal patterns can prove (or disprove) the importance of religion for the consumption of fish generally and *bacalao* in particular.[97] Especially increased fish consumption during the pre-Easter Lent period is interpreted as a clear sign that religion, rather than market forces and secular preferences, determined overall consumption. The strongest evidence for such a pattern of seasonality comes from a study of consumption patterns in late eighteenth-century Madrid, which found that the seasonal variation of consumption of *bacalao* and beef was almost perfectly inverse.[98] Cod demand rose strongly for a limited period around Christmas and for the entire pre-Easter period while beef consumption declined at the same times.

The author deduced from this that religious restrictions, rather than economic factors, were the main force driving fish demand. Interestingly, however, the inverse relation between cod and beef prices remains intact throughout the year. This begs a number of questions. While the Easter and Christmas highs do confirm the impact of the religious calendar, the complete synchronization suggests that *bacalao* had developed into an almost perfect substitute for beef—the single most important animal foodstuff in Spain. In other words, when cod demand rose, beef demand fell and vice versa. The availability of a close substitute meant that consumers could react immediately to price changes.

[94] On the seminary, see Sarrailh, *España ilustrada*, 212.
[95] Purchasers had to buy the *bula de la cruzada* in addition to the meat indulgence (*indulto de carnes*) but were still required to keep fasting on Ash Wednesday, the four Fridays during Lent, the last four days of the Easter week, and the four of Christmas, Pentecost, Ascension day, and Sts. Peter and Paul.
[96] López Losa, "Aproximación"; Cubillo de la Puente, *El pescado*.
[97] See López Losa, "Aproximación," 26–27, and Bernardos Sanz, "Abastecimiento."
[98] Bernardos Sanz, "Abastecimiento."

There is another reason to doubt that seasonal patterns are a good indicator of religious fasting as the main reason for *bacalao*'s spectacular rise as a staple foodstuff. As seen in figure 3.1, the seasonal nature of imports was not necessarily a function of demand conditions but reflected some fundamental features of the supply side in the early phases of the expansion of the transatlantic trade. The characteristic in question was the Spanish preference for New England supplies rather than those from Newfoundland that became a permanent feature of the trade. In its origin in the mid-seventeenth century, the resulting seasonality had been a response to the demand of Englishmen for Iberian wool, which conditioned the decision making of English merchants. The seasonal cycle of New England fisheries combined more easily with that of wool exports from Spain. In Portugal by contrast, the annual cycle of the wine trade fit more easily with imports from Newfoundland.

These supply-side-induced structures of consumption, however, proved durable over time, with most imports of cod, especially into northern Spain, still arriving from New England in the later eighteenth century. It also meant that in some towns, notably in Bilbao, most *bacalao* shipments arrived after the main New England fishing season, which happened to coincide with the Lent fasting period (compare figure 3.1). There seems no good reason to argue that the Portuguese, who received most of their fish in the autumn, were less observant Catholics. Hence, rather than fasting driving fish demand in Spain, cod supplies from Puritan New England made popish fasting habits a possibility in Spain's inland regions. The seasonality of the trade resulted in more supplies and reduced prices that led naturally to increased spring consumption. Pronounced increases in cod sales in spring could thus be a consequence of religious restrictions, geographical origin of the catch, or both. In short, seasonality is not the clear-cut indicator for religious motives that it has been made out to be.

What about the claims of Spanish enlightened thinkers that the rise in cod demand was the fault of the great numbers of unproductive nuns, monks, and priests? In some ways, the very data used in this book would support their allegations. Throughout the archival search for series of *bacalao* prices I have not come across a single account book of a religious institution that did not contain any references to substantial amounts of cod bought by the institution. The amounts might vary, but all spent a notable share of their monthly food outlays on this fish. Cod was such an obvious staple supply of religious institutions that it became the object of charitable giving. The faithful traditionally tended to give grain or candles. Nevertheless, by the late seventeenth century one regularly finds entries in the account books such as the following from February 2, 1694, in the Franciscan monastery (Franciscanos Menores) Reina de los Angeles in Cadiz: "the syndic received 300 *reales* silver that a devout person gave for *bacalao*."[99]

---

[99] AHN, Clero Libro, 1837.

Table 3.1. Average annual per capita consumption of *bacalao* in Spanish convents and monasteries, eighteenth century

Year	Place	No. of institutions	Gender	Average consumption (kg)
1752	Province Galicia	73	M	18.19
1752	Province Galicia	24	F	14.76
1752	Province Leon	34	M	17.97
1752	Province Leon	19	F	6.84
1784–98	Bergara	1	M	23.00

Source: Galicia: Meijide Pardo, *Comercio*; Leon: Miguel López, *Mundo*, appendices 19, 20; Bergara: López Losa, "Aproximación."

Nevertheless, a quick back-of-the-envelope calculation of the consumption attributable to religious institutions also illustrates that Enlightenment disdain for the allegedly large numbers of religious institutions driving cod consumption should be taken with a grain of salt. As mentioned above, estimates derived from supply figures suggest a per capita consumption of *bacalao* around 3.3 kilograms annually by the late eighteenth century. Members of religious orders and lay clerics indeed consumed far more than the average person as the estimates for per capita consumption in about 150 monasteries and convents in table 3.1 illustrate. Some monasteries in Galicia consumed reportedly up to 34 kilograms per person and year.[100] If such amounts expressed purely religious motives, these consumers were very zealous about their faith, indeed.

It is hard to assess what the size of an average portion of *bacalao* was. Modern-day portions are in the order of 80–100 grams before the *remojado*, or rehydration. Such a portion would cover the daily protein needs of an adult male. The seminarians of Bergara in the 1780s consumed 250 grams per fish day, presumably in two meals.[101] Given those portions, 34 kilograms of fish would guarantee two fish meals on about 120 days a year, or 240 days if they had just one fish meal per day.

Yet no matter how seriously religious "professionals" took their fish days and fasting, their numbers were limited even in Spain, no matter how loudly eighteenth-century Enlightenment voices protested that the high number of monks and nuns was "the real cancer of the Spanish Commonwealth." The papal nuncio to Spain felt obliged to ask bishops to report on their numbers and income; the resulting 1764 survey showed regional differences with high numbers in Andalusia and Extremadura and very low ones in Galicia and

[100] Meijide Pardo, *Comercio*.
[101] López Losa, "Aproximación," 26. A 1631 estimate from Guipúzcoa calculated 360 grams per person and day, though it is not clear whether this meant dry or watered. In any case this quantity seems almost impossible to consume. Fernández Albaladejo, *Guipúzcoa*, 68.

Asturias.[102] A large share of monks, nuns, and priests lived in the urban areas. In the small town of Leon they made up about 6 percent of the population in 1757.[103] In Madrid "church related professions" allegedly accounted for 11 percent of the population at the same time.[104] However, overall, nuns, monks, and priests accounted for only 0.7 percent of the Spanish population in 1591, at most 1 percent in 1752, and 0.3–0.7 percent in 1800.[105] Despite their high average consumption, members of religious orders consumed less than 3 percent of overall *bacalao* imports.[106] This was not a small number, but clearly religious "professionals" were not the main culprits for what eighteenth-century pamphleteers saw as a disastrous habit of importing a staple foodstuff.

The exaggerated estimates of religiously motivated fish consumption hence served a political point. The high consumption of fish by religious communities was not large enough to have an effect on the overall availability of cod to the population. More important, it cannot explain the pattern of imports observed in the long run. The share of Spaniards devoting their life to religion hardly changed over time. In addition, there were fewer Church-enforced fish days in the eighteenth century (and dramatically fewer ones in the nineteenth) than there had been in the seventeenth century, as shown above. Thus religiously motivated consumption by the population at large did not account for the pace at which overall per capita consumption of cod continued to rise.

Bacalao *as Food for the Poor*

Terreros y Pando was not alone among contemporaries in asserting that *bacalao* was an essential complement in the diet of the poor. In 1661 a member of the Cabildo of Jaén (Andalusia) claimed that "*bacalao* is the only food of the poor."[107] Only anchovies and pilchards were considered less attractive because they were literally "small fry." During 1659 Jaén experienced one of the many food riots that Spain saw throughout the seventeenth century. However, this time the crowd did not target the granaries or bakeries, the usual object of ire for urban food rioters across early modern Europe. Instead, it went for the merchant in charge of supplying the town with cod.[108]

---

[102] Barrio Gozalo, "Clero regular," 126–27.

[103] Cubillo de la Puente, *Comer*, 17.

[104] Ringrose, *Madrid*, 68.

[105] My own elaboration based on Barrio Gozalo, "Clero regular," 124; Comín, Hernández, and Llopis Agelán, *Historia económica*.

[106] Estimate based on per capita consumption of 15 kilograms (the maximum likely amount for the overall group consisting of men and women), 70,000 members, and around 30,000 tons of cod.

[107] Quoted in Coronas Tejada, "Abastecimiento de pescado," 40.

[108] Ibid., 42ff.

The circumstantial evidence in favor of either religious and economic motives as driving forces for increasing consumption is in the end inconclusive and another approach is needed. However, data for the food intake of the lower classes are notoriously difficult to come by. Consumption historians often rely on records from charitable institutions to gain insights into the food intake of the poor. One might, however, doubt that the food coming out of the kitchens of institutions reflected what poor people up and down the country ate. Studies of consumption in various hospitals and asylums in Madrid in the early nineteenth century found a diet that was surprisingly rich in meat and contained very limited quantities of *bacalao*.[109] By contrast, the Hospice of Leon consumed about six kilograms of *bacalao* per capita in the late eighteenth century.[110] Given what we know about meat and fish consumption generally, neither estimate would seem representative. The problem with data from these sources is that the sample is usually too small to allow a clear identification of the causes driving the composition of the food basket. Maybe cod was no longer cheap in Madrid, or maybe Spanish society was just very generous with its infirm; there are some indications that hospital patients were considerably better fed than they would have been outside the hospital.[111]

Nevertheless, there is one way to control for the impact of religion in consumption and test the hypothesis that economic reasons played a major role. This is to focus on economic differences within a group that can safely be assumed to take religious observance seriously. Members of religious orders ate far more fish than the average person, as seen above. Yet the high averages mask remarkable differences between religious institutions as revealed by data for the consumption of Galician monasteries in 1752 collected by Antonio Meijide Pardo and presented in figure 3.3. There was a wide divergence of per capita consumption of cod between monasteries of the same order. The box graph plots all observations underneath the main box. The left and right borders of each box represent the 25th and 75th percentile values and the vertical line in the box the median. The smallest observation is 4.7 kilograms per head for one of the Benedictine monasteries, the largest, a Dominican monastery, with 34.3 kilograms. Notwithstanding the variation within orders, the mean consumption of Benedictines and Jesuits on the whole was lower than that of Augustines, Dominicans, and Franciscans.

The 1764 survey undertaken by the papal nuncio mentioned above makes it possible to estimate the economic well-being of monasteries belonging to

[109] Fernández García, *Madrid*, 179ff.
[110] Miguel López, *Mundo del comercio*, 179.
[111] The only contemporary account of the share of income spent by laborers on various items suggests, notably, a very low proportion given to bread compared to some estimates provided in the recent literature. That, of course, would make sense, since the taxation system shifted the fiscal burden from the most basic necessity, bread, to other goods such as wine, meat, and fish. Sureda Carrión, *La hacienda castellana*, 14.

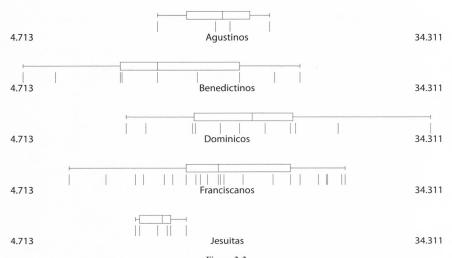

Figure 3.3
Annual consumption of *bacalao* in Galician monasteries,
1750s–1760s (kilograms per capita). *Source*: My own elaboration
based on Meijide Pardo, *Economía marítima*.

each of these orders very broadly. The survey contains data on only two
of the Galician dioceses, Lugo and Mondoñedo, reported in table 3.2. In
both, the survey considered Benedictine monasteries rich, as were the Jesuits
of Lugo. Though the latter refers to only one diocese, it is consistent with
results from elsewhere in Spain that indicate that Jesuit congregations were
economically more successful than those of other orders. Still, these results

Table 3.2. Economic status of monasteries in the Galician Dioceses Lugo and
Mondoñedo by religious order, 1764

Order	Dioceses	Monasteries	Monks	Economic Status
Agustinos	Lugo	1	16	sufficient
Benedictinos	Lugo	2	75	rich
Benedictinos	Mondonedo	1	39	rich
Dominicos	Lugo	2	54	sufficient
Dominicos	Mondonedo	3	41	sufficient
Franciscanos	Lugo	2	73	sufficient
Franciscanos	Mondonedo	6	194	poor
Jesuitas	Lugo	1	18	rich

Source: My own elaboration based on Meijide Pardo, *Economía marítima*, and Barrio Gozalo, "Clero
regular."

Table 3.3. Annual consumption of *bacalao* of individual Galician convents and monasteries, 1750s–1760s

Order	F/M	Place	Members	Bacalao (kg/pc)	Economic status
Dominicos	F	Lugo	64	11.31	rich
All (average)	F	Galicia		14.76	
Benedictinos	M	Villanueva Loren.	41	7.06	very rich
Hosp. S Juan de Dios	M	Lugo	7	18.61	poor
Franciscanos	M	Ribadeo	31	26.15	very poor
All (average)	M	Galicia		18.19	

Source: See table 3.2.

should be interpreted with caution, given their regional limitations and the reduced sample available for the assessment of economic status.

It is reassuring, however, that data for three monasteries and one convent that could be identified by name and location in both sets of data would strengthen the argument. Table 3.3 shows that both the rich Dominican nuns of Lugo and the even richer Benedictine monks of Villanueva ate far less *bacalao* than the average Galician nun or monk. By contrast, the poor monks of the Hospital de San Juan in Lugo consumed more than the average, and the unfortunate Franciscans in Ribadeo seem to have seen few other food-stuffs on their plates. It is unlikely that regional differences in the number of fish days played a large role in these figures, since they are all from the same region. Assuming generous 125-gram portions and 90 to 100 fish days in the mid-eighteenth century, 11 or 12 kilograms per head fulfilled the "religious quota." The conclusion must be that economically affluent Benedictines and Dominicans ate *bacalao* only on fasting days or may even have substituted expensive fresh fish for *bacalao*. But poor monks ate *bacalao* on many days that were not religious fish days.

Spanish monks made their economic decisions like everybody else. One way this can be illustrated is by their reaction to price changes. Economists call this the "own price elasticity," that is, how quickly consumers change the amount of a good they purchase when its price is altered. If cod con-sumption was predominantly a function of religious observance, the faithful would probably continue purchasing it even if prices rose sharply. If, how-ever, increasing consumption was a response to *bacalao*'s being a relatively affordable source of scarce protein, price changes should quickly translate into changes in the quantity of cod purchased.

An estimation on the basis of the particularly complete list of purchases from the account books of the monastery of the Agustinos Calzados Nuestra Señora de Gracia in Cadiz between 1700 and 1813 results in an own price elasticity of −0.5. In plain language, the faithful Augustinian monks bought

5 percent less *bacalao* if its price increased by 10 percent.[112] Clearly, cod consumption was responsive to price changes. In fact, the degree of adjustment estimated here is very close to the order of magnitude observed by economic historians for grain in various European countries in the early modern period. In this respect, too, *bacalao* was a staple food.

Once controls for the religious consumption pattern are introduced, it becomes clear that dried and salted codfish was considered an inferior good by the mid-eighteenth century at the latest. Poor monks ate *bacalao*; rich ones bought indulgences to eat meat or bought fresh fish. The Basque defender of the Spanish Enlightenment Arriquibar described precisely this process when he remarked in the late 1770s that "our consumption of this commodity, instead of diminishing, rises furiously because of the shortage of meat, so much, that the poor people of the countryside have introduced it even on meat days, because of the shortage of meat, as well as the ease of preparation."[113]

[112] Estimation based on a loglog OLS regression of quantities purchased on prices, with an N of 86 and an $R2$ of 0.14. If a time trend is included, the result changes to $\varepsilon = 0.8$ with an $R2$ of 0.23. The analysis of the residuals suggests no omitted variable bias in either case. Income or other data to overcome the simultaneity problem are not available. Yet the data were derived from only one monastery in a large port town, and it is safe to assume that the decision maker was a price taker. In other words, it is unlikely that the OLS results are biased.

[113] Arriquibar and País, *Recreación política*.

Chapter 4 _____

The Tyranny of Distance

Transport and Markets in Spain

SPAIN SUFFERS FROM a particularly unforgiving geography by European standards. Within its present borders the average altitude above sea level is about 660 meters, which also happens to be the altitude of Madrid. That makes Spain the country with the second-highest average elevation in Europe after Switzerland.[1] In terms of landmass it is just smaller than France, but it has only two navigable rivers, the Ebro and the Guadalquivir, and even these become unnavigable barely 100 kilometers from the sea. Fast currents and abrupt changes in water levels resulting from the large elevations render other rivers useless for transport purposes. To complicate things further, the central high plateau is separated from the coastlines in every direction by mountain ranges. The natural passes through these often exceed 1,000 meters in height—a veritable challenge given early modern transport technology. Anyone who has taken the modern motorway through the Desfiladero de Despeñaperros (Gorge Where the Dogs Are Hurled Down) from Andalusia to Madrid has an appreciation of just how difficult some of those passages must have been.

It is thus hardly surprising that market integration in Spain was haphazard, slow, and regionally diverse in the early modern period, it could be argued. Spain was just unlucky; its geography did not lend itself easily to the technologically available means of improving transport either on water or land. But the extent to which unfavorable transport conditions contributed to Spain's overall predicament and restricted market integration is poorly understood. It is not very clear at all thus far what the trends and cycles in market integration were in the first place. This chapter will hence first turn to analyzing the actual state of market integration, followed by an analysis of the role played by transport in this state of affairs using the *bacalao* market as an empirical tool.

Market Integration in Spain: What We Know

Until the 1990s, the overwhelmingly negative view of Spanish economic development in the early modern period led to an unproven, generalized

[1] Madrazo, *Comunicaciones*, 20–24.

assumption that the process of market integration mirrored the overall fortunes of the Spanish economy: a short-lived apogee in the sixteenth century, misery in the seventeenth, and little more than stagnation in the eighteenth. When this chronology was transposed onto market integration it was argued that Spain had a relatively well-integrated network of commercial towns, especially in the Castilian interior in the sixteenth century, whose economic decline from the seventeenth century onward was accompanied by the disintegration of internal markets. In the eighteenth century, outward-oriented port towns supposedly slowly dragged the backward hinterland out of its hibernation.

There were compelling reasons for the picture of decline and disintegration in the late sixteenth and seventeenth centuries and moderate resurgence in the eighteenth. The late sixteenth-century collapse of northern Spanish woolen textile trades with the Netherlands, northern France, and England went hand in hand with the implosion of the famous commercial fairs of northern Castile.[2] This brought an end to an intense phase of commercial expansion that had been underpinned by an organization based on large internationally integrated commercial firms organized in the famous merchant guilds of Bilbao and Burgos.[3] It was assumed that the decline of the powerful commercial institutions and organizations was an expression of a general disintegration of markets within Spain.[4]

The signs of severe strain in the Castilian economy throughout the first half of the seventeenth century seemed to lend support to the argument of deepening disintegration. Although some have argued that the seventeenth-century agrarian sector was subject more to transformation than to outright decline, it is fairly obvious that there was indeed a serious crisis of agricultural production.[5] In addition, the distribution of population within the Peninsula began to shift. Formerly successful towns in the Castilian interior, Burgos, Avila, Segovia, and many others, lost a substantial part of their population, while at the same time population density in the coastal areas increased.[6] Most important, historians have been fascinated by the emergence of Madrid, a large new urban center in the heart of Castile. Temporal coincidence between a decline in population in the old Castilian towns and the rise of the new capital Madrid was constructed in one seemingly convincing step into a causal relationship between the two developments.[7] Thus, the rise of the capital was held responsible for fracturing the markets in the hinterland. But were internal markets really disintegrating?

A short survey across Spanish regions shows that both qualitative and quantitative studies cast doubt on this interpretation. The collapse of Castilian

---

[2] Abed al-Hussein, "Trade and Business."

[3] Grafe, *Mundo ibérico*; Phillips and Phillips, *Spain's Golden Fleece*; Priotti, *Bilbao*.

[4] Ringrose, *Madrid*.

[5] Yun Casalilla, *Sobre la transición*; Yun Casalilla, "De Molinos."

[6] For a discussion, see chapter 8.

[7] Ringrose, *Madrid*.

external trade with northern Europe during the late sixteenth and early seventeenth centuries led to a breakdown of the large international commercial firms and the fair economy that had articulated it.[8] This was part of a larger reorganization, however, that favored smaller operators in both external and internal trade rather than a sign of market fragmentation per se. Commercial activity now experienced the sort of agglomeration process that had been slowed down by the incumbent players. Former commercial towns like northern Castilian Burgos, once known as the *caput castellae* (head of Castile), declined rapidly. At the same time in the northern coastal regions, activity shifted from two dozen small ports supported previously by inland Burgos toward concentration in one main port, Bilbao, and one intermediate one, Santander. The northern region within became more, not less, integrated, and the emergence of a more articulated urban hierarchy was one outcome of this process. From the 1630s onward external trade experienced a notable upsurge through newly established links with England and New England. Since recently arrived foreign merchants had little inland contact, locals shifted their investment into domestic trade networks supporting the new foreign trades.

Overall it seems likely that the structure of domestic trade between the Castilian interior and the commercially very important northern coast was transformed in a direction of less power for the large merchant guilds, less influence for a reduced number of trading houses, and more trade being conducted by small and independent operators. Even though domestic trade volumes must have declined in the worst decades of the late sixteenth and early seventeenth centuries, there is little evidence that the northern coast was less integrated with the Castilian hinterland in 1650 than it had been in 1570. If anything, the involvement of corporate organization declined over this period, lowering barriers to entry, and the market became more competitive.

A similar development was underway in Catalonia. García Espuche's beautiful account of the transformative period in Catalan history between the mid-sixteenth and mid-seventeenth centuries traces the resurgence of Barcelona not just as a commercial town but now also as the center of an integrated region.[9] The sixteenth and seventeenth centuries used to be a stepchild of Catalan historiography, sandwiched between medieval splendor and the beginning of industrialization in the eighteenth century, which was precocious by Spanish standards. The traditional narrative of a Catalan commercial crisis in these centuries was in its origin strongly linked to the notion of exclusion from the American trades.[10] As the commercial center of gravity of Spain moved southward toward Seville and Cadiz, it was argued that the famous exclusion of non-Castilian merchants through a decree issued by

---

[8] The following discussion relies on Grafe, *Mundo ibérico*.

[9] García Espuche, *Un siglo decisivo*.

[10] For a discussion, see Delgado i Ribas, "América y el comercio"; García Espuche, *Un siglo decisivo*, 343–47.

Isabella of Castile had placed those from the Crown of Aragon at a disadvantage. Except for a short period during Isabella's lifetime, however, historians have found little evidence for an outright exclusion of the Aragonese.[11]

To be sure, merchants from anywhere in the Peninsula other than Seville or Cadiz were discriminated against through the incorporation of the American trades. Yet it seems that merchants from Barcelona in particular found their way into the American trades through Andalusian intermediation in the same way as did northern Spanish (and international) merchants.[12] According to García Espuche, between the second half of the sixteenth century and the first half of the seventeenth century, the Catalan economy reoriented itself in a way that lay the foundation for its eighteenth-century expansion. Manufacturing began to emerge in the countryside that became much better integrated with Barcelona.[13] Merchants in the Catalan capital, in turn, increasingly exported these products to Atlantic rather than Mediterranean destinations. Beginning in the 1680s, Catalan participation in trade with the Indies picked up. Initially it took the form of coastal trade with Cadiz, where Cadiz merchants took over as agents, partners, or intermediaries. After 1740 Catalan ships sailed in the official fleets to the Americas.[14] In short, the notion that the Catalans were excluded from the Indies trade and that this contributed to commercial disintegration is difficult to maintain in the light of recent research.

Further down the coast in Valencia, the outlook was gloomier, especially in the seventeenth century. The 1609–14 expulsion of the Moriscos, who accounted for a third of the population, left a terrible imprint on the regional economy for at least a century.[15] In contrast to Castile, feudal institutions had survived into the early modern period in Valencia. The massive decline in population in some parts of Valencia after the expulsion did not lead to improvement for the remaining rural population or those resettling the former Morisco villages but on the contrary has been blamed for a tendency toward re-feudalization.[16] A combination of high rural dues and repeated demographic shocks like the severe plagues of the 1640s and 1690s followed by a delayed rebound in population contributed to this stagnation. A recent econometric analysis essentially confirms what historians have been arguing for a long time: faced with a severe drop in income, Valencian *senyors* (feudal lords) were disinclined to offer better conditions so as to resettle land more quickly. Production recovered only very slowly.[17]

[11] Martínez Shaw, *Cataluña*, 72–198, 246–69.
[12] In the early years of the Carrera de Indias the very large Basque and Navarrese participation in the trade was legendary. This was also true in the eighteenth-century trades with the Philippines and the River Plate.
[13] García Espuche, *Un siglo decisivo*.
[14] Martínez Shaw, *Cataluña*, 72–198, 246–69.
[15] Casey, *Valencia*.
[16] Palop Ramos, *Hambre*, 117.
[17] Chaney, "Ethnic Cleansing."

Valencia was also negatively affected by a lack of regional agglomeration. Until the late eighteenth century the political and commercial center was Valencia town, which had no working deep port and thus relied on the politically less powerful and capital-poor town of Alicante for its access to the sea.[18] Valencia, however, remained strongly integrated with its Castilian hinterland (the main outlet for its silks) and especially across the Mediterranean with Sicily, from where it received much of its grain supplies. By the late eighteenth century, up to 75 or 80 percent of Valencia's grain was imported from Italy in bad years.[19] Further south, the old Reino de Murcia and its main port, Cartagena, struggled probably even more than Valencia. Yet here there is evidence of war-related spikes in internal trade and external trade, probably driven by the upsurge in wool exports to Italy between the 1580s and 1620s when Castile's northern European wool trade was almost entirely interrupted.[20] Yet again, there is little evidence of an outright disintegration from the hinterland.

Much has been written about Andalusian trade and external integration in the three centuries after Spaniards first set foot in the Americas. The cycle of activity, the fast-rising trade volumes of the sixteenth century, and the relative and absolute contraction of the late sixteenth and first half of the seventeenth centuries are some of the best-documented features of Spanish economic history thanks to the Chaunus, and there is little merit in summarizing what others have analyzed with much greater skill and erudition.[21] What is worth stressing is the effect that the enormous expansion of commercial activity in Seville had on coastal trade with other regions on the Iberian Peninsula. One outcome of the transatlantic expansion and the integration of Spain with the American and Pacific markets was a notable increase in *cabotaje*, or coastal trade. As Basques, Cantabrians, Catalans, Portuguese, and others increased their investment in trades that indirectly supplied the Carrera de Indias, coastal communications between the various peripheral regions became notably more regular.

A journey through the Spanish regions in the late sixteenth through eighteenth centuries thus suggests a multitude of local and regional problems but not necessarily an overwhelming trend of disintegration in the late sixteenth and seventeenth centuries. The existing quantitative studies of market integration based on grain (mostly wheat) prices offer some additional information. David Reher suggests that there was indeed a slight tendency toward better-integrated regional markets in New Castile, Barcelona, and Valencia during the sixteenth century, albeit on the basis of fairly heterogeneous data. Over the course of the seventeenth century he observed hardly any trend in

[18] Palop Ramos, *Fluctuaciones*, 72ff.

[19] Casey, *Valencia*, chapter 4; Palop Ramos, *Fluctuaciones*, 59–60.

[20] Velasco Hernández, *Auge*.

[21] To name but a few: Bernal, *La financiación*; Bernal Rodríguez and García-Barquero, *Tres siglos*; Chaunu, Chaunu, and Arbellot, *Séville*; Lorenzo Sanz, *Comercio*; Stein and Stein, *Silver*.

these three regions or in Andalusia, Segovia, Leon, and Navarra, suggesting stagnation rather than decline. His analysis also suggests that in the eighteenth century market integration rose significantly.[22] But these results have to be interpreted in the context of grain's peculiar political economy discussed in chapter 2, and it is not obvious how representative they are for the non-grain part of the economy.

In a commendably careful study, Llopis Agelán and Jerez Méndez show that within the region of Castile and Leon, that is, the north-central *meseta*, grain markets were quite integrated by the eighteenth century; but the authors argue that the volatility of prices remained high nevertheless.[23] Whether this was a consequence of market interventions or idiosyncratic supply shocks is hard to determine. More important, levels of volatility between regions continued to be vastly different with the coastal regions enjoying much more stable prices, indicating better-integrated grain markets than those of the interior. This would suggest that there was a substantial and increasing degree of market integration *within* regions, but integration *across* regions remained weak even in the eighteenth century. At the same time, coastal regions like Barcelona and Valencia were more linked with external suppliers of grain than with the interior, which in turn exhibited a reasonable degree of integration across some close-by internal regions but next to none with the coasts.[24] Grain markets became really integrated in Spain only after about 1830; and, ironically, they probably became less integrated in the later nineteenth century, a time when the railways could have been expected to drastically improve the situation.[25]

Market Integration in Spain: What We Did Not Know

The lack of information on how markets developed in early modern Spain either with regard to Spain's integration with the rest of the world or within the Peninsular territories and regions has made discussions of what caused markets to become more or less integrated fraught with problems. It is tempting to simply cite the hostile geography, as much of the literature has done. But at present this is essentially a hypothesis that remains to be tested. Turning back to the cod market, it is now possible to establish a common indicator for all of these markets and trace the trends of market integration across time and space much more clearly in a first step toward understanding what drove trends over time. We will start with the development of the fast-increasing transatlantic trades, which can serve as a proxy for understanding how the

[22] Reher, "Producción, precios e integración," table 2.
[23] Llopis Agelán and Jerez Méndez, "Castilla y León," table 6.
[24] Reher, "Producción, precios e integración," table 3; Palop Ramos, *Fluctuaciones*, 24.
[25] Barquín Gil, *Precios del trigo*; Barquín Gil, "Transporte y precio." On the surprisingly low social savings from the introduction of railways, see Herranz-Loncan, "Infrastructure Investment."

larger, global markets were changing. Then we will turn to trade within the Peninsula and finally ask if it was really the case that Spain's high transport costs had subjected markets to an insurmountable tyranny of distance.

Transatlantic Market Integration

One of the distinctive features of cod was that it was a staple commodity and at the same time part of the new and expanding transatlantic exchange that brought new goods to European consumers. Beyond their impact on the balance of trade, these commodities also provided a few more pleasures and somewhat improved nutrition to Europeans. But to what extent did they alter European markets? At least two sets of issues need to be addressed. First, there is a legitimate debate about how one should define and measure increased market integration on an interoceanic scale. Second, how much a given degree, or trend, of market integration in these intercontinental exchanges affected European economies domestically depended crucially on the comparative development within domestic markets.

Global and economic historians have struggled with the question of whether world markets became more integrated over the early modern period. On the one hand, most historians assume that globalization started in the 1500s at the latest and that all regions involved were transformed in significant ways.[26] Those studying the commodity chains of cacao, coffee, tea, or *bacalao* have shown the impact of interoceanic trade on social and economic relations in producing regions, as well as on trade circuits, political power, and consumer culture at the other end.[27] They would argue that the quantitative expansion of a transatlantic trade like that in *bacalao* is witness enough to the increasing integration across large distances. Quantitative economic historians, on the other hand, have taken issue with this view. While they acknowledge the growth in the volume of intercontinental trades, they argue that market integration only began to leave its mark on the choices producers and consumers could make when it affected prices, something for which they have found little evidence.[28]

The differences between qualitative and quantitative concepts of globalization go beyond definitions and semantics or arcane details of treatment of price data. The volume of global trade undoubtedly increased massively over the early modern period. The debate has so far largely centered on the role played by global, often colonial, commerce in the "rise of the West"

[26] Osterhammel *Globalisierung*.

[27] See, e.g., Mintz, *Sweetness*; Clarence-Smith, *Cocoa*; and Topik, Marichal, and Frank, *From Silver to Cocaine*.

[28] Broadberry and Gupta, "Monetary and Real Aspects"; O'Rourke and Williamson, "Globalisation"; O'Rourke and Williamson, "Once More."

and the Industrial Revolution.[29] Yet the outcome of an expansion of commerce driven by either increased import demand in Europe or export supply outside Europe was different from that of intercontinental trade driven by price convergence, as quantitative economic historians rightly stress.[30] Higher transatlantic trade volumes affected Spanish consumption possibilities by increasing the availability of nutrients—and pleasures. But price convergence in transoceanic markets had the potential to shift *relative* prices of supplies within European markets. In other words, it mattered how the pace of interoceanic integration compared to that within European markets.

This then leads to the second important issue. If a decline in transatlantic shipping costs was accompanied by a similar fall in domestic trading costs, this would, economically speaking, just have increased consumer welfare. All goods became cheaper at about the same rate because the part of the price represented by transaction costs would fall. If all prices fell by about the same proportion there is little reason to assume that it would have affected choices *between* goods. Thus it would have been very good news for Iberian consumers, and producers of competing domestic goods would have been indifferent. If on the other hand domestic markets integrated faster (or slower) than transatlantic ones, domestic goods became more (or less) competitive compared to imported ones. As we will see, this comparative development was more significant for trends in Spanish market integration in the eighteenth century than the absolute increase in transatlantic market integration.

The question of whether trade led to price convergence has remained almost intractable for lack of data that would make it possible to look at any of the statistical standard measures of market integration, volatility, price co-movements, or price convergence. Few price series exist before the late eighteenth century that can be compared across the oceans; and those that do exist are often for commodities that are hardly representative. O'Rourke and Williamson, for example, analyzed transoceanic price differentials of very high value-per-weight goods such as spices. Yet, like all luxuries, they are a poor indicator of trade costs.[31] There is a similar lacuna with regard to freight rates, which could alternatively be used to gauge transoceanic trends in price convergence. If we knew only that freight rates fell, it would be likely that prices on either side of the ocean moved closer together.

---

[29] This debate evolved over the question as to whether the "contribution of the periphery," as the supply of new foodstuffs from beyond Europe was dubbed by one economic historian, was small or if it was large because it supplied "ghost acreage" (and ghost fishing grounds) that could feed European consumers. O'Brien, "The Contribution of the Periphery." O'Brien has reversed his position on the issue substantially in the meantime. For the idea of ghost acreage, see Pomeranz, *The Great Divergence*.

[30] O'Rourke and Williamson, "Globalisation," 23.

[31] Ibid. Scarcity was what defined them as a luxury, and where demand was totally price inelastic, lower transport costs were unlikely to translate into lower consumer prices.

Even the patchy information for either freight rates or price differentials that does exist is hard to interpret. The reason is one of the classic dilemmas of economic history: how to deflate nominal prices, in this case transport and transaction costs. Did it matter if transport costs decreased compared to a large basket of goods, a kind of consumer price index (CPI)? Or should one look at what is sometimes called the freight factor, that is, the percentage of the price of the transported good that was made up of transport costs?[32] As a consequence, quantitative historians disagree on how much progress there was in long-distance market integrations. Walton and Shepherd argue that transatlantic freight rates in the Chesapeake tobacco trade fell substantially between 1620 and 1775 with efficiency improving by about 0.7 percent per year. They also claim that transport costs in the sugar trade from the British Caribbean to London fell notably between 1678 and 1717.[33]

Menard contends, by contrast, that freights were stagnant between the 1650s and the 1760s in the Barbados sugar trade—if compared to English consumer prices—leaving little room for the assumption that there was much price convergence.[34] O'Rourke and Williamson have argued that there is even less evidence for a transatlantic "transport revolution," when freights are deflated by sugar prices in Barbados, which fell by more than the overall English price.[35] To the best of my knowledge there are no estimates for the Spanish Atlantic in part because historians always assumed that American trade was subject to monopoly organization in Seville and Cadiz and thus exposed to too few pressures to increase productivity.

The data on *bacalao* prices offer a unique opportunity to shed some light on the debate. As mentioned above there are three standard ways of estimating market integration: the volatility of prices in a given location, the correlation coefficient, and the actual price wedge between towns. In the first case, the intuition is that more integrated markets should mediate more quickly between locations that experience short-term supply shocks. If, for instance, a particularly severe storm made it impossible for *bacalao* to be delivered to the port of Bilbao (Vizcaya) but instead drove ships into the Cantabrian port of Santander, prices would rise sharply in Bilbao and drop in Santander. In well-integrated markets this effect should, however, be very short-lived. As news of the shortage in Bilbao arrived in Santander, local merchants would take advantage of the opportunity and arbitrage away the price differential very quickly. Prices in both towns would return to "normal" levels, or in other words there should be overall low price volatility in both towns.

The second measure looks at the "co-movement" of prices. In integrated markets a rise (fall) of the price of cod in Bilbao should be mirrored by a rise (fall) of the price in other towns. As price differences open the possibility for

---

[32] For the definition of the freight factor, see North, "The Role of Transportation," 214.
[33] Shepherd and Walton, *Shipping*, 68–69.
[34] Menard, "Transport Costs," 264ff. Menard used the Brown-Hopkins CPI for 1981.
[35] O'Rourke and Williamson, "Globalisation," 28–29.

Table 4.1. *Bacalao* price volatility in North America and Spain, 1650–1800

	North America	Bilbao	Barcelona	Cadiz
1650–1699	0.090	0.249	0.260	*0.250
1700–1749	0.111	0.228	0.204	0.142
1750–1800	*0.063	0.163	0.158	0.308
Average	0.088	0.213	0.207	0.233

Source: See the data set of this volume.
Note: Values reported are standard deviation of $\Delta p_t^i = \ln p_t^i - \ln p_{t-1}^i$ where p is the price, t the time period, and i the town. Results based on 16–29 observations marked *; all other results based on 30–50 observations.

arbitrage profits, merchants will make sure prices in two locations move in the same direction. The final measure is price differences between two locations; the closer integrated markets are, the lower the price difference should be. The underlying assumption is that the three ways of estimating market integration would move in similar ways: lower volatility of prices in a town should be associated with stronger association between prices and smaller price differentials across two towns. Each measure just reflects slightly different aspects of the same process: market integration.

Table 4.1 displays the volatility of *bacalao* prices in North America and Spanish coastal towns in fifty-year periods. Volatility was consistently lowest in the New England market. It has been shown empirically that markets for commodities, raw materials, agricultural products, and especially fish are generally more volatile than those for manufactures. Jacks, O'Rourke, and Williamson have recently estimated that the average standard deviation (our measure of price variability) across twenty-seven commodities in England between 1700 and 1819 was 0.143.[36] The standard deviation of cod prices in New England never exceeded 0.111, indicating a surprisingly stable fish market at the source. In the Spanish ports, Bilbao, Barcelona, and Cadiz, variability of prices was much higher. Not surprisingly, the transatlantic journey introduced a notable amount of volatility. But in Bilbao and Barcelona prices became notably less volatile over time, suggesting better integration between Spanish and North American ports. In Cadiz they started with a lower level of volatility, which fell further till the mid-eighteenth century but then rose sharply in the second half of the eighteenth century.

In order to analyze the co-movement of prices in these four locations, table 4.2 summarizes the pairwise correlation coefficients. On a transatlantic level,

[36] Jacks, O'Rourke, and Williamson, "Commodity Price Volatility," table 3. Their estimates are based on annual data for England reported by Clark, "Working Class." The methodology is therefore comparable to the one employed here.

Table 4.2. *Bacalao* prices: Pairwise correlations North America and coastal Spain, 1650–1775

	North America	Bilbao	Cadiz	Barcelona
North America	1.000			
Bilbao	−0.001	1.000		
Bilbao+1	0.344			
Cadiz	−0.189	0.321	1.000	
Cadiz+1	0.227			
Barcelona	−0.011	0.180	0.163	1.000
Barcelona+1	0.330			

Source: See the data set of this volume.
Note: Correlation coefficients over 0.3 in bold; variables denominated +1 are lagged by one year.

the prices in none of the Spanish ports were correlated with prices in the same year in North America: not only are the coefficients small, but they also have the "wrong" sign; prices in Bilbao actually fell when they had risen in New England. Yet most of the cod shipped from North America to Spain would of course be on sale in the year after it was fished and processed, as we saw in chapter 3. Sure enough, when prices in a given year in New England are compared with those in the following year in Spanish ports, the correlation is quite strong for Bilbao and Barcelona, a little weaker for Cadiz.

Llopis Agelán and Jerez Méndez argue convincingly that values over 0.3 indicate substantial integration by the standards of the early modern period.[37] The pattern of price variability would thus suggest that North American and Spanish coastal markets were fairly well integrated in this period. Remarkably, the level of price correlation on the transatlantic scale (with one time lag) was—if anything—higher than that at the domestic level between Spanish port towns. While price movements in Bilbao and Cadiz were almost as strongly correlated as those across the Atlantic, those between Bilbao and Cadiz on the one hand and Barcelona on the other had correlations that were notably weaker.

Finally, we can see the trends in transatlantic market integration in even more detail when looking at the convergence of prices in grams of silver per kilogram on either side of the Atlantic in figure 4.1. Price differentials are presented in six-year moving averages to smooth some of the volatility, which makes the annual data hard to read. Given the straightforward nature and direction of the cod trade, the markup that was paid in Spanish ports such as Bilbao in the north, Cadiz in the south, or Barcelona on the Mediterranean can be interpreted as the total transaction costs of the trade between North America and the Spanish ports. These included shipping and

[37] Llopis Agelán and Jerez Méndez, "Castilla y León," 34.

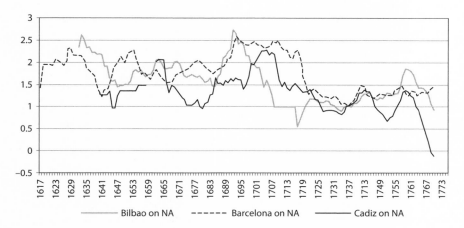

Figure 4.1
Price markup between North American and Spanish ports (eleven-year moving average in grams of silver per kilogram). *Source*: See data set of this volume.

other trading costs, as well as customs at port and various other port and lighting duties. The international and Peninsular wars of the late seventeenth and early eighteenth centuries clearly drove up price differentials; the period before the Treaty of Utrecht (1713) was notorious for trade interruptions, and the War of the Spanish Succession (1701–15) did not help supplies either. The effects of the war lasted longest in Barcelona, as can easily be seen, and this is consistent with the history of the war. In the long run, however, prices between North America and the main Spanish import ports were converging; the markup paid for cod in Spain over prices in New England was falling.

From 1650 to 1775 the estimated fall in price differentials (controlling for war) was 0.6 percent per annum for trade with Bilbao, 0.7 percent with Barcelona, and about 1 percent with Cadiz, as reported in table 4.3. The Cadiz figures are somewhat puzzling because of the precipitous fall in the late 1760s and early 1770s to a level that at times was even below North American prices. It seems likely that this was caused by a change in local taxation, since the municipality introduced a much more generous system of drawbacks for ecclesiastical institutions in 1765.[38] Here we encounter for the first time the impact that local taxes could have. But even if we exclude those and concentrate on the Bilbao and Barcelona estimates, total transaction costs between North America and Spanish ports fell to about half between the mid-seventeenth century and the last quarter of the eighteenth century.

This was a moderate decline to be sure. Yet by comparison with what we know about sixteenth- to nineteenth-century transport technology, it was notable nonetheless. It is remarkably close to Walton and Shepherd's estimate of 0.7 percent improved efficiency in the Chesapeake to London tobacco

---

[38] Bustos Rodriguez, "Hacienda municipal gaditana," 49.

Table 4.3. Annual rate of change in trade costs between North America and Spanish ports (1650–1775)

	Change in trade costs annual rate (%)	Impact of war (%)	N	R2
North America to Bilbao	−0.57	34	90	0.35
North America to Barcelona	−0.67	58	86	0.26
North America to Cadiz	−1.00	73	88	0.40

Note: All estimations based on OLS regressions of the natural log of the price differential in grams of silver on time trend and war dummy. All coefficients are significant at the 1 percent level.

trade, or to Menard's freight index for the intra-European wine trades from the late sixteenth to the mid-eighteenth centuries.[39] The price convergence between North American cod markets and Spanish ones does not allow us to distinguish freight and other costs. However, because the packaging and lading techniques of cod hardly changed over this period, much of the decline must have come from more efficient shipping and port services.[40] In addition, as discussed in chapter 3, mid-seventeenth-century exports of cod were only just breaking even for (New) England merchants. This biases the trend against the main result, namely that transatlantic trade costs really fell at a modest but steady rate, interrupted only by war hikes.

Transatlantic trade costs fell no matter which of the deflated measures discussed above are used. The share of trade costs in the final price of cod in the Spanish port, the "freight factor," was 58 percent in Bilbao in the 1650s, 55 percent in Barcelona, and 49 percent in Cadiz. It fell to 36 percent (Bilbao) and 46 percent (Barcelona) in 1765–75, while in Cadiz it even turned negative as mentioned above. More realistically it was about 35 percent in the 1750s before the unusual decline in prices of the late eighteenth century. Or to use O'Rourke and Williamson's preferred measure: the Bilbao price of cod was 2.45 times the North American price in the 1650s but only 1.56 times the price at origin in 1766–75. *Bacalao* was the fourth most important export commodity for North America in this period.[41] Measured by what went on in this very substantial trade, the Anglo-Spanish Atlantic was indeed shrinking in the seventeenth and eighteenth centuries.

[39] Menard found that costs fell about 0.7 percent per annum. Menard, "Transport Costs," 272. For the nineteenth century Harley estimated that between the 1810s and the 1850s English freight rates per ton declined on sail ships by about 0.9 percent per annum. Brautaset and I have argued that Norwegian freight rates on sail ships between 1830 and the 1860s might have declined by as much as 1.5–2.5 percent per ton-mile. Harley, "Ocean Freight Rates"; Brautaset and Grafe, "Quiet Transport Revolution."

[40] This contrasts with the cotton and tobacco trades, where changes in packing technology accounted for much of the productivity improvement. See Harley, "Ocean Freight Rates," who corrected North, "Ocean Freight." See also Menard, "Transport Costs," 263.

[41] Magra, *The Fisherman's Cause*, 128.

The claim made by quantitative historians that trade costs in the Atlantic in the seventeenth and eighteenth centuries stagnated at best was always counterintuitive. After all, we know that manning ratios, that is, the number of tons shipped per crew member, were rising during this period in all trades except for those of the armed and monopolized Asian companies where the men were needed as gunners, not as sailors. Since wages accounted for a substantial part of total costs on sailing vessels, higher manning ratios, implying smaller crews, must have increased productivity.[42] Historians were probably too quick to identify the nineteenth century and the technological revolution of steam as a breaking away from a stagnant early modern period. The back extrapolation from the fast changes of the nineteenth century to a supposed seventeenth- and eighteenth-century stasis is unconvincing.

Transatlantic trade with Spain, at least, was slowly and unspectacularly becoming cheaper between 1650 and 1800. All three of the measures commonly used suggest the same trend. Volatility was decreasing over time. Prices *between* North America and Spanish ports were quite strongly integrated and notably more so than *among* some of the Spanish ports. And the study of price convergence shows that the somewhat more volatile Cadiz market in fact experienced the strongest fall in the markup merchants paid in Cadiz's port over New England prices. But how did these intercontinental trends compare with domestic ones?

Market Integration within Spain, 1650–1800

Table 4.4 looks at the full set of volatilities of cod prices for the Spanish towns in the sample across the three fifty-year intervals. On the way inland, markets actually absorbed some of the variability. Generally volatility was lower in the interior than in the ports probably because consumers could use the durability of cod to wait out the more extreme price movements resulting from too many or too few vessels arriving. The very low levels of volatility in Madrid and Toledo illustrate how relatively stable these large markets were already in the mid-seventeenth century. Yet volatility trends between the coast and the interior diverged toward the second half of the eighteenth century. On the coast volatility declined (with the already noted exception of Cadiz) while in the interior the trend toward more stable markets was inverted to an extent in the later eighteenth century in all towns except Albacete. Something was reversing the tendency toward more integrated markets in the interior.

In Seville and Pamplona volatility was slightly higher than in the central *meseta*, especially in Seville in the first period. But their trends were similar

---

[42] Grafe, Neal, and Unger, "The Service Sector." For manning ratios in the Jamaican, Charleston, and Asian trades, see Menard, "Transport Costs," 251, 266, 270. Even in the mid-nineteenth century wages accounted for one-third of all costs on sailing vessels. Brautaset and Grafe, "Quiet Transport Revolution."

Table 4-4. Price volatility in Spanish markets: *Bacalao* and grain, 1650–1800

Bacalao

	Bilbao	Barcelona	Cadiz	Toledo	Madrid	Seville	Pamplona	Albacete	Sahagún
1650–1699	0.249	0.260	*0.250	0.127		0.233	0.167		
1700–1749	0.228	0.204	0.142	0.099	*0.100	0.116	0.118	0.223	0.156
1750–1800	0.163	0.158	0.308	0.134	0.137	0.144	0.166	0.203	
Average	0.213	0.207	0.233	0.120	0.119	0.164	0.150	0.213	0.156

Grain

	Barcelona	Segovia	Pamplona	Leon
1650–1700	0.297	0.349	0.220	0.326
1700–1750**	0.116	0.254	0.209	0.286
1750–1800	0.123	0.242	0.191	0.269
Average	0.179	0.282	0.207	0.294

Sources: For *bacalao*, see dataset of this volume; for grain, see Reher, "Producción, precios e integración," 550.
Note: Results based on fewer than 16 observations omitted, those based on 16–29 observations marked *; all other results based on 30–50 observations.
**Reher does not specify in which period 1700 and 1750 are included.

to those of Madrid and Toledo. Among smaller places closer to the coast, Sahagún in the north fared almost as well. Albacete in the southeast, however, suffered much higher volatility. We will return to this later, but it should be noted that Albacete's consumers obtained their cod from ports situated in two different *reinos*, Valencia and Castile, and were thus subject to different tax and currency systems.

How do these values compare beyond Spain and beyond this one commodity? Compared to the average price volatility cited above for England in the eighteenth century of 0.143, all Spanish interior towns except Albacete exhibited lower or similar volatility over the last two periods. This is certainly remarkable considering the deep-seated idea that Spanish markets were very poorly integrated by European standards. Nor was the variability of cod prices in Spanish towns too dissimilar from that of other Spanish commodity markets. David Reher performed a similar analysis for grain markets, but because he used some of the aggregate series constructed by Hamilton discussed in chapter 2, only a few of his results are comparable. For Barcelona and Pamplona we can compare his results for grain directly with the cod results. For Sahagún and Toledo we can compare with geographically fairly close Leon and Segovia.[43]

The overall similarity between grain markets and cod markets in terms of volatility is evident, though cod markets were somewhat less volatile. That could be a consequence of more political interference in the grain markets or more exposure to local production shocks. As discussed in chapter 2, this is hard to tell in the case of grain. Differences between the grain and cod results opened up in the late eighteenth century, however, when grain markets exhibited a clear trend toward lower variability even in the interior. Indeed, most historians of the grain market have suggested that prices in coastal towns experienced less volatility.[44] Yet in the cod business the opposite was true. The analysis is hardly conclusive but certainly suggestive. The main difference between grain and cod markets was that the former were not subject to the vicissitudes of Spanish consumption taxes. Is it possible that this explains the diverging trends between grain and cod prices on the one hand and between cod prices in the interior and on the coast on the other? That would suggest that the negative impact of trade and consumption taxes was increasing in the second half of the eighteenth century.

The results for the correlation analysis reported in table 4.5 underscore the notion of relatively well-integrated markets. Here a higher coefficient expresses a stronger association between the markets. Overall the table

[43] Reher also reports values for Andalusia and New Castile as well as Valencia. But these are based on Hamilton's data and therefore *regional* aggregates. Notably he finds much higher volatility in Andalusia in the grain markets than the *bacalao* estimate suggests, presumably because of the aggregation problem. Reher's data were de-trended in a slightly different way, but the author claims that results based on the technique employed here were practically identical. Reher, "Producción, precios e integración."

[44] Palop Ramos, *Fluctuaciones*, 24ff.

Table 4.5. Pairwise correlations between *bacalao* prices, 1650–1800

	Bilbao	Cadiz	Barcelona	Sahagún	Albacete	Pamplona	Seville	Madrid	Toledo
Bilbao	1.000								
Cadiz	**0.321**	1.000							
Barcelona	0.180	0.163	1.000						
Sahagún	**0.312**	**0.484**	0.260	1.000					
Albacete	**0.380**	**0.337**	0.142	0.075	1.000				
Pamplona	**0.320**	0.036	0.139	−0.053	0.132	1.000			
Seville	**0.351**	0.272	0.105	−0.007	0.174	0.079	1.000		
Madrid	**0.551**	0.212	0.247	0.240	**0.466**	−0.008	**0.398**	1.000	
Toledo	**0.431**	**0.306**	0.232	0.261	0.220	0.215	**0.337**	**0.385**	1.000

Source: See data set of this volume.
Note: Correlation coefficients over 0.3 in bold.

reflects a high degree of integration between these markets; a top value of 0.55 for the coefficient of correlation between Bilbao and Madrid indicates strong integration by the standards of early modern Europe. Bilbao was the one market that articulated integration of cod markets within Spain, with pairwise correlation coefficients in excess of 0.3 in any pairing except that with Barcelona. That is not surprising given Bilbao's role as the main import port.

Finally, we can follow *bacalao* from its coastal points of entry into the interior in figures 4.2a–d, which display silver prices for North America and the Peninsular towns. Figure 4.2a reflects the relatively strong degree of price convergence between markets in coastal Andalusia, the Basque Country, and Aragon. The falling costs of transatlantic trade in the long run are again visible: while North American prices show no trend, those in the Spanish ports trend down slowly until the 1770s, after which date they rise sharply. Also notable are the periods of high volatility around the turn of the seventeenth century and during the Seven Years' War (1754–63). Yet price trends fell toward the last third of the eighteenth century. The last quarter of the eighteenth century saw very high volatility and high absolute prices, with the exception of the 1770s in Cadiz as noted above. This explains the return of higher volatility of prices on the coast in the last part of the eighteenth century.

A massive price hike in Barcelona during the early 1650s is explained by its secession to France, monetary chaos, and the following siege of Barcelona. Markets in all towns were severely affected by the closing of New England supplies between 1775 and 1783. Prices fell somewhat thereafter, but renewed war and the turmoil of the late 1800s kept prices at a substantially higher level. Looking at the coastal towns from the perspective of price convergence helps qualify the results above: while in terms of volatility and correlations Bilbao, Cadiz, and Barcelona seemed rather less well integrated than the interior towns, price convergence would suggest that the price levels in these three towns moved very closely together. The three measures of market integration seem to diverge in various ways.

How well coastal markets were integrated in terms of price convergence becomes obvious only when they are compared to integration with the hinterland. Figure 4.2b compares prices in the main northern port of Bilbao with those in Madrid and Toledo, that is, at the center of the Peninsula. As the crow flies these were at distances of 322 and 385 kilometers, respectively, though following the road network the distances would have been closer to about 400 and 490 kilometers. These figures illustrate a few expected characteristics. At practically all times (except for a few years during the War of the Spanish Succession [1701–14]) it remained more expensive to trade cod from the port to the interior than it was to take it from North America to Spain. This huge absolute and relative superiority of shipping over land transport is often taken for granted, but its impact on *relative* prices is rarely explicitly discussed.

From 1650 to 1800 the markup between Bilbao and Toledo fell by an annualized rate of 0.24 percent, evidence of a painfully slow process of price convergence between the northern coast and the very heart of Castile (see table 4.6). The rate implied a fall in trading costs by about a third over a century and a half, considerably less than the decrease in transatlantic trade where rates were closer to 0.6 or 0.7 percent (see table 4.3). Not only was maritime trade absolutely a lot cheaper at any one time, but price convergence occurred faster than in the overland cod trade between Bilbao and Madrid or Toledo, the most important port of entry and the most important consumption centers of the interior. Maritime trade's relative advantage increased all the time.

As a consequence imported goods, the price of which included both interoceanic and domestic trade costs, became ceteris paribus relatively cheaper than domestically produced goods. This had at least two implications. First, for coastal regions obtaining supplies from without the Peninsula and marketing domestically produced goods outside the Peninsula became *relatively* more attractive than enhanced exchanges with the interior over the seventeenth and eighteenth centuries. Second, cheaper access to larger markets increased the natural advantage of the coastal regions compared to the interior. The opportunity cost of geographic features, such as distance to the coast, was changing over time. This is often forgotten in a literature that assumes that a "difficult" geography was an unchanging liability on the path to market integration.

Seville, on the other hand, seems to have been on an altogether different path (see figure 4.2c). True, the price differentials between Seville and its natural port of supply Cadiz fell at a rate of 0.7 percent annually (see table 4.6). Price convergence at that rate was otherwise only seen in transatlantic

A

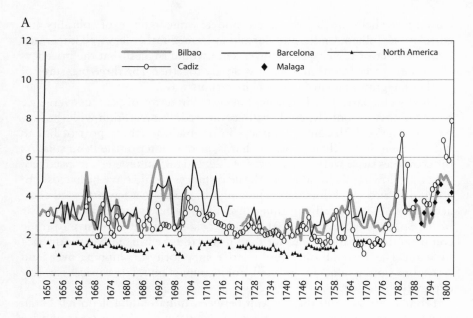

B

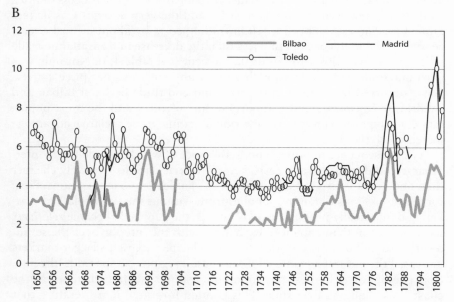

Figures 4.2a–b
Bacalao prices in Spanish towns and North America (grams of silver per kilogram):
(A) North America and maritime Spain: Bilbao, Cadiz, Barcelona, Malaga;
(B) northern coast and central *meseta*: Bilbao, Toledo, Madrid;

C

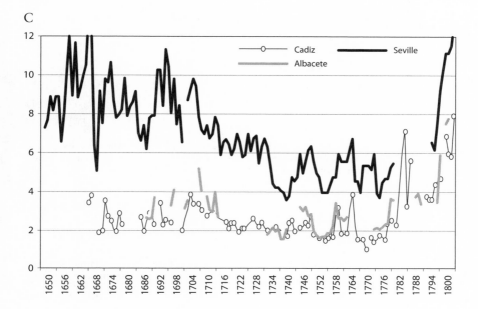

D

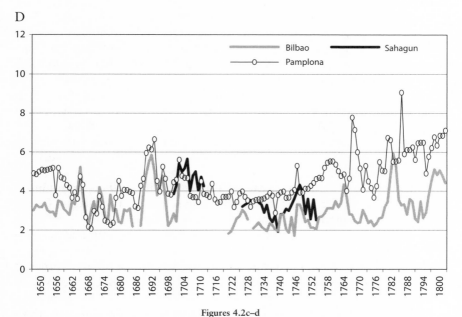

Figures 4.2c–d

Bacalao prices in Spanish towns and North America (grams of silver per kilogram):
(C) southern coast, La Mancha, and Andalusia: Cadiz, Albacete, Seville;
(D) northern coast, Old Castile, and Navarra: Bilbao, Pamplona, Sahagún.

Table 4.6. Annual rate of change in trade costs between Peninsular ports and selected interior towns, 1650–1800

	Change in trade costs annual rate (%)	Impact of war (%)	N	R^2
Bilbao to Toledo	–0.24	–17	116	0.14
Cadiz to Seville	–0.72	10	107	0.41
Bilbao to Pamplona	0.48	–6.5	132	0.27

Note: All estimations based on OLS regressions of the natural log of the price differential in grams of silver on time trend and war dummy. All coefficients are significant at the 1 percent level, except war coefficient for Pamplona, which is not significant at 10 percent.

transport. That would seem to confirm claims by Anes based on grain markets that prices in Seville rose appreciably less in the eighteenth century than those elsewhere.[45] But appearances are deceptive. Price differentials between Cadiz and Seville fell so quickly because they were extremely large at the outset. Seville's market in 1650 was completely out of sync with any other market in this sample in terms of price levels. The apparently strong trend toward convergence between Seville and Cadiz over the century and a half after 1650 was more akin to Seville's "return" to its Andalusian surroundings. This is truly astonishing if we consider that in terms of volatility and correlation with prices in other towns, Seville looked absolutely *unexceptional*.

The extraordinarily high price level in Seville presents historians with a number of challenges. The most obvious is that there was no such thing as "Andalusian" prices (or wages for that matter) in the early modern period. The market was clearly for a long time deeply unsettled by the altogether exceptional economy of the town of Seville.[46] In the largest southern Spanish town, prices were 30–40 percent above those in centrally located Madrid or Toledo in the mid-seventeenth century. *Bacalao* prices in Seville were four times those in the closest large seaport, Cadiz. This is why Hamilton's interpretation of his "Andalusian" series, which mixed prices in Seville and Cadiz, was highly problematic.[47] It is one thing if the price and wage levels in Seville were out of sync with its own hinterland, as the data suggest, and another if there was a general "price revolution" affecting the Spanish economy as a whole, as Hamilton implied. The results suggest that one should proceed with the utmost caution when arguing on the basis of Seville prices, which were clearly exceptional by Spanish standards. Hence the use of Hamilton's so-called Andalusian price series in all kinds of international comparisons in

[45] Anes, *Crisis agrarias*; Palop Ramos, *Fluctuaciones*, 28–29.
[46] That Seville was exceptional in terms of wage levels as well is shown by Reher and Ballesteros, "Precios y salarios."
[47] Hamilton, *War and Prices*, xxiv–xxv.

lieu of "Spanish" prices is even more problematic.[48]

Beyond the historiographical implications, however, the case of Seville demonstrates the continuing intractability of market integration in Spain. In the cases of Madrid and Toledo, low volatility and high price correlations were accompanied by convergence of price levels, as one would expect. However, this was not true in the case of Seville. Nor was this a difference between a more integrated central Castile and a disintegrated southern market, as the Albacete series confirms. Judging on the basis of price variability or co-movement, Seville was as integrated into Spanish markets as most places. Yet its extremely high price level requires explanation.

It is, of course, tempting to attribute the Seville exception directly to the impact of the Indies trade on this Andalusian town. As the *de iure* single port for the Americas trade from the 1580s to 1717, Seville experienced a well-documented economic boom during the sixteenth century.[49] The trend toward price convergence in the eighteenth century could be ascribed to the transfer of the Indies entrepôt from Seville to Cadiz after 1717 and to the relative decline of Seville. However, such an interpretation is unconvincing for at least two reasons. First, if the location of the Americas trade drove prices up because of the inflow of American silver and that of people attracted by it, there should have been upward pressure on prices in Cadiz after 1717. But that was clearly not the case. Cadiz prices remained the lowest in the Peninsula for much of the eighteenth century (see figure 4.2c). Second, the same mechanism should have led to a fall in prices in Seville that was centered more sharply on the early eighteenth century when trade was moving to Cadiz. That is not the case either.[50] Seville prices hovered around 8 grams of silver per kilogram until the turn of the eighteenth century, when they began to decline steadily, reaching a level of about 4 grams around the mid-eighteenth century. The standard explanation of a locally much more severe price inflation in Seville caused by the Americas trades is at best a half truth.

Nor were trends in market integration more clear-cut on the northern side of the Peninsula, as demonstrated in figure 4.2d. Prices in the Navarrese capital Pamplona were hardly higher than those in Bilbao in the turbulent years of the late seventeenth century. However, after the 1730s cod prices in Pamplona rose dramatically, accounting for an overall trend over the century and a half under consideration of an *increase* in price differentials by almost 0.5 percent per annum (table 4.6). Yet Pamplona had none of the attributes

---

[48] The same is true for his series denominated "Old Castile." Hamilton's 1500–1650 Andalusian series (as opposed to the 1651–1800 series) apparently only uses Seville sources, which solves the inconsistency problem but makes them wholly unrepresentative of anything but the town of Seville. Hamilton, *American Treasure*, xxix–xxx. The use of Hamilton's series has had a tremendous impact on the notion of the price revolution as a source of industrial failure in Spain.

[49] Domínguez Ortiz, *Orto y ocaso*.

[50] De facto much of the shipping had moved to Cadiz from the 1670s onward. Thus prices should have declined even earlier. Stein and Stein, *Silver*.

of Seville. It was a reasonably prosperous regional town, but it did not experience the windfalls associated with the Indies trade in Seville or Cadiz. As in Seville, the volatility measure as well as the correlation coefficients suggested a relatively high degree of market integration for Pamplona, especially with the port of Bilbao. Yet the trend toward price divergence says the opposite loudly and clearly.

The structure of the cod trade has made it possible to compare for the first time the more commonly employed indicators for market integration, price volatility and co-movement, with the actual trends in price convergence, something that is impossible when looking at grain (as discussed in chapter 2). There are two main conclusions. First, there were no "national" trends. Second, the three measures of market integration were not always driven by the same processes. The seemingly confusing outcomes explain why historians have tended to disagree about the state of market integration in early modern Spain. In the words of a Spanish pop song, *depende, todo depende*: it all depends on what measure one chooses. Overall price movements suggest that the level of market integration was considerable by the standards of the period. However, in some cases, most notably Seville and Pamplona, something was driving a very large wedge between the price levels in the various towns. This led to the contradictory results for price convergence, as opposed to price volatility or correlations.

The Transport Question

Transport costs should be the first suspect when trying to explain the large price wedge between otherwise reasonably integrated markets. Contemporary travelers complained incessantly about slow and cumbersome transport in Spain. Inns and other infrastructure along the road also had a poor reputation. The French traveler and writer Madame d'Aulnoy observed with astonishment in the 1680s that "it seems very strange to us that in the inns which are the nearest to this great town [Madrid] you are worse used than in those which are a hundred leagues distant; you would think you came rather into deserts, than near a town where resides so great a monarch."[51] Spanish mercantilists and statesmen agreed that high internal transport costs and poor roads held back the development of internal markets.[52] The foremost study of Spanish early modern transport by Madrazo argues that the road network was not only in bad shape but that there was very little progress between the sixteenth and the mid-eighteenth centuries.[53]

---

[51] Aulnoy and Foulché-Delbosc, *Travels into Spain*. D'Aulnoy's accounts mixed fact and fiction, but there is little reason to doubt that her descriptions of Peninsular roads and inns interspersed throughout her stories are accurate since they coincide with most other accounts.

[52] See, e.g., Uztáriz, *Theorica*. Jovellanos, *Informe de la Sociedad Económica de esta Corte al Real y Supremo Consejo de Castilla*; Ward, *Proyecto económico*.

[53] Madrazo, *Comunicaciones*.

While geography accounted for a tough starting point, political economy is blamed for the lack of progress. There are two sides to this story. On the one hand, there is the narrative of the supposed disintegration of the Castilian hinterland economy as a consequence of the politically fostered rise of Madrid. It argues that the growth of the "artificial" capital broke the backbone of a fragile transport system. On the other hand, historians of transport cite a familiar set of factors as reasons for the poor development of the transport sector in Spain: feudal disinterest, an ineffective Crown distracted by other priorities, and patrimonialism, which made the implementation of any concerted effort in improving the infrastructure impossible. These two are examined in turn.

The Political Economy of Spanish Transport

In his highly influential book *Madrid and the Spanish Economy*, Ringrose has argued that Madrid's parasitical growth after its elevation to capital status in 1561 dislocated a previously integrated network of Castilian interior towns.[54] The city's population exploded from about 30,000 inhabitants in the 1560s to 130,000 by 1617, creating a supply nightmare.[55] The growing needs of the urban populace pushed suppliers of vital foodstuffs further and further into the Castilian hinterland in search of grain, meat, and wine. Given poor road communications, all available resources were sucked into supplying the new capital, and the trading networks between smaller Castilian towns broke up under the pressure.

The deficient Castilian transport system, which in the absence of river or canal transport had to rely on a poorly maintained network of roads that were often not even suitable for wagon transport, proved for Ringrose to be the Achilles' heel of the Spanish economy and the proximate cause of disintegration. However, the underlying source of the fracturing of the markets was a political one: the creation of a new, artificial capital in the very center of the Iberian Peninsula. Ringrose's story dovetails nicely with the traditional notion of a disintegration of Spanish markets in the seventeenth century examined above. Yet neither a closer look at regional histories nor the quantitative evidence offers much support for this disintegration story, as we have seen. Nevertheless, the conclusions he derived from his impressive research on Spanish markets and transport remain the dominant view.

Ringrose has argued that direct intervention in the transport market through requisitioning of wagons and draught animals in return for strong support for the corporate organization of transport providers distorted the private carrying trade early on. He offered the first empirical study of the carter's guild and thus initiated modern research on the topic. His depiction, however, tapped into an earlier literature that argues that the absolutist

---

[54] Ringrose, *Madrid*.
[55] Ringrose, "Government and the Carters," 51.

Crown had unduly favored certain guild monopolies, most prominently the association of the owners of Spain's huge migratory sheep flocks, the Mesta, those of long-distance traders, the Consulados, and lastly a "national" guild of "teamsters," the Cabaña Real de Carreteros.[56]

This historiographical tradition, associated with the names of the U.S. historians Julius Klein, Robert Sidney Smith, and Earl Hamilton, flourished from the 1920s to 1940s at a time when concern about the rise of fascism and neo-corporatism in Spain and elsewhere in Europe was at its height. Contemporary reviews of these scholars' books demonstrate that they were read as a cautionary tale about the present as much as the past.[57] Still, at the time, these were standard-setting works of economic history. But as with much historical research, time and a great many modern studies have disproved the main conclusions of every one of these monographs.[58] Surprisingly, however, their portrait of the Spanish economy as being subject to a particularly nefarious form of Crown-protected corporate monopoly has survived. Uncritical quotations from these authors still appear with astonishing regularity in the references to Spanish economic history by Anglophone authors.[59]

Ringrose's research showed that the Cabaña Real de Carreteros was not a "national" guild. Yet he accepted and extended the view of a strong corporate relationship between carters and Crown in which the Crown made the carters "its captive employees."[60] Starting in the late fifteenth century, but in particular in the late sixteenth to about the mid-seventeenth centuries, the Crown extended a number of privileges to carters. They were exempted from most local tolls and consumption taxes and, crucially, given access to grazing on village commons with legal recourse through specialized courts that were presumably stacked in favor of the carters.[61] Though the Crown reduced its support for these transporters in the second half of the seventeenth century, their rights largely remained on the books. Ringrose has claimed that throughout the eighteenth century the symbiotic relationship between these

---

[56] Ibid., 45–47; Klein, *The Mesta*, 22–23. Klein referred to the teamsters in his book as an institution that was similar to the Mesta. See also Smith, *Spanish Guild Merchant*.

[57] Hanney, "The Mesta," 316–17. Hamilton's contribution was to the history of mercantilism and the impact of silver imports.

[58] For updated research on the Mesta, see, e.g., González Enciso, *El negocio*; Phillips and Phillips, *Spain's Golden Fleece*; Ruiz Martín and García Sanz, *Mesta, trashumancia y lana*; and Drelichman, "Licence to Till." The only more recent survey text on the "Price Revolution" is Pieper, *Preisrevolution*. For an English survey, see John Munro's review of *American Treasure* at http://eh.net/bookreviews/library/munro (accessed March 29, 2010) and Munro, "Money, Prices, Wages." For a recent attempt to gauge the impact on Spanish tradables versus non-tradables, see Drelichman, "Curse of Moctezuma." For a population-based explanation, see Goldstone, "Urbanization and Inflation."

[59] Most recently Acemoglu, Johnson, and Robinson "Rise of Europe" rely on Hamilton's 1948 article "Role of Monopoly" for their characterization of Spanish overseas trade. Douglass North's account of Spanish history rests also on the Mesta and merchant guild interpretations, which in more recent versions of the argument were coupled with a reference to path dependence. See North, *Institutions, Institutional Change*, 113–15.

[60] Ringrose, "The Government and the Carters," 52.

[61] Ibid.

transporters and the government persisted; the carters fulfilled most of the government's needs (read the supply of Madrid) and in return they "spent most of their time working for public or semi-public agencies."[62]

The transport system in early modern Spain was in fact articulated by two parallel subsystems. On the one hand, there was a relatively small sector of professional transport specialists.[63] These could mobilize substantial numbers of carts or wagons drawn by oxen to be used on suitable roads, or mule caravans in the many parts of the interior that could not be passed by anything but a pack animal.[64] The much larger share of transport services, however, was provided by seasonal labor, both human and animal. In the agricultural low season peasants with a few mules or oxen would use their animals for some extra income in the transport sector. Wagons and other wheeled transport probably accounted for only about 2.5 percent of all transported volume; the rest was moved on pack animals.[65]

Given that the opportunity cost of these peasant transporters was close to zero—in other words, had they stayed at home they would not have been able to augment their income at all—this was a flexible and cheap supply of transport means. On the downside, it was unreliable and of course seasonal, though arguably intense local demand in harvest seasons tended to be followed by, rather than coincide with, demand for long-distance services. There is also some evidence to suggest that toward the eighteenth century even this small-scale business became a year-round activity, reflecting increasing specialization.[66] Still, it was at times a poor substitute for more regular transport services. For this reason, Ringrose argued that the government's increasing reliance on the relatively small professional transport sector had a disproportionately large negative effect on the rest of the economy which had to make do with the irregular and seasonal supply provided by part-timers.[67] Even worse, privileged carters who were allowed to access most of the fodder needed at the expense of village commons essentially levied a tax on the countryside; the government could benefit urban consumers in Madrid without having to actually charge a subsidy.[68]

This depiction of a transport system pressed into service by a powerful, increasingly absolutist government in the interest of a useless bureaucratic capital city through the means of corporate structure fit perfectly into the

---

[62] Ringrose, *Transportation*, 36.

[63] The best-studied group of muleteer traders were the *maragatos*. See Cubillo de la Puente, *El pescado*, and Rubio Pérez, *Arrieros maragatos*.

[64] Ringrose, *Transportation*.

[65] Estimate based on Madrazo, *Comunicaciones*, 77, who claims that professional wagons account at any one time for two million kilograms, while pack animals carried 40 million kilograms. If we add to that that the former moved at 12–18 kilometers per day and the latter 30–40, then in the seventeenth century only 2.5 percent of all transport was supplied by wagon.

[66] The example of the Argolleros from Leon seems to suggest this: see Cubillo de la Puente, *El pescado*, 57–58.

[67] Ringrose, *Transportation*.

[68] Ringrose, "Government and the Carters," 52. See also Ringrose, *Transportation*, 124.

historical narrative of the political economy of Spain at the time of Ringrose's writing. It rings less true today. Ringrose's qualitative and (partial) quantitative evidence on transport and trade was integrated into the accepted normative understanding of the political economy. Hence, the supply of grain to the municipal grain storage (*posito*) of Madrid was labeled a "government service," although Ringrose acknowledged that much of the grain arrived without "government encouragement."[69] The Crown's support for carters and muleteers was interpreted in a corporatist light, and requisitions of carts, wagons, mules, and oxen were seen as the norm rather than the exception. The Crown also allegedly relied on the carters rather than peasant transporters and their mules because the direct link between the more organized carters and the Crown confirmed the view of Crown-supported guild abuses.

Few of these interpretations have been confirmed by subsequent research. The authorities in charge of supplying the municipal *positos* relied, in all but famine years, on private contractors who entered into perfectly voluntary contracts. They used carters, but also peasant muleteers (*arrieros*), who in the winter months were the only ones able to supply the cities, since oxen were taken to winter grazing far away and roads were often impassable for carts and wagons anyway.[70] That is not to say that in times of scarcity grain transporters of all kinds were not drafted into service against their will, and the Madrid *posito* did have the right to sequester both grain and transport at fixed prices in extreme situations. Even other *positos* like that of Valencia created in 1770 had limited powers, such as preferential buyer's rights at market prices.[71]

Officials acknowledged, however, that sequestering transport led to plenty of evasive and fraudulent behavior, and thus the authorities tried to avoid it. Muleteers in a region where Crown officials, the *corregidores*, attempted to press-gang transporters into supplying Madrid at the fixed rate disappeared from sight only to reemerge in the capital with a lading of grain they had shipped either on their own account or for someone paying a higher rate. Others skimmed off smaller amounts or adjusted the official price of transport to the market rate by having the grain weighed when wet, thereby adjusting the weight when they could not negotiate the price. Even if the evidence for prices charged per *fanega* (weight) and *legua* (distance) transported is limited, it is very clear that prices were often adjusted seasonally and according to the demand and supply of grain and transport.[72] Intervention in the transport market at the hands of municipal (and rarely Crown) authorities probably mattered in famine years.[73] Yet to conclude on this basis that political intervention dislocated the transport system altogether requires an argumentative Olympic long jump.

If royal folly and the establishment of Madrid as Spain's first capital were

[69] Ringrose, *Transportation*, 40–41.
[70] Palop Ramos, *Fluctuaciones*, 42–45.
[71] Ibid., 11.
[72] De Castro, *El pan de Madrid*, 287–95.
[73] Llopis Agelán and Jerez Méndez, "Castilla y León," 39–57.

not to blame for the supposedly miserable transport, what was? Transport historians have been less concerned with Madrid's (the city's) rise than with Madrid's (the government's) inability to foster infrastructure. Once again, one encounters the traditional narrative that is so obviously contradictory: the central power, the absolutist state in Madrid, had supposedly all the means to induce improvements, but whenever it tried to move something, local resistance—or at least the lack of local support—could stop it without a problem.

The transport historian Madrazo, for instance, argued that infrastructure experienced no substantial changes because

> roads were not subject to any rationalization, no administrative organism and technicians capable of analyzing the problem and planning a communication and transport network, no specialists were sent, no rules for roads were created . . . without attention from the State [capital letter in the original] and without regular finance the little impetus [*braserillo*] from the *corregidores,* councils, *cortes*, guilds and *consulados de comercio* went nowhere.[74]

This is the familiar storyline of the failure of the central state to act. The author, however, goes on to outline with exemplary clarity the way in which road building was actually organized, financed, and put into practice. The pivotal role was not played by the Crown but by the towns. Before 1750 "the [central] state took no part in the construction, financing or oversight [*dirección facultativa*], leaving the initiative in the hands of the municipalities under the responsibility of the *corregidores* who generally could not impose the realization of works on the collective, which the latter did not consider their immediate interest."[75] All of a sudden the *corregidor*, the powerful arm of the state, was apparently unable to impose the realization of works if the locals were not interested? Undeterred, Madrazo blames seigneurial and urban disinterest, but his own research shows that the main problem lay somewhere else entirely. Towns financed the construction and repair of bridges and roads in the same way they financed everything else: with local trade and consumption taxes.[76] Not surprisingly, when the *cortes* discussed transport in the sixteenth and seventeenth centuries, they mostly focused on how the towns could raise the money for infrastructure, not on whether or not it was desirable.[77]

The problem was not simply that towns were too parochial in their outlook or that local nobles stood in the way of progress. There is plenty of evidence that towns up and down the country were hugely concerned with access to infrastructure, be it ports, roads, or bridges. The Castilian towns of Valladolid, Medina del Campo, and Medina de Rioseco dedicated about 10 percent of their expenditure to infrastructure in the mid-eighteenth century,

[74] Madrazo, *Comunicaciones*, 67.

[75] Ibid., 18.

[76] They were supposed to defray the costs of the *repartimientos*, their share of larger road works, and sometimes labor services, the so-called *sextaferias* or *zofras*.

[77] Madrazo, *Comunicaciones*, 18–19, 71, 339–53.

an important outlay.[78] Since the late fifteenth century infrastructure and safe transport were a prime concern of the *hermandades* of Castilian towns, and they remained so into the nineteenth century.

Yet towns often lacked the fiscal means to undertake larger projects, and from the mid-sixteenth century onward they were deep in debt as we will see in chapter 6. The travails of the Mediterranean port of Valencia to get royal support for the construction of a desperately needed pier to accommodate larger vessels are a case in point. Conscious that poor accessibility was its weakest point, the town planned and lobbied the Crown for the project from the late seventeenth century onward. However, building could not start until the last decades of the eighteenth century when royal support was finally secured. Even well-to-do Valencia could not afford major harbor works on its own.[79]

Historians have argued that improvements to the bottlenecks of the Iberian transport system, mostly mountain passes and some rivers, had to wait until pockets deeper than those of the municipalities could be reached into.[80] Yet this view is problematic, too. It is true that the central hacienda in Madrid began to get involved with a few particularly crucial projects only in the mid-eighteenth century. During the years 1749–51 a paved mountain pass was built across the 1,500-meter elevation of the Sierra de Guadarrama at Gudillos, the main obstacle separating Old Castile from Madrid. The hacienda established a toll that was subsequently used to keep the road in a decent state. Between 1750 and 1753 a road suitable for wagons was built from the northern port of Santander to Reinosa through the Cantabrian Mountains.

Only in 1762 did the Crown apply a general consumption tax on salt that was earmarked for road improvements and was explicitly meant to relieve the pressure on the towns. But yet again the tax was far from uniform; surcharges and exceptions applied in some regions, notably in Galicia and Valencia. Nor did this result in much road building; by the later 1770s only about 200 kilometers of paved roads had been built. The last three decades of the eighteenth century saw the creation, abolition, reestablishment, and alteration of a variety of bodies and commissions that were supposed to plan, supervise, and pay for the building of a network of "national" trunk roads. At the same time there were repeated requests sent to the municipalities asking them to take care of their part of the local and regional networks.[81] But at the end of the century there were hardly 300 kilometers of paved roads and the vast majority of road and bridge building was undertaken by the towns and villages through which they passed.[82]

---

[78] García García, *Crisis*, 80.
[79] Palop Ramos, *Fluctuaciones*, 72–75.
[80] Madrazo, *Comunicaciones*, 339–47.
[81] Ibid., 97–99.
[82] Ibid., 165.

Not a Problem After All?

Given the geographical reality of Spain and contemporary concerns about communications it is understandable that historians identified transport as a major issue. Spain, the argument goes, was suffering the tyranny of distance. But closer inspection of the evidence creates more puzzles than answers. First, Madrazo's assertion that next to nothing changed in Spanish transport between 1500 and 1750 is exaggerated. Despite all their shortcomings, towns and municipalities apparently did do a lot to improve transport even if there was a total absence of eye-catching projects. Second, if transport bottlenecks explain the sorry state of market integration in Spain, distances and travel times should be the crucial explanatory variables that explain the pattern of price convergence, or the lack thereof, in early modern Spain. As it turns out, they are not. Let us look at these arguments in sequence.

While it is almost impossible to measure the cost of travel with any degree of certainty, it is possible to establish roughly how long it took to get from one place to another. It seems a fair assumption that time should be a good proxy for transport costs, which were largely about wages, the use of animals, fodder, food, and accommodation along the road. Contemporary guidebooks reflect the journey times travelers had to allocate. Almost certainly people traveled faster than goods, but there is good reason to assume that passenger transport and—more important—its trend over time can at least offer a guide to how the speed of all types of transport changed since it depended on the state of roads, bridges, and the like in similar ways.

Table 4.7 uses data for various routes at three points in time: 1641, 1775, and 1850. Traveling did become considerably faster over this period. In 1641 the daily stages between Spanish towns described in the *European Mercury* were about 13 kilometers.[83] By 1775 this had risen to 46 kilometers a day. Travel speed thus increased noticeably, though in terms of international comparisons Spain lagged behind. In the mid-eighteenth century British stage-coaches covered about 50 kilometers a day from London to out-of-the-way Edinburgh but reached up to 100 kilometers a day on some of the south-western routes out of London, such as the one to Ipswich.[84] Nevertheless, this kind of difference is much less dramatic than much of the historiography would suggest.

Maybe it was all due to the fact that travelers in Spain had a strong incentive to get to the next inn quickly. That is at least what the chaplain of the English ambassador to Spain, the Reverend Edward Clarke, thought. He claimed that travelers were rushing their horses because Spanish inns would fill their rooms on a first-come first-served basis. Thus he was appalled to find that a gentleman of distinction might have to sleep in the stables while

---

[83] Wadsworth, *The European Mercury.*
[84] Daunton, *Progress and Poverty*, 285ff.

Table 4.7. Travel times between Spanish towns according to contemporary guides

Year		1641				1775	1850
From	To	km/day	From	To		km/day	km/day
Laredo	Sta. Maria del Paular	10.59	Madrid	Irun		47	196
Laredo	Vitoria	12.50	Madrid	Zaragoza		46	200
Laredo	Leon	19.25	Madrid	Barcelona via Zaragoza		44	190
Logrono	Tudela	19.00	Madrid	Valencia via Utiel		50	160
Madrid	Guadalajara	17.50	Madrid	Valencia via Albacete		47	141
Palencia	Salamanca	13.13	Madrid	Barcelona via Valencia		48	140
Santiago	La Coruña	8.75	Madrid	Cadiz		50	151
Seville	Leon	11.22	Madrid	Granada		46	195
Seville	Cordoba	11.50	Madrid	Badajoz		50	133
Seville	Malaga	11.94	Madrid	La Coruña		38	111
Seville	Granada	9.33	Madrid	Oviedo		40	150
Granada	Cordoba	11.00	Madrid	Bilbao		39	158
Granada	Malaga	9.50	Madrid	Pamplona		49	195
Murcia	Granada	17.50	Madrid	Santander		39	158
Cuenca	Granada	13.74	Madrid	Valladolid		42	190
			Madrid	Segovia		58	174
Average		13.10	Average			45.81	165.1

Source: My own estimates based on Wadsworth, *European Mercury*, 1775 and 1850; Madrazo, *Comunicaciones*, 548.
Note: Distances for 1641 converted from leagues at 1 league = 7 km based on average league in Wadsworth, *European Mercury*.

a humbler traveler occupied the beds—evidently a wholly unacceptable state of affairs for an eighteenth-century Englishman.[85]

The good reverend's embarrassment over this Spanish egalitarianism notwithstanding, it seems safe to conclude that the fall in travel times had more to do with slowly improving infrastructure than with the competition for a decent bed at the inn. The notion of a stagnant transport network in Spain

[85] Clarke, *Letters*. English and French travelers repeatedly complained about Spaniards' lack of respect for their social betters. Cf. Brunel and Aerssen, *Journey into Spain*, 22.

before the mid-eighteenth century does not hold up to scrutiny. The way in which Spanish towns and municipalities took charge of the transport network, berated by contemporaries and historians alike, seemed capable of producing quite reasonable progress. It would appear that fixing small bridges over rivers that tended to flood and potentially stop a mule caravan for several days over time did make a difference. In the nineteenth century this slow and incremental progress finally gave way to a more systematic approach. Road building accelerated in the 1820s and showed its impact by 1850 when coach travel reached 165 kilometers per day on the main routes out of Madrid. The average travel speed had thus increased by a factor of 3.5 between the mid-seventeenth and the third quarter of the eighteenth century or at an annual rate of about 0.9 percent. Between 1775 and 1850 it increased again almost by a factor of four, or an annual 1.7 percent.

Admittedly, time was only one factor that determined total transport costs, albeit a very large one. There is a host of ancillary evidence that would suggest that other cost factors were either constant or not rising fast enough to counteract the time factor. A rare series for the cost of hiring mules, the largest capital input in any Iberian transport business, suggests that the cost fluctuated violently in the late seventeenth century but hardly increased overall, even in nominal terms, between the mid-seventeenth and the late eighteenth century.[86] The few available series of freights for a homogeneous product on a comparable route would equally suggest that the freight factor, that is, the cost of transport compared to the price of the transported good, was falling. This was true in eighteenth-century Galicia as well as in Catalonia.[87] Even Ringrose's estimate for the price of transport of grain in Extremadura between the 1760s and 1780s would suggest that the nominal price was stable as grain prices increased; in other words, the freight factor was falling.[88]

More generally, if price differentials of the same good in different locations were a function of transport costs, transport times and/or distances should be reasonably correlated with those differentials. Yet neither travel times nor distances are good predictors of price differences in the Spanish *bacalao* markets. Table 4.8 analyzes the relationship between price differentials among towns in the data set expressed in ten-year averages, reporting the distances between these markets and the number of days it took to travel between them, where available. For the second half of the seventeenth century prices are reported for different decades due to missing observations.[89] In the cases of the pairs Cadiz-Albacete, Bilbao-Sahagún, and Bilbao-Pamplona, alternative estimates are offered based on the distance from the closest port, that is,

---

[86] Feliu, *Precios y salarios*, vol. 2, 141.

[87] Eiras Roel and Gelabert, "Contabilidades hospitalarias como fuentes de los transportes internos"; Feliu, *Precios y salarios*, vol. 2.

[88] Ringrose, *Transportation*, table 11, p. 80.

[89] Distances between towns are defined "as the crow flies." That overstates the costs per 100 kilometers significantly, but as long as we have no clear evidence on the length of the route that was actually taken, it is the soundest way of comparison.

Table 4.8. Cost of transport per distance and days traveled in the seventeenth and eighteenth centuries

	Years	Price differential (gr of silver/kg)	Cost per 100 km	Years	Price differential (gr of silver/kg)	Cost per 100 km	Cost per day of travel (1775)
Bilbao-Madrid	1673–82	1.74	0.54	1766–75	1.83	0.57	0.18
Bilbao-Toledo	1651–60	3.21	0.83	1766–75	2.03	0.53	0.18
Cadiz-Seville	1667–76	7.38	7.61	1766–75	2.27	2.34	0.76
Cadiz-Albacete	1701–11	0.83		1766–75	0.59		
Alicante-Albacete		0.83	0.61		0.59	0.43	0.15
Bilbao-Sahagún	1702–11	3.88	1.99	1744–53	0.92	0.47	0.18
Santander-Sahagún		3.88	2.47		0.92	0.59	0.23
Bilbao-Pamplona	1651–60	1.77	1.49	1766–75	2.70	2.27	0.90
San Sebastian-Pamplona		1.77	2.85		2.70	4.35	1.35
Average of seven routes		3.14	2.30		1.72	1.44	0.49

Source: For prices, see the data set of this volume. For travel times, see Madrazo, *Comunicaciones.*
Note: Missing observations: Madrid, 1675–76, 1771–73; Seville, 1769; Albacete, 1704–6, 1709, 1766–70.

Alicante, Santander, and San Sebastian, respectively. For Albacete the sources confirm that cod supplies were almost always brought in from Alicante, and in the case of Pamplona, it is likely that cod was obtained from San Sebastian even if it was after transshipment from Bilbao given cheap and readily available coastal shipping. In Sahagún it is less obvious; both Bilbao as well as geographically closer ports like Santander were used. The values for direct deliveries from the large ports function as the lower-bound estimate, those to the closer small ports as higher-bound estimates.

In any case the wide range of price markups per 100 kilometers in the seventeenth century is quite evident: the lowest range from 0.5 to 1 gram of silver/100 kilometers between Bilbao and the central *meseta* or the coast and Albacete, to 2–3 grams of silver/100 kilometers for the inland journey to the Old Castilian town of Sahagún and to Pamplona and, finally, a breathtaking 7.6 grams from Cadiz to Seville. By the second half of the eighteenth century the average cost per 100 kilometers had been reduced by about a third. Costs had also overall become more uniform: on most routes they amounted to around 0.5 grams of silver/100 kilometers. The decline on the route to Seville had lowered the cost to 2.5 grams, but that was still five times the cost elsewhere. In the case of Pamplona the cost per 100 kilometers had *increased* by about 0.36 percent per annum over a century and quarter in which the average time it took to travel had fallen by 0.9 percent per annum.

The Tyranny of Distance

The emergence of the transatlantic and pan-Iberian markets for *bacalao* offers a unique way to revisit the debates about the impact of geography, technology, and distance on the torturous Spanish path toward more integrated markets. Between the mid-seventeenth and the late eighteenth centuries the establishment of a very large new transatlantic trade that supplied a basic foodstuff like cod bears witness to the impact of early globalization. It illustrates that there was more to the expansion of interoceanic trade than increased volumes. Quantitative expansion was accompanied by a convergence of price levels on either side of the Atlantic. The recent literature on globalization has played down this effect too much. Transatlantic price convergence was definitely good news for Spanish consumers. Yet the cod markets also demonstrate that transoceanic integration changed the relative prospects of "domestic" and "international" market integration in Spain: in terms of price convergence, integration *without* proceeded at a faster rate than integration *within*. This in turn changed the competitiveness of domestic production vis-à-vis supplies from outside the Peninsula, especially for the coastal regions. It also changed the incentive structures for these areas as we will see in chapter 8.

That Spain was saddled with a complicated geography that increased the costs of creating a functioning transport network is a commonplace.

This should not tempt us to exaggerate the effects and fall for geographical determinism, however. Spanish road transport was considerably slower—and therefore less efficient and more expensive—than English road transport. And the differences in road transport understate the real issue. Spain lacked the alternative of river and canal transport that accounted for much of the bulk transport in northern Europe, though it had a very active coasting trade.[90]

Nevertheless, communications were hardly as stagnant as Spanish historians of transport from Ringrose to Madrazo have claimed. Travel became faster and cheaper. There was a trend toward slow price convergence in several markets, notably between either the northern or the southern coasts and the central *meseta* around Toledo and Madrid, but also between the ports and old Castilian Sahagún and Albacete in La Mancha. The rise of Madrid converted the communication network into a radial one. Yet the often repeated statement that this essentially cut other Castilian towns off the network, notably Toledo, is not borne out by the data.[91] If anything, Toledo experienced increased price convergence with both Madrid and the ports over this period.

These markets represented the sort of development toward slow price convergence that might have been expected, even though it has to be noted that the rates of convergence observed were slower than those of improvements in transport times. The real puzzles in the data are towns that do not follow any common trend, like Seville and Pamplona. The traditional argument that the Indies trade monopoly was the only cause for Seville's high price levels does not sit easily with the evidence. The data on distances covered per day in the mid-seventeenth century presented in table 4.7 offer some clues. Southwestern Andalusia suffered more than other parts of the Peninsula from poor road networks, and with it Seville. This is reflected in the below-average distances for the daily stages between Seville and other towns in the 1640s reported by Wadsworth. Still, the extraordinary price of *bacalao* in Seville cannot be explained by poor roads, as shown in table 4.8. The case of Pamplona is even harder to explain. On the one hand, the state of roads in the Basque Country and Navarra was reputedly rather better than elsewhere and improving in the eighteenth century. On the other hand, a divergence of price levels clearly contradicts all results expected from improving internal communications.

The results obtained for volatility of prices and from the price correlations between different towns suggest a different picture from those implied by the price convergence data. Seville and Pamplona were *not* poorly integrated with other markets by Peninsular standards. The ports suffered higher volatility. Barcelona stands out as a market with low price correlation with the other ports or the interior. Indicators that are commonly used by economic

---

[90] The Canal de Castilla, a 200-kilometer canal constructed in the provinces of Palencia, Burgos, and Valladolid, eventually served to facilitate the transport of grain from this major producing region to the coast. Contruction began in 1753, but it was not inaugurated until 1842. Guerra Garrido, *Castilla en canal*. On the coasting trade, see O'Flanagan, *Port Cities*.

[91] Ringrose, *Madrid*, 252–77; Madrazo, *Comunicaciones*, 152.

historians in order to gauge market integration, price convergence, volatil-ity, and price correlation do not point in the same direction: the price wedge between markets that were fairly well integrated was sometimes huge.

One conclusion follows quite naturally. Distance was but one factor in Spain's problems with market integration. Spanish communications were not desperately worse than roads elsewhere in Europe as often claimed, nor was there total stagnation in the system. The road network continued to depend on the initiative and fiscal health of the municipalities for much of the period under consideration. For reasons that go deep into the constitutional struc-ture of Spain, as we will see in chapter 6, towns were the location of fiscal power and the only providers of public goods other than defense—and they provided some of that, too. In spite of their state of indebtedness from the late seventeenth century onward, the progress in communication they effected surprisingly suggests that they kept up with their infrastructure duties to a reasonable degree. The few more centralized road projects executed between 1750 and 1780 generally cleared some of the most grievous bottlenecks in the communications network, normally mountain passes like the one over the Sierra de Guadarrama, with limited impact on the "national" system. Spain was not suffering from a crippling tyranny of distance. Still, relatively high transport prices contributed to sheltering local and regional economies from the pressure for more market integration, as will soon become clear.

Chapter 5

Distant Tyranny

The Historic Territories

DOMESTIC MARKET INTEGRATION IN SPAIN was indeed slow; more specifically, it was much slower than Spain's integration with the international economy over the long run, and its progress was regionally extremely diverse. That much should be clear from the results of chapter 4. Poor transport technology and bad roads did not help matters and provide some of the background for understanding Spanish markets. Still, transport itself exhibited a trend toward slow but steady improvement over the century and a half under consideration here, and this progress proceeded faster than the overall trend of price convergence proxied by the time it took to travel from one place to another. In short, transport was at most one part of the problem. This suggests that the impact of the political economy of Spanish markets should be moved into the foreground.

Chapter 1 has shown that there is little evidence that Spain's political economy suffered from the sort of expropriatory failings of supposedly centralizing, all-powerful "absolutist" states that earlier NIE literature had diagnosed. As historians of the Spanish Empire have long pointed out, in the Spanish monarchy "even in its European core Absolutism was [merely] a political aspiration."[1] The contrast with parliamentary systems was also easily overdrawn. One of the greatest historians of Spain, Elliott, put it aptly: "parliaments could be just as arbitrary and intrusive as kings."[2]

European rulers governed over territories in the plural, not the singular, and multiple levels of authority coexisted.[3] Far from being absolutist despots of the unified and centralized state, rulers were subject to several levels of authority sharing with corporate bodies, such as provincial estates, towns, guilds, and the Church. All of these demanded that the Crown respect their ancient corporate "freedoms," that is, privileges and again the plural, and not to be mistaken for the abstract idea of freedom in the singular, that is, the universal freedom of the individual, which had formed the intellectual underpinning of the NIE model.

Indeed, sixteenth- and seventeenth-century political theorists saw absolutism as the opposite of arbitrary government, a guarantee for life, liberty, and

---

[1] Halperin Donghi, "Backward Looks," 221.
[2] Elliott, "Empire and State," 380.
[3] Epstein, *Freedom and Growth*.

private property.[4] Absolute power was about the drive of the monarchy to overcome competing claims to political autonomy by rural seigniors and the noble estate as a whole. It was about liberating society from the historical "freedoms" (read privileges) of estates and corporate bodies. The disciplinary focus of historical sociology and economics on absolutism as the rule of a monarch with near total control of the executive and legislative branches of government, that is, as the opposite of the modern freedom of the individual, is an anachronistic perspective.[5]

Fragmented sovereignty complicated the political economy of early modern states. Economic historians have argued that in France the main drawback was the incompatibility of revenue and expenditure decisions. Yet, as shown in chapter 1, that was *not* the main problem in eighteenth-century Spain where the Crown kept spending under control, relatively speaking. Jurisdictional fragmentation also meant different monetary, tax, customs, and political systems, and many more smaller and larger differences across territories and towns that added to the cost of exchanging goods. In Spain this was the real problem.

In order to understand why and how Spanish patterns of divided authority affected the efficiency of markets, this chapter will first take one step back and consider more carefully where power was located, how it was exercised, and how it was legitimized. More specifically, we need to probe more deeply into the political foundations and the ideology of power that underpinned jurisdictional fragmentation and made it so much harder to surmount than the mountain passes of Iberia. It will become clear that there were deep ideological and constitutional reasons why monarchical rule in Spain remained wedded to the notion of a contract between Crown and subjects. There were also important institutions that supported this conception.

Second, this chapter revises the actual attempts at unification and centralization undertaken in the later seventeenth and eighteenth centuries. The research strategy employed is based on a comparative approach that assesses the actual outcomes of reforms and would-be reforms, especially of the early eighteenth century. This comparative perspective is all-important: The argument I have been putting forward is *not* that there was no trend toward centralization at all. Instead, I argue that by the standards of the wider European experience the unification process was very slow, incomplete, and haphazard in Spain, not just in the Habsburg period but at least into the nineteenth century. This was not a "failure" to centralize, however. Rather, what I have called the *Verfasstheit* of society (the way it was constituted), which depended on social relations, political thought, religious conceptions of society and rule, and the political economy underpinning the viability of rule, was incompatible with an abolition of the sources of jurisdictional fragmentation because they were also the source of legitimacy of rule. Or,

---

[4] Henshall, *Myth*, 130–32.

[5] See, e.g., Ertman, *Leviathan*.

to put it another way, the nature of governance in the Spanish monarchy by and large could not solve the coordination problems that hindered market integration in Spain throughout this period because doing so would have also done away with its own legitimacy.

Focusing primarily on outcomes rather than aims and intentions of reforms enables us to distinguish more clearly if, where, and to what extent a tendency toward centralization and unification came into place. If there was such a tendency, it should be clearly visible in the structure of the monetary, customs, and fiscal systems, as well as in tax and price data. Monetary disturbances caused by multiple currency systems should have declined. Internal customs borders should have disappeared or at least become less important. The tax system and the tax burden should have become more uniform across territories and towns. The authority to tax should have become more centralized. As a consequence, over time, transport costs, rather than such jurisdictional obstacles, should have become the main explanatory variable that determined price variations across places. A quantitative analysis of the market confirms what the historical narrative suggests: even the most radical attempt at change, the Bourbon reforms of the early eighteenth century, could not set the trends in market integration on a different trajectory or erase the impediments. In this chapter the focus will be on the role of the historic territories in the Peninsula. The next chapter will look at the role played by towns.

The Foundations of Composite Kingdom

Spain emerged as a dynastic conglomerate of Castile, Aragon, and Navarra, adding Portugal, the Netherlands, Naples, Sicily, Sardinia, and Milan at times, never mind the largest (until the mid-eighteenth century) European empire in the Americas and the Philippines. It is a commonplace that Spain never overcame this heritage of "composite kingdom" in the Habsburg period. By the mid-seventeenth century, neither Castile nor Aragon was unified as they contained historic territories that maintained their own political representations. In the old Kingdom of Aragon the Crown had to negotiate with separate *cortes* in Catalonia, Valencia, and Aragon, plus Mallorca. Here the estates survived as a formidable force integrating a society with stronger feudal roots across estamental boundaries to the end of the Habsburg period— though they were not (in Valencia and Catalonia) or rarely (in the province Aragon) called in the second half of the seventeenth century.

In the Basque Provinces, where the juntas were differentiated along a rural-urban divide (all Basques were considered legally noble, thus traditional estates were meaningless), and in Navarra, where they consisted of the *brazo militar,* the *brazo eclesiastico*, and the *brazo de las universidades* (nobility, clerics, towns), representations survived beyond the end of the ancien

régime protected by their historic freedoms, the *fueros*.[6] In Castile, power
was devolved back to the towns, and there it remained until the end of the
old regime order and beyond.[7] To a lesser extent, exceptions applied to the
former kingdoms of Granada and Murcia and to Galicia. Many historians
see the Bourbon eighteenth century as an era of internal centralization. Yet
Spain ultimately failed to make a transition to a "nation," much less a nation-
state, in the early modern period and struggled throughout the nineteenth
and twentieth centuries with the task.[8] Some would argue it still does; even
in 2010 "Spanish" courts and society discuss the preamble of the Catalan
statute, which invoked a Catalan nation (and thus implicitly denied the existence of a Spanish one).

Constitutional Constraints: Legitimizing Power

A tension between attempts at unification, what we commonly refer to as
the early stages of nation-state building, and local, regional, and corporate
resistance against this tendency was a general feature of European history
between the sixteenth and early nineteenth centuries. Why centralization
never took root in Spain is thus a *comparative* question, not an absolute one.
The historiographies of early modern Britain and even more so of France
have been at pains to rescue the survival of local agency, linguistic diversity,
and regional economic trends from an earlier literature that had written
national stories into the pre- or proto-national histories as part of a creation
of the imagined national community, to use Benedict Anderson's very helpful
concept.[9] But there can be little doubt that England (and Wales) and even
France exhibited earlier than Spain a stronger degree of economic, social, and
cultural integration and cohesion as well as political centralization.

   The source of legitimacy and the nature of rule and power in Spain are
important ingredients in a better understanding of the extraordinary resistance in Spain to the formation of a more unified, and therefore more powerful, governance structure—something economic historians pay too little
attention to. The very basis of all ancien régime corporatist polities was the
diffusion of power across corporate bodies, ranging from estates to regulated
companies, towns, guilds, religious confraternities, and others. The location
of power was decentralized across corporate entities. The overall tendency

<hr>

   [6] Solbes Ferri, *Rentas Reales de Navarra*, 38. See also Agirreazkuenaga, "Abolition." The
Navarrese representations continued to function until 1841. In addition, the rules for the
approval of taxation differed from territory to territory. In the *cortes del reino* de Aragon all
chambers had to approve the grant unanimously. In Navarra, it was sufficient for the Crown
to gain a simple majority in each chamber. Solbes Ferri, *Rentas Reales de Navarra*, 45–46.
   [7] Fernández Albaladejo, "Monarquía"; Thompson, "Absolutism in Castile."
   [8] Elliott, "Composite Monarchies."
   [9] Anderson, *Imagined Communities*. See also Gellner, *Nationalism*.

between the sixteenth and late eighteenth centuries in Europe was toward a hierarchical ordering that would eventually place the central government, be it monarchical or parliamentary, firmly at the top as the ultimate source of power that was its own, either devolve or centralize. However, this process was certainly not linear, and in Spain it remained a game of one step forward two steps back. Strategies of co-optation, for example, always involved a degree of devolution of power to regional political elites that needed to be co-opted. As Thompson has shown, by the second half of the seventeenth century in Spain, devolution had won out over the creation of "national" institutions, be they estates or the Crown, or even a national representation of the clergy.[10]

The resistance to a political and fiscal—and hence economic—unification in Spain was empowered partly by the survival of unusually strong contractual elements in Spanish conceptions of rule and governance. Spanish historiography over the past two decades has started to reinterpret the relationship between ruler and ruled in both theory and practice. Spanish kings were clearly not absolutist in the sense that political economy has tended to use the term—namely as unlimited autocrats. Like most European monarchs, they were subject to natural law and divine order, and they were also seen as being subject to the traditional laws of the land.[11] Yet cultural and intellectual historians have noted a number of ways in which the Spanish monarchy stood out for its limited powers at both the ideological and practical levels. These limits ranged from the lack of divine elements in court ritual to the ideological foundations of the *potestas populi*.

Spanish court life was noted for the absence of pomp and circumstance, and it clearly did not resemble the model of French ostentation and representation of power which, following Elias's seminal work half a century ago, has come to be seen as standard political practice.[12] In the absence of representative state functions and military displays, the court ceremonial was evidently not directed toward a legitimization vis-à-vis the king's subjects but served as little more than diplomatic exercise. The royal family remained private, in contrast to France where royal birth and death and everything in between took place in full view of court society. Instead, the subjects' favor was wooed at public processions and bullfights on the Plaza Mayor and in expanding festivities for the masses.[13] Spanish monarchs also enjoyed few of the divine elements of legitimization commonly ascribed to their English or French colleagues.[14] Coronation rituals, important acts of emphasizing

[10] Thompson, "Absolutism in Castile."

[11] On the coexistence of an "office theory" of rule, that is, one that interpreted the king as merely fulfilling a mandate with proprietary practices that implied a hereditary, divinely justified possession of power, see Rowen, *The King's State*. For a more detailed discussion of the Spanish monarchy, albeit with a focus on New Spain, see Cañeque, *King's Living Image*, especially chapter 2.

[12] Hofmann, *Hofzeremoniell*, 289–92; Elias, *Die höfische Gesellschaft*.

[13] Hofmann, *Hofzeremoniell*, 292.

[14] Reinhard, *Staatsgewalt*, 67.

the divine origin of monarchical rule elsewhere, did not exist in either early modern Castile or Aragon, much less in the Basque Provinces or Navarra. Leftovers of a Castilian coronation ritual, which was probably of Moorish origins, were abolished in the fifteenth century.

Indeed, to talk about the "Crown" as a synonym for the monarchy is a bit of a misnomer in the Spanish context. Spanish documents speak about the *rey/reina* or *real persona,* rarely about the *corona,* and the modern historiographical use is largely a transfer of an English concept onto Spanish history. In fact, strictly speaking, there was no "Crown"; the kings of Castile had no regalia, no scepter, no throne, and no crown, and they were neither consecrated nor crowned, as Paul Monod has stressed.[15] The Crown was a defender of the Catholic faith but not the representation of the divine on earth. The Spanish Jesuit Pedro de Rivadeneira (1526–1611) argued that "No king is absolute or independent or proprietary, but is a lieutenant and minister of God."[16] Like their royal peers elsewhere, Spanish kings engaged in public acts of devotion, for example, the washing of the feet of paupers, as a demonstration that they were subject to a higher law. Yet unlike their European peers, they lacked the "royal touch": they were never thought to have healing powers or other sacred attributes.[17]

Monod has suggested that the Iberian reluctance to accept the notion of divinity of the king was rooted in an Islamic heritage that rejected personified divinity as blasphemous.[18] More generally, Giovanni Levi has argued that the survival of a popular conception of justice was common to Mediterranean Catholic traditions, as well as Jewish and Islamic ones. Reciprocity remained the source of legitimacy and required a sovereign that would perform his/her duties and was thus far from absolute. It implied an expectation of equity that shaped distributive justice within a corporate hierarchical society and that circumscribed the consolidation of social and legal institutions.[19] Whatever the origins of these elements in Iberia's long multireligious and multiethnic past, what matters for the present discussion is that this lack of a divine source of legitimacy shaped kingship and aristocracy and helped sustain the notion of contractual power not only in ideology but also in the practice and exercise of power.

It has been repeatedly noted that just as Jean Bodin was laying the foundation of the doctrine of absolute power of the French kings in his *Six livres de la Republique* (1576), Juan de Mariana's *De rege et regis institutione* (1598) defended the right to tyrannicide. The Frenchman argued that power had been transferred to the kings as an irrevocable, hereditary right that

[15] Monod, *Power of Kings,* 42–43.

[16] Quoted in ibid., 51. See also Cañeque, *King's Living Image,* 72–77.

[17] Bloch famously pointed out that "royal touching" in order to heal scrofula was practiced in Britain until the Hanoverians came to the throne in 1714, though Stuart pretenders clung to their touch longer. In France the practice disappeared only with the revolution and was shortly revived as late as 1825. Bloch, *The Royal Touch,* 220, 226, 228.

[18] Monod, *Power of Kings.*

[19] Levi, "Reciprocidad mediterránea," 126.

could not be revoked under *any* circumstances, even if he was a despot or tyrant. Mariana, by contrast, replied like much of Spanish political thought: only a fool would argue that it was not just and according to law to kill a tyrant.[20] The people had delegated authority to the king but had not alienated their *potestas populi*.[21] Nor was Mariana's view the exception; his was supported by most of his contemporaries like Domingo de Soto (1494–1560), Jerónimo Molina Lama y Guzman (1650s–?), Francisco Suarez (1548–1617), Gabriel Vásquez (1550–1604), Fernando Vázquez de Menchaca (1512–69), and Domingo Báñez (1528–1604).[22] "You Monarchs are but laborers; you deserve as much as you work for," the poet and royal advisor Francisco de Quevedo (1580–1645) told Philip IV (1605–65).[23]

For most Spanish thinkers of the sixteenth and seventeenth centuries good qualities in a king were not a desirable add-on, they were the essence of kingship; moral authority was the source of legitimacy, and a tyrant was no longer king and could rightfully be removed.[24] Perhaps more surprisingly, the notion of *potestas populi*, of the legitimacy of rule being established by a transfer, but not alienation, of power from "citizens" [*vecinos*] to the monarch was as early as the mid-sixteenth century extended to apply to the indigenous *pueblos* of the Americas.[25] It should also be noted here that the basis of political power was the *vecino*; Spanish political thinkers departed from the idea of the town as the location of political life. It is possible that the absence of religious conflict within Spanish Christianity created less need for a more absolute definition of monarchy, especially when we consider how religious divisions bedeviled French and English monarchical succession in the sixteenth and seventeenth centuries and dominated controversy about the role of the monarchy.[26] Be that as it may, Mariana's work was publicly burned in London and Paris but hardly raised eyebrows in Madrid or Barcelona.[27]

[20] Mariana, *De rege et regis institutione*, book 6.

[21] Quijada, "*Potestas Populi*," 198, 200. Cañeque, *King's Living Image*, 72–73.

[22] Skinner argued that Suarez should be seen as a predecessor of Locke and Hobbes and the Salamanca School as one basis of the idea of the modern state rooted in popular expression. But he also insisted that Suarez had conceived of power as being "transferred absolutely" to the king. Skinner, *Foundations*, 2:174–84. Quijada has recently shown that the focus on Suarez has distracted from more radical thinkers such as Vázquez de Menchaca, Mariana, and Pérez de Mesa, and that the Neo-Scholastics diverged from their Thomist origins by refusing to accept that the king was not subject to the regulations of positive law; instead they argued that the individual maintained full control over his/her own liberty. Quijada, "*Potestas Populi*," 204ff.

[23] *Política de Dios, y gobierno de Christo*, part II, chap. XIII, in de Quevedo Villegas, *Obras*. My translation.

[24] Maravall, *Estado*, 402–5; Quijada, "*Potestas Populi*," 198; Thompson, "Castile: Polity," 145.

[25] Quijada, "*Potestas Populi*," 204–12. On the idea of the town as an expression of good government, see Escobar, *Plaza Mayor*, 192–216.

[26] Rowen's account would seem to support this argument, though he does not make it explicit. Rowen, *The King's State*, especially chapters 2 and 3.

[27] Kamen, *Imagining*, 41.

The subjects of the Spanish king meanwhile entertained themselves at public performances of Lope de Vega's famous play *Fuenteovejuna*, first published in 1619. Monod observed that it was very unlikely that it could have taken place in France or England.[28] As the villagers of *Fuenteovejuna* shout "Long live the King," they kill their abusive landlord, fully expecting that the king will accept their taking justice into their own hands for the abuse of power they suffered. And pardoned they are.[29] Nor was this just the stuff of fancy plays or restricted to Castile. The inhabitants of the small Valencian town Elche took advantage of the general protests in more than seventy Spanish towns in the wake of the 1766 Esquilache riots in Madrid to rid themselves of their seigneur and declare Elche part of Crown lands (*realengo*). They called in the scriveners to testify to the procedural correctness of the public act of transfer and fully expected to be pardoned. In the event, the Madrid Councils reversed the transfer. But the Councils also overturned the (few) sentences passed by local judges. The worst punishments imposed on a very serious act of rebellion orchestrated by around two thousand inhabitants, who had unilaterally expropriated their lord, were relatively mild *destierros* (banishments) and terms in the army; and it would seem that many of those were not even implemented.[30]

In a similar vein Catalonia saw the dissemination of the legend of Sobrabe in the late sixteenth century. The myth traced the origin of the establishment of a Christian polity that would be the nucleus for the Kingdom of Aragon to this mountain region located in today's province of Huesca. With the Sobrabe story the so-called Oath of the Aragonese appeared, claiming that since earliest times the kings of Aragon were obliged to swear an oath to respect the traditional freedoms *before* their subjects would swear them allegiance. The Oath of the Aragonese appeared in at least four independent publications in Italy, France, and Spain between 1565 and 1593 but was also mentioned by Jean Bodin and others.[31] Though important variations existed in the wording, the best-known version became the one reported by Antonio Pérez, the fugitive secretary of Philip II, of 1593.[32]

---

[28] For a contrasting interpretation of Lope de Vega's play, see Forcione, *Majesty and Humanity*, 17.

[29] Monod, *Power of Kings*, 131.

[30] Palop Ramos, *Hambre*, 152–53.

[31] Giesey, *If Not*. In France the alleged oath became part of the religious conflict when it was used by Francis Hotman in his *Francogallia* (1573) as a means to legitimize Huguenot resistance against the Catholic monarchy defended by Bodin. See Rowen, *The King's State*, 36–43.

[32] Antonio Pérez was an interested party in celebrating Aragonese political independence. Following political intrigues in Madrid and having ordered the murder of Juan de Martínez Ruiz (he alleged with the assent of Philipp II), the king eventually had him and his accomplices put under arrest and ordered a judicial process to begin. Pérez escaped to his native Aragon, where he was legally protected, though he had been convicted to death in absentia in Madrid. Attempts to have him arrested by the Inquisition caused an uprising in Aragon, and Pérez eventually fled to France and England. Marañón, *Antonio Pérez*.

Nos que valemos tanto como vos
Os hazemos nuestro Rey y Señor
Con tal que nos guardeys nuestros fueros, y libertades
Y syno, No[33]
[We, who are worth as much as you
Make you our King and Lord
So that you guard our ancient freedoms and liberties
And if not, Not.]

The oath was neither constitutional theory nor historical practice. Instead, it was part of a process of invention of the past. The mythical origins of the Kingdom of Aragon were fused with the *fueros* (traditional liberties) of Navarra and with the actual tradition of an oath being taken first by the heir to the throne and then by the king himself at accession. Yet the fact is that the myth was propagated in defense of Aragonese rights vis-à-vis the Crown. A contemporary Venetian diplomat cited the oath in reports to the doge in order to explain why the Aragonese were so impossible to handle for the Crown, reflecting the view of disinterested contemporaries that Aragon enjoyed an unusual degree of independence by the standards of the time.[34]

In Catalonia, the notion of a contractual monarchy was particularly deeply embedded in the political culture and practice as has often been pointed out. Municipal office in Barcelona continued to be assigned by a lottery among the ruling class, the *insaculaciones*, mirroring the practice in the Italian republics. The Crown's ability to grant status as an "honored citizen," part of the urban patriciate, was relatively limited until 1714.[35] Since Giovanni Botero's *Relationi universali* (1596–1602), Catalan history has been contrasted with an allegedly far more absolutist Castile.[36] Generations of modern historians trained by Elliott's magisterial *Imperial Spain* have grown up with this notion.[37] Also, the Aragonese nobility and bourgeois elites might well have felt that Castile was more "absolutist," especially given the evident political weakness of the Castilian aristocracy. With feudal rights determining social relations to a much larger degree in Catalonia, and especially in Valencia, even the most prosperous Castilian *mayorazgos* (entailed estates) were more limited in their seigneurial rights than were their Aragonese cousins.

Yet contemporary foreign observers were disparaging of the Iberian aristocracy in all territories and made fewer distinctions between Castilian and Aragonese aristocrats:

[33] Giesey, *If Not*, appendix 1.
[34] Soranzo, "Relazione di Spagna."
[35] Amelang, *Honored Citizens*.
[36] On Botero's assessment, see Gil, "Republican Politics," 263. The *relationi* were translated into Spanish as early as 1603.
[37] Elliott, *Imperial Spain*.

The Grandees of Spain appear such only at a distance: here they seemed to me very little, and without any other advantages than to put on their hats, and sit down in the Kings presence; in other particulars I never observed less inequality in the most popular Republick.

Such was Brunel's view.[38] Notably, these observers thought of the Hispanic kingdoms in the Peninsula as "deficient" because social hierarchies were too flat for their taste. In this light, the absence of divine providence and the permanent reassertion of strong elements of contractual rule and devolved fiscal control are less surprising, and it is likely that the difference between Aragonese "constitutionalism" and Castilian "absolutism" has been over-drawn.[39] The Spanish Crown depended on a large degree of approval by its subjects in all of its territories, including Castile, in comparison to its European peers.

From Ideology to Institution

The concentration of power at the center was limited by the practice of power as much as by the ideology of power. The interplay between multiple loca-tions of power, the underlying conception of power, and the actual practice of power is most clearly illustrated in the existence of a veto against any form of central authority, be it that of the Crown or its Councils, contained in the famous phrase "la ley se obedece pero no se cumple" (the law will be obeyed but not complied with).[40] Its constitutional (as well as economic) significance can be illustrated by a small incident that occurred when the Crown tried to introduce an unpopular new trade registration in Bilbao in 1628 in an attempt to use a uniform customs and registration policy in its international competition, especially with the Dutch and English. The representative of Vizcaya replied that

> In . . . the said *fuero* . . . it is said that any royal decree which would be directly or indirectly against the *fuero* of Vizcaya should be obeyed but not complied with (*sea obedecida y no cumplida*). I, in the name of the said *señorio* [Vizcaya], with due respect obey the said decree as our King and natural sovereign has sent. But inasmuch as this is in any way against our *fueros* . . . I submit humbly before his royal person . . . and I refuse to execute and comply with the said royal decree in everything prejudicial."[41]

As is obvious from this the *pase foral*, the special privilege contained in the *fueros*, amounted to a real veto, not merely a temporary suspension of a

---

[38] Brunel and Aerssen, *Journey*, 22.
[39] Thompson, "Castile: Absolutism," 201–3.
[40] Phelan, "Authority."
[41] AFB, CB, Libro 65/59 Antonio de Landaverde 1628.

decree, as Gil has claimed.[42] And to assume that this veto right only applied in Vizcaya or the Basque Country would be a mistake.[43] The *pase foral* was simply the institutionalized expression of a constitutional tradition in the Spanish monarchy that defined the relation between Crown and territories, towns, and corporate bodies in general. Every official, corporation, or individual could invoke the famous phrase "la ley se obedece pero no se cumple."

The veto power implied in this was functionally very different from a centralized veto power residing in one or even multiple "parliaments," or representations of estates, in that it was fully decentralized. It is better conceptualized within Levi's concept of reciprocity and rule as the administration of justice and hence deeply embedded in corporate society, which it defended from Crown encroachment. At the same time, it gave local and regional opposition against changes in economic governance, as in the case of the foreign trade registers mentioned above, a foundation in legal process.

The notion of *se obedece pero no se cumple* was born out of what MacLachlan calls a "philosophical matrix," which argued that the king or queen could not will anything that would prejudice his or her subjects.[44] Ergo, any royal decree perceived locally as prejudicial could be resisted perfectly legally under the constitutional pretext that the Crown would not have issued it if only it had full information about its consequences. The veto translated the notion of contractual rule contained in the political writings of the sixteenth and seventeenth centuries into an administrative and legal form that persisted. In Vázquez de Menchaca's words, the prince's decree only "has the force of true law, as regards its implementation, if it is aimed at the public good," or in the words of Bartolomé de las Casas (1484–1566), "the king's decisions that are harmful to the people will be null and void."[45]

In the last consequence, the possibility of a veto gave unparalleled powers to the political elites in the historic territories and to town oligarchies because they could and did use it against any policy that would restrict their regional decision-making powers. In addition, the veto power built into the traditional liberties of territories (and towns as we will see) significantly helped protect these special rights. At the same time, an ideology of power

---

[42] Gil, "Republican Politics," 268.

[43] In fact, the *fueros* of Navarra were codified earlier than those of the Basque Provinces, where initially only Vizcaya had a written code. Kasper has argued that the stronger feudalization of Navarra, where the *sobrecarta* fulfilled a similar function, contributed to the difference. Kasper, *Baskische Geschichte*, 52, 55. The Basque province of Alava was only formally granted the *pase foral* in 1703, i.e., under the Bourbons. It was formally revoked in 1766 in the wake of the second *matxinada*, a popular uprising that coincided with the Esquilache riots elsewhere, but reinstated in 1780. Porres, "Hermandad a la provincia," 290.

[44] MacLachlan, *Spain's Empire*, chapter 1. See also Cañeque, *King's Living Image*, 74–75. Most of the literature has focused on the legacy of the phrase *la ley se obedece, pero no se cumple* in Spanish America, where it was supposed to be an expression of a general disregard for the law. However, as Cañeque has pointed out the phrase *was* the law.

[45] Vázquez de Menchaca, *Controversiarum*, book 1, introduction 121, p. 179; las Casas, *De regia potestate*, quoted in Quijada, "*Potestas Populi*," 199, 209.

that maintained surprisingly strong notions of contractual rule long after they had been sidelined in other western European territorial states also helps explain what constrained the Spanish central monarch's exercise of power in the absence of a formal "constitutional" constraint. Spanish kings had to rely on negotiation and bargaining to affect changes to the existing order. That turned out to be a contradiction in terms.

Bourbon Challenges and the Survival of the Composite State

Historians have long argued that there was a significant break between the Habsburg and Bourbon periods in terms of the Crown's willingness and success in pushing for an abolition of the historic freedoms of Spain's corporate society. They broadly agree that in the Habsburg period the Crown made only very limited efforts to unify the legal systems, political institutions, fiscal structures, currencies, or languages of the constituent parts of the composite monarchy that was Spain. The distinct rules of bargaining over fiscal resources in each of the constituent territories, for instance, survived the nominal unification under one Crown and created a degree of complexity that set the Hispanic monarchy apart from its European neighbors.

The interpretation of Bourbon policies after 1705 is far more controversial. An early wave of reforms, most prominently the *decretos de Nueva Planta*, which ended Aragonese "self-government" by abolishing the *cortes* and other representative institutions in the four territories of the Crown of Aragon, was a clear break with tradition. Yet they should not be taken out of historical context. Shortly before his death in November 1700, the heirless Carlos II of Habsburg had decided to pass the Crown to Philip duc d'Anjou, grandson of Louis XIV, and thus relegate the Archduke Charles of Austria to third in line after Philip's younger brother. In the "Second Partition Treaty" (1699), France and England had agreed that Charles of Austria should succeed to the throne of Spain while France would keep much of the Italian territories. Yet upon Carlos II's death, Louis XIV instead decided to accept the former's testament in favor of his grandson, thus further destabilizing the already unbalanced European power system. This international context of the ensuing War of the Spanish Succession (Queen Anne's War to North Americans) with primarily France on one side and Austria, England, Portugal, and the Dutch Republic on the other is well-known.[46]

Within Spain, however, the War of the Spanish Succession was a civil war, as Lynch has pointed out.[47] What became a conflict within the reigns of the Hispanic monarchy allied with one side or another started largely with strong disagreements between social groups within reigns, especially in Valencia and

[46] Kamen, *Succession*.
[47] Lynch, *Bourbon Spain*, 37–46.

Catalonia.[48] The outcome of these conflicts was not inevitable. The fragile pro-Habsburg coalition in Valencia and Catalonia and the equally uncertain pro-Bourbon public in Castile were contingent developments. There was hardly any spontaneous rejection of Philip d'Anjou in his new Spanish territories. Upon his arrival in Spain in 1701/2 Philip followed time-honored tradition (and his grandfather's advice) in traveling from territory to territory to fulfill the succession customs as his Habsburg predecessors had done.[49] The towns of Castile were summoned to the Convent of San Jerónimo in Madrid for the swearing in of the new King Philip V of Castile. Elsewhere in the monarchy the viceroys followed the existing protocol, and the Aragonese sent a delegation to Madrid to welcome their king-to-be. Only in Naples and Caracas were there incidents following the proclamation of Philip V, none of them of much consequence.

While Austrian troops in support of Charles of Austria's rival claims to the Spanish throne had already entered Italy and engaged Franco-Spanish troops, Philip V swore his oath in the Catalan town of Lérida (Lleida) in May 1701. He went on to call the Catalan *corts*, which the Crown had avoided calling since the revolt of the 1640s and 1650s, and was voted a *servicio* of 1.5 million Catalan pounds. Philip named the queen governor in Barcelona. He called for a *corz* in Aragon, which duly assembled in Zaragoza and at which the queen represented Philip. By December the towns of Navarra and the Diputados of the Basque Provinces, their permanent representation, proclaimed Philip king.[50] So did the Parlamento of Palermo soon thereafter.

In short, Philip's accession to the throne closely mirrored long-established traditions of ruling the composite kingdom. He had sworn to uphold the traditional rights of the historic territories just as his Habsburg predecessors had done. He had negotiated for grants of taxation and given in to the demands of territorial representations. The *cortes* of Navarra, for example, succeeded in defending the increased fiscal autonomy they had wrestled from their kings in the later seventeenth century.[51] Indeed, in some of the historic territories, Philip V continued to strengthen their position vis-à-vis the Crown. In 1702 he formally acknowledged the recently written *fueros* of Guipúzcoa.[52] Through a decree in August 1703 he transferred to the province of Alava the same rights to their *fueros* and the right to resist royal legislative prerogative contained in the *pase foral* that Vizcaya and Guipúzcoa had enjoyed. In 1708 the province's rights were extended to reflect the larger independence enjoyed

---

[48] Ibid.

[49] What follows is based on Artola, *Monarquía*, 548–49.

[50] Zabala Uriarte, *Mundo urbano*, 30.

[51] In Navarra the Crown tried through the viceroy to return to the early seventeenth-century system of *cuarteles y alcabalas*, which were more regular, but was rebuffed by the *cortes* of 1702. The *cortes* only acceded to new taxes once they were levied as *donativo*, which they had to concede on each occasion. Solbes Ferri, *Rentas Reales de Navarra*, 102–3.

[52] Gorosábel and Echegaray, *Las cosas memorables de Guipúzcoa*, book 4, 302–5.

by the province of Guipúzcoa in general.[53] In constitutional terms there was initially nothing very unusual about Philip's accession.

By early 1705, however, the mood in Barcelona had turned decidedly against Philip. Anti-Gallic sentiment ran high in Catalonia, which had been invaded by the French only a few years before. The Catalans had bitter memories of the French bombardment of Barcelona in 1691 and the earlier intervention and dismemberment of Catalonia during the Catalan secession (1640–52).[54] Yet Francophobia was also instrumentalized during the civil war. Conflicts between the Crown and the Catalan elites over such themes as the right to determine the *insaculación* (the right to determine who could participate in the lottery for public offices) were longstanding.[55] But so were disagreements within the Catalan ruling groups, which now turned into open disputes between "Philipistas" and those in favor of Charles, who was proclaimed king of Spain in Vienna in 1703. The self-confident merchants of Barcelona bargained with both Philip and Charles, and both promised generous privileges. A slightly different social cleavage opened up within Valencia where the fraught relations between a very powerful landowning nobility and a hard-pressed peasantry had led to revolt as recently as 1693. Here, too, longstanding discord now took the shape of pro-Habsburg versus pro-Bourbon sentiment.

Preexisting social conflicts made allegiances aleatory. The Valencian peasantry looked to the archduke for deliverance from their hated, powerful noble masters, while the Castilian populace at large mostly supported Philip. Castilian grandees and nobles in turn openly sided with the archduke in large numbers, possibly in reaction to their feeling of marginalization in the political process.[56] In contrast, the upper nobility in Catalonia sided with Philip and the lower with the archduke.[57] In Bilbao, the largest port in the northern Basque Provinces, a resurgent local mercantile elite was decidedly pro-French and used the situation to move for the expulsion of English and Dutch resident merchants in an attempt to remove their main competitors.[58] Their Catalan counterparts eventually decided to throw in their lot with the Austrian side, partly in expectation of commercial advantages derived from an alliance with the English and Dutch whom the Basque merchants had just tried to expel.[59]

It is important to remember that neither side in this war fought at least initially to dismember the Spanish monarchy. Instead they fought to impose

[53] Porres, "Hermandad a la provincia," 289–91.

[54] Kamen, *Spain, 1665–1700*, 381.

[55] Amelang, *Honored Citizens*.

[56] For the relatively weak position of the Castilian aristocracy, see, e.g., Windler, *Lokale Eliten*, 22ff.

[57] Kamen, *Succession*; Lynch, *Bourbon Spain*, 29, 44–45.

[58] Zabala Uriarte, *Mundo urbano*, 30ff.

[59] Mercantile interests in Barcelona thought that the British alliance might help their commercial expansion, especially into the American trades. Lynch, *Bourbon Spain*, 42.

"their" king on all of the composite kingdoms. In the event, the pro-Habsburg mercantile and artisan interests of Barcelona carried the day in Catalonia. After a formal agreement signed in June 1705 in Genoa between the Catalans and the English, Archduke Charles and his troops entered Catalonia and Valencia unopposed. Depending on the point of view, this act eventually gave Philip a valid reason, or a welcome pretext, to suppress the traditional liberties of all Aragonese territories once the war had turned in his favor.

The real or alleged legitimization for the suppression of the *foral* institutions of the Kingdom of Aragon is subject to debate. Some historians argue that the explicit support of the various Aragonese representative institutions for Charles did constitute a breach of the basic compact between territory and Crown and was in effect high treason.[60] The archduke established his parallel government in Barcelona and undertook his campaigns, including the occupation of Madrid, from there. The Catalan *corts*, abandoned by their international allies at the Utrecht peace talks in 1713, eventually declared war against Castile in 1714. The suppression of the traditional governing institutions of Valencia and Aragon in 1707 and those of Catalonia after the final siege of Barcelona in 1714 is thus interpreted as a harsh, yet completely justified, punishment within the Spanish notion of compact between king and subjects. In other words, the Catalan institutions, not the Crown, had ripped up the contract. One of the problems with this view is that the opposition to Philip was largely concentrated in Barcelona and a few other places, while the rural areas in Catalonia remained loyal to him.[61]

Other scholars argue that the military victory over the Aragonese simply provided an unusually good opportunity to rein in the strong institutional independence of that realm, something the new dynasty had been hoping for all along. Once the archduke had abandoned his claims and Philip had demonstrated in Valencia and Aragon that he would punish those who had rebelled against him, the motivation for fighting on changed. Now, Catalonia fought for its traditional *fueros* within a Spanish monarchy. Certainly Philip's decree of 1707 abolishing the *fueros* in Aragon and Valencia can be read that way. The rebellion and the fact that the population had failed "entirely in the oath of allegiance that they offered me as their legitimate King and Lord" as well as the "right of the conquest that my Arms recently made of them" was the context (and maybe a pretext) to revoke "all those *fueros* and privileges, customs and form of government observed up to now."[62] Philip's stated aim was to "reduce all my reigns of Spain to the uniformity of the same laws, practices, customs and Courts, ruling all through the laws of Castile."[63] Thus the *decretos de Nueva Planta* of 1707–16 were an effective expression of a unifying drive that sought to establish an absolutist polity along the lines of

---

[60] Artola, *Monarquía*, 550–52.
[61] Kamen, *Spain, 1469–1714*, 291–92.
[62] "Novissima Recopilacion, Libro 3, Titulo 3, Ley 3. (1707)," reproduced in Díaz-Plaja, *Documentos: Siglo XVIII*, 71–72. My translation.
[63] Ibid.

Louis XIV. Indeed, some argue that the decrees were an active attempt to suppress a path toward "federal" government in Spain that would have been possible.[64] Yet this view, too, has its problems.

The new dynasty undoubtedly brought with it a number of administrators, first foreign but increasingly Iberian, that were keen to reform Spanish institutions at every level.[65] Yet the simplistic notion of Bourbon, or French-style, centralization has in some ways persisted far longer in the Spanish historiography than in the French tradition, where historians have debunked it fairly successfully.[66] Twentieth-century history goes a long way to explain that difference. Center-periphery relations are possibly the single most important political issue in Spain today, and the historiography has not been alien to the political debates. An extraordinarily violent civil war (1936–39) followed by thirty-six long years of a fascist, centralist dictatorship and the brutal suppression of all languages (and other regional expressions) but Castilian during those years have created strong associations in people's minds between the "rights" of the traditional territories and political freedom. Even today, three and a half decades after Franco was allowed to die peacefully in his own bed while still in power, those notions are ever-present in political debates. In some cases they have become more powerful as Basque, Catalan, Valencian, and Galician nationalists in particular have busied themselves strengthening their own "imagined communities." One cannot hope to understand the historiography without this context of the creation of Basque, Catalan, and other "national" histories set against the very concept of a Spanish history.

Part of this process was an obvious and very fruitful resurgence of an interest in researching the history of the traditional territories and reigns that made up the Spanish composite monarchy. Thus, paradoxically after Franco's death, Spanish historians overcame the problematic heritage of "national" histories earlier than their colleagues in other European countries because what constituted the nation remained contested. Historians can today draw on an exciting literature for individual regions and territories that has successfully exploited the exceptional richness of Iberian archives. However, this head start came at a price. Perhaps uniquely in Europe, Spanish history has often been written from the periphery to the center. Strong regional academic traditions have shaped historical research since the later eighteenth century and even more so in the post-Franco era. Catalan historians have been particularly productive, but strong historiographical traditions have also emerged in the Basque Country, Valencia, the south, and elsewhere.

Seen from the periphery, and in the context of Spanish history of much of the twentieth century, the center seemed to be continuously encroaching upon traditional liberties and forms of self-government from the late Middle

[64] Albareda i Salvadó, *Felipe V.*

[65] To name but a few: Jean Orry, Michel-Jean Amelot, the Princess des Ursins, Jose Patiño, and Melchor de Macanaz.

[66] For a recent overview of the literature, see Beik, "Absolutism."

Ages to the nineteenth century. And it was, of course. Spain was, as I have argued above, part of the European process of the creation of nation-states, and a trend toward stronger and more hierarchical power was one feature of that process. Yet caution is warranted. In the face of francoist oppression, regionalists collapsed "traditional liberties" in the plural in their meaning into universal liberty, the modern concept in the singular. As we have seen, however, the former were essentially corporate special rights that had very little to do with a modern concept of universal freedom of the individual. This is as anachronistic as economists' use of the concept of individual freedom when modeling the economies of the early modern period. The politicization of this discourse has muddied much of the historical debate for perfectly understandable reasons that nevertheless compel the historian to disentangle a complex set of contemporary and historical circumstances.

Much has thus been written on reform projects discussed, planned, and sometimes introduced by the Bourbons in eighteenth-century Spain, on the protagonists at court and elsewhere, and on their implementation or failure in Latin America and the Peninsula.[67] Questions of intent, motivation, plan, and project have taken center stage in that literature. However, for the purpose of the argument discussed here, I will focus primarily on the outcomes on the ground. Did the implementation of reforms, such as it was, result in a substantial unification of the political economy of the Spanish monarchy and thus reduce jurisdictional fragmentation and hence coordination failure?

The analytical means will be a brief discussion of some of the key reforms with their impact (or the lack thereof) on the monetary, customs, and fiscal systems and on market integration. The latter continues the quantitative analysis begun in chapters 3 and 4. Ultimately, market integration can be interpreted as an aggregate measure of the outcome of reforms across geographical units once other important factors, such as distance from port and time trends in transportation costs, are taken into account.

Using the same database of cod prices across Spanish territories and towns, one should thus be able to understand better how and how much the political economy of Spain contributed to the large unexplained differences in market integration indicators observed in chapter 4. It will also help clarify whether the supposed drive toward centralization in the eighteenth century reduced such political economy obstacles.

Money

One of the most fundamental economic rights of European rulers since the Middle Ages was the right and the power to coin their own currency.[68] It

---

[67] For example, Paquette, *Enlightenment, Governance, and Reform*; Lynch, *Bourbon Spain*; Domínguez Ortiz, *Carlos III*; and Onaindía, *La construcción de la nación Española*.

[68] This was a European but not a global phenomenon; Chinese emperors did not claim the monopoly of issue. Irigoin, "Silver Era."

was a basic part of what Europeans understood to be sovereignty, and it was jealously guarded: counterfeiting was equal to high treason and led to capital punishment in practically every polity.[69] The move toward a more unified control over the issue of currency is thus an important indicator of the larger trends. By the mid-seventeenth century, the Iberian monarchy had not experienced any significant unification of its monetary system since the merging of Aragon and Castile in the late fifteenth century. Castile, Aragon, Catalonia, Valencia, Mallorca, and Navarra all issued their own currencies, while the Basque Provinces relied on Castilian coins.[70] The latter were based on a system of a peso of eight *reales* and 272 *mrs*, though different gold coins, accounting units, and small coins complicated the system. In Navarra the unit of account was the *real sencillo*, equivalent to just over half a *real vellón*.[71] The Aragonese territories instead based their currency system on a pound (*libra* of 20 *sueldos/sous* and 240 *dineros*), though here, too, other denominations circulated.

In Castile the circulating medium officially consisted of silver coins and fiat coins made of a copper-silver mix (later without silver), the infamous *vellón*.[72] It is well-known that the latter was subject to long-term severe inflation starting around 1600 and lasting until 1685, interrupted only by violent deflationary measures in 1628, 1642, 1652, and 1664. In the late eighteenth century, inflation returned with the ill-fated attempt at the introduction of the *vales reales*.[73] The *vales* performed as monetized bonds that in practice circulated as fiduciary paper money. Large issues under the pressure of war translated after 1794 into depreciation, and inflation accelerated dramatically after 1800.[74]

Notwithstanding this history of expansion (and subsequent depreciation) of fiat and fiduciary money, Castile was one of the few European polities that experienced hardly any debasement of its silver currency until 1808, save for a very brief period in 1642 and a one-off debasement in 1686 in the context of a reform that eventually achieved the stabilization of the *vellón* currency.[75] The logical outcome of the coexistence of a high-quality silver coin with fiat

---

[69] Private mints were outlawed in Castile in 1494 and the number of royal mints limited to seven. García de Paso, "Estabilización," 49.

[70] A very helpful overview is Feliu, "Monedes de Compte."

[71] The *sencillo* was exactly 64 *mrs*, i.e., 0.53125 *reales vellon*. See Yanguas y Miranda, *Diccionario*, 2:386.

[72] Fiat coins have an intrinsic metallic value that is lower than their face value.

[73] Sardá, *Política monetaria*, 33–42; Tedde de Lorca, "San Carlos."

[74] The bonds traded at face value in the 1780s, yields began to rise in the mid-1790s, and discounts on face value reached about 20 percent in 1798. After massive emissions in 1800 this rose to 50 percent. Stein and Stein, *Edge of Crisis*, 535, 536; Tedde de Lorca, "San Carlos."

[75] García de Paso, "Estabilización." This debasement of Peninsular *reales* also created the double standard that would be maintained until the end of the eighteenth century, whereby Peninsular silver coins, so-called *provinciales*, had 20 percent less silver content than the American ones, the *nacionales*. Smaller changes to the *nacionales* were undertaken in 1726–28, 1737, 1772, and 1786. Vicéns Vives has argued that the latter two were indeed devaluations in all but name. Vicens Vives, *Economic History*.

coin inflation was the disappearance of silver from circulation as Castilians hoarded silver and spent *vellón*. Just as Gresham's law would predict, the bad money drove the good out of circulation.

Economic historians have understandably concentrated on the inflationary effects of the large emissions of fiat currency and the impact monetary instability had on Crown finance and the development of manufacturing and agriculture.[76] Yet it is also clear that the monetary confusion during much of the seventeenth century disintegrated Spanish markets. Silver premia, though broadly moving in the same direction, differed significantly between regions. In 1641 the average premium stipulated for contracts denominated in *vellón* at the Court in Madrid was almost 78 percent over silver, while in Bilbao (Vizcaya) it was 66 percent.[77] For the same year, Feliu has suggested that the premium was 96 percent in Andalusia, 94 in New Castile, and 88 in Old Castile.[78]

In addition to these market distortions *within* the Castilian currency area (which included the Basque Country), *vellón* inflation introduced a further complication into exchanges between Castile, Valencia, Catalonia, Aragon, and Navarra. An example of this effect was illustrated in chapter 4. Prices for *bacalao* in Albacete were markedly more volatile than those in other interior towns, even though the town seemed to be fairly well integrated with the ports and enjoyed some of the lowest price levels. Yet in Albacete, located in southeastern La Mancha on the borders of Valencia and Murcia, the account books of the religious institutions vividly illustrate the complications resulting from multiple systems of coinage and coins, even in the eighteenth century when rates were nominally fixed. Conversions rarely worked at a set rate, and the lack of one or another coin in transactions created multiple sources of error and, one suspects, the occasional opportunistic fraud.[79] The evidence reflects local transactions and suggests that diverse coins and currencies and rapidly changing exchange rates caused at least some transaction costs, though this was possibly more in the form of price volatility than in terms of actually raising price levels.

The rights of the Crown to issue new currency differed substantially between the historic territories. Though the *cortes* of Castile regularly called on the king to limit the issue of *vellón* in order to tame inflation in the sev-

---

[76] Motomura, "The Best and Worst of Currencies"; Drelichman, "Curse of Moctezuma"; Sargent and Velde, *Small Change*, 230–54.

[77] For Madrid, see Serrano Mangas, *Vellón*, appendix 1; for Bilbao, see AHPV, Leg. 5018, s.f.

[78] The comparisons are based on Hamilton's price data and therefore should be used with caution, as mentioned in chapter 2. Feliu, *Precios y salarios*, vol. 2.

[79] The account books of the Monastery of the Franciscanos Menores Descalzos Nuestra Señora de Llanos in Albacete refer constantly to conversion issues. Occasionally prices and their conversions between currencies were patently incorrect, such as in 1725. AHN, Clero Libro 23, s.f.. Monetary issues also repeatedly gave rise to conflicts with supplies such as those the monastery settled with Fernando Espinoza over a load of fish in 1750. See AHN, Clero Libro 38, s.f.

enteenth century, they had no direct power to stop the monarch from issuing more coins. Instead, they had to negotiate lower seigneurage for other forms of taxation. The Basques had no rights to issue coin but could outlaw the use of particular Castilian coins, which in effect meant they could veto royal policy but not shape it. In Navarra and Aragon (until 1707), by contrast, the right to determine the issue of new coins rested squarely with the *cortes*.[80]

This had unintended consequences. Strictly speaking Castilian petty coins were not legal tender in Aragon, and small change was constantly in short supply.[81] Refusing the demands of the Crown and of the town of Zaragoza to issue more or debased currency, the Diputación of the Aragonese *corz* had the Zaragoza (Aragon) mint produce coins of such high quality and stable silver content that they were immediately driven out of circulation, hoarded under people's mattresses, or, more often, shipped over the French border.[82] A constitutional conflict ensued between the estates, which represented largely the interests of recipients of money rents, and the town of Zaragoza, which wanted to foster trade through monetary reform.

The Crown sided with the town but proved unable to override the estates. The Aragonese population paid dearly for their *corz*'s monetary "prudence." As they repeatedly complained, the only circulating coins in the later seventeenth century were particularly debased Valencian ones or *peruleros*, a heavily debased Peruvian coin.[83] In monetary matters basic market forces were much stronger than in trade because other transaction costs, such as transport, were so low. Smuggling coin was easy and small change was perennially short in early modern Europe, giving an added incentive to the illegal introduction and circulation of coins that were not legal tender.[84] This and the workings of Gresham's law made the theoretical autonomy in minting an illusion for the small Aragonese territory, situated as it was between Catalonia, Valencia, Castile, Navarra, and France.

Various measures between 1680 and 1686 eventually brought *vellón* inflation in Castile down sharply. The silver premium was stabilized through the issue of coins with higher intrinsic value. Silver was coaxed back into the market through a measured debasement of the silver *real*.[85] From the late 1680s until 1794, Castile experienced no serious monetary fluctuations. Catalonia, too, had experienced severe monetary disturbances in the second

---

[80] The *cortes* of Navarra and the king agreed to issue small coin in the cortes of 1724–26, 1743–44, 1757, 1766, 1780–81, and 1794–97. Indeed as in the 1780s it was often the king who needed extra convincing before giving in to the *cortes*' proposed legislation. Navarra, *Cuadernos*, 1:635–36, 2:132–633.

[81] Mateos Royo, "Burden."

[82] Ibid.

[83] Ibid. For Valencian coins, see Feliu, "Monedes de Compte," 463.

[84] On the problem of small coin, see Sargent and Velde, *Small Change*.

[85] Vilar, *Oro*; García de Paso, "Estabilización," 70–76. However, the debasement created two types of pesos, old ones of 10 new *reales* and new ones of 8.

half of the seventeenth century, reaching their worst period during the Catalan secession from the Spanish monarchy in the early 1650s. As a consequence, the valuations of silver and regional *vellón* currency, the minting of which was controlled by the Consell de Cent of Barcelona, were permanently uncoupled and silver was repeatedly debased.[86] However, it appears that the post-1686 stabilization of the Castilian currency began to have an impact on the reigns of the Crown of Aragon, increasingly stabilizing the exchange rates.[87] As in Navarra, in monetary matters market forces limited the power of territorial institutions.

During the War of the Spanish Succession Charles of Austria's government used the Barcelona mint to issue his own Castilian *reales*, thus emphasizing his claim to sovereignty over all possessions of the Spanish monarchy.[88] Yet between 1705 and 1714 Philip V, the new Bourbon ruler, successively asserted his sovereignty over the minting of circulating medium. He restricted the issue of coins in the mints of the Aragonese territories, while at the same time closing all mints in Castile except those of Madrid, Segovia, and Seville.[89] Catalans, Valencians, Aragonese, and Mallorquins continued to use valuations in pounds/shilling/pence, and throughout the eighteenth century a bewildering number of diverse coins continued to circulate. Yet in 1737 and 1751, respectively, the exchange rates of Catalan and Valencian fiat currencies to Castilian silver were fixed.[90] For the most part, exchange rates between coins were stable and by 1741 José Inocencio Aparicio could offer readers a printed manual that allowed them to manageably "reduce" an impressive number of "effective, as well as imaginary [units of account], extinct, or non-existing" coins to their value in any other form of legal tender still circulating in the reigns of Castile, Catalonia, Valencia, Aragon, and Mallorca.[91]

The historical record suggests that the territories of the Spanish Crown became indeed more integrated in monetary matters from the late seventeenth century onward and moved a little closer to Philip V's aim to "reduce all [his] reigns of Spain to the uniformity of the same laws, practices, customs and Courts." However, more direct royal control over the mints of the Crown of Aragon was only one factor in this development. Market forces were more important. Monetary historians of Spain agree that the crucial stabilization of the 1680s in fact created a Castilian monetary standard that would become the point of reference for the non-Castilian territories.[92] Monetary stabilization was an achievement of the Habsburg period, not the early Bourbons.

[86] Feliu, "Monedes de Compte," 459.

[87] Mateos Royo, "Burden."

[88] The use of the power to mint by competing authorities as a means of establishing sovereignty as well as a source of income was repeated during the Napoleonic Wars. See Sardá, *Política monetaria*, 27–42.

[89] Ruíz Trapero, "La reforma monetaria," 390.

[90] Vilar, *Crecimiento*, 227.

[91] Aparicio, *Norte fixo*, 4.

[92] Vilar, *Crecimiento*.

Notably, neither Philip nor his successors ever established a unified coinage system.

Though European historians still largely associate Castile with the inflationary episodes of fiat currency between 1600 and 1680, the unparalleled stability of the Spanish silver peso meant that by the eighteenth century at the latest it became the international exchange standard par excellence.[93] Indeed, the history of the peso is another powerful reminder that the NIE story of a predatory Spanish state flies in the face of the facts. Spanish coins articulated not only European trade but also global commerce between Europe, South and North America, and Asia. Merchants and rulers from China to the newly independent United States obviously trusted the Spanish Crown to maintain the silver standard of its coins until the end of the ancien régime.[94] Therefore, it is difficult to see how, notwithstanding formal control over the currency, any of the non-Castilian territories could have maintained an independent monetary policy. The Aragonese experienced this already in the late seventeenth century. The markets for circulating medium were too easily integrated for artificial barriers, erected between monetary systems as an assertion of political sovereignty, to survive.

The government of the much-maligned last Habsburg, Carlos II, had laid the basis for a notably more integrated and stable monetary system already in the 1680s, two decades before the Bourbon takeover. The Castilian reforms rather than a decreed formal unification of the monetary standards provided a stable monetary anchor. In money matters market forces were much stronger than in trade. Transactions costs associated with the illegal introduction or export of coins were minimal. In the bad years of Castilian *vellón* inflation coins could always be slipped over borders. The incentive to take good coin out of circulation played into the hands of the smugglers, too. At the same time, reforms in the larger Castilian economy evidently had a salutary effect on the non-Castilian territories, enabling the territorial authorities to reestablish a standard. In border towns, such as Albacete, the costs associated with the physical coexistence of different coins continued to be visible in higher volatility. Beyond that, however, in money matters jurisdictional fragmentation mattered little as soon as the largest currency area adopted a stable standard. In other words, the transaction costs associated with jurisdictional fragmentation in the currency markets were reduced effectively because reform in *one* territory was enough to let the market do the rest.

[93] For an excellent recent investigation of the relatively (by European standards) minor adjustments in silver content, see Nogues-Marco, "Bullionism."

[94] Irigoin, "Silver Era." The almost complete confidence that the Spanish peso inspired has gone almost unnoticed among monetary historians. When the North American Continental Congress began issuing the continental dollar after 1775, it naturally promised the bearer to receive its equivalent in "Spanish milled dollars" (pesos) at the date of maturity. Contemporaries quickly came to distrust the ability of the U.S. revolutionary government to repay its debt and discounted the paper. Yet nobody doubted that the Spanish milled dollars against which the issue was pegged would retain their silver value.

Internal and External Customs

If monetary integration was more market driven than institutionally designed, the internal customs and tax borders within the Spanish monarchy were a clear object of political debate and decision making. Eighteenth-century observers paid particular attention to two issues: the so-called *puertos secos* (dry ports: inland customs points) and the external customs tariffs and rights to trade in the seaports. The internal barriers had attracted criticism from influential advisors such as the Conde de Gondomar and Juan Ortiz as early as the sixteenth century.[95] By the eighteenth century mercantilists like Uztáriz lauded Colbert's attempts to free internal trade from all sorts of levies and taxes, lamenting the lack of similar efforts in Spain.[96] A number of tariff and tax reforms occurred in the later seventeenth century and especially under the Bourbon dynasty after 1705, but as we will see, assessing their impact is a complex affair.

In an ideal world, we would study the short- and long-term impact of Bourbon reforms on trade diversion and revenue collection, as well as that on territorial tax incidence and costs of administering the system. Such a comparison before and after individual reforms were introduced could help us understand the transaction costs imposed on the economy by the jurisdictional fragmentation inherited from the Habsburg age. Unfortunately, many of the reforms, those that became permanent as well as those that were short-lived, took place during or immediately after the War of the Spanish Succession. In this environment of severe military, political, and economic turmoil it is virtually impossible to assess the short- and medium-term results of any reform. Thus, a second-best research strategy is required. This is a comparison of the trends of the impact of taxation and customs over the long run, which will be the center of the analysis that follows. Did the cumulative effect of the reforms substantially alter the burden customs and tariffs placed on different parts of the economy? Did they change the overall tax burden in the various territories toward a more uniform and "rational" system? Again, the underlying assumption is that both fiscal data and measures of market integration can serve as proxies for the aggregate results of reforms.

The interior customs, or dry ports, that separated territories of the Spanish monarchy internally rather than on the coast or at a foreign border had emerged out of a variety of historic processes. Some originated in the Middle Ages, others in the period of the unification of the Hispanic reigns under the Crown of Castile in the late fifteenth century.[97] Two different paths had led toward fiscal fragmentation between the regions. The first and more obvious one was that represented by the four territories of the Crown of Aragon on

---

[95] Grice-Hutchinson, *Early Economic Thought*, 159–60. For Gondomar, see Sureda Carrión, *La hacienda castellana*, 123.

[96] Grice-Hutchinson, *Early Economic Thought*, 163.

[97] For a description of the main lines in 1646, see Larraz López, *Mercantilismo*, 149–52.

the one hand and Navarra (and Portugal until 1640) on the other. Here the terms of unification through dynastic marriage in the case of the Aragonese Crown (1479) and military conquest in the case of Navarra (1515) and Portugal (1580) stipulated clearly that existing fiscal and representative systems would not be changed and the traditional "liberties" (*fueros*) not touched. Thus by the late seventeenth century the formerly "international" borders still functioned essentially in the same way, with export and import duties being charged—and spent—by the Castilian, Navarrese, and Aragonese treasuries independently. But there were also still interior customs functioning on the boundaries between the old reign of Castile, on the one hand, and Galicia, Cantabria (known as *Cuatro villas de la mar*), and Asturias on the other.[98] Also, in the southern half of the Peninsula some *puertos secos* seem to have survived until the end of the Habsburg era between Castile and Murcia, though probably not between Castile and Andalusia.[99]

The second source of fiscal fragmentation is exemplified by the Basque Provinces. These were often referred to as the "exempted provinces," a somewhat misleading label since they were not exempted from all taxation; however, although all three provinces had become a part of the Castilian Crown by the thirteenth century, they were explicitly exempted from Castilian customs.[100] Historically their poor agricultural basis had served as justification for their privileged position; early on they depended on maritime supplies of grain and other staple foods.[101] These rights had been enshrined in the *fueros* and meant that goods entering (leaving) the Peninsula through Basque ports had to pay their customs not at port but when passing the internal border between the Basque Provinces and Navarra or Castile. Since there were no customs points between the three Basque Provinces or on their coasts the territories were de facto a large free-trade zone.

Isabella of Castile failed in the late fifteenth century to alter the Basque status of exemption, and none of her Habsburg successors dared touch the rights to their own customs and taxation in Aragon, Navarra, and the Basque Country again beyond minor adjustments.[102] Philip V's decision to abolish the *puertos secos* in the northern half of the Peninsula between 1707 and 1721

[98] Muñoz Pérez, "Mapa," 773. For the fish trade from Galicia, see Cubillo de la Puente, *El pescado*, 220.

[99] It is possible that a number of taxes that only applied in the former Reino de Granada, the last Moorish polity in the peninsula until its conquest by Castile in 1492, resulted in selective customs posts on its interior boundaries, though Muñoz Pérez found no evidence for such posts. Muñoz Pérez, "Mapa."

[100] Kasper, *Baskische Geschichte*, 30–60.

[101] This remained a standard defense even if trade data clearly show that at least Vizcaya stopped importing large amounts of grain after the 1620s and 1630s. Grafe, *Mundo ibérico*, 129–30.

[102] These included the stationing of *jueces* or *alcaldes de saca* in some of the larger ports of the exempt provinces and on the French Navarrese border who were entitled to search and apprehend goods that fell under the category of "forbidden exports," mainly bullion, horses, and other military equipment. Torquemanda Sánchez, "Los Puertos Secos."

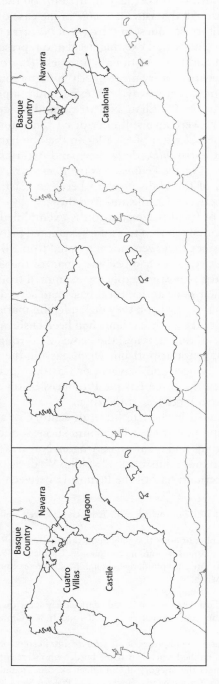

Figure 5.1
Internal customs borders pre-1707 (left), in 1718 (middle), and after 1722 (right).

was thus the first attempt at reform in over two hundred years. Decrees of 1707 effectively abolished the customs borders between Valencia, Aragon, and Castile. After the capitulation of Barcelona this was extended to Catalonia, and in 1717 a famous Real Instrucción of the king to the administrator of customs demanded that *all* internal customs be relocated to the coastline.[103]

The abolition of the internal customs quickly ran into problems in all of the affected territories, however, which were also home to many of the most important trade networks. Catalan external tariffs were much lower for some products than those of Castile, Aragon, and Valencia. The abolition of the internal customs thus enticed trade diversion when Castilian, Aragonese, and Valencian merchants began to take advantage of the more moderate Catalan customs. The Crown, worried about lower revenues, was paradoxically forced to erect new internal customs borders between Catalonia and its neighbors, Aragon and Valencia, in 1722.[104] The episode laid open an obvious problem that was to persist in various parts of the Peninsula throughout the eighteenth century. As long as the Crown did not have full control over the maritime and overland external tariffs, the abolition of internal *puertos secos* had complex, unintended consequences. It stimulated trade, but this was not revenue neutral from the point of view of the Crown. On the one hand, trade flowed increasingly through low tariff ports in Catalonia. On the other hand, the Crown had limited control over the revenue produced in Catalonia even after the abolition of the Catalan representative institutions.

Thus trade diversion affected the aggregate revenue of the *real hacienda*. In addition, trade diversion was likely to erode the political support for the abolition of the *puertos secos* especially in the regions that bordered Catalonia. Add to this that external customs differed not only between the historic territories but also, especially before the 1740s, within Castile thanks to the different application of tariffs by the tax farmers.[105] Though it is virtually impossible to quantify the degree of trade diversion caused by the reforms, the establishment of the new set of *puertos secos* in 1722 offers at least some evidence that regional authorities thought the problem was serious. Nevertheless, in the case of the Aragonese kingdoms the abolition of the internal customs was there to stay. From the later 1710s onward customs barriers between the territories of the Aragonese reigns and those of Castile had largely disappeared.

That was more than could be said about the internal customs further north. The 1717 decree also ordered that the *puertos secos* of the Basque Provinces were to be transferred to the Gulf of Biscay, effectively abolishing the free-trade-zone-status of the territories. The king anticipated opposition and insisted with his administrator of customs (*administrador de las rentas*

---

[103] "Real Instrucción de 31 Agosto 1717."
[104] Torquemanda Sánchez, "Los Puertos Secos," 1029–30; Muñoz Pérez, "Mapa," 755; Mercader Riba, "Organismo piloto 2," 538.
[105] Muñoz Pérez, "Mapa," 765.

generales), the Marqués de Campoflorido, that he was determined to break any Basque resistance.

> If [the Basques] will not accede voluntarily [*buenamente*], you shall make them understand that I will have to take all those measures that are most convenient to my royal service . . . , diverting the trade of Bilbao, including the wool trade as well as all other goods, to the port of Santander, . . . and you will make sure that its implementation is tight [*estrechar las diligencias cuanto sea posible*].[106]

The king effectively blackmailed the Basques with the threat of diverting all legal trade from the largest northern Spanish port, the Basque town of Bilbao, to Santander in Cantabria (Castile), where the transfer of the internal customs to the coastline had created less resistance.

Notwithstanding royal determination and bullying, the reform had a short life in the Basque Country. Implemented in the spring of 1718, it was all but abandoned by 1721. The transfer of the customs posts almost immediately provoked popular unrest in Vizcaya and Guipúzcoa, the so-called *matxinada* of 1718.[107] In March the boats used by the customs officials in the small Vizcayan ports of Bermeo and Algorta went up in flames.[108] Historians of the *matxinada* disagree about the origins of the popular response, which was driven by laborers from the rural areas. Fear—justified or not—that the introduction of Castilian tariffs would increase prices seems to have been involved.[109]

The highest representative of the Crown in the *señorio de* Vizcaya, the *corregidor*, instantly ceded to the demands of the crowd. He also wisely affirmed his opposition to the transfer of the customs posts and effectively undermined the royal instructions, invoking the right to refuse execution of harmful royal orders. The local elites, by contrast, resisted the crowds of irate workers likely because a transfer of the major export trade to another town was a real threat to their prosperity. Unrest lasted a week in the larger towns, and though it flared up again occasionally during the summer, it was over altogether within six months. Yet by the time the *matxinada* had run its course, fifteen people in Vizcaya had met a violent death. The victims were all local officials, among them the highest representative of the *señorio*, the mayor of Bilbao, and the town's first alderman. Here and in Guipúzcoa the challenge was to the local elites, not the Crown. The populace looted and burned down buildings owned by the local oligarchy, whom they blamed

[106] "Real Instrucción de 31 Agosto 1717." The king to the Marqués de Campoflorido, quoted in ibid., 774. My translation.

[107] Otazu, *Igualitarismo*, 225–58.

[108] Porres, "Hermandad a la provincia," 294–95.

[109] In Vizcaya in particular the revolt seems to have been driven by the decline of the rural iron-producing sector. The name *matxinada* was derived from the local term for iron workers. Otazu, *Igualitarismo*, 253. Zabala argues that the revolt was instigated by the mercantile elites, who kept a low profile to avoid punishment in the form of a diversion of trade to Santander. Zabala Uriarte, *Mundo urbano*, 93–94.

"for selling out the fatherland [*patria*] in consenting to them [the decrees that transferred the customs to the coast]."[110] The Crown eventually grew concerned enough to dispatch three thousand royal troops to the territory in the autumn according to some historians, but by then the revolt had apparently run its course.[111]

This unrest was enough for Philip's government to repeal the reform and restore the customs to the borders between the Basque Provinces and Castile. The government justified its *volte face* with both rising collection costs of the new regime as well as falling customs receipts, but it was clear that the real cause of both of these was popular resistance. The king also wisely and publicly restated his respect for the Basque *fueros*.[112] By 1727 a formal agreement was reached with Vizcaya and Guipúzcoa, in which the Crown recognized their "exempt" status; a similar accord with Alava had come into effect in 1723.[113]

For a while resolute royal initiative coupled with threats to the dominant Bilbao mercantile interests seemed to have a substantial effect on the political oligarchy, especially in the *señorio* of Vizcaya. Royal victory over the rights of the traditional territories seemed almost in reach. However, the notion of traditional local representation was too strong for the oligarchy to become an effective enforcer of the king's demands. The royal representatives in the Basque territories seem to have grasped this very quickly. The hierarchies of power were too flat for the Crown to instrumentalize the regional oligarchy, even if the latter had responded to the threat to its livelihood on this occasion.

Attempts to abolish the *puertos secos* separating Navarra from Aragon, Castile, and the Basque Provinces were equally stillborn. In Navarra, as in the Basque Provinces, fiscal independence had traditionally been justified with the poor agricultural base. In addition, Navarra was an inland territory with no access to the sea and thus relied on Guipúzcoan, Aragonese, Castilian, or French imports.[114] There were no tariffs at all for Navarrese merchants importing goods, none on victuals in general, but ad valorem customs on other imports and exports.[115] Navarra was thus not "exempt" but

[110] Report by Don Enrique-Antonio de Arratabe about the revolt in Escoriaza (Guipúzcoa) cited in Otazu, *Igualitarismo*, 247. My translation.

[111] According to Porres the fifteen assassinations resulted in thirty-two death sentences, though it is not clear if these were executed. While the Basque historiography tends to refer to the reaction as severe repression, it seems moderate given the large number of high-profile murders. Porres, "Hermandad a la provincia," 295.

[112] Zabala Uriarte, *Mundo urbano*, 91–96.

[113] Porres, "Hermandad a la provincia," 296. Muñoz Pérez, "Mapa," 776, argues that an agreement with Alava was not reached until in 1748.

[114] For this and what follows, see Solbes Ferri, *Rentas Reales de Navarra*, 57–87.

[115] Imports of all items that were "eatable, drinkable or could be burned" (timber) were free of charge also if imported by a non-Navarrese. Other imports paid 3 percent ad valorem. The treasury of Navarra (*comptos*) imposed a 5 percent ad valorem tariff on all exports. Exceptions applied to the most important exports, wool, wine, and iron, which paid much lower duties, and to grain, the export of which was essentially prohibited without special permit.

maintained its own administration of its customs, known as *tablas*. Castile and Aragon levied tariffs through their respective administrations at their borders with Navarra (the *diezmos*) of around 15 percent ad valorem. Tariffs on the border with Guipúzcoa were probably minimal for most but not all goods, while the French tariffs were levied on the border in the Pyrenees. This special privilege turned Navarra into an obvious conduit of goods smuggled from France via Navarra into Castile and into a permanent headache for the Castilian hacienda.

Its privileged access to the French markets meant that Navarra probably benefited greatly from the War of the Spanish Succession. The general insecurity affected maritime transport, which made the otherwise cumbersome transport across the Pyrenees worth merchants' while.[116] The 1718 decree thus changed the economic situation fundamentally in Navarra by transferring the customs points to the French border at the Pyrenees while declaring free trade between Navarra and its Iberian neighbors. The implementation was placed in the hands of the new office of *intendente*, one of the administrative novelties the Bourbon monarchy sought to introduce across the Peninsula and to which we will return.[117]

In contrast to the Basque Country, the resistance against the new customs borders and the *intendentes* was not popular but carried by the *foral* institutions in Navarra. But it achieved the same result: by January 1, 1723, the *intendentes* were abolished and the collection points of the customs returned to the former interior location on a line along the river Ebro. Navarra offered the Crown a few concessions aimed at reducing rampant contraband from France into Castile via Navarra. Navarrese were still exempt from most import duties but were henceforth required to submit to checks by the customs officials. Also, a new tariff schedule was introduced that covered more goods and limited the time-honored tradition of individual agreements between merchants and tax farmers. Yet the abolition of the internal customs with Navarra was there to stay until the second half of the nineteenth century.

It stands to reason, however, that the institutional resistance in Navarra was not the only motive for the Crown to go back on its own reform agenda. Customs revenues were the *only* tax income levied in Navarra that by right belonged to the Royal Treasury rather than to the Navarrese. Hence Madrid used them to defray the costs of the royal administration of the Reino de Navarra and to finance some military expenditures.[118] Thanks to the receipts from the customs, the Crown's apparatus of governance in Navarra was almost self-financing. Any shortfalls had to be covered out of royal customs revenue of Castile.[119] Lower tariff returns in Navarra thus presented the Royal Treasury with the prospect of having to increase substantially its trans-

---

[116] Solbes Ferri, *Rentas Reales de Navarra*, 95.

[117] Ibid., 155–61.

[118] García Zúñiga, *Hacienda*, 41; Solbes Ferri, *Rentas Reales de Navarra*, 96–97.

[119] García Zúñiga, *Hacienda*, 41.

fers to the Reino. In view of the tight fiscal situation of the royal hacienda, the Crown could simply not afford the abolition of the internal tariffs of Navarra as long as no alternative stream of income was available.

Overall the new Bourbon dynasty had achieved only a very limited fiscal unification of the territories. Its intentions ran into trouble with the traditional particularism of its subjects on the one hand and fiscal reality on the other: if territories were supposed to be self-financing, they had to be given the possibility to raise revenue. Customs between territories of the former Crowns of Aragon and Castile had been permanently abolished. Elsewhere, resistance to the abolition of the *puertos secos* had proved too strong. For less than two years in the late 1710s it looked as if these internal collection points might become a thing of the past in the Iberian reigns of the Spanish monarchy. Alas, they were never fully abolished in Navarra and the Basque Provinces and were officially reinstated by late 1722. The open revolt against the new dynasty in Aragon, Catalonia, and Valencia allowed Philip to portray his subjects as having reneged on the compact between king and subjects and thus to invoke the right of just conquest. This "treason" was instrumental in overriding their traditional privileges. In Navarra and the Basque Provinces, which had remained loyal, no such claim could be made, and it seems that without this justification the Bourbon king was back to where his Habsburg predecessors had been: he would have to negotiate.

Even in Catalonia, however, the abolition of internal customs proved impractical since the Crown could not impose a common external tariff. Thus trade diversion, customs avoidance, and smuggling were rife and increasing over the eighteenth century.[120] Ironically, the end of the *puertos secos* made the port of Barcelona more attractive: it now combined the lower Catalan external tariffs with free imports into Castile from Catalonia. When the Royal Treasury created new internal customs in Fraga, on the Aragonese-Catalan boundary, and in Tortosa, on the Catalan-Valencian boundary, in order to collect the difference between Catalan and Castilian external tariffs, it implicitly acknowledged its own failure.[121] As Mercader Riba has pointed out, the abolition of political institutions of the principality of Catalonia had only a limited impact on the ability of the Crown to change the regulation of commerce: "The spirit of the decree of suppression of the internal borders was thus debilitated [through the introduction of the *puertos* in Fraga and Tortosa]. With the *Generalitat* [the old *foral* institution] or without it, things apparently continued the same way."[122]

Throughout the Bourbon period the Crown and its treasury continued to choose ways of alleviating the most egregious fiscal injustices without removing their origin, usually the traditional rights of territories or towns. Instead it created additional institutions, such as the new customs between Catalonia

---

[120] Muñoz Pérez, "Mapa."

[121] Ibid., 755n724.

[122] Mercader Riba, "Organismo piloto 2," 538. My translation.

and the other Aragonese territories, to remedy its inability to achieve real unification. The result was often not a simplification, unification, and centralization of the fiscal system but yet another layer of rights devolved that would in
due course turn into "traditional" freedoms that were ever harder to remove
and with it further fiscal fragmentation. This was a feature of reforms in the
local context, as in the larger regional setting; the port of Cartagena (Reino
de Murcia) had obtained a reduction of its customs rates in return for its
role in the construction of the navy yard it supported. The consequence was
predictably trade diversion from nearby Alicante (Reino de Valencia), and
its aggrieved town authorities did not cease to point out the injustice. Alas,
instead of revoking Cartagena's privilege, the Crown issued the Real Cedula
of September 29, 1742. This established a new "customs border" on the main
road out of Cartagena to protect Alicante from the unfair competition.[123]

The outcome of Bourbon reforms of internal and external customs was
complex and often contradictory. The actual administration of customs
improved markedly; by mid-century the Crown had managed to regain
control over the collection of external customs (*puertos de mar*) from tax
farmers in Castile, for example. But superior administrative technique went
hand in hand with additional layers of complexity. As Muñoz Pérez has
pointed out, the first Bourbons had embarked on an ambitious program of
customs reform to alleviate the burden that domestic trade and consumption
taxes placed on their Spanish subjects. By the 1760s and 1770s this strategy
had failed entirely. Customs receipts accounted for only 15 percent of total
Peninsular Spanish Crown income in 1770 (compared to about 30 percent
in Britain), and exemptions granted to new industries aggravated the trend
in fragmenting and lowering the yields further.[124] Insistent attempts made
by reformers to use a more active mercantilist tariff policy along the lines
practiced by the English and the French only exacerbated the impact of
the *puertos secos* because the Spanish system allowed too much local and
regional decision making for such efforts to work as they did in France or
England.[125] In the end, the inability of the Crown to overcome the resistance
of historic territories and towns ensured that the fiscal burden remained
overwhelmingly on the backs of local consumers.

Taxation and the Historic Territories

The Crown's continued need for negotiation is even more obvious when looking beyond customs and at the tax system established in the historical territories of the Spanish Crown more generally. Historic precedent was strong, but

---

[123] Ibid., 755n724.

[124] Estimate represents percentage of revenue from customs and wool taxes out of total
receipts minus transfers from the Americas and carryovers based on Merino Navarro, *Las
cuentas*. For Britain, see O'Brien, "Political Economy," 9.

[125] Muñoz Pérez, "Mapa."

contemporary political interests not only protected these but applied them to entirely new taxes as well, as we will see. In the sixteenth century different constitutional structures in Naples, the Low Countries, and Castile had produced vastly different outcomes in their fiscal negotiations with Charles V.[126] In each territory some form of representative assembly existed, but their role and interests were strikingly different. In the Netherlands, both the large towns and the provinces were invested with authority to negotiate with the Crown or its representative in Brussels, making it virtually impossible to extract revenue beyond that used within the territory. Charles V famously complained that in the Low Countries, "everyone demands privileges that are contrary to my sovereignty [*hauteur*], as if I were their companion and not their lord."[127] In Naples, the nobility was far more powerful and could be co-opted by the Crown more easily against towns and territories.[128]

In the seventeenth century these problems persisted unabated even though it is clear that the Crown, its *validos,* and public commentators were increasingly concerned with equitable and moderate taxation. Indeed there were several well-known projects to achieve a more uniform tax contribution of the various territories.[129] The first systematic attempt was undertaken by the *valido* of Philip IV, the Conde Duque de Olivares.[130] Under the increasing financial and military pressure of the Thirty Years' War (1618–48), Olivares tried to vastly raise the general fiscal contribution of the non-Castilian territories, which had been either nonexistent or minor.[131] The Catalan and Portuguese representations in particular, however, refused to vote additional taxes beyond anything used in their own territories. Unable to overrule provincial opposition, Olivares proceeded to allocate the costs of raising troops directly to the historic territories under the "Union of Arms" in an attempt to avoid the thorny issue of raising taxes. The result of his endeavors to circumvent what the historic territories considered their right to refuse contributions was that both Portugal and Catalonia rose in revolt in the 1640s, and Palermo and Naples in 1647.[132]

Portugal was eventually lost at the end of a long and costly struggle. The Masaniello Revolt in Naples was suppressed only after it had run its course. Meanwhile, Catalonia seceded for a time, shortly as a republic then as a territory controlled by France, but returned to Spain in 1652 after a less than pleasant experience with domestic strife and French indirect rule that turned out to be considerably more meddlesome than "Spanish" notionally

[126] Tracy, *Emperor Charles.*

[127] Ibid., 53.

[128] Ibid., 56–62.

[129] Sureda Carrión, *La hacienda castellana,* 77–78, 113–17.

[130] Elliott, *Olivares*; Elliott, *Catalans*; Valladares, *Felipe IV.*

[131] Gelabert, *La bolsa del rey.*

[132] Considerable uncertainty exists around a purported secessionist uprising under the leadership of two of the most powerful Andalusian grandees, the Dukes of Medina Sidonia and Ayamonte, which allegedly failed to muster much regional support.

direct rule. The Spanish Crown's reaction to the Catalonian experiment in secession was surprisingly mild and mirrored that in Naples. A few leaders were punished severely, but for the second half of the seventeenth century the Crown largely left Catalonia to its own devices in what has been described as the *neo-foral* period.[133] As Elliott argued, paraphrasing the seventeenth-century *arbistrista* González de Cellorigo, "such strength as it [the Spanish monarchy] possessed derived from its weakness."[134]

In the aftermath of the turbulent and damaging 1640s and 1650s, the monarchy explicitly respected the *fueros* and traditional rights of Catalonia, Valencia, Aragon, Mallorca, Navarra, Castile, Guipúzcoa, Vizcaya, and Alava, as well as the traditions of less independent Galicia and Murcia in the second half of the seventeenth century. In some cases this period actually saw a strengthening of regional rights, not just de facto but also *de iure*. The most notable instance was Guipúzcoa, which for the first time issued a written version of its privileges in 1696.[135] Elsewhere, increased control of *foral* institutions, over taxation in particular, created a similar shift in power toward the regions and away from the center.[136] The later seventeenth century, possibly the worst moment for early modern Spanish Crown finances, saw many proposals on how to reform the tax system and achieve more interregional equality, but they were rarely acted upon.[137] The Crown was unable even in this most dire fiscal situation to overrule the resistance from the historic territories.

The counsel from mercantilist advisors was, however, still to achieve at least some fiscal integration among the historic territories. Brunel's *Voyage* commented on the increasingly desperate attempts of the Crown to raise money in the 1650s in the face of resistance in all reigns, including Castile.

> Before the King went to Aranjuez [the royal summer residence], he assembled the Estates of both Castiles, which consist of the Deputies of 22 Towns, each Town sending two. Such Assemblies are called las Cortes. The King made them a Speech, and told them, that of the ten Millions of Gold, his Kingdoms yearly supply him with, not above three came into his Coffers, and necessities of State considered,

---

[133] There was a pattern. Revolts elsewhere from the Basque Provinces (the *matxinadas* of 1642, 1719, and 1766) to Valencia (the Second Germania, 1693), to Alto Peru (the Tupac Amaru Rebellion, 1780) and New Granada (the Comuneros, 1779) always elicited a similar response: severe violence against the perceived leaders (especially in Alto Peru) and an attempt at reconciliation with the territory. This could even be maintained for the *motín de Esquilache* (1766), which was accompanied by uprisings in about seventy cities and involved as many as 30,000–40,000 people. The king had to flee skirmishes between troops and townspeople in Madrid that left forty dead. Eight "leaders" were garrotted in Zaragoza before the king asked to stay all executions.

[134] Elliott, *Imperial Spain*, 352.

[135] Gorosábel and Echegaray, *Las cosas memorables de Guipúzcoa*, book 4, 302–5; *Nueva Recopilación de los fueros de Guipúzcoa*.

[136] See, e.g., for Navarra, Solbes Ferri, *Rentas Reales de Navarra*, 55–56, and Mugártegui Eguia, *Hacienda*. For Guipúzcoa, see Bilbao, "Provincias exentas," 76ff.

[137] Matilla Tascon, *La única contribución*, chapter 1.

it was his pleasure they should consult of wayes to bring the entire sum into his hands. That to this purpose every Town and Province should take care themselves to bring their proportion into his Exchequer, where he willed them to suppress many of the Officers that managed his Revenue, and devoured the greatest part of it: after this he also demanded some augmentation. The Cortes met, and laboured in this affair, but it was much feared they would not consent to such a suppression, . . . it was believed they would not think the people able to pay any more, the miserie and poverty of the Country considered. In the mean time this King, (his ten Millions of crowns excepted) draws little or nothing from the People; and Navarre, Aragon, and the Kingdom of Valentia, (not united to the Castiles) are not thought to bring up above two Millions.[138]

In the late 1680s, a new attempt was made to remedy the situation under the direction of the Conde de Oropesa, *valido* of Carlos II. But by then the emphasis had changed substantially. Whereas Olivares's plans assumed that equalizing the fiscal contribution of the territories would increase the total tax take and thus strengthen the Royal Treasury, Oropesa's thoughts implied the opposite.

> It seems to me against reason, Christianity, convenience, and politics that the poor Castilians are not free [from over-taxation] just as the Aragonese, Catalans, Valencians, Navarrese and Biscayans, no matter how obedient they are, how miserable and most rigorously [fiscally] oppressed, given that they preserved these kingdoms in far away places fighting with their blood and contributing with their properties.[139]

Oropesa had essentially accepted the impossibility of increasing non-Castilian taxation. In order to achieve a degree of fiscal equality between territories it was therefore necessary to *decrease* Castilian taxation. The foundations for the lowering of the tax burden in the late seventeenth century, discussed in chapter 1, and the subsequent (relative) prudence of the Crown's treasury directly emanated from the realization that a "just" fiscal system in a governance system of such flat hierarchies was always going to be at the lowest common denominator.

Oropesa formulated the contradiction between fiscal ambition and Spanish political economy with notable clarity. Political and fiscal unification were advocated by contemporary mercantilist writers everywhere in Europe because they were seen as a means of increasing the fiscal revenues of the Crown by wresting taxes from towns, historic territories, and other corporate bodies, and this is how economic historians have approached the topic. The strong political rights of the historic territories in the Spanish composite state, however, made it impossible to unify *and* increase taxation. A degree of unification could only be achieved at the expense of lower overall taxation. Paradoxically, mercantilist policies threatened to make the state fiscally

---

[138] Brunel and Aerssen, *Journey.*
[139] Quoted in Artola, *La hacienda*, 216–17n211. My translation.

weaker rather than stronger in Spain. They were thus often a practical impossibility in a time of extreme fiscal distress, and that meant in Spain at least for the entire seventeenth century.[140]

The question remains if the abolition of some of the *foral* institutions (1707–14) was a game changer in fiscal policy. The creation of a new institutional setup in the Aragonese territories under the Nueva Planta presented the new Bourbon regime with the possibility of increasing the share of revenues derived from those territories for the first time. Fiscal reforms, however, necessitated the introduction of new intermediate royal administrations, which Spain lacked. The Nueva Planta left territorial borders unchanged (with a few exceptions), but the top political posts were reformed. The viceroys of Aragon, Valencia, Catalonia, and Mallorca were replaced with captain generals and governors, though these had to share power with the highest legal court, the Audiencia, just like the viceroys had done.[141] As Artola has argued, the transition from viceroy to governor was not so much a real power shift as an ideological change in the conception of rule.[142] The viceroy had been a representative of the king in the reign. The governor's power, by contrast, emanated from a delegation of power to him from the Crown. On the ground, however, that transformation might be less visible. The English traveler Swinburne thought that the governor of Catalonia, the Marques de Mina, had "long governed Catalonia more like an independent sovereign, than like a subject invested with delegated authority."[143]

Attempts to introduce French-style *intendentes* directly responsible to the king's new ministers met with little more success in Castile than they had in Navarra. First introduced in some places in 1711, they became functional only after 1749 when the ministry of the Marques de Ensenada doubled efforts.[144] Yet by 1767 the intendents had become one of the victims of the *motín de Esquilache*, the popular uprising that also ousted Carlos III's first minister, the Italian Marchese di Squillace. In its wake, unpopular reforms were repealed. Hence the intendents were stripped once again of all functions that were not military or fiscal.

The creation of the intendencies was the clearest attempt to institute administrative centralization. The traditional role of the Castilian *corregidores*, previously the main royal officers in each district, was the administration of justice rather than direct governance at a local level (though of course they constantly negotiated for indirect influence). The model of the intendents, by contrast, suggested a direct government of local district affairs.

---

[140] Grafe, "Mercantilism."

[141] In Aragon, Valencia, and Mallorca the title was *comandante general* or *capitán general* (1711/15), in Catalonia *gobernador y capitán general*.

[142] Artola, *Monarquía*, 582ff.

[143] Swinburne, *Travels*, 86.

[144] Kamen has stressed the importance of the intendent system in shaping the careers of some of the key reformers, which seems to have been more important than the actual creation of the post. Kamen, "Intendents."

However, it was not to be, and the opposition to the reforms once again reveals that the problem was not bureaucratic failure but a result of how representation and governance functioned.

Opposition to the intendants was surprisingly not carried primarily by the traditional territories. Instead it pitched two views of governance against one another that competed for predominance throughout the territories of the Spanish monarchy in the eighteenth century.[145] The traditional administration through *corregidores*, *chancillerias*, and the Consejo Real (Royal Council) still conceived of governance primarily as the provision of justice. Its objective was equal access to the law in all territories, whether local or "provincial" law, or the law of the kingdom. Practical considerations of what we might call *government* as distinct from *governance* were immaterial to this vision. Reformers from Macanaz and Patiño to Ensenada and Esquilache, by contrast, emphasized the effectiveness and efficiency of *government*; hence their attempts to create more equal fiscal and administrative jurisdictions both geographically and in terms of their structure. But their success was clearly limited. The important point is that opposition to a more coordinated system of government was not based exclusively in the territories but existed also at the center of the monarchy itself. In fact, one of the key measures introduced in the Crown of Aragon with the *decretos de Nueva Planta* ironically ended up strengthening the position of the Royal Council in Madrid vis-à-vis the reformers; that was the case of Madrid's transformation of the traditional Aragonese district officers into *corregidores*.

The notion of governance as the administration of justice by the king and his Councils was still powerful, even in eighteenth-century Spain. It embodied an ideology of power that gave little incentive to centralize the location of the day-to-day exercise of power. Justice was after all largely guaranteed by an ex post legal process that reviewed local decision making, not by ex ante hands-on intervention from the top. This explains at least in part why the abolition of some of the most powerful traditional territorial institutions in the Crown of Aragon did not simply sweep away the legacy of negotiated rule. This was still governance by royal veto, not by legislative initiative at the center.[146]

One of the consequences was that the relative fiscal burden in the various Spanish territories remained highly uneven under the Bourbons. Estimates are subject to intense discussion; the problem is technical as well as one of political interpretation. On the technical side, the persistence of different types of taxes in the various territories and distinct patterns of exemptions create a large margin of error when estimating the fiscal burden. While the total amount collected can be established with reasonable precision, it is often not clear who paid the taxes, and how the burden was distributed. It is, for instance, open to debate how much of the customs (*tablas*) collected in Navarra were rolled over onto Navarrese consumers and how much was

---

[145] Artola, *Monarquía*, 588–98.
[146] Irigoin and Grafe, "Bargaining for Absolutism."

paid by Castilian consumers purchasing French goods that had to travel through Navarra, or indeed by French producers.

Calculations of the tax burden per capita are also a poor guide to what the Crown actually received and, more important, what part of the collected sums had already been subtracted for local use, as illustrated by the example of the Navarra customs. Since customs revenues financed the royal administration locally, they were almost permanently in deficit.[147] Transfers to the central treasury out of Navarra's customs were thus negative while much of the revenue raised in the territory was fed back into the regional economy right away in the form of wages and purchases. The reinvestment of royal revenue in the territories where they had been raised was a feature of Spanish fiscal governance in the Peninsula as well as in the Americas and further complicates the interpretation of the relative fiscal burden.[148]

Most of the historical debate has, however, understandably centered on the direct contribution of each territory to the Spanish monarchy.[149] Although this constitutes a more straightforward measure, even this debate might never be resolved satisfactorily. However, in terms of the impact of varying tax regimes on market integration, it is instructive to see how the tax burden differed from territory to territory, creating very different market conditions in each region. Figure 5.2 displays estimates representing the total tax burden per capita in *reales vellón* in Castile, Catalonia, Navarra, Guipúzcoa, and Vizcaya in the 1770s and the 1790s (1800 to 1802 in the case of Vizcaya). The basis of the estimate is simply the tax take divided by the population. The figures presented here exclude revenue from customs duties for the reasons mentioned before: it is difficult to assess how much of these fell on consumers in the respective territory.

These numbers are admittedly a crude proxy for how successful the Bourbon regime was in unifying the fiscal system across Spanish regions. Yet no matter how rough the estimates are, they are a testimony to failure. In the 1770s, before a phase of sustained increases caused by the pressure of the wars against France after 1793, the average tax burden in Castile, Catalonia, Navarra, and Guipúzcoa was 32, 25, 6, and 2 *reales*, respectively. Though in the last two decades of the eighteenth century Guipúzcoans experienced the largest increase in their taxes, their burden was even in the 1790s equivalent to less than 10 percent of the average burden in Castile. Vizcayans' tax burden refers to a slightly later period and is almost certainly an overestimate. It also includes export duties; even so, it barely reached 8 *reales*, confirming what all contemporaries took for granted: the Basque Provinces and Navarra were even in the late eighteenth century subject to a much lighter fiscal burden than the rest of the Peninsula.

[147] García Zúñiga, *Hacienda*, 41; Solbes Ferri, *Rentas Reales de Navarra*, 96–97.

[148] Grafe and Irigoin, "Stakeholder Empire."

[149] From the point of view of the individual merchant who traded across these boundaries and that of the consumer who sourced supplies from beyond boundaries, that historiographical focus on fixed territories was actually meaningless.

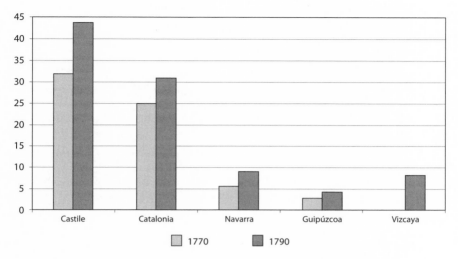

Figure 5.2
Per capita tax burden by reign in the 1770s and 1790s (*reales vellón*). *Source*:
Castile, Catalonia, Navarra, Guipúzcoa: García Zúñiga, Mugartegui Eguía, and de
la Torre, "Evolución de la carga tributaria," 85. Vizcaya: taxes from Bilbao Bilbao,
"Provincias exentas," 78 (for 1800–1802) and population from *Censo de Flor-
idablanca 1787*, INE, vol. 6 (Madrid: Artes Gráficas Sorual, 1991).

Since the Basque Provinces and Navarra had effectively been left untouched
by the reforms of the early eighteenth century, their lighter fiscal burden could
hardly surprise. Yet why had the Crown not succeeded in effectively equalizing the burden between Castile and the former Crown of Aragon? In the
wake of the Nueva Planta, attempts were made to introduce the system of
Castilian consumption taxes known as *cientos* and *alcabalas* in Valencia. This
soon failed. The amount was then commuted to a fixed sum apportioned to
each locality, to be charged locally by traditional means, that is, in any way
a town saw fit.[150] Similar to the Valencian example, a so-called *equivalente*,
supposedly equivalent to Castilian consumption taxes represented in the
rentas provinciales, was introduced in Catalonia and Aragon.[151]

Initially this hiked up the effective tax rate so much that Uztáriz, who
knew Spain's public accounts better than most, acknowledged that the *equivalente* was hard on the population despite immediate rebates.[152] Because
the nominal amount due was fixed, however, the real yield was eroded over
the century by population and economic growth as well as moderate inflation. In Figure 5.3 the trends are clearly visible; the *equivalente* remained
unchanged while Castilian trade and consumption taxes were effectively

---

[150] The town of Valencia (as opposed to the territory of the same name) was possibly an
exception since the tax was converted here into an ad valorem sales tax of 8 percent, which
consequentially rose with economic activity. Palop Ramos, *Hambre*.
[151] Artola, *La hacienda*, 224–46.
[152] Uztáriz, *Theorica*, 347–48.

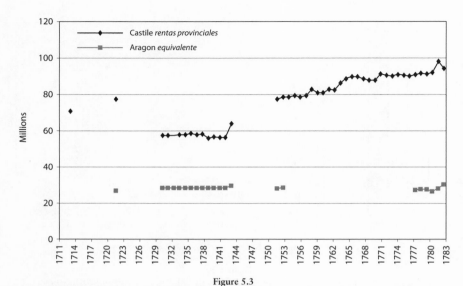

Figure 5.3
Total nominal revenue from Castilian *rentas provinciales* and Aragonese *equivalente* in the eighteenth century (*reales vellón*). *Source*: Artola, *La hacienda*, 304–8.

indexed to population and economic growth. Thus Garcia Zúñiga, Eguía,
and de la Torre argue that the tax burden in Catalonia was probably higher
per capita than that in Castile in the 1730s but had by mid-century become
lower and continued to fall.[153]

Reform remained more nominal than substantive. In addition, the Basque
Provinces and Navarra, both of which had supported the winning French
side in the War of the Spanish Succession, obtained guarantees that their
entirely autonomous fiscal system would be left largely untouched. Spanish
reformers kept on trying to tackle the differential tax burden. In the 1750s,
the government tried yet again to replace the very uneven provincial taxes
through an *única contribución*. This project, too, failed. Yet the data it produced vividly illustrate that the tax take was not just different between the
historic territories but also within Castile.[154]

The most powerful example for this persistence of negotiated rule under
the Bourbons was the tobacco monopoly. Royal taxes came in various forms.
In Castile the traditional importance of the *alcabalas* (sales taxes) was sur-
passed by the *millones* (usually financed through local consumption taxes) by
the seventeenth century and in the eighteenth century the *estancos* (monopolies). The introduction of the monopolies in Spain's European territories, as
well as the American and Asian possessions, is the fiscal measure most closely

---

[153] García Zuñiga, Mugartegui Eguía, and de la Torre, "Evolución de la carga tributaria."
[154] Grafe, "Epstein Memorial Lecture."

associated with the notion of a transformative Bourbon fiscality.[155] And of all of the *estancos* the tobacco monopoly experienced the fastest expansion. Yet, even this supposed showcase of Bourbon reformism and centralization was subject to the same rules of the game that applied to more traditional taxes as its application in the different territories reveals.

In Castile the *estanco del tabaco* was actually introduced in 1636 under the Habsburgs, not the Bourbons. From the point of view of the Royal Treasury it was a success. By the second half of the eighteenth century it accounted on average for about 15 percent of Castilian revenue, equal to all customs.[156] The tobacco monopoly was, like every new tax, an expansion of state authority, but its implementation lay as often in the Hispanic polities in the hands of private investors.[157] The yield was used to service the obligations arising from the *millones* and was thus initially controlled by the same administration, the *sala de millones*, which had become the permanent representation of the *cortes* towns since the mid-seventeenth century. However, in 1701 with the beginning of the Bourbon reforms this *de iure* control of the *reino* as represented by the *sala de millones* was abolished, and the tobacco tax was reorganized.[158]

Nevertheless, eighteenth-century attempts to unify the administration in the Castilian regions failed repeatedly. To some extent they were hamstrung by being part and parcel of the haphazard introduction of intendencies. As a consequence, provincial jurisdiction over the tobacco monopoly remained vested in various officers of the existing administrations—sometimes the *corregidor*, sometimes the president of the Chancilleria—and even after *intendentes* were finally introduced, the administration of the tobacco tax remained differently organized across the regions.[159] In sum, the *estanco de tabaco* mirrored the development of Castilian taxes in the eighteenth century. Administration improved slowly, and tax farmers were increasingly pushed out of the system and disappeared by 1731. The legal umbrella that once originated from the formal representation of the towns in the supervisory body, the *sala de millones*, was transformed into one in which provincial representatives were endowed with local control over the collection and administration of these taxes. As a recent historian of tobacco in Castile points out, the tobacco monopoly, an entirely new and very lucrative tax, was rolled out on the basis of preexisting fiscal structures and shaped around the reforms of the intendent system. But in the end its local and provincial structure was a result of renegotiations at the local level over practicability and historic preeminence.[160]

---

[155] Cf. de Jesus, *Tobacco Monopoly in the Philippines*; Deans Smith, "The Money Plant"; Fradera, *Filipinas*; Nater, "Cuba and Tobacco."

[156] Average of tobacco revenue as share of net Castilian revenue in 1763–1807 was calculated on the basis of Merino Navarro, *Las cuentas*.

[157] Norton, *Sacred Gifts*, 201–28.

[158] The representation was indirect since the representative of the sala de millones was a member of the junta de tabacos until 1701. Escobedo Romero, *Tabaco*, 30–40.

[159] Ibid., 47–74.

[160] Ibid., 74–75.

The slowly improving administration of the monopoly in Castile was, however, not the main problem for the Royal Treasury. Smuggling was much more problematic because it threatened the revenue by effectively undermining the monopoly. As the price of tobacco rose, the incentive for the illegal introduction of tobacco via France, Lisbon, or Genoa increased as well. Jurisdictional fragmentation between the historic territories thus posed an even larger dilemma in the case of the monopoly than it did for customs. It was paramount that the monopoly be watertight. This should not have posed an insurmountable challenge in principle. Spanish America, in particular Venezuela and Cuba, could serve the increasing Spanish demand, and in order to increase its grip on the supply chain the Crown tried to monopolize the purchasing of tobacco in Havana after 1707.[161] Unfortunately the administration of the tobacco monopoly had to rely on the collaboration of the historic territories, a large obstacle.

In Catalonia the local merchant oligarchy had succeeded in the mid-seventeenth century in stopping a monopoly from being introduced. Catalan traders were early on involved in the European tobacco trades and thus adamantly against a Crown monopoly.[162] In 1701, however, the Catalan corts, still favorably disposed toward the Bourbon Philip V, offered the new monarch a tobacco monopoly, overriding local resistance. Alas, as the principality fell out of love with its new monarch nothing came of it until Philip's reconquest of the territory. In the 1710s the tobacco monopoly was introduced, mirroring the earlier Castilian reforms.

The pattern of consumption of tobacco in eighteenth-century Catalonia as studied by Torres Sánchez suggests, however, that the estanco was never much of a monopoly in this territory. Even though Catalonia experienced faster population and economic growth than Castile, the per capita consumption of tobacco supplied through the estanco fell over the century. It was also curiously biased toward high-quality snuff.[163] Evidently Catalan merchants used their involvement in the legal trade for cheaper Brazilian, North American, or French smoking tobacco supplied via Lisbon or Genoa to circumvent the monopoly. Enterprising small traders crossing the French border increased supplies of "free" tobacco further.

Thus a two-tiered market emerged with low-quality smoking tobacco mostly purchased outside the monopoly and high-quality snuff within. The shortfall in revenue was observable to all; Catalans' official consumption— and thus tax payment per capita—was only half that of Castilians in the later eighteenth century.[164] Yet there was little the Madrid government could do. Whenever sufficient numbers of troops were stationed on the French border smuggling declined, but the costs of running the monopoly exploded. As

[161] González Fernández, "Tabaco y poder."
[162] Instead a tax was adopted, with relatively modest fiscal returns.
[163] Torres Sánchez, "Failure," 737–48.
[164] Ibid., 747.

soon as the troops left, smuggling into Catalonia rebounded. As long as local magistrates were willing to tolerate the situation, revenues from the tobacco tax kept declining in Catalonia while they rose spectacularly in Castile.

In the Basque Provinces, meanwhile, the problem was not revenue; given their exempt status the Crown had no right to introduce the lucrative tobacco monopoly here anyway. Instead negotiations with the provinces centered on how to limit smuggling from the provinces to Castile rather than into the provinces in the first place.[165] The administration of the tobacco monopoly wanted to create an additional cordon of tobacco customs on the internal border between Alava and Castile, duplicating not only the customs administration in the ports but also those administering other taxes in the *puertos secos*. This expensive and generally unpopular measure—the Basques were loath to let the tobacco guards patrol inside their territory—was then replaced by a quota of tobacco to be imported outside the monopoly. The amount was supposed to suffice for the Basque population but meant to restrict contraband.

Since the Royal Treasury could not levy any tax or monopoly in the Basque Provinces, its best strategy was to minimize costs by delegating even more authority. Henceforth the provincial administration was responsible for the suppression of contraband. Thus the Royal Treasury traded control for lower enforcement costs; the provincial authorities expanded their remit by combating contraband under their own legislation. Finally by the late eighteenth century the Basque authorities were given full control over the import, sale, and consumption of tobacco. Some time around 1803 the province of Guipúzcoa created a new formal *caja* to manage what was now a provincial monopoly, the *adehala de tabaco*.[166] Over the course of the century the provinces had succeeded at wresting control of the new tax away from Madrid.

It was in Navarra, however, where the limits of royal reformism became most apparent. Navarra had introduced its own tobacco monopoly in 1642, which it had farmed out from the very beginning.[167] In principle this should have lowered the incentive for smuggling in comparison with the Basque Provinces. However, ample supplies from France, which could be authorized by the *cortes* of Navarra or brought over long, hardly controlled borders, turned Navarra into a serious breach in the Castilian monopoly.[168] Having lost its fight against the Navarrese *cortes* over control of the customs after the War of the Spanish Succession, the Royal Treasury looked for ways to consolidate at least the tobacco tax that were compatible with the privileges of Navarra. At stake were not only the cost of maintaining yet another interior line of guards but also the loss of income from the monopoly in Castilian regions close to the Navarrese border.

[165] Angulo Morales, "Estanco."
[166] Mugártegui Eguia, *Hacienda*, 168–69.
[167] Solbes Ferri, "Renta del Tabaco," 196.
[168] Solbes Ferri, *Rentas Reales De Navarra*, 135–43.

The solution was nothing short of creative. Unable to rein in Navarra's control over its own customs (or rather Navarra's unwillingness to exert this control), the Royal Treasury bid in 1716 for the farm of the tobacco monopoly in Navarra at the same price that the previous tax farmer had paid. The *cortes* of Navarra agreed but insisted on a term of eight years for the agreement, lest anyone should forget that the treasury of Navarra, not the Royal Treasury, was the legal owner of this income stream. With a short interruption in the 1740s, this then became the way in which the Bourbons dealt with the threat to their most precious monopoly. The Crown became a tax farmer in the service of the *cortes* of Navarra.[169]

Ironically, this excursion into private enterprise was not even profitable for the Royal Treasury. Since the costs of controlling the French and Guipúzcoan borders were so high, the tobacco monopoly of Navarra was in deficit throughout almost the entire eighteenth century. Grudgingly, Madrid met the losses acknowledging two facts: one, it could not extend the tobacco monopoly successfully into any of the historic territories; and two, it actually had to subsidize the administration of the tax at least in Navarra and the Basque Provinces if it wanted to successfully exploit its profitable Castilian monopoly.

Once more it is hard to overstate the contrast with the state of affairs north of the Pyrenees. Michael Kwass has recently offered a fascinating account of the criminalization of ordinary Frenchmen at the hands of a repressive tobacco monopoly that clearly achieved a degree of control that was quite remarkable. With a machinery consisting of twenty thousand guards and a judicial process that sent hundreds to the gallows and many thousands to the galleys, a coalition of the powerful tax farmers' cartel and the Crown created a control mechanism and popular resistance at the same time. Kwass argues convincingly that the repression succeeded only at juxtaposing in consumers' minds "an underground capitalism of illicit (yet morally legitimate) trade and a court capitalism of licit (yet morally illegitimate) fiscality."[170]

By contrast, in Spain the tax farm remained largely under the control of the historic territories; in Castile its administration was integrated into the existing regional structures. Over the course of the eighteenth century conflicts over smuggling increased on the borders of the historic territories.[171] However, Angulo Morales found a total of only 236 cases against tobacco smugglers brought to court in all of Spain over the entire decade of the 1750s, and it is unclear how many were convicted. Most of these concerned cases on the southern coast, presumably the illicit introduction into southern seaports rather than through the *puertos secos* in the north. On the borders of the historic territories local authorities refused to collaborate with the guards of

---

[169] See, e.g., *Arrendamiento general del tabaco propio del Reyno de Navarra a Su Magestad en los mismos terminos, y con las propias clausulas, y condiciones, que el anterior, con aumento del precio que refiere.* Navarra, *Cuadernos,* 2:156–58.

[170] Kwass, "The First War on Drugs."

[171] Angulo, "Estanco"; Angulo Morales, *Puertas.*

the tobacco monopoly, who were perceived as infringing on territorial self-administration even though the organization of the monopoly was much less centralized than in France to begin with.[172]

The reaction to widespread resistance in Spain was still a negotiated solution in the medium term. The result was an uneven and murky application of the taxes and a differential tax base across territories. Contemporary observers pointed to the loss of legitimacy this created and the limits it imposed on the tax rate. However, paradoxically, this haphazard system was more legitimate locally and regionally in the eyes of consumers than the French apparatus—at least within Castile. Indeed, in Spain tobacco contributed twice the share of revenue to overall Crown receipts as in France at much lower enforcement costs.[173] Faced with widespread evasion and resistance, the French state and its tax farmers created a formidable repressive apparatus; the Spanish Crown negotiated and if necessary cut its losses—and costs.

The Consequences of Composite Kingdom

Leaving aside the political implications and the ostensible failure to create a more unified Spanish fiscality even after the abolition of the Aragonese institutions, contemporaries were convinced that the uneven incidence of taxation in the historic territories had an impact on the integration of markets. However, the aggregate outcome was not always predictable and might differ from commodity to commodity depending on a variety of factors. In those territories that were still separated by *puertos secos*, domestically produced goods enjoyed relatively lower prices than those that had to be "imported." At the same time, the effective protection of domestic goods could drive up prices of domestically produced goods. It appears, for example, that a consumption basket for a family in Navarra was slightly cheaper during the period 1718–23 when Navarra's customs border with the other territories of the Spanish Crown were abolished for a short time.[174]

In the Basque "exempt" provinces the lack of external customs complicated the equation even more. A lower total amount of revenue collected per capita suggested ceteris paribus lower consumption taxes *and* lower retail prices. But since consumption taxes tended to concentrate on a few particular foodstuffs like wine, meat, fish, and oil in particular, their outcome could again diverge. What is obvious is that market prices reflected the uneven surcharges levied in the form of external and internal customs duties as well as different tax regimes in the various territories.

[172] Angulo Morales, *Puertas*, 187, 204.

[173] Seven percent of French Crown revenue and 15 percent of Spain's revenue came from tobacco. Kwass, "The First War on Drugs"; Merino Navarro, *Las cuentas*.

[174] Fernández Romero, *Gastos*, 157–61. This should be interpreted with utmost caution, however, since the end of the war might have distorted prices.

Table 5.1. Determinants of the price of *bacalao* in Iberian territories, 1650–1775 (%)

	1	2	3	4	5	6
Price North America −1 (1gr/kg)	16.97	22.73	15.89	17.67	23.20	14.04
Distance to port (100 km)	14.06	14.02	14.40	11.57	11.66	10.90
War		12.03			11.60	
Catalonia				−6.39	−5.92	−12.19
Navarra				−16.47	−16.47	−19.75
Vizcaya				−13.06	−12.19	−16.47
year fixed effects	no	no	yes	no	no	yes
Constant	85	73	106	93	81	22
R2	0.22	0.23	0.38	0.24	0.26	0.41

Note: OLS regressions using natural logarithm of silver prices of *bacalao*, n = 693. All coefficients significant at the 1 percent level, except Price North America −1, which is not significant at the 10 percent level in equations 3 and 6, and Catalonia, which is not significant at the 10 percent level in equations 4 and 5. Coefficients for dummies transformed $(EXP(\beta) - 1)*100$. Omitted region: Castile.

The *bacalao* data set again clarifies some of the issues. Their structure allows us to identify more precisely the relative contribution of a variety of factors including transport costs and transaction costs created by territorial fragmentation using simple regression techniques. The results are reported in table 5.1.[175] The basic ingredients of equations 1 to 3 (columns 1 to 3) are quite obvious: price at origin in North America, distance from the coast to the consumer, and trade interruptions caused by war. The coefficients can be read as the percentage change in price associated with a one-unit change in the explanatory variable.[176] Thus, an increase of the price of *bacalao* at the source in North America by one gram of silver increased the price at destination in Spain by somewhere between 14 and 23 percent. Every 100 kilometers that the fish had to be transported inland drove up the price by another 11 to 15 percent. War, too, had an impact, adding about 12 percent to the final price. As an alternative to the somewhat blunt war variable and the falling but hard to model trend in transport costs (observed in chapter 4), fixed effects for each year (equations 3 and 6) probably control better for the presence of year-specific factors not captured by any of the other explanatory variables.

Equations 1 to 3 therefore contain the most obvious sources of price variation. Yet as the R2 in specification 3 shows, the price at origin together with the distance of the consumer from the ports of arrival, the incidence of war, and possible time trends explain at best only about 20 to 40 percent of the

[175] Prices were standardized to silver in order to account for different currencies in circulation.

[176] For comparison: given an average price of 2.71 grams of silver per kilogram in Cadiz (1650–1800), for example, a 10 percent rise is equivalent to a 0.27-gram increase in price.

variation in the final price of cod in Iberian towns.[177] Or to put it another way, 60 to 80 percent of the variation in prices was apparently not associated with the cost of buying cod at its point of origin and transporting it to the final destination but rather determined by some other factor.

The Costs of Interior Boundaries

Dummies representing the historical territories can be used to gauge the extent to which prices diverged from the Castilian level in the historical territories of Catalonia, Navarra, and Vizcaya. At first sight the results seem to confirm the pervasive notion in the historiography that these were somehow "privileged," that is, that historic freedoms translated into a lower tax burden and into lower consumer prices. No matter if war is included as a dummy or year fixed effects, apparently the simple fact that a consumer lived in Catalonia cut the final price by between 6 and 12 percent, in Vizcaya by 12 to 16 percent, and in Navarra by 16 to 20 percent. Indeed, the order of magnitude suggests that being located in the non-Castilian territories outweighed an increased distance of somewhere between 50 and almost 200 kilometers from the coast.

Caution is in order, however. The addition of the territorial dummies seems to add very little to the goodness of fit ($R2$), leaving somewhere between 60 and 75 percent of price variations still unexplained. In addition, the results reported here would suggest that Navarrese consumers were rather better-off than most others in the Peninsula. However, in chapter 4 we saw that prices in Pamplona were rising strongly and unusually after the 1730s. Although the results seem to confirm the traditional narrative about the advantages enjoyed by the non-Castilian territories, they still do nothing to explain the contradictions between different indicators for market integration observed in chapter 4. Chapter 6 will show that there is still one element missing for understanding the restriction of markets in Spain: the towns.

However, the data permit an analysis of the impact of the changes occurring in the early eighteenth century and therefore of the hypothesis that the Bourbon reforms overcame the jurisdictional fragmentation of the Habsburg period at least partially. The fiscal position of the Basque Country and Navarra changed relatively little after the accession of the new Bourbon dynasty, as we saw earlier. I have also argued that the economic impact of the dramatic legal changes in the former Crown of Aragon on the ground can easily be overestimated. In fact, an analysis of the pairwise correlation of Barcelona prices before and after 1714, when the *decretos de Nueva Planta* came into effect in Catalonia, shows some surprising results. The abolition

---

[177] The $R2$ is a measure of the goodness of fit of the regression line. An $R2$ of 0.22 in specification 1 can be interpreted as 22 percent of the variation in the final price being explained by the explanatory variables.

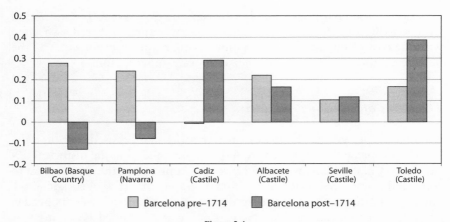

Figure 5.4
Pairwise correlation between *bacalao* prices in Barcelona and selected towns pre-
and post-abolition of the Aragonese *foral* institutions.

of the *puertos secos* with Castile should have increased integration with
Castilian towns, reflected in a higher correlation coefficient in the longer
run. Undoubtedly, even if the reforms had been a resounding success at help-
ing integrate Spanish *bacalao* markets, the "treatment" effect of the reform
might have taken quite some time to become visible in higher correlation
coefficients. However, on the whole, successful reform should have meant
that price correlation between Aragonese and Castilian towns between 1650
and 1714 was visibly lower than between 1714 and 1800.

Figure 5.4 illustrates that the actual development was more complicated.
The correlation coefficients for Barcelona-Albacete actually declined further,
while that for Barcelona-Seville increased minimally to a still low level of just
over 0.1. Measured through correlations Barcelona and Toledo for the first
time became well integrated. The single largest improvement, however, can
be seen between Barcelona and Cadiz. That certainly justifies much of the
historiography that has stressed an increasing engagement of Catalans in the
Andalusian trade, both in its own right and as a point of intermediation for
the American trades.[178] However, that in turn suggests that the abolition of
the internal customs had very little to do with this. Indeed, what was hap-
pening was a long-delayed increased integration among the Mediterranean
coastal regions rather than across the former boundaries of the historic territories. As far as one can tell from the data on the fish trade presented in
figure 5.4, the long-term outcome of the *decretos de Nueva Planta* was at best
mixed in terms of the degree of integration between Catalonia and Castile.

At the same time, Barcelona clearly became considerably less integrated
with the "exempt" *señorio de* Vizcaya (Basque Country) and Navarra. There
is no obvious reason why that should be the case. After all, the legal situa-

[178] Martínez Shaw, *Cataluña*, and chapter 4.

tion of the latter two had changed little after 1714. It is possible, however, that attempts to control for trade diversion after the abolition of the internal customs between the former *reinos* of Aragon and Castile reinforced the fragmentation between Aragon and Navarra. That would have affected trade with the Basque Country too because it had to pass through Navarra. The picture that emerges is less than positive with regard to market integration trends before and after the political watershed of 1714. While the abolition of the internal customs with Castile had a mixed effect, the surviving borders seem to have become more damaging to market integration if we take the fish market as an indicator.

Territories and Markets

The origins of the composite state in Spain and elsewhere reach back into the late medieval process of unification. However, the ideological foundations of contractual rule were particularly strong in Spain, and they protected the rights of historic territories (and towns, as we will see) much more success-fully. Strong territorial *foral* institutions, such as the *juntas generales* of the Basque Provinces or the Navarrese *cortes*, continued to force the Crown to negotiate on an equal basis with these territories. A tradition that gave even the Crown's own officers a strong power to veto Crown decrees—and this is essentially what the *pase foral* amounted to—strengthened territorial rights further.

Historians have long argued that reform proposals under the Habsburgs were hardly ever actually trying to change the governance structure that underpinned the composite state. Some of the Bourbon reforms were more ambitious, and the *decretos de Nueva Planta* changed the legal situation permanently in the Crown of Aragon. However, in terms of their impact on the political economy on the ground they were only a limited success. Thus negotiation among near equals was the predominant mode of political interaction between each of the constituent parts of the monarchy and the Crown in Madrid, its ultimate arbiter.[179]

The lack of a clearly defined political hierarchy in which the Crown could have mandated changes worked most of the time. A compromise had to be found on most important issues. On the upside, there was little need to expend money, military might, or political capital on enforcement. The Spanish Crown was notable for its lack of internal enforcement mechanisms, and where resistance arose, whether in the Basque Provinces over the reform of the customs border or in the towns of Castile and Valencia during the Esquilache riots, the Crown generally ceded enough ground to maintain its

---

[179] For an in-depth study of fiscal negotiation from the mid-sixteenth century to the first half of the seventeenth, see Dubet, *Hacienda*. For the "ultimate arbiter," cf. Irigoin and Grafe, "Bargaining for Absolutism," and Halperin Donghi, "Backward Looks," 222.

legitimacy. At the same time, where compromise could not be achieved, stalemate and the inability to affect reform was the most likely outcome. Most important, the outcome of negotiations was not easily predictable but had to be worked out on a relatively costly case-by-case basis. What historians and political economists have sometimes interpreted as the "failure" of the Spanish Crown to raise revenue extraction as far as it possibly could during either the Habsburg or the Bourbon period was, in most of these territories, not a matter of administrative malfunction or rampant patrimonialism but a reflection of the composite monarchy's very constitution. Not surprisingly, it affected new taxes like the tobacco *estanco* just as much as old ones.

The jurisdictional fragmentation between Spain's territories did not affect all areas of economic activity in the same way. The persistence of different currency systems mattered relatively little. Once the largest area, Castile, had stabilized its rampant small coin inflation in the later seventeenth century, market forces in the currency markets, where other transaction costs were low, did the rest. Internal customs were an altogether bigger problem and the Bourbon reforms made limited headway here. Even in the Crown of Aragon where the *puertos secos* were abolished, the impossibility of also reforming external customs created mostly trade diversion. Judging from the *bacalao* market, the aggregate effect of the Bourbon reforms of customs and taxation were a mixed bag. There was a little more integration between Aragon and Castile, but the negative impact of the remaining borders increased. Nor were tax burdens becoming more equal in the longer run. However, the quantitative results should be examined with a measure of caution. While they suggest that both transport costs (measured as distance from the coast) and the role of the historic territories had a substantial impact on prices, a large share of the variation in prices between Iberian towns remains yet unexplained.

Chapter 6

Distant Tyranny

The Power of Urban Republics

WRITING ABOUT WIDESPREAD RIOTS in Spain in the autumn of 1854, a German journalist and incisive commentator on European affairs tried to trace the deep historical roots of the "revolutions" Spain had experienced since the turn of the century. In a series of articles for the *New York Daily Tribune* he quipped, "Spain has never adopted the modern French fashion . . . of beginning and accomplishing a revolution in three days." Instead it experienced revolutionary upheaval during the periods 1808–12, 1820–23, and 1834–43, and of course again in 1854. The writer traced the social origins of these protracted conflicts back to three major events in the sixteenth century: the suppression of the Revolt of the Comuneros, an urban uprising in 1521; the Catholic reaction; and the discovery of the Americas. It was then that "Spanish liberty disappeared under the clash of arms, showers of gold, and the terrible illuminations of the auto-da-fe [*sic*]." There was just one thing that perplexed him:

> How are we to account for the singular phenomenon that, after almost three centuries of Habsburg dynasty, followed by a Bourbon dynasty—either of them quite sufficient to crush a people—the municipal liberties of Spain more or less survive? That in the very country where of all the feudal states absolute monarchy first arose in its most unmitigated form, centralization has never succeeded in taking root?[1]

How indeed?

The journalist in question, Karl Marx, was a very keen observer and in the habit of asking good questions. Born and raised in German-speaking Trier, which had preserved its independence until Napoleon put an end to it and which had been unwillingly incorporated into Prussia only in 1815, he witnessed firsthand the slow process toward the unification of the German states, free cities, and principalities. From this vantage point, he probably perceived more acutely than others the lack of centralization, the absence of a political hierarchy that could be recognized as a nation-state, and the reality of fragmented sovereignty in Spain, a country that history suggested had been unified three and a half centuries earlier. His bewilderment stemmed of course

---

[1] Reprinted in Marx and Engels, *Revolution in Spain*, 295, 303.

in part from the erroneous starting point he shared with many modern political economists: Spain was not particularly "absolutist" under the Habsburgs, and the Bourbons proved quite insufficient to crush a people—even if they had tried. Yet Marx was right in pointing out that centralization never took root, and he sensed correctly that this had a lot to do with municipal liberties, which had survived in Spain far into the nineteenth century.

A Community of Communities

I have argued that in Spain power was predominantly invested in bodies representing well-defined spatial sub-units rather than the corporate representations of a society of estates (such as the Crown and aristocracy), which at least theoretically were "national" in nature.[2] This system of governance protected Spanish conceptions of contractual rule. It was a multilayered structure, but it was polycentric, not hierarchical. In other words, just as rule was not exercised from the top down from the Crown to the territories, it was not exercised from the territories to the towns. As we have seen, the historic territories had powerful means at their disposal to defend rights *to* provincial taxation and *against* taxation through their monarch. However, arguably the single most important locations of power in Spain were the towns.

Towns and cities were the basic unit of Spanish civic life, and as Nader and others have shown, being a town *vecino/a* (householder/citizen) was a fundamental part of early modern Spanish identity.[3] Towns came in all shapes and sizes. There were royal towns, towns that were under ecclesiastical control, and towns under seigniorial control. Yet no matter their status or size, towns controlled much of their hinterland and with that Spain's rural areas. The notion of the town as the site of "civilization" was so essential to Spanish conceptions of social organization that town foundations became the most important step in the Spanish colonization of the New World; not surprisingly the urban cultures of Meso- and South America inspired admiration among the *conquistadores*.[4] The architecture of the *plaza mayor*, the town square, with its array of buildings representing the Church, royal sovereignty, the power of the town council, and other corporate institutions literally set in stone Spanish conceptions of multipolar hierarchies of power.[5]

---

[2] Nader, *Liberty*, 6.

[3] For the concept of the *vecino*, see Herzog, *Defining Nations*. The legal rights of women, especially those who were heads of household, differed across the territories of the Spanish monarchy. In the Basque Country, for instance, married women could act as full representatives of the household if they held a *poder*, and there is little evidence that they were excluded from economic activity. But in principle all women would self-identify in documents in the same way as the men, and start every declaration with "I Maria García, *vecina* of Toledo."

[4] Lockhart and Schwartz, *Early Latin America*, chapter 3.

[5] Escobar, *Plaza Mayor*; Lockhart and Schwartz, *Early Latin America*.

Towns and the Spatial Exercise of Power

Municipalities were the site of "representation," an anachronistic term I use once again in the absence of a better alternative. The *vecinos* were represented through their town institutions. It was no accident that at the heart of the Spanish monarchy the Castilian estates were in turn a representation of the most important towns of the realm. The Castilian *cortes* ceased to meet initially because a weak Crown feared the towns' might in 1665. Their functional end, however, simply meant that for the rest of the century the forum of negotiation between towns and Crown shifted from the *cortes* to the *sala de millones*, the body created in the early seventeenth century to administer the important new *millones* tax. The *sala*, however, was an integral part of the Council of the Treasury (Consejo de Hacienda). Therefore, the reform turned the *cortes*-voting towns into a direct part of the governmental council structure, while at the same time they retained their right to negotiate individually and directly with the Crown, as Thompson and Fernández Albaladejo have shown.[6]

Now the towns were surely sitting in the front row. Negotiation moved from debates between the king and his Councils on the one hand, and the estates on the other, directly into the king's Councils. The "King in Parliament" was replaced by a "King in Council," but this did not mean that the royal denial to call the *cortes*—that is, the towns—implied that the Crown had gained "absolute" power as historians used to claim.[7] Instead, power had reverted from the town-dominated *cortes* to the towns directly. This precluded the possibility that the estates could develop into a truly "national" representation.[8] However, it did not end the might of the towns nor was it the end of representation because towns embodied a long tradition of participatory politics. More power given to the municipalities thus implied in some way an expansion of representation, not a curtailment.

Most Castilian towns were of course small, but they nevertheless required a substantial number of elected or designated officeholders. Nader has pointed out that as a consequence most male householders in Castile outside the large cities (and many within their large city neighborhoods) would at one point in their lives have held some kind of public office.[9] Their participation in governance as mayors, council members, or treasurers of the central institution of Castilian political organization, the municipality, shaped their notion of their role in society and of the constitutional nature of rule.

---

[6] Fernández Albaladejo, "Monarquía"; Thompson, "Castile: Absolutism," 191.

[7] Maravall, *Estado*, 281. See also Kamen, *Spain, 1665–1700*, chapter 2. The claim by historical sociologists like Ertman that Spain lacked participatory structures in the towns and regions, that the Crown derived much income from the sale of offices, and that the fiscal system was land based, all of which led to patrimonialism and absolutist structure, is simply factually wrong. Ertman, *Leviathan*.

[8] Thompson, "Castile: Absolutism."

[9] Nader, *Liberty*, 36–39.

Recent research has also shown that longstanding traditions, such as open assemblies of all householders voting important decisions about the legal status of their municipality or reacting to local emergencies, remained common throughout the old regime order in spite of the "oligarchization" of municipal government.[10]

In the other historic territories, in the Crown of Aragon (until 1707–14), in Navarra, and in the Basque Provinces, the towns were not as strongly represented in the territorial institutions. Indeed the towns were relatively weak in the Basque juntas in particular. Yet urban freedoms were nevertheless very strong. Barcelona, the largest and most powerful town in the Crown of Aragon, had until the early eighteenth century an urban government with prerogatives that Amelang has called "unrivalled by any other city in the peninsula."[11] The Nueva Planta decrees left civil law, in particular those bits of it that were administered by the municipalities, unchanged.[12] Yet the Crown did increase its influence in Barcelona decisively by assuming the right to select the aldermen who previously had been selected in a lottery draw among a select oligarchy.[13] The power of the *honored citizens* of Barcelona, as they were known, was severely cut back—but the cuts had started from a level of virtual independence.

Not surprisingly, towns were also the exception to the rule that patrimonialism and the sale of offices were notably more restricted in Spain than in comparable monarchies. The sale of municipal "power offices," primarily *regimientos* (aldermanships), led to a well-studied tendency to create powerful urban oligarchies. This did limit popular representation but it arguably also reinforced already strong urban power.[14] As Tómas y Valiente points out, if a mid-eighteenth-century *regimiento* in Salamanca with an annual salary of 88 *reales* 8 *mrs*, was sold for 20,000 *reales*, this tells us at least two things about the buyer: one, he or she—offices were quite often purchased by women—must have had money to spare, and two, he or she must have seen it as an investment in collateral advantages rather than a job.[15]

Yet we ought to be careful not to overestimate the pecuniary, as opposed to social and political, benefits officeholders derived: the same office had sold for about 12,000 *reales* in 1690 and had thus realized a meager rate of annual return on capital of about 0.85 percent per annum in the meantime. Had the officeholder instead invested in a *censo* (a private debt obligation), he or she would have received 3–4 percent annual interest over the same period, or the equivalent of 70,000 *reales* in 1750.[16] More to the point, an aldermanship in

[10] Palop Ramos, *Hambre*; Thompson, "Castile: Absolutism."

[11] Amelang, *Honored Citizens*, 19.

[12] Kamen, "Melchor de Macanaz," 705.

[13] Barcelona's municipal government was replaced by the more common form of twenty-four aldermen; in smaller towns eight aldermen were considered sufficient.

[14] Cf. Madrid: Hernández, *Sombra*.

[15] Tomás y Valiente, "Ventas." See also García García, *Crisis*, 85.

[16] For interest rates, see chapter 8.

one of Castile's most important towns was evidently not yielding the sort of returns in fees and/or kickbacks suggested by the rise in the value of offices that Doyle has documented for France.[17] This much is obvious: in Castile, power was up for sale at a municipal level, but venality and nepotism were subject to clear boundaries even here. Aldermanships of Spanish towns were not primarily attractive because of the immediate economic benefits that officeholders derived but because of the access it gave them to the exercise of legal and fiscal power.

Even if most Castilian towns were too small to enjoy many of the social, economic, and cultural attributes of urban life, they were administratively and politically independent and handled their own fiscal affairs at least until the 1760s and to a lesser degree thereafter. This notion of the legal rights of the urban corporation translated what I have called "representation" into real-life decision-making powers. One of the fascinating features of Peninsular life was its famed litigiousness, and towns played a crucial role as both plaintiffs and defendants. They negotiated and/or litigated over rights to taxation, use of commons and water, contributions to public works, and countless other issues. They sued neighboring towns, individual citizens, corporate bodies, such as guilds or the Mesta, or their seigneur; in a remarkable number of cases they took the king in his role as the seigneur of the *realengo* to court.

Economic historians tend to think about widespread litigation as a sign of a poor definition and enforcement of contracts and/or a high level of social conflict. It also reveals, however, that Castilians from all social groups felt entitled to be heard before the law. MacKay has shown how Castilian towns and individuals refused and renegotiated the terms of being conscripted into the army in the sixteenth and seventeenth centuries.[18] Even the most humble and miserable subject of Philip IV (1621–65) "wrote to the king as if they expected to be listened to, and their confidence was often rewarded."[19] The existence of such institutions as the *defensores de pobres*, ex-officio lawyers for the poor, seems to support a notion of equal access to the law, though not equality before the law. The latter would have contradicted the fundamental understanding of a society based on freedoms, that is, special rights assigned to corporate entities, rather than a nineteenth-century concept of the freedom of the individual. At least higher appellate courts were also surprisingly willing to defend villages and towns against the aristocracy or poor peasants against urban oligarchs on the basis of their freedoms.[20] As Nader has rightly observed, "Castilian's famed litigiousness might be seen as a sign of their confidence in their capacity for self-administration and their essential faith that the monarch or lord was not their enemy."[21] The king was an "ultimate arbiter" of interests in the Peninsula and in the

[17] Sánchez Belén, *Política fiscal*, 291; Doyle, *Venality*, 225ff.
[18] MacKay, *Limits of Royal Authority*.
[19] MacKay, *Myth and Reality*, 2.
[20] Kagan, *Law Suits and Litigants*, 102–4.
[21] Nader, *Liberty*, 9.

"stakeholder empire" he ruled in the Americas, not an absolutist ruler in the traditional definition.

How stable were such conceptions of governance during the sixteenth, seventeenth, and eighteenth centuries? As in the case of the relation between Madrid and the historic territories, the traditional historiography has assumed that the ascent of the Bourbon monarchy after 1700 changed the rules of the game dramatically. Kamen argues, for example, that rising levels of litigation were a sign of increasing absolutism in the late Habsburg years and insinuated that this trend continued under the Bourbons. However, the assumption of a strong break between the Habsburg and the Bourbon period has come under scrutiny in this case, too. Windler has recently shown that in the late eighteenth century the tide of litigation turned decisively in favor of towns and against the seigneurs in lower Andalusia, arguably the Castilian region where large aristocratic estates had been a territorial power, if anywhere.[22]

Crown-town relations took more clearly the form of patron-client networks in the later eighteenth century, transforming an earlier model of the towns as autonomous bodies. Yet client networks, too, preserved the basic notion of a contractual relationship. Indeed, there is overwhelming evidence that the practice of power continued to evolve within the limits created by contractual ideology in all Peninsular territories and that towns continued to exert local political and fiscal power until the early nineteenth century. It is telling that while historians of the last Habsburg, Carlos II (1665–1700), have increasingly seen his reign as foreshadowing Bourbon governance, historians of the Bourbon period (1700–1808) argue now that early talk of decisive reform by French advisors quickly gave way to incremental changes of limited substance. When Marx wrote about Spain in the mid-nineteenth century, municipal liberties looked remarkably strong even for an observer from the German territories who was familiar with "free" towns and hanseatic city-states.

Legitimizing Governance in Times of Crisis

The clearest sign that towns had not lost their role in Spanish political organization and conceptions of rule is found in the events that unfolded after 1808. After Napoleon's troops invaded Spain, the French emperor took the Spanish monarch prisoner and placed his brother Joseph on the Spanish throne as a puppet king. As is often the case, crisis revealed underlying structures that are hard to trace in the day-to-day exercise of governance. Bereft of a legitimate ruler, the Spanish king's subjects reverted to the source

---

[22] Kamen, *Spain, 1665–1700*; Windler, *Lokale Eliten*, 425ff.

of power and legitimacy they knew, the *vecinos* represented in their town.[23] Towns in Spain and the Americas held open *cabildos*, assemblies of the *vecinos*. Juntas were formed in towns on either side of the Spanish Atlantic comprising broad representations of society: corporations, citizens, members of the urban institutions, representatives of the peasants in the rural hinterland, and so forth. *Cortes* were called in Cadiz to bring together the juntas of the towns.

In the Americas where the process has been studied much more intensely as part of a literature on the origins of the Spanish American national states, these assemblies included the urban and the rural, whites, mestizos, indigenous peoples, and blacks—in short, the entire *pueblo* (municipal population).[24] The recent Spanish American historiography has focused much more attention on the origins of Spanish American political organization that seemed to spring up spontaneously in the Independence period than that of the metropolis. Historians have increasingly come to argue that there was nothing very spontaneous about the assemblies and political decisions taken by Spain's American subjects. Instead, they were rooted in Peninsular conceptions of the *pueblo* and the *vecino*.[25]

Even though the legitimate king was now absent, imprisoned by the French, the traditional guarantees of a veto were upheld. When the Juntas Generales de Sevilla that governed "free" Spain ordered Cuba to close its port to foreigners, the Cuban authorities obeyed and thus accepted the Juntas' legitimacy as the provisional ultimate arbiter. However, they eventually "suspended the compliance with the decision" since the local situation did not allow its application. In an early sign of the troubles that Spanish and Latin American governments would face in the nineteenth century, the Cubans limited the power of the Juntas in just the same way in which they had limited the power of the Crown before; they obeyed but refused to implement regulation they objected to.[26] Now more than ever the location of power was the town, the exercise of power lay with municipal corporate entities, and their exercise was robust (even in the midst of war) and self-confidently grounded in a contractual ideology of power. "Spain's" Declaration of War against the Napoleonic occupation was famously issued on behalf of all Spaniards by the judge of Móstoles, which was at the time a three-hundred-household

---

[23] Quijada, "Pueblo." See also the recent collection of essays in Chust Calero, *1808*. There is a debate among political historians of Latin America as to whether the constitutional figure was a *retroversion* of sovereignty or a deposit. See Chiaramonte, "'Ancient Constitution,'" and Portillo Valdés, *Crisis atlántica*.

[24] Dym, "Soberanía transitiva."

[25] An exception is Portillo Valdés, *Crisis atlántica*. Cf. Rodriguez O, "Origins of Constitutionalism."

[26] De la Sagra, *Historia económica*, 144, 366–68. See also Irigoin and Grafe, "Bargaining for Absolutism," 200.

town that today forms part of Madrid's exurbs.[27] Small wonder the French occupiers underestimated resistance in Spain.[28]

The Political Economy of Urban Republics

Urban representation had important consequences for the fiscal system and through the fiscal system on market integration. Until the end of the ancien régime it determined what kinds of taxes dominated, who was liable to pay them and at what rate, and how they were collected. The urban-centered Spanish fiscal system challenges a number of larger interpretations of comparative European fiscal development that have underpinned the hypothesis of the superiority of "parliamentary" over "absolutist" states. One element of the supposed advantages of the British fiscal state, as well as that of the Netherlands, was a shifting of the fiscal burden from direct taxes on land and wealth toward indirect taxes on trade and consumption. Indirect taxes allowed the state to profit from increasing economic activity and—by taxing consumers rather than wealth holders—they did not discourage investment. As long as they were levied on "revenue" goods, that is, commodities that had no close substitute, they were unlikely to distort the market substantially, and they were supposed to be more equitable though probably not fairer.

Once more, economic historians read the evident difference between British and Dutch fiscal systems on the one hand and the French situation on the other as a paradigm of "parliamentary" versus "absolutist" regimes. In Britain the increased reliance on customs and excise taxes was said to be made possible by parliamentary control after the Glorious Revolution of 1688, and in the Netherlands the Estates had pushed in this direction even earlier.[29] This contrasted with France, which relied more on direct agrarian taxation, notably the *taille*.[30] Little surprise, too, that comparative studies of European fiscality extrapolated the French case and argued that Castilian taxes were inefficient because they were extracted mainly as direct taxes from an unproductive agricultural sector.[31] This is simply incorrect. Once again economic historians have looked at best at one half of the story.

Spanish history demonstrates that contrary to NIE arguments, the different structures of fiscal systems in Europe, in particular whether they relied

[27] Nader, *Liberty*, 11.

[28] The historiography suggests that Joseph Bonaparte made serious attempts to understand Spanish governance but found little empathy for this approach in Paris. Esdaile, *Peninsular War*; Esdaile, *Fighting Napoleon*; Fraser, *Napoleon's Cursed War*; Tone, *The Fatal Knot*.

[29] Ashworth, *Customs and Excise*.

[30] Hoffman, "France," 230, 239, suggests that by the mid-seventeenth century direct taxes accounted for 56 percent of total revenues in France.

[31] The myth of an agrarian-based Castilian tax system is still part of most standard comparative texts (e.g., Brewer, *Sinews of Power*, 66ff; Ertman, *Leviathan*, 16), though more recent comparative research has begun to reflect that this is wrong. Cf. Pamuk and Karaman, "Ottoman State Finances."

on direct or indirect taxes, depended originally much more on the degree of traditional urban autonomy (and early urbanization rates) than on questions of political regime. Where towns took control over revenue collection, indirect taxation on trade and consumption was the obvious choice. This is clearly visible in the transformation of the fiscal base in Navarra. The main traditional taxes, the *cuarteles*, were originally a direct tax on property. But as soon as their collection was turned over to the municipalities they were converted into indirect consumption taxes.[32]

In Castile, as in the Burgundian lands (including the Netherlands) where towns were also very strong, indirect taxes dominated very early on precisely because they were quintessentially urban taxes levied on activities that characterized the town economy. By contrast, only about 5 percent of the taxes on Castilian agricultural production were charged by the Crown, though peasants possibly lost about one quarter of their output to various dues, taxes, and rents in the mid-eighteenth century.[33] Furthermore, land taxes were almost unknown in Spain. By the eighteenth century substantially less than 20 percent of revenues, including those paid to the Church rather than the Crown, were charged through any form of direct taxation.[34]

Compare this setup to England's where indirect taxation only became important during the Civil War, that is, earlier than NIE writers have actually claimed but centuries later than in Spain. As late as the first decade of the eighteenth century, land and other direct taxes made up 35 to 40 percent of total revenue. The dramatic rise in excise in England began only after 1720, and direct taxes eventually fell to Spanish levels in the 1780s.[35] Thus, in terms of shares of indirect taxation, eighteenth-century England with its weak urban traditions was catching up with Spain and the Netherlands, not forging ahead thanks to a parliamentary revolution.

However, the differential origin and development of indirect taxation in England, the Netherlands, and Spain had lasting consequences on the way in which indirect taxes were applied. Their application in turn explains why the impact of indirect taxation was beneficial in England but harmful to market integration in Spain. In centralized England indirect taxation was collected by a unified national excise administration at uniform rates and was charged at the production site rather than at the point of sale or consumption. Faced with the need to assess and measure production, the excise collectors thus became agents of standardization and knowledge transfer across certain

---

[32] Solbes Ferri, *Rentas Reales de Navarra*, 48.

[33] Yun Casalilla, *Sobre la transición*, 461. Yun estimates that "lay" dues accounted for 3 percent, ecclesiastical ones for 5.5 percent, local land rents and municipal rents for 6 percent, and royal ones for 5.

[34] Torres Sánchez, "Possibilities," table 3, implies that direct taxes made up 24 to 30 percent of Spanish revenue in the later eighteenth century. He apparently subsumes under direct taxes the *rentas provinciales*, the largest share of which were *alcabalas*, *sisas*, and *cientos* and other consumption taxes, i.e., clearly indirect taxes.

[35] O'Brien, "Taxation," table 2.1.

industries.[36] In the Netherlands, too, what had originally been municipal taxes were consolidated at least into provincial taxes in the sixteenth century under the pressure of a war against an overwhelmingly more resourceful enemy, Spain, thereby improving the efficiency of the fiscal system notably.[37]

Financing the State, One (Taxed) Cod at a Time

In Spain, by contrast, indirect taxes continued to be collected at the municipal level and were never unified. *Alcabalas*, *cientos*, *arbitrios*, and *sisas* were levied by municipalities on manufactures, wine, meat, dried cod, oil, vinegar, and other staples. In theory *alcabalas* and *cientos* were royal taxes that applied across Castile perpetually while *arbitrios* and *sisas* were strictly municipal dues often granted for a limited number of years. They were raised initially as a means to defray a particular outlay such as infrastructure or an army contingent, the buying of a town privilege, a legal process to stop a village in the hinterland from buying its "independence," or to pay for the *servicios ordinarios* and *extraordinarios* of the Crown.

Yet *sisas* and *arbitrios* had a way of becoming permanent and were often still in place two hundred years after they had first been introduced.[38] At the same time *alcabalas* and *cientos* were collected at the municipal level just like the *sisas* and *arbitrios* and not at a uniform rate. Though towns needed royal permission for imposing additional taxes, the Royal Council could hardly stop them from raising the money the Royal Treasury demanded in the seventeenth century. In the eighteenth century, the government positively encouraged the towns to raise income to pay off their debt. In other words, no matter their legal and administrative origin, these taxes were de facto hard to distinguish. They had a tendency to simply become a multitude of urban sales and consumption taxes that once introduced rarely disappeared.[39] There was one remarkable exception already noted: bread, which was exempted.

Castilian cities and towns were usually apportioned a block grant, a particular share of all taxes voted by the *cortes* or by the representatives of the voting towns after 1665. But the decision on how these taxes were raised was taken at the municipal level by town councils, no matter if a town was part of the royal demesne (*realengo*) or belonged to the Church or nobility. These decisions included the kinds of activities or goods that would be burdened as well as the mechanism through which taxes were raised; for example, if

---

[36] Ashworth, "Manufacturing Trust."

[37] Fritschy, "Efficiency."

[38] Theoretically towns relied on two kinds of income streams, *propios* and *arbitrios*. The former were legally a town's property, while the latter theoretically needed royal approval and became increasingly important. In reality the distinction was blurred. García García, *Crisis*, 33ff.

[39] Ibid. Cf. also for the collection of *alcabalas* and *almojarifazgos* in Seville, Martínez Ruiz, *Finanzas municipales*, 49–69.

they were farmed out to an *arrendador* (tax farmer) or levied by municipal agents or if they were charged as an ad valorem consumption tax or, less often, apportioned according to some criteria of wealth in a poll tax.[40] Indeed the much-criticized reliance on tax farming, often seen as an indicator of the advance of patrimonialism in Spain, had little to do with that. For many Peninsular municipalities outsourcing the administration of fragmented taxes was likely the most efficient way of collection given their large role in the fiscal system. The source of inefficiencies in the fiscal system was not so much collection techniques but the role of the towns as such, as we will see.

The role played by towns within the fiscal system also finally explains one of the issues raised in chapter 1: How did the Spanish Crown continue to finance the enormous expansion of the state in the sixteenth century, how did it managed to hang on in the seventeenth, and how did it behave so fiscally prudently in the eighteenth? Given the highly autonomous jurisdiction of towns over (non-ecclesiastical) taxation, the Habsburgs naturally secured initially many of the loans by offering its creditors rights to the proceeds of urban revenues as both security and interest payment rather than against income received by the royal hacienda.[41] The Crown's financiers were consequentially hardly concerned about the dire straits of the Habsburg Royal Treasury. What mattered was that the tax earmarked for interest payments was effectively collected. That might be the wine tax of Granada, the fish tax of Leon, or both, or a share of either.[42] Unsurprisingly, the common heritage of strong urban institutions meant that this, too, mirrored more closely the management of public debt in the Netherlands than in France or England, which relied on a process of "bureaucratic delegation."[43]

Here then is another reason why North and Weingast's famous model of the link between "constrained monarchs" and "successful development of the private market" fails to convince empirically. The credit-worthiness of the Spanish Crown often made no difference to the Crown's creditors; what mattered in the Castilian context was how well towns and their rural hinterland were managed because they were the source of debt service. Constraints at the level of the Crown were of little importance. This explains why the political

[40] For a detailed example, see the discussion about the administration of the very important *millones* in Andrés Ucendo, *Millones*, chapter 4.

[41] For Seville, for instance, see Martínez Ruiz, "Crédito público," and Martínez Ruiz, *Finanzas municipales*.

[42] For the variations in how seventeenth-century *repartimientos* were raised, see Artola, *La hacienda*, 146–57.

[43] The term is used by Stasavage, *Public Debt*, 65, 66. France used the *rentes sur l'hôtel de Ville* of Paris after 1522, but by the late sixteenth century they had degenerated into forced loans. Hoffman, "France," 233. In the eighteenth century, it increasingly drew on financing through the surviving *pays d'état* as intermediaries in raising debt. The purpose here was clearly to take advantage of the better credit rating—and consequentially lower interest rates—they enjoyed. The difference is, however, not only in the historical timeline but in the fact that the Spanish Crown dealt literally with thousands of urban units *in addition* to the non-Castilian composite territories.

economy model's focus on sovereign (that is, Crown) borrowing is actually anachronistic.

Yet this also explains why the Crown continued to negotiate over rights and resources not only with the historic territories but also with individual towns. In 1623 the Count Duke of Olivares, the *valido* of Philip IV, was desperate for money to send to the troops fighting in what would become the Thirty Years' War. He contemplated a measure that would replace the indirect taxes of the *sisas* and *alcabalas* with a direct tax on each town and village in Castile. Alas, the Count Duke estimated that royal officials would in this case have to deal directly with more than fifteen thousand municipalities.[44] Small wonder the plan came to nothing, even though it would not even have touched thousands of municipalities in the non-Castilian parts of Spain.[45]

The Crown in its role as "ultimate arbiter" could intervene in municipal finances, but it did so only when urban government was badly mismanaged, as in the case of a number of Valencian towns in the first half of the seventeenth century.[46] The cost for Madrid to intervene in individual towns was notable. An investigation of fiscal accounts that reflected the myriad distinct taxes entailed mountains of requests for information on traditional rights and duties to be provided by the incumbent town officials. The *corregidores* were supposed to be royal officers and thus independent, but one should not forget that they, too, were paid out of the urban purse.[47] If the Councils wanted any unbiased insights, they had to pay a salaried outsider to perform an investigation. The necessity of judging the administration of a municipality against its own locally determined fiscal and municipal rights placed a very high burden of proof of wrongdoing on the Crown or Councils. Hence, Madrid usually refrained from investigating unless internal strife within municipalities over fiscal and political rights threatened the public peace.

Royal Prudence and Urban Debt

As a consequence, the legacy of Habsburg spending was not high interest rates that crowded out private investment or hindered the development of financial markets, as current political economy models of the predatory state would suggest. We saw in chapter 1 that sovereign interest rates were remarkably low most of the time. Instead, an enormous debt, shouldered by cities like Madrid, Seville, and Valladolid, resulted in severe constraints on towns' expenditure on public goods.[48] This was a real problem because municipali-

[44] Nader, *Liberty*, 129; Elliott and de la Peña, *Memoriales y cartas*, 1:16.
[45] Nader, *Liberty*, 4.
[46] Díez Sánchez, *Hacienda municipal*, 54–55.
[47] García García, *Crisis*, 84.
[48] Andrés Ucendo, "Herencia"; Gutiérez Alonso, *Estudio sobre la decadencia*; Martínez Ruiz, *Finanzas municipales*; García García, *Crisis*.

ties were not only raising much of the revenue, they were also responsible for practically all public goods except defense; and they usually paid for some of the military costs, such as the maintenance of buildings, too.

They provided safety and infrastructure and paid for the salaries of almost all public officers. Lower court judges (and sometimes even those in the Audiencias, the appellate courts), some lawyers, public order officials (*alguaciles*), and the jailers were on municipal payrolls, as were the tax administrators, elementary school teachers, surgeons, and matrons. Towns provided basic public health measures and financed, or co-financed with the Church, "welfare" in orphanages and hospitals. Paid elected town officials also enforced market rules, weights and measures, and hygiene in slaughterhouses and fishmongers, and, as we have seen, larger cities often maintained granaries and provided emergency supplies of basic food, especially grain, in times of famine.

As debt service began to consume increasingly large shares of the total revenue over the course of the seventeenth century, many municipalities drastically multiplied dues and cut all other expenditures. Martínez Ruiz has estimated that between 1612 and 1693 the funds available in Seville for the maintenance and improvement of municipal services and infrastructure fell by almost 80 percent, if compared to the ordinary expenditure of the city.[49] The situation was particularly severe in Seville because revenue was falling continuously. Yet by the late seventeenth century most large municipalities, and quite a few midsized ones, were in a dire financial situation, and the *hacienda real* regularly had to write off huge amounts of arrears in taxes owed by the towns for such concepts as the *servicio ordinario* and the *servicio extraordinario*.[50]

No wonder then that the interest rates on the Crown's debt as represented by the *juros* shot up in the late seventeenth century, as seen in chapter 1. The limited debt forgiveness constituted a partial default of the towns on their debts to the Crown. Paradoxically, restructurings of the Crown's debt in the late seventeenth century in particular were in fact the result of another restructuring of debt, namely that of the towns with the Crown and of the "haircut" the Crown suffered in these negotiations. In a multipolar system of governance even the financial losses of public indebtedness were fairly evenly distributed. Town aldermen might just prefer to service their own loans first before standing in for the Crown's *juros*, and there was not a lot the *hacienda real* could do about that.

Nevertheless, the mountain of debt that Madrid had taken on in the second half of the seventeenth century on behalf of the Crown meant that 58 to 66 percent of its municipal revenue over the entire eighteenth century was spent on interest payments, according to one estimate.[51] The three largest

---

[49] Martínez Ruiz, "Crédito público," 143.
[50] Garzón Pareja, "Carlos II"; Sánchez Belén, *Política fiscal*.
[51] Andrés Ucendo, "Herencia."

towns of the province of Valladolid spent about 14 percent on salaries, 11 on schooling, health, and welfare, 10 on military and royal service, 9 on infrastructure, 6 on Church festivities, and less than 1 percent on seigneurial dues in the mid-eighteenth century. That was after expending 48 percent on debt service.[52]

Indebted towns were hard-pressed to maintain basic services and perform the functions of coordination of legal, fiscal, regulatory, and infrastructural oversight over the market. Remarkably, Castilian municipalities managed to increase their spending on infrastructure in the second half of the eighteenth century. The improvement in road travel documented in chapter 4 is thus even more notable. Spanish towns were performing small miracles in continuing to improve transport at a time when interest payments and salaries severely restricted what could be spent on investments. This came undoubtedly at the expense of other public goods.[53] Cash-strapped towns were also more easily co-opted by urban officeholders and local oligarchies who could promise to anticipate some of the tax take. David Stasavage's recent work shows that a tight-knit town oligarchy that was willing to bankroll the debt of their home town in return for political control was the single best way of reducing "sovereign" (that is, municipal) interest rates.[54] Yet another reason why the Crown was well advised to tread carefully when it came to reining in urban freedoms.

The Bourbons did make attempts to introduce reforms that could affect the towns in three different but overlapping ways. One was the introduction of intermediate administrative units between the towns and the Crown, that is, the attempt to establish a more hierarchical power structure. Municipalities were stripped of some powers, and intendents installed in the cities supervised royal taxation.[55] However, the plans to create proper territorial units in the shape of Intendencias on a French blueprint were implemented in a haphazard way as we have seen and remained largely unsuccessful in breaking the autonomy of the towns.[56]

The second set of reforms affected the towns by trying to replace the locally controlled trade and consumption taxes with alternative sources of revenue and thus reduce the fiscal might of the towns. An early eighteenth-century attempt to shift the tax burden to foreign customs was blocked by the *cortes* towns within Castile and by the historic territories beyond Castile, as mentioned above. First in the 1750s and again in the 1770s, the Crown tried once more to replace at least one large group of indirect taxes, which formed part of the *rentas provinciales*, with a direct tax on wealth

[52] García García, *Crisis*, 80–108.

[53] Ibid., 94.

[54] Stasavage, *States of Credit*.

[55] In 1717 a decree officially reordered Spanish administrative regions into *partidos* and *superintendencias*.

[56] *España dividida*; Nader, *Liberty*, 10–11.

and income streams, the *única contribución*. Again, it failed in the face of concerted resistance from local town oligarchies.[57]

A third strategy was for Madrid to devise reforms that tried to rein in town finances more directly between 1738 and 1766.[58] In 1760 the Crown enacted one of the most ambitious reform programs of the Bourbon period. It created the Contaduría General de Propios y Arbitrios, which brought urban finances under a single supervisory body to which towns had to submit their accounts for revision.[59] For the first time the municipalities were to be formally integrated into the fiscal structure of the *reino*, even though they had been the backbone of that structure for centuries. New rules on the administration of expenditure and revenue theoretically took away the towns' autonomy to manage their own finances.[60] For instance, surpluses now had to be used to pay off urban debt by law. Unfortunately, this only succeeded in sacrificing the Crown's own policy that was trying to reduce local trade and consumption taxes to that of reducing urban debt.[61]

Local historians have interpreted the urban reforms of the 1740s to 1760s as a decisive encroachment on local autonomy in parallel with the historiography of the alleged disempowerment of the historic territories.[62] Yet there is myopia in that view, which emanates from a notion that anything less than total urban autonomy equals abusive royal power. Castilian towns were on a shorter leash than they had been; the quality of their administration of local finances in particular was under closer scrutiny. Reformers pushed for improved administrative skills at the municipal level and a consolidation of the multitude of parallel administrations for each and every tax. Accounting manuals directed at municipal treasurers began to appear. The Basque economic reform society published treatises on what kind of training was required so that a town's *vecinos* would become good municipal administrators.[63]

But, yet again, even the creation of new offices and bodies had only limited effects on the ground. More often than not, old administrators and treasurers

---

[57] The aristocracy, too, seems to have resisted the idea that all Castilians would be charged the same kind of taxes rather than the actual amount charged. The Spanish upper nobility was in fact subject to quite a few taxes—either specific to their *estamento* like the *lanzas* or as a result of their economic activities. Cf. Cremades Griñán, *Borbones*, 74. On the *única contribución*, cf. Matilla Tascon, *La única contribución*.

[58] These included the Real Junta de Valdíos y Arbitrios (1738), a decree of 1745, parts of the ordinances for the intendencies (1749), the creation of the Contaduria General de Propios y Arbitrios (1760), and the introduction of the *síndicos personeros* and *diputados del comun* (1766). See also Martínez Ruiz, *Finanzas municipales*, 67.

[59] Windler, *Lokale Eliten*, 30ff.

[60] Ibid., 29–30.

[61] García García, *Crisis*, 221.

[62] See, e.g., Martínez Ruiz, *Finanzas municipales*, 67–71. The author claims unconvincingly that the result of the reforms was a deliberate and almost complete control over Seville's municipal finances.

[63] Verbedel, *El contador moderno*; Sarrailh, *España ilustrada*, 245.

simply acquired new titles, and the abolition of existing taxes proved impos-sible.[64] Madrid acknowledged implicitly that it had no power to break the dominance of the urban oligarchies that ran the fiscal system when they created the *personeros del comun* in the municipalities, elected defenders of the lower social ranks.[65] At no time were the towns subject to checks to see whether their revenue was equivalent to their potential sources of revenue.[66] While municipalities now had to forward their accounts for supervision to the Council of Castile, most were rubber-stamped *en bloc* and in any case only looked at with year-long delays. This was hardly effective control from the center.

In the late eighteenth century the suggestion that the royal administra-tive apparatus could supervise the nearly fifteen thousand municipalities' finances, all of which relied on separate tax structures, was entirely unrea-sonable. Most of the council's suggestions for changes concerned the expen-diture side, not the revenue side. Even if towns' accounts were admonished, the municipalities could often successfully ignore and delay interventions or sue the administration. Windler has argued that in Lower Andalusia, for example, the main outcome of the reform was to strengthen urban elites in an area where powerful aristocrats had controlled "their" towns more than elsewhere in Castile by giving them more direct representation and access to the Crown and Council.[67]

Administrative reforms of municipalities in the 1760s took away some of the control over municipal taxation *de iure*, but they did little to consolidate the plethora of municipal consumption and trade taxes that drove a wedge between the price levels in various towns. Municipalities were still the most important tax collection agencies and thus, by definition, still enjoyed large autonomy over fiscal management. Worse still, thanks to the sale of town privileges starting in the sixteenth century and continuing right up to the end of the ancien régime, the Crown and treasury were dealing with an ever-increasing number of self-administrating towns. The number of legal towns in Castile probably increased by another 30 percent between the early seventeenth century and the end of the eighteenth, and every new town rep-resented yet more devolution of central power.[68]

Jurisdictional Fragmentation and the Market

The jurisdictional fragmentation across territories seen in chapter 5 was therefore compounded by divided authorities *within* territories. The inter-

[64] Cf. Bustos Rodriguez, "Hacienda municipal gaditana"; Pozas Poveda, *Ciudades castellanas*.

[65] Windler, *Lokale Eliten*, 427ff.

[66] For what follows, cf. García García, *Crisis*, 223ff.

[67] Windler, *Lokale Eliten*, 425.

[68] Estimate based on data provided for New Castile by Nader, *Liberty*, table 4.2.

pretation of the quantitative results for the costs that the historic territories imposed on the market (table 5.1) is hence somewhat equivocal and reveals only part of the story. The data set contains only one town in Navarra, Vizcaya, and Catalonia but seven in Castile. The uncomfortable question is whether Pamplona, Bilbao, and Barcelona are good proxies for the situation in each of these territories. In addition, we have also seen that there are legitimate questions about the existence of a Castilian "average" against which to compare the other territories (see figure 5.4).

In the absence of price series for other towns within the non-Castilian territories, the discussion has to rely at least in part on indirect evidence. There can be no doubt that municipal finances across the Peninsula exhibited an enormous variety of trajectories in the late seventeenth through the eighteenth centuries. As anchor for the heavily indebted Royal Treasury, municipalities had retained a large amount of control over their finances into the eighteenth century.[69] Yet that came at a price of heavy debts as we have seen. The total debt stock of Spanish municipalities (excluding the Basque Country and Navarra) was equivalent to at least ten times their current revenue by 1769—no wonder interest payments often accounted for half of all the expenditures of larger Spanish towns. If overdue interest is included, the ratio was probably closer to 20 to 1.[70] This translated almost invariably into yet more indirect taxes that further burdened trade and consumption at the local level.

For local consumers, how well their town managed its debt thus became paramount. The solvency of municipalities depended on a large number of highly idiosyncratic factors: the functioning of urban political institutions, the quality of their administration, the amount of municipal revenue derived from income streams to which the town had full property rights (*propios*), the ability to borrow at low interest against their value or revenue, the tax base that could sustain additional *arbitrios*, and many others. The diversity this gave rise to is clearly visible in a number of excellent recent studies on the urban finances in the seventeenth and eighteenth centuries. Towns like Cordoba, with a relatively healthy amount of municipal property, could afford lower taxes than nearby Seville, which struggled to finance its debt.[71] The lower overall tax burden in the Basque Provinces translated initially also into low municipal taxes. In the Basque Provinces, however, the successive move away from taxes levied directly on each household to regular indirect consumption taxes began to show in higher municipal indebtedness and even higher consumption taxes in the later eighteenth century, which would become equally unsustainable in the nineteenth.[72]

[69] García García, *Crisis*, 40ff.

[70] These estimates are based on the returns of over ten thousand municipalities to the *catastro de Ensenada*. Ibid., 41–42, 110–11.

[71] Pozas Poveda, *Ciudades castellanas*; Pulido Bueno, *Consumo y fiscalidad*; Martínez Ruiz, *Finanzas municipales*.

[72] Mugartegui Eguía, *Estado*, 117–20.

The Costs of Urban Republics

An in-depth study of the municipal finances of each of the towns in our sample is beyond the means of this enterprise as it would involve dozens of distinct, often poorly documented taxes and other measures in each of them. However, the price data once again offer an indirect way of understanding the impact of variations in urban taxation. Table 6.1 repeats the regression analysis reported in table 5.1, but it now substitutes town dummies for those of the historic territories. The most obvious result is that the goodness of fit ($R2$) is notably better. In specification 9, which again includes the price in the previous year in North America, a measure of distance, and year fixed effects, the regression now explains about 70 percent of the observed price variation compared to the price of *bacalao* in Cadiz. As the only Castilian port with a long series in the data set, Cadiz serves here as the yardstick, and thus it is the omitted category.

Remarkably, the coefficients for the dummy variables for some of the Castilian towns are tiny and in any event not statistically significant at the

Table 6.1. Determinants of the price of *bacalao* in Iberian towns, 1650–1775 (%)

	7	8	9
Price North America −1 (1gr/kg)	11.65	18.07	20.40
Distance to port (100 km)	20.48	20.55	19.91
War		14.12	
Madrid	1.51	1.71	4.71
Toledo	dropped	dropped	dropped
Malaga	dropped	dropped	dropped
Albacete	−17.30	−18.94	−15.63
Sahagún	13.88	11.63	18.53
Seville	141.09	141.09	136.32
Barcelona	36.34	37.71	32.31
Bilbao	25.86	27.12	24.61
Pamplona	15.03	15.03	12.75
year fixed effects	no	no	yes
Constant	63	49	67
R2	0.68	0.70	0.81

Note: Estimation based on OLS regressions using natural logarithm of the silver prices of *bacalao,* n = 693. All coefficients significant at the 1 percent level, except Price North America −1, which is significant at the 5 percent level in equation 9, Sahagún, which is significant at 5 percent level in equation 8, and Madrid, which is not significant at the 10 percent level in equations 7, 8, and 9. Omitted town: Cadiz.

10 percent level. This suggests that differences in prices in Madrid, Toledo, and Malaga in comparison to those in Cadiz were to a large degree explained by distance to the port and the year fixed effects. Differences between towns not associated with those two variables did not matter much. Lest one is tempted now to overestimate the degree of jurisdictional integration within Castile, a look at other towns comes as a sobering reminder. In Albacete the estimates suggest that prices were 16 to 19 percent lower. In Sahagún they were 12 to 18 percent higher. As in all calculations, prices in Seville were entirely out of proportion. The simple privilege of living in Seville came throughout this period at a cost of having to pay a surcharge of about 140 percent.

The coefficents for all of the non-Castilian towns are significant, though as noted there is an identification issue: it is impossible to distinguish whether this was an effect of jurisdictional fragmentation at the territory or town level. Yet what seemed the expected cost advantage outside Castile in table 6.1 all of a sudden looks far less rosy for non-Castilian consumers in Bilbao (Basque Country), Barcelona (Catalonia), and Pamplona (Navarra) if compared to Cadiz rather than the Castilian average.

The explanation is simple. The outlier Seville drives up the average estimate for the Castilian price of *bacalao* in the earlier estimations (reported in table 5.1). Once the sample is broken down to the town level, it turns out that prices were on average 32 to 38 percent higher in Barcelona, 25 to 27 percent higher in Bilbao, and 13 to 15 percent higher in Pamplona. It should be remembered that the Bilbao series is derived from a monastery that was located a short distance into the interior, but the difference is far too large to reflect transport costs to that location. The Barcelona prices by contrast represent the port itself. It is possible that shipment from North America deep into the Mediterranean was more expensive, but it is unlikely that this accounted for the large difference compared to Cadiz.

Few historians have tried to compare the situation of consumers across the historic territories. In general, studies tend to limit themselves to the territory in question while comparisons across Castile exclude the non-Castilian regions. The result of this first comparison across territories and towns is thus surprising. Far from being privileged, consumers in the historic territories outside Castile, at least in the case of *bacalao*, paid a surcharge once we account for other cost factors such as prices in North America, naval conflicts, and the distance from the port of introduction. Obviously the effect might derive from the local taxation system in the three towns represented here, Bilbao, Barcelona, and Pamplona. Unfortunately, this last question is impossible to disentangle with the present data set. For now what is clear is that a combination of differential customs, port fees, costs imposed by the *puertos secos*, and municipal consumption taxes account for much of the difference.[73] The inclusion of the town dummies that proxy these specific political economy costs explains a large part of the price variation.

---

[73] For the large differences in port fees, see Caballero y Estevan, *Aduanas*, appendix 2.

More important, the result seriously questions a notion that was as strong in contemporary political discourse as it is in the historiography. The elites in the Basque Country, Navarra, and to a lesser extent the former Crown of Aragon defended their differential tax and customs systems tooth and nail, usually alleging the advantages for consumers. Few historians have questioned whether consumers in fact benefited from the external customs exemptions because they were meant to lower prices. Notwithstanding that the results here represent only one staple food, albeit an important one, at the very least the analysis casts doubt on this interpretation. On the basis of this evidence, the championing of consumer interests by regional elites begins to sound a little hollow.

One way to begin distinguishing between the town-specific variations in prices and those caused by the fragmentation between historic territories is to look again for the "treatment" effect of the *decretos de Nueva Planta*. Table 6.2 displays the results of an analysis along the same lines as before only now the regressions are split into pre-1714 and post-1714 estimations.[74] In all towns except Toledo, the town-specific effects encapsulated in the dummy were very large in comparison to the impact of a rise of prices in North America or that of increased distance from the coast. In the seventeenth century the size of the town effects outweighed the impact of a rise of 1 gram of silver per kilogram in North America, itself the equivalent of a 70 percent rise in the average price.[75]

In the eighteenth century this remained true in Seville, Barcelona, and Pamplona, but the change elsewhere was largely driven by a more nuanced impact of the North American price on Spanish prices. In fact, integration across the Atlantic had increased as we know, while the town-specific differences had hardly declined anywhere. An additional 100 kilometers of transport from the coast added about 20 percent to the final price, slightly less in the eighteenth century. Here the results provide us with another indirect way of estimating the freight factor, which confirms that it was falling slowly. Given a maximum distance from the coast of about 400 kilometers as the crow flies for any location in Spain, transport costs could thus have added an absolute maximum of about 80 percent to the final price of cod in the very center of the Peninsula—in Toledo, for instance.

Elsewhere the town-specific contribution to variations in prices equaled or exceeded the cost of transport. Albacete (Castile) is the one town that seems to have been able to purchase its supplies cheaper overall than even Cadiz. In chapter 3 we saw that prices were low but quite volatile in Albacete. It seems likely that this pattern was explained by its location on the Castilian-Valencian internal border; being able to play suppliers from Alicante (Castile)

---

[74] Arguably the analysis for the entire country could use any year between 1700 and 1714 as a cutoff point, i.e., between the start of the reforms and the abolition of the *fueros* of Aragon. A number of alternative years have been tried with little impact on the estimates.

[75] Average price 1650–1775 in Essex County: 1.37 grams of silver per kilogram.

Table 6.2. Determinants of final price of *bacalao* in Iberian towns before and after the Nueva Planta decrees (%)

	pre-1714	post-1714
Price North America −1 (gr/kg)	8.84	27.41
Distance to port (100 km)	20.44	19.11
War	16.38	15.80
Albacete	−16.67	−16.32
Toledo	0.00	0.00
Sahagún	21.61	15.43
Seville	169.39	109.33
Barcelona	28.56	33.35
Bilbao	23.30	23.88
Pamplona	−15.24	44.80
R2	0.85	0.75

Note: Estimation based on OLS regressions In $p_i^t = \alpha + P_{NA}^t + Dist_i + war + \beta_i + \varepsilon$ with i towns. Pre-1714: $N = 293$, all coefficients significant at the 1 percent level, except Price North America −1, which is significant at the 10 percent level; post-1714: $N = 400$, all coefficients significant at the 1 percent level. Omitted towns: Madrid, due to multicollinearity, and Cadiz.

and Valencia against one another probably lowered the average price, but it also increased volatility.

Pamplona (Navarra) stands out again in this analysis because the town-specific price factors actually changed sign. In the seventeenth century, inhabitants of Pamplona spent on average 15 percent less on a given quantity cod. By the eighteenth century this advantage had experienced a dramatic reversal. Buying cod in Pamplona rather than Cadiz now added 45 percent to the price even after transport costs and year effects are taken into account.

In part Navarra paid the price for not having a coastline. *Bacalao* was introduced from Bilbao (Vizcaya) or more likely from San Sebastian (Guipúzcoa). In either case, it had to pay the Guipúzcoan *bacalao* tax. The tax was introduced in 1629 when the Crown first gave the province rights to level provincial taxes as opposed to having to finance itself exclusively through taxes collected by the municipalities. According to Mugartegui the duty rose from 68 *mrs* to 255 *mrs* per *carga* (load) by 1703.[76] Mugartegui assumed that it was a typical consumption tax falling mostly on Guipúzcoan pockets. However, it is likely that in a territory that had a privileged supply of fresh fish, it was the Navarrese on the other side of the border—and without alternate

[76] Mugartegui Eguía, *Estado*, 84–85.

suppliers—who paid the tax. They also paid not once but twice: since the cod was in transit the levy was due at the point of entry and the point of exit.

This Navarrese subsidy to the Guipúzcoan public purse can, however, explain only part of the price difference. Though the conversion of the "load" is subject to some doubt, the tax likely accounted for less than 10 percent of the premium paid for cod in Navarra in the eighteenth century.[77] Even if the estimate is conservative, the absence of a substantial price hike in the price of cod in Navarra as evidenced by Pamplona prices (figure 4.2c) around the time of the tax increase in 1703 seems to confirm that Guipúzcoan taxes were not the main driving force in the reversal of Pamplona's convergence trends. And since imports of foodstuffs into Navarra were not subject to import tariffs on the Navarrese side, these cannot explain the difference either. Yet another surtax on cod was introduced in Navarra directly in 1797 in order to help finance the repairs needed on the main road to Castile, the *camino real*.[78] Prices rose further in the following years, but that charge cannot explain the long-term divergence of Navarrese *bacalao* prices either. The only reasonable explanation for the massive increase in prices in eighteenth-century Pamplona is local consumption taxes or other types of market interventions.

The surcharge paid by Seville consumers illustrates vividly the massive impact of local consumption taxes. Seville was particularly indebted; the Crown had used the town as a means of finance since the early days of the sixteenth century, in return granting Seville a remarkable level of independent power. Its debt peaked in the late sixteenth century and fell dramatically in the first half of the seventeenth century. It rose steadily again until the 1730s, when it was stabilized but remained high for the rest of the century.[79] As a consequence, Seville imposed legendary burdensome consumption taxes on its population. In the case of *bacalao* this tax regime resulted in prices that would have been the equivalent of moving the city 800 kilometers further from the coast—in other words, twice as far away from the next port as geographically possible in the Iberian Peninsula. By comparison, Pamplona's surcharge in the eighteenth century was a little less dramatic, equal to 250 kilometers from the coast. But in this case we cannot say with any certainty if the difference was caused by territorial or municipal features.

Both cases clearly show how multifaceted the problem of market integration was in Spain. Transport costs were indeed important but less so over time. The degree to which they explain the final price of an imported commodity like cod also depended on where the consumer lived. In Madrid, Toledo, or Sahagún it is likely that general transactions costs accounted for much of the price increase as the fish was taken into the interior. Moving goods between

---

[77] Based on 1 *carga* = 123 kilograms and 5 grams of silver tax per *carga*, the tax would have added 0.15 to 0.2 grams of silver per kilogram. Mugartegui's figures for total taxes would suggest the total import of *bacalao* did not exceed about 140 tons in the late eighteenth century. This seems very low and would suggest that the measure of the cod *carga* was actually smaller.

[78] Navarra, *Cuadernos*, 2:115–27.

[79] Martínez Ruiz, *Finanzas municipales*, passim.

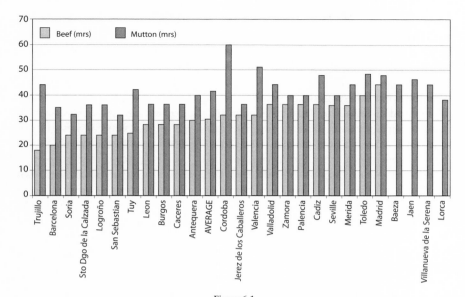

Figure 6.1
Beef and mutton prices in different cities (1764–66) (*mrs*). *Source*: Palop Ramos, *Fluctuaciones*, 85–86.

historic territories added to the cost. However, given the general reliance of the tax system on local consumption taxes, it is hardly surprising that in some towns the impact of the local tax regime dwarfed transport costs.

In the end, cod connoisseurs in Toledo or Madrid paid the additional costs of transport but not much beyond that. Once more it is clear that the markets at the center of the Peninsula, Madrid and Toledo, are not the problematic markets in seventeenth- and eighteenth-century Spain. If anything they were more closely integrated with nearby towns and the coast. Non-Castilian consumers paid a surcharge for cod, even if their overall tax burden was much lower than that of Castilians, as we saw above. This is a reminder of the complications arising from the multiple levels of jurisdictional fragmentation that superimposed territorial and municipal divergences. It also calls into question the notion that the exempt Basque Provinces enjoyed much lower import prices. In fact, given the high level of transatlantic market integration observed in chapter 3, it is possible that cod exporters and/or importers in the exempt Basque Provinces captured the tax advantage by rolling it over at least in part to the Basque consumers.

How representative were the patterns seen in the cod market for the relative cost of transport and jurisdictional fragmentation in general? In one sense they were very representative. *Bacalao* was a staple, and as opposed to grain, it was at the receiving end of the predominant features of the political economy of early modern Spain. Local and regional customs, taxes, and dues applied to cod as they did to meat, wine, oil, and a large number of other staple products. What the study of *bacalao* reflects very clearly is the large

impact of local and regional political economy factors on price levels in Spain
and thus on market integration.

In another sense, cod is not representative. It would be very dangerous to
assume that a high price of cod in town A could be interpreted as an indica-
tion that all prices in town A were high. Figure 6.1 reflects an attempt by
Palop Ramos to estimate the price of beef and mutton across Spanish towns
in the mid-1760s. The picture reflects the one for *bacalao*, which was studied here in much more detail. The average price of beef was 30 *mrs*, that of
mutton 41. Yet the beef price ranged from 18 to 44 *mrs*. In the graph, towns
have been ordered from left to right according to the price of beef, the most
important meat in Spain. This illustrates clearly that mutton prices were not
necessarily following the same pattern across towns. Another point is noteworthy. Beef and mutton prices in Palop's sample were quite high in Seville,
but they were actually slightly lower than those in Toledo and Madrid.

Distant Tyranny

The Bourbon reforms did try to effect some unification. Yet, as we saw, their
impact on the ground was severely circumscribed no matter how one judges
their aspirations. The final outcome—a very uneven tax burden between
territories (as seen in chapter 5) combined with divergences at the town
level—was such that their impact on individual products was almost unpredictable. The estimates in chapter 5 suggested that *bacalao* was about 5 to 20
percent cheaper in Catalonia, Navarra, and Vizcaya than it was in Castile.
However, when we move to the town level, it becomes considerably more complicated. In the case of Barcelona and Bilbao in particular it is hard to tell the
urban from the territorial effects, but the Castilian towns illustrate that town
effects were probably at least as important as those of the historic territories.

In chapter 4 a curious picture emerged: towns that were quite integrated
with others in terms of their price movements and volatility seemed to be on
a different plane altogether when looking at their price levels. The evidence
provided in table 5.1 makes this picture much clearer. Geography was not
to blame. The historical territories and their customs and tax systems mattered and can explain the differences between some towns. But in some cases,
town-specific factors do most of the explaining. In this sample this is clearly
the case for Seville. It is close to impossible to follow to the smallest detail the
system of local dues—*sisas, arbitrios, alcabalas*, and *cientos*—that municipalities used to finance themselves. The evidence thus has to be indirect. But
it is well-known that heavily indebted municipalities like Seville burdened
their inhabitants with ever more consumption taxes.

In the end two points stand out. First, the most serious distortions in Spanish Iberian markets were not caused by transport costs but by the combined
effect of jurisdictional fragmentation at the level of the historic territories and
the towns. Seen from the bottom up through the eyes of *bacalao* consumers,
the eighteenth-century state did not markedly improve its role as coordinator

of the internal market across the historic territories. This of course is not an entirely new insight. But given the tendency in the historiography to continue stressing the break between the Habsburg and Bourbon periods, it is worth noting. The consumer paid for this through the detrimental effects of less integrated markets that limited consumption choices.

There was more reform zeal after 1700 to be sure. Yet its effect on market integration was muted. The data do not suggest a substantial step change in market integration between, or tax unification across, historic territories after 1700 or 1714. Variations across towns remained almost unchanged over the eighteenth century. The process of urban reform was certainly more drawn out over the century than the change in the legal status of the Crown of Aragon had been. However, the lack of any trend toward a harmonization of prices across towns in the eighteenth century would suggest that the urban reform program did little to overcome the fragmentation of markets. Nor should we be surprised. Reforms designed to keep a closer eye on urban finances might have improved the quality of fiscal administration. Yet at the same time, the requirement to pay off urban debts increased the need for local taxation even further.

Second and more important, while the potential costs of jurisdictional fragmentation have now been generally acknowledged, the analysis presented here allows us to asses them in comparison with transport costs for the first time. Not surprisingly, their impact was uneven, but in some places the costs of jurisdictional fragmentation outweighed all other transaction costs, including transport, by a factor of 8. Notwithstanding the large margins of error, the order of magnitude is such that one cannot but acknowledge that overall jurisdictional fragmentation was a much larger problem than geography. Furthermore, transport was steadily improving, though painfully slowly. The costs imposed by jurisdictional fragmentation by contrast showed no clear trend at all. Finally, the methodology employed herein has made it possible to compare the impact of jurisdictional fragmentation at different political levels. The results suggest that while the historiography had paid considerable attention to the power located in the historic territories, quantitatively the negative consequences of strong urban autonomy on market integration were even larger. Marx had been on to something all along.

The analysis of the *bacalao* markets in Spain between the mid-seventeenth century and the end of the eighteenth century has thus helped clarify quite a few of the apparent contradictions of market integration. The political economy of Spain was ill suited to overcome jurisdictional fragmentation because the deeply ingrained notion of local and territorial representation was protected by institutional structures and a fiscal system that underpinned the sovereign rights of territories and towns, even in some cases where those had been abolished *de iure*. However, why did this jurisdictional fragmentation stifle economic growth in Spain to such an extent? To understand this we need to return to the questions of where the growth potential of early modern European economies lay, why it was so hard to mobilize in Spain, and what the slow and haphazard growth of the market that did occur look like.

Chapter 7

Market Growth and Governance in Early Modern Spain

> I have ever thought it a useful and entertaining Study, to enquire into the Trade and Manufactures of a Country, and to note down whatever was excellent or defective in either, from hence a valuable Lesson is learned, of imitating the one, or avoiding the other. I therefore applied myself to understand the foreign Commerce of the Minorquins [inhabitants of the island of Menorca], and considered the Manufactures they raised from their native Commodities, with the Attention they deserved.
>
> Upon a nearer View, I discovered with Astonishment and Concern, that these poor people trifled away their Time in childish Amusements, and neglected almost every Advantage of their Climate and Situation, and were contented to import a thousand Necessaries, and twice the Number of Superfluities, from foreign Countries, for which they paid ready Money."[1]

CAUGHT BETWEEN ANXIETIES about Anglo-Spanish imperial rivalry and their own hubris, English travel writers of the eighteenth century had few charitable things to say about their Iberian competitor. Spaniards were "lazy, improvident people," taunted one observer. Another thought that "the listless indolence equally dear to the uncivilized savage, and to the degenerate slave of despotism, is no where more indulged than in Spain; thousands of men in all parts of the realm are seen to pass their whole day, wrapped up in a cloak, standing in rows against a wall, or dosing [*sic*] under a tree."[2] The author of the first passage, the British engineer John Armstrong, who had been stationed on the Balearic Island of Menorca in 1738, was at a loss to comprehend why the islanders had not embraced more enterprising ways, given that they had been under British rule since 1708.[3]

Leaving aside time-honored British chauvinism, descriptions of Spain in the eighteenth century are intriguing for their accounts of perceived indolence, or more generally of a people who failed to take advantage "of their Climate and Situation." Taken at face value these observations convinced

---

[1] Armstrong, *Letters from Minorca*, vii–viii.

[2] *A Trip to Spain*. See also MacKay, *Myth and Reality*, and Swinburne, *Travels*. For an excellent analysis of these writings, see Hontanilla, "Images."

[3] Menorca was officially ceded to Britain in the Treaty of Utrecht (1713) and with shorter interruptions held by the British until the Treaty of Amiens (1802).

contemporaries and historians that Spain was simply producing less than it could have. Alleged idleness was a well-rehearsed theme in Europe's Protestant north whenever the mores of southern European papists (or non-Europeans, for that matter) were described. Swinburne thought that

> The poor Spaniard does not work, unless urged by irresistible want, because he perceives no advantage accrue from industry. As his food and raiment are purchased at a small expence, he spends no more time in labour, than is absolutely necessary for procuring the scanty provision his abstemiousness requires.[4]

This observation is more revealing than it might seem. First, Swinburne argued that Spaniards worked fewer hours and days than he thought they ought to. Second, unwittingly perhaps, Swinburne intuitively provided one possible explanation for such behavior. Spaniards simply did not believe they could benefit from higher levels of "industry," that is, effort. What he was describing was the paradox of "backward" societies: the underutilization of available resources, in this specific case, underemployment.

Living Below Their Means

It would be dangerous to blame the remarks of Swinburne or Armstrong solely on the well-studied cultural arrogance of British writers. Spanish sources of the early to mid-eighteenth century agreed in principle.[5] They regularly supposed that agricultural laborers would only have work 100 to 120 full days per year. For artisans they assumed 180 days of full employment, while in the service sector 250 days might have been the norm.[6] Even in the later eighteenth century agricultural laborers were probably employed for only 150 to 200 days a year, and a workday outside the main agricultural

---

[4] Swinburne, *Travels*, 150–51. The comments reflected the notion of a backward-bending labor supply curve, that is, a situation where the effects of increased income dominate the substitution effects of work for leisure that higher salaries could induce. To put it simply: workers would reduce their labor offer if wages increased. The empirical evidence of the existence of such labor market behavior at low-income levels is thin, but most eighteenth-century contemporaries believed this to be true.

[5] In her marvelous work on the attitudes toward work in eighteenth-century Spain, Ruth MacKay rightfully points out that the problem was not that Spaniards refused manual labor, as so often claimed, but that Enlightenment writers stumbled over their own prejudices. MacKay, *Myth and Reality*. The argument presented here adds an economic dimension to MacKay's work in social and cultural history but agrees entirely on the general point.

[6] When the Crown tried to reform the Catalan tax system after 1714 it calculated the *tributo personal* to be paid by individuals on daily incomes multiplied by 100 and 180 days of full-time work, respectively. See Fernández de Pinedo, "Cataluña," 195. The Catastro de Ensenada of the 1750s used 120, 180, and 250 days for agricultural laborers, artisans, and services, respectively.

season might not have exceeded five hours of actual work time.[7] According to the director of the largest cloth manufacturer in Segovia, workers put in three to four hours less a day than in a comparable French establishment.[8]

The contrast with northern Europe, where by the second half of the eighteenth century traditions like the work-free "Saint Monday" were rapidly disappearing, was increasingly obvious.[9] In northern Europe most workers probably put in close to 300 days, a number that was reached in Spain only in the late nineteenth century by Catalan industrial workers.[10] Agricultural workers in the 1840s across Spain worked about 240 days, but regional differences seem to have been large: in Andalusia the average number of workdays in agriculture was probably only 120 even in the late nineteenth century.[11] Though there are intense debates about the actual length of the working day and week in northwestern Europe, it seems certain that effective working hours increased there much earlier and faster than in southern Europe generally and in Spain specifically.[12]

Choices?

Historians have concentrated on two possible mechanisms that could explain different patterns of labor efforts over time: on the one hand, religious changes led to the abolition of Catholic holidays, which in turn increased the number of *potential* workdays. On the other hand, the introduction of new consumer goods increased the incentive to augment the family income that could be spent on desirable new products. The former is well documented. Protestant regions often experienced a strong discontinuity following the abolition of saint's days, but it is clear that a similar though slower and more continuous

---

[7] Peiró Arroyo cites some evidence that Aragonese laborers were on average unemployed for about four months and that another 50 days fell on religious holidays. He concludes that the work year was about 200 days. But laborers would also rest on Sundays, so the real number was probably closer to 150 days. Peiró Arroyo, *Jornaleros*, 74–77. Alvarez Nogal and Prados de la Escosura have also recently estimated that agricultural workers had 150 days of work around 1800, while artisans worked about 200. Alvarez Nogal and Prados de la Escosura, "Rise and Fall," 8–9, with permission from the author. Fernández Romero suggests that in Navarra male adults might have worked between 215 and 229 days a year, in part because of the relatively high labor demand of Navarra's viticulture and combining various sources of employment. Fernández Romero, *Gastos*, 53.

[8] García Sanz, "Competitivos," 423.

[9] Thompson, *English Working Class*; Voth, "The Longest Years."

[10] Allen, "The Great Divergence," assumes 250 days across Europe in the early modern period. Domenech argues that Catalan textile workers put in 282 days in 1870–80 and 291 days in the early nineteenth century. However, even these were low by international standards for the time. Domenech, "Working Hours," 472.

[11] For Andalusia, see Simpson, "Technological Change."

[12] For an in-depth discussion of northwestern European patterns, see de Vries, *The Industrious Revolution*, 87–92.

process occurred in Catholic areas.[13] The latter mechanism is demonstrated most fully in Jan de Vries' magisterial recent work on the "Industrious Revolution." De Vries argues that the promise of increased consumption of "new luxuries," affordable and standardized but fashionable goods, drove families to raise and specialize their labor input. Northwestern European families were smaller, which made it easier to coordinate their consumption wishes within the household. This in turn gave them an incentive to try to increase the family money wage. They broke out of a world that knew only leisure for the rich and coercion for the poor, the world of antiquity (and the U.S. South before the abolition of slavery), or indeed leisure and poverty for all.[14] The lure of consumption made families work more, harder, and in a more specialized way. In doing so, they set the Netherlands and Britain, in particular, on a path of economic growth that was faster than that of the rest of Europe and the rest of the world.

De Vries has given us an elegant and convincing account of families' choices: how they allocated their time between leisure and work, and how they allocated their income between the "bare necessities" and modest amounts of conspicuous consumption in response to market incentives. He makes, however, one crucial assumption almost *en passant*. His "industrious" people needed markets that were integrated enough for new goods to be readily available and more work to be on offer; they had to be the kind of markets that allocated resources efficiently and where workers chose how, and how much, to work and consume. It is thus not surprising to observe this process earliest and most intensely in the Netherlands and Britain, which exhibited very high degrees of internal market integration very early on.

Or No Choices?

Elsewhere, such choices of labor supply or consumption patterns were only rarely available. In the absence of well-integrated markets both the demand for labor and the supply of goods were typically very inelastic. Most underemployed agricultural laborers in Spain were not bound to the land and could vote with their feet in search of more working hours—and some of them did. Spanish commentators were greatly concerned about the evident depopulation of large agricultural regions in the Castilian interior. They alleged that land was falling fallow while there always seemed to be too few employment opportunities for the swelling, idle, urban masses, most of whom were

---

[13] Ibid., 88. Though de Vries does not discuss the decline in feast days in Catholic countries, it might have been demand driven, i.e., where workers were interested in increasing their labor supply, objections to the abolition of religious holidays waned. Voth, by contrast, stresses government intervention reforming the number of feast days. Voth, "Physical Exertion."

[14] Ibid., 41.

migrants from the depopulating agrarian hinterland. Migration evidently served as an adjustment mechanism, but it was a very blunt and limited one.

Even if migration left behind empty interior villages and created mounting supply problems in a few large cities, notably Madrid, factor markets for labor and capital were as slow to integrate as goods markets.[15] The share of total urban population in Spain hardly increased at all between the 1650s and 1800, bearing witness to the limited contribution that internal migration could make to overall market development. Like external migration, it would only start to have a real impact on the Spanish economy in the late nineteenth century.[16] At the same time, we will see that capital markets suffered similarly from fragmentation and that in the goods markets the introduction of new commodities into the Spanish markets beyond large towns took a very long time, inevitably limiting consumer choice.

Understanding the relation between underutilization of resources and poorly integrated markets is vital to shed light on the sort of backwardness that afflicted early modern Spain. A simple graphic tool used in economics known as the production possibility frontier (PPF) can help. It illustrates the maximum output of goods and services that a society can produce (the "GDP"). For simplicity one can assume that society produces just two goods or services. This is depicted in figure 7.1: the further to the right society moves, the more of good/service 1 is being produced; the further to the top, the more of good/service 2 is produced.[17] The frontier delimits the maximum amount of all products/services that can be produced given the available natural resources, labor, and capital (the "factors of production") and given the available technology.

Along the frontier a society can reallocate these resources to produce different combinations of various goods and services—the equivalent of moving from point B to point B' or any other place on the curve. Yet unless available resources increase or technology improves, society has to stay within the frontier. The problem is that premodern societies were usually not *on* but far *inside* the PPF. Because capital, labor, and natural resources were allocated inefficiently, society produced maybe at point A, far away from their potential output at B or B'. To put it simply: premodern societies were really a lot poorer than they ought to have been.[18]

This is not to say that early modern societies in general, or in Iberia in particular, were economically stagnant in the early modern period. What de Vries termed aptly the "the revolt of the early modernists" has shown beyond any doubt that earlier ideas of a stagnant premodern world were ill-conceived.[19] A large body of empirical research has illustrated a slow and intermittent, often

---

[15] For contemporary comment on the lack of agricultural and artisan population outside the large towns, see, e.g., Ward, *Proyecto económico*, 204–6.

[16] Rosés and Sánchez-Alonso, "Regional Wage Convergence."

[17] The PPF is generally assumed to be strictly concave to the origin.

[18] Epstein, "Rise of the West," 253–55.

[19] De Vries, "The Industrial Revolution and the Industrious Revolution," 253.

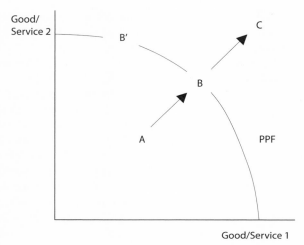

Figure 7.1
The society-wide production possibility frontier.

geographically diverse but eventually substantial expansion of the European economy for centuries before the Industrial Revolution.[20] The argument is no longer whether there *was* growth in the early modern world but *what kind* of growth. The nature of growth in many parts of Europe, including Spain, was of the sort based on the eradication of inefficiencies rather than the pushing out of boundaries. It was about getting from A to B, not from B to C, most of the time.

In theory, there are three ways in which premodern economies could grow.[21] One was to expand the PPF through more factors of production, more population, more capital, more natural resources. More population, however, often lowered per capita income. Early modern societies still occasionally faced the threat of the Malthusian trap, and population growth, though a stated aim of eighteenth-century mercantilists, was a mixed blessing. Where the degree of market integration was low, population increases put pressure on the agricultural sector. Hence, population-induced growth was probably most of the time extensive rather than intensive.[22]

De Vries' concept of the "Industrious Revolution" charts a more promising path taken by the likes of the Netherlands and England. If the existing population could offer more labor input with only a slight increase in the need for the production of foodstuffs, labor could be employed in more efficient ways and society might be on its way to a factor-driven expansion of

[20] For recent estimates of Spain in the European context, see Llopis Agelán, "La 'revolución de los modernistas,'" and Alvarez Nogal and Prados de la Escosura, "Rise and Fall."

[21] Growth here is meant to be intensive growth, i.e., per capita growth.

[22] This held true unless in a process first considered by Boserup the pressure on agricultural resources actually induced improved techniques in farming and animal husbandry. Boserup, *The Conditions of Agricultural Growth.*

the PPF (point C).[23] More capital might have also mattered, but as we will see, there is little reason to believe that a lack of investible capital kept the Spanish economy in check. Finally, land and natural resources were difficult to expand by the early modern period. Most land was used for some form of agriculture. Institutional factors such as land markets circumscribed by the near-inalienable holdings of municipalities, large ecclesiastical institutions, and noble *mayorazgos* probably limited agricultural development, though their impact in Spain is hotly contested.[24] By the late eighteenth century, there was evidence in Spain that some land previously used as commons had been taken under the plow for more intensive use.[25] But Spain had only limited possibilities for the kind of "reclamation" projects that expanded agricultural land in some parts of northern Europe in the eighteenth century, even if it is not clear whether the potential for irrigation was fully exploited.[26]

The second way to push the PPF from point B to point C was through improved technology. The role of knowledge and technology in early modern society used to be underestimated, mainly because technological change in hindsight seemed so slow by the standards of the modern period. Readily applicable macro-inventions that would expand the economy's limits were rare. But new processes and products often helped remedy existing allocative inefficiencies. Chapter 4 offered some proof of this. Transport technology did not experience any fundamental macro-inventions in this period. It continued to employ mules and oxen, as well as small carts or wagons that changed only slowly in design. Yet small improvements in the organization of transport and limited road building drove down travel times across the Spanish geography in sustained ways, if very slowly. Technological progress and more efficient markets were thus intimately related. "Useful" knowledge, or knowledge that had a relatively direct practical application in technology and processes, underpinned a more efficient use of resources and thus helped society inch closer to its frontier as the example of transport illustrates.[27]

However, beyond the very important interplay between technological change and better-functioning markets, allocative efficiency was more than anything else a function of market integration. This third path to economic growth was unglamorous but fundamental. As long as skills, labor, capital,

[23] De Vries, *The Industrious Revolution*, 112. De Vries' model is, as the author acknowledges, an expansion of a Boserupian model that introduces a non-agricultural sector (77–78).

[24] For an in-depth account of rural land markets and use, see Yun Casalilla, *Sobre la transición*, 455–504.

[25] Herr, *Rural Change*; Simpson, *Siesta*, 64–67.

[26] Neither the yield per hectare nor labor productivity or the total amount of cultivated land increased between the mid- and late eighteenth century. They did, however, roughly double over the nineteenth century, suggesting precisely the kind of underutilization of resources discussed here. See Bringas Gutiérrez, *Productividad*. For long-term trends since, see Yun Casalilla, *Sobre la transición*, 505–6. The creation of more irrigated land with the construction of the Canal Imperial de Aragon in the 1780s was one of the few larger projects undertaken.

[27] Mokyr, *Gifts of Athena*.

and other inputs into production could not be matched in the same place, they remained useless. In the 1740s, a pamphlet on fiscal reform put the problems this way: Catalonia had plenty of cloth-making establishments, which produced a quality that could compete well with foreign manufactures. The fine wool needed for their manufacture was produced in Segovia, in old Castile generally, but also in Extremadura and more northern areas.[28] Alas, the transport of wool over land from Old Castile to Catalonia on mule back made the finished textiles uncompetitive compared to international imports by the time they were taken back into the interior. The obvious solution was coastal shipping. Yet the pamphlet pointed out that wool could not be taken to the coast and from there by coastal shipping to Catalonia because customs were charged as soon as it reached the port.[29] Only in 1746 did a reform allow the shipment of wool free of the specific tax from a limited number of Spanish Mediterranean ports.[30] This system, however, still required the placement of sureties to be reimbursed on presentation of proof that the wool had remained on Spanish soil in the Peninsula. Even then the most important ports in the north were still excluded.

How much textile-making know-how the Catalans had acquired, how much capital they had at their disposal, and how skilled they were at distributing their wares across the Peninsula did not matter. As long as it was prohibitively expensive for them to obtain the necessary wool, a raw material produced in larger quantities and higher qualities in Spain than anywhere else in Europe, their production could not compete with imports.[31] Obtaining wool, however, was not expensive just because overland transport was dear; rather, overland transport had to be chosen because the customs regime in the seaports translated into internal customs barriers between Castile and Catalonia. This was the case as late as the 1740s after the land internal customs had finally disappeared.

This example illustrates a simple issue well-known to Spanish historians: the problem was not scarcity of skills, capital, or natural resources per se but "matching" or allocative inefficiency. The latter could be mediated to a degree by the substitution of factors of production and inputs more generally. Mules could sometimes substitute for coastal shipping. But there were obvious limits to that sort of substitution. Thus, more integrated markets for labor and manufactures, for skills and agricultural products, were probably the single most important way in which early modern societies slowly moved

[28] For an estimate of regional production, see García Sanz, "Competitivos," 401.

[29] Zabala y Auñon and de Loynaz, *Sobre el modo de aliviar los vasallos*, 132. See also Madrazo, *Comunicaciones*, 80–81.

[30] Real Orden, 15 de marzo 1746, quoted in Muñoz Pérez, "Mapa," 761n733.

[31] García Sanz has argued that Spanish cloth making was in fact competitive in lower qualities but could not compete in higher qualities due to poor technology, high monitoring costs, and high wages rather than transport. Given that he looked at production in Segovia, transport costs would be low. But here skills and other inputs were in short supply. García Sanz, "Competitivos."

toward reaching their actual potential—and "industriously" began to push the boundaries of what was thought possible.

Poor allocation meant not only shortages, however, but also the opposite. Early modern European economies were full of slack.[32] This was particularly but not exclusively true in the agrarian sector. Grantham estimates that existing technology could have produced an agricultural output that was 60 percent above the actual output of eighteenth-century French agriculture.[33] Barquín argues that Spain produced too much grain most of the time, not too little.[34] This was not out of foolishness but bare necessity. The target production had to be so high because the minimum supply had to be guaranteed even in years of bad harvests. In good years the excess could simply be fed to animals. As long as it was prohibitively expensive to make up the often quite regionally restricted harvest shortfall with supplies from neighboring regions, peasants had to err on the side of caution. As a French traveler observed in 1655:

> The provinces of the interior are too distant from profit in order to share in the work [available in the coastal areas]. This fault also creates a monstrous inequality in the wealth of the Provinces, and a real danger for those in the center of the realm to die of famine, or to [just] save themselves through depopulation in the case of famine, at the same time that neighboring provinces may be overflowing with grain and necessary victuals, without being able to supply [the interior provinces].[35]

In other words the only insurance against famine was overproduction in "normal" years. Fields that could have been used for grazing and the production of more profitable meat, or milk, or wool had to be given to grain production as an implicit insurance against the possible havoc caused by poor weather.[36] The prime problem of early modern societies was not poverty but inefficiency. Inefficiency, however, was largely the result of poorly integrated markets.

The Economic Consequences of Representative Governance

Consequentially, economic progress in early modern societies was to a considerable extent about the elimination of slack. Technology that would have

---

[32] The potential role of slack in both economy and politics is discussed in detail by Hirschman, *Exit, Voice, and Loyalty*, 12–15.

[33] Grantham, "Divisions of Labour."

[34] Barquín finds that the elasticity of demand for grain was much higher than most historians have thought and argues convincingly that the only reasonable explanation is overproduction. Barquín Gil, "Las elasticidades."

[35] Claverie, "Voyage," 458. My translation.

[36] McCloskey has shown most clearly how the persistence of agrarian practices long described as obsolete such as open fields become intelligible when seen in the context of insurance against harvest fluctuations. Donald McCloskey, "Enclosure of Open Fields."

drastically reduced transport costs, by shifting goods onto waterborne trade, for example, could remove slack. Yet a technological step change in transport was impossible in a country that was ill-suited for canals and river shipping. In such relatively poorly integrated markets, institutional and organizational solutions to problems of matching and coordination were thus paramount.

These could be of a private nature, for example, an agreement between a convent in central Castile and a muleteer trader to supply *bacalao* to the interior on the basis of a risk-sharing agreement. Such contracts allowed cash-strapped mule owners to act as agents for transactions that were otherwise impossible to finance, thereby overcoming the mismatch in capital markets.[37] Private actors could also employ collective action, as in the case of the Spanish merchant guilds, the *consulados*, that pooled resources to organize, protect, and monitor their trade.[38]

Yet much of the coordinating activity fell to political institutions that established a monopoly of power and administration over a particular territory and with it determined taxes, market rules, customs, and regulations. Chapter 1 argued that economists have zoomed in largely on how powerful political regimes distorted incentives by favoring some at the expense of others. The predominant political economy model with its focus on the predatory state always assumed (but rarely investigated) that the fiscal system in polities like Spain was extractive because the Crown was not constrained in its actions across the board. Where the monarch had undivided sovereignty, subjects and their economic activities were liable to be fleeced. Restrictions emanating from divided sovereignty just made matters worse because the burden of abusive central states would fall disproportionately on a few sectors of society and the economy.

However, as we have seen, the early modern Spanish polity in fact failed to acquire the sort of monopoly of power ascribed to it by the traditional narrative. The location and exercise of power remained multipolar to an unusual degree. The problem was not so much the active intervention of a central state in the Spanish economy or the existence of coercion that distorted incentives. Instead, economic historians and political economists have underestimated the challenges that early modern European states faced on their way to becoming autonomous strong actors in the first place. The lack of a powerful, centralizing state in Spain was not simply a matter of poor implementation of nominally centralist policies based on "a wealth of analysis [of economic and political problems] and poverty of execution."[39]

---

[37] For the wool trade in the first half of the seventeenth century, see Grafe, *Mundo ibérico*, chapter 7. Ramos Palencia provides a fascinating discussion of small-scale and larger trading networks and mechanisms that slowly integrated the town and hinterland of Palencia into pan-Iberian markets. Ramos Palencia, "Pautas," chapters 7 and 8.

[38] Guilds and other producer and merchant organizations could of course also be an obstacle to more integrated markets. For the recent debate, see Epstein, "Craft Guilds"; Ogilvie, "Rehabilitating the Guilds"; and Grafe, "Guilds, Innovation, and the European Economy."

[39] Stein and Stein, *Edge of Crisis*, 3.

The analysis of where power was located (that is, the corporate entities endowed with jurisdictional rights), how power was exercised (that is, who were the historical actors), and how power was legitimized socially, religiously, and ideologically has broken out of the teleological models of the predatory fiscal-military state. It suggests a polity where a lot of power continued to be located in the municipalities and historical territories but also in a number of other corporate entities, such as the merchant guilds. The Crown was a crucial element in this, as it was needed to negotiate the interests of a multitude of players who perceived themselves as possessing "special" but essentially equal status. Not surprisingly, control over these bodies was a continuous political contest; Spain's lower nobility, for instance, became almost inseparably entwined with urban government.

Local and regional autonomy allowed for decision making based on direct knowledge and created a political competition that made the emergence of a more coercive political force impossible. It also made coercion unnecessary most of the time. Spain was a polity that experienced few serious challenges to its governance. Within its governance structure local and regional concerns were prioritized. Spanish territories and corporate bodies, for instance, defended the moral economy of the right of a population to affordable food with an armory of legal challenges. This helps to account for the relatively low incidence of food riots in Spain even at times when agricultural crises hit large parts of the Peninsula and Spain's poor market integration aggravated local misery.

Yet local and regional autonomy came at the expense of further limiting market coordination in an economy where relatively high transport costs already slowed down the deepening and widening of the market. The outcome was that local and regional representation protected Spain from coercion but paradoxically hindered economic development. Every local rejection of the Crown's attempts to intervene in affairs of taxation, market regulation, and provision was another step away from unification. The relatively flat hierarchies of political and social organizations in Spain's corporate society resulted in an insufficient coordination of activity.[40]

Different types of jurisdictional fragmentation shaped economic outcomes. The Spanish structure of governance affected market integration so unevenly for two major interrelated reasons. First, the historical territories resisted the abolition of their "historic freedoms," their collective rights which, truth be told, consisted in restricting the freedom of individuals. Second, the strength of the "urban republics" added another formidable layer to the equation. Even if these two levels were notionally autonomous from one another, in effect they were not. The Crown's inability to override the resistance of the historic territories to an abolition of the *puertos secos* and to the creation of a more effective external tariff or a more effective tobacco monopoly (seen in chapter 5) made it impossible to shift the tax burden away from indi-

[40] Epstein, "Rise of the West," 255.

rect consumption taxes. With strongly circumscribed control over "national taxes" such as customs and excise (*rentas generales y estancos*), consumption taxes had to remain the backbone of the fiscal system. However, those were under the control of the municipalities and strengthened the role of the towns within the overall system of governance. They were also even more fragmented with grievous consequences for market integration.

This lack of coordination thus revealed itself at all levels of organization. The slow and uneven process of economic integration between the Spanish historic territories was one element, but the actions of "urban republics" were another. The large share of price differences explained by local and regional sovereignty over the prime source of fiscal income, trade and consumption taxes, restricted consumer choice. Early modern Spanish municipalities had enough real-life fiscal experience to single out those goods for taxation that consumers found harder to substitute: oil, meat, fish, vinegar, prominent local products such as silks in Valencia, or most important in many towns, wine. Yet as long as bread was not taxed, everything had a substitute. With their debts sky high, town councils often acknowledged that they were effectively shutting down markets for certain products. Many town aldermen also knew three centuries ago that tax revenue on consumption behaved like the Laffer income tax curve: revenue would first rise with higher rates but then higher rates would discourage consumption so much that aggregate revenue would fall. However, at the local level the town *regidores* had few choices.

Tax rates not only differed between towns or territories but also across goods. "National" markets were hard to establish if a charge was imposed at the city gate on *bacalao* in town A, while in town B mutton was the town treasurer's favorite victim. It did not help if fish on its way to Pamplona had to pass either two inland customs points if it came from the port of San Sebastian or one external and one internal customs point if it came from Barcelona. Paying taxes was in itself a cumbersome and costly process and open to corruption and bribes. Papers had to be produced to document payment of dues, notaries had to be paid to produce the papers, sureties had to be deposited, which bound up capital. And in the end the aggregate cost of delivering *bacalao* to the consumer might simply be prohibitive, such that no market existed at all. Where there was no supply there was little incentive for local laborers to maximize their working hours either.

Contemporaries were well aware of the issues. In the 1720s, Uztáriz thought that the price of Spanish manufactures was driven up by "the *millones*, which have also risen a lot, and the *sisas*, and the municipal *arbitrios*, practically all levied on foodstuffs, which the workers consume," with detrimental effects for the whole economy.[41] His analysis was not novel. Alvarez de Toledo had argued exactly the same in the early seventeenth century, only he blamed the *alcabalas* (sales taxes) since the *millones* had only just been

[41] Uztáriz, *Theorica*, 320–21.

introduced.[42] The ultimate result was a quagmire: consumption taxes drove up prices and wages, hurting both the competitiveness of manufactures and agricultural products. At the same time their localized impact stymied market integration, making it hard to eliminate both shortages and slack. Poor allocation in turn reduced the choices of workers and consumers alike. No matter how industrious Spaniards felt, more often than not there was no work to do and nothing to consume.

Reaching Spanish Consumers

And yet new goods like *bacalao* would eventually make it into the market, even in Spain. Much of the mercantilist disdain for cod imports was alarmist, but as seen in chapter 3, there was no mistaking the expansion of the consumption of *bacalao*, or that of tobacco, or chocolate, or coffee, or cotton fabrics, or many other novel goods associated with the creation of a new consumer culture in the later seventeenth and eighteenth centuries. Was it possible that an industrious revolution occurred in such a backward economy? Or was this just a result of the conspicuous consumption of the few who chose to consume and not invest rather than the virtuous consumption of the many who would work harder for their share of the new world of goods?

Seen exclusively from the supply side, the apparent contradiction between increasing imports of these new commodities and the disappointing pace of market integration is hard to resolve. The conventional analysis of market integration using prices that we have relied on up to this point cannot explain why Spanish consumers increased their purchases of cod. The introduction of *bacalao* proceeded from coasts toward the interior. One explanation for why consumption continued to increase over time even though domestic market integration between the towns of this sample improved only haltingly was precisely that more consumers became part of the distribution networks.

Town and Country

Like most market integration studies, we have so far looked primarily at large towns, and it is for towns that we have the best data. Yet arguably some of the most important changes were not occurring at the level of intertown integration but through the expansion of networks into the hinterland of these towns. There are very few studies of food consumption outside towns, and existing price data only reflect urban markets.[43] As a consequence, existing market integration studies arguably tell us little about 60–80 percent of the

---

[42] Sureda Carrión, *La hacienda castellana*, 183–84.
[43] Again the very extensive study by Cubillo de la Puente is a case in point, as it hardly mentions differences between urban and rural consumption. Cubillo de la Puente, *El pescado*, 302. Most of the articles he cites on consumption focus on the supply of towns.

early modern population that lived in rural areas. One way around this problem is to compare the existing figures for urban demand with the estimates for overall per capita supply. The logic is simple: since urban consumption was higher than average per capita consumption, rural spending on *bacalao* must have been lower than average.

Tax data, which are systematically biased to underestimate consumption, indicate that Madrileños consumed a minimum of 3.5 kilograms in 1629, 3.7 kilograms in 1789, and 2.5 kilograms in 1848.[44] Thus the absolute lower-bound estimates are slightly higher than our estimates for per capita supply (minimum of 3.0 kilograms in the late eighteenth century). Coronas Tejada argues that in the town of Jaén in the second half of the seventeenth century, per capita consumption was as high as 10.5 kilograms per capita, a figure that seems too large.[45] Cubillo de la Puente reports that during the entire eighteenth century the inhabitants of urban Leon got a minimum of 2.3 kilograms provided only through the town's system of *obligación*, in which a merchant supplied a fixed quantity at a set price. Since this took care of supply mainly during the Lent fasting period while outside that season private muleteer traders and fish merchants supplied the urban market, the total consumption was probably about twice that amount.[46] In the 1830s a simple average of nine towns in Castille-Leon indicates a per capita consumption of 4.4 kilograms per inhabitant.[47]

A few figures available for very small localities confirm that they consumed less. Table 7.1 shows relatively reliable late eighteenth-century consumption figures for a number of places in Castille-Leon that had between 900 and 3,000 inhabitants. Average consumption was only about 1.7 kilograms, clearly below the national average. The exception was Villamañan (almost 4 kilograms). The reason for this is that the village's weekly market specialized in *bacalao* for the entire region. Something similar happened to the 2,800 inhabitants of Astorga, another small place in Castile and Leon that happened to be located on the main route from Galicia to the fish fair in Benavente.[48] Relatively lower rural consumption resulted directly from an insufficient integration into the supply networks; villages close to these networks had consumption patterns resembling more closely the ones observed in towns.[49]

---

[44] Bernardos Sanz, "Abastecimiento," 10ff. Figures for 1629 are based on the assumption that the share of *bacalao* in overall fish consumption did not change until the late eighteenth century.

[45] Coronas Tejada, "Abastecimiento de pescado," 44. This was 5,250 grams during Lent fasting and about the same amount over the rest of the year.

[46] Cubillo de la Puente, "Carne y pescado."

[47] Cubillo de la Puente, *El pescado*, 293–94. The towns are Avila, Burgos, Leon, Palencia, Salamanca, Segovia, Soria, Valladolid, and Zamora.

[48] Miguel López, *Mundo del comercio*, 179ff.

[49] It is possible that urban consumption was also encouraged by the lack of fresh meat in towns. However, the relatively higher consumption of *bacalao* in small villages that were integrated into the trading networks suggests that access to markets rather than problems of meat supply in large towns explains *bacalao* consumption.

Table 7.1. Average per capita consumption of *bacalao* in small localities in Castille-Leon, 1780s–1790s

Place	Year	Bacalao (kg)	Inhabitants	Bacalao (kg/per capita)
Pancorbo	1785	2,185	1,194	1.830
Agreda	1786	4,842	3,212	1.507
Valencia de Don Juan	1791	2,300	1,047	2.197
Villamañan	1791	5,290	1,373	3.853
Toral de los Guzmanes	1791	690	883	0.781
Alba de Tormes	1793	4,338	2,468	1.758
San Felices de los Gallegos		1,357	1,869	0.726
Piedrahita	1796	4,721	1,699	2.779
Average (excl.Villamañan)				1.654
Average Spain overall	1780s			3.300

Source: Miguel López, *Mundo*, 179.

Since dried and salted cod was over-represented in the urban diet, increasing rates of urbanization would explain the overall increase of imports. In other words, the rise in total consumption might not have had anything to do with market integration. However, this is clearly not the case. Iberia was one of the most urbanized parts of Europe by the sixteenth century, but urbanization stalled thereafter until the nineteenth century as shown in table 7.2. This is even true if we use a threshold for defining urban centers as having as few as five thousand inhabitants, which biases Spanish urbanization rates upward thanks to the large number of small towns. Hence, imports and thus consumption increases cannot be explained by rural-urban migration.

Consequentially, the increasing imports of *bacalao* must have been absorbed by an ever-increasing number of consumers in smaller towns and villages. I have argued that dried, salted cod was a staple food across Spain

Table 7.2. Urbanization rate estimates in Iberia, 1500–1850

Year	Spain (%)	Portugal (%)
1500	18.4	15
1600	21.3	16.7
1700	20.3	18.5
1750	21.4	17.5
1850	19.5	15.2

Source: Bairoch, Batou, and Chèvre, *Population*, 259. Urbanization rates are the share of population in towns with over 5,000 inhabitants.

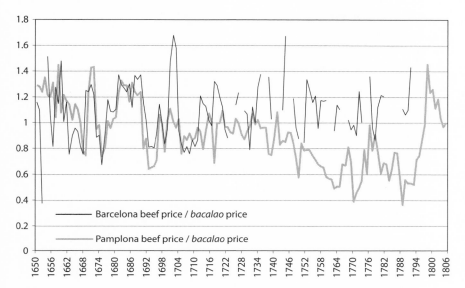

Figure 7.2
Ratio of beef and *bacalao* prices in Barcelona and Pamplona, 1650–1800.
Sources: The data set of this volume and Feliu, *Precios y salarios*, vol. 1;
and Fernández Romero, *Gastos*.

by the mid-seventeenth century. That statement now needs qualifying. It was certainly part of the diet of most inhabitants of Spanish towns, but in smaller villages and rural areas consumption was still much lower a century and a half later. Rural Spaniards were not worse Catholics—or at any rate their slowness to adopt *bacalao* was not driven by lax religious observance. As we saw in chapter 3, religious fasting shaped in part the seasonality of consumption but does not explain *bacalao*'s rise to prominence in Spain. Instead, cod became a staple because it was a cheap supply of animal protein in a country where large parts of the population went short of meat. That made *bacalao* especially attractive for consumers of small means, urban *or* rural. It is tempting to think that cod consumption was lower in the countryside because the rural population had better access to meat. Yet the opposite was true. Meat consumption in towns was systematically higher than outside urban areas. If rural consumers were on the whole poorer, as they likely were, they should have consumed, relatively speaking, even more cod.

Comparing the price of beef and cod for a few towns for which data exist is thus instructive in terms of understanding consumer choice. Figure 7.2 suggests that the relationship between prices of cod and beef remained largely stable for nearly a century and a half in Barcelona. Consumers were willing to pay a small premium of 8 percent on average for beef over *bacalao*. Notwithstanding large fluctuations, the curve has no time trend that is significant at all. The same was true for Pamplona until the 1730s, and the cycles of higher relative prices of beef or cod are remarkably synchronized. However, between the 1740s and the 1780s things went horribly wrong for *bacalao* consumers in Pamplona. Beef was now up to 40 percent cheaper, and only at the end of the century was unity reestablished.

The extraordinary cost of cod observed in some towns like Pamplona illustrates how changes in local taxation could affect consumer choice dramatically. This was not an isolated event, nor was it necessary that a particular good, such as fish, be directly taxed. Given the availability of close substitutes, local prices of fish might rise because meat was taxed. Up to the 1730s even in Pamplona the market was working to the extent that substitutes were available to the consumer who had a certain amount of arbitrage. In other words, before the 1740s it was likely that the town used consumption taxes but not measures that caused rationing.

After the 1740s matters turned worse for consumers. Though no detailed information is available, the complete distortion of the market in Pamplona was probably caused by a combination of measures from the tool kit of early modern Spanish towns. Town councils faced two mutually contradictory tasks. On the one hand, they had to raise sufficient income to finance local and supra-local expenses, as well as often sizable debt. On the other hand, public order depended crucially on the town being supplied with staple food at prices that did not push the population below the survival threshold. Both tasks tended to encourage not only the introduction of consumption taxes, which affected prices, but also interventions in the quantities supplied. Towns could pay merchants to provide supplies, create stocks, or restrict sales.[50] In addition, tax hikes in one good might be accompanied with price ceilings in another. For example, a particularly unfortunate coincidence of consumption taxes levied on fish and price ceilings on meat, which probably led to meat rationing and rising demand for fish, could explain what happened in Pamplona.

In addition, the generally stable relationship between prices of cod and meat did not mean that the *relative* price was identical across places. All other factors being equal, cod depended on import markets and was cheaper closer to the port. Meat was supplied locally or regionally, and its price before taxes was a function of local agricultural conditions and the size of the market rather than distance from the coast. Hence beyond the massive differences in price levels introduced in some places by the tax system, the relative price of cod compared to beef moved in favor of beef with distance from the coast. In Leon (130 kilometers from the coast), for example, cod was still a good choice for the consumer if one compares the cost of a unit of protein that either fish or meat could deliver.

Figure 7.3 illustrates this. Given the margin of error in converting the weight of watered fish into protein content in this case, it reports upper- and lower-bound estimates for the price ratio between animal protein from beef

[50] Palop Ramos, *Fluctuaciones*, 84.

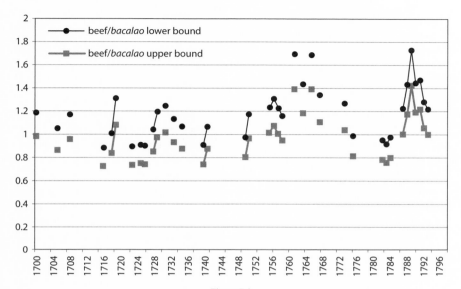

Figure 7.3
Ratio of cost of protein provided by beef and *bacalao* in Leon, 1700–1794.
Source: Cubillo de la Puente, *Comer*.

and *bacalao*. In Leon this still made cod a sensible purchase from a nutritional point of view; alas early modern inhabitants of Leon clearly had fewer consumption choices than did their contemporaries closer to the shore.[51]

Spanish consumers used their choices to arbitrage between goods to the extent that they could. But the important point is that local taxes and market interventions in combination with relatively high transport costs severely restricted these choices. For a product that had to be shipped from the coast to the interior, distribution networks needed to exist that linked the smallest hamlet to the large international ports. These were slow to develop. Small localities even in the eighteenth century were mostly served by the irregular supplies of ambulant fish vendors.[52] The slow development of local distribution networks stymied the integration of rural consumers into transregional markets. Nevertheless, the rise of the overall imports of *bacalao* also bears witness to the fact that eventually rural Spaniards became plugged into these markets. The increasing integration of rural consumers absorbed slowly but steadily the rising amounts of fish that arrived in Spain. In the absence of a game changer in transport or better political coordination, this wholly

[51] In fact, in terms of its protein content, the period of high cod prices from 1740 to 1790 in Pamplona reported in figure 7.2 also meant that beef-based protein and cod-based protein were equally expensive. Given the high protein content of cod, beef was more expensive from a nutritional perspective in most places in Spain, though this was obviously not clear to contemporaries.

[52] Cubillo de la Puente, *El pescado*, 202.

unspectacular process was the essence of Spanish market integration for much of the early modern period.

Consumer Evolution

Such a pattern was a long way from the kind of consumer revolution observed in northwestern Europe in the seventeenth and eighteenth centuries. Obstacles to market integration slowed down the process of urbanization, while an expansion and deepening of the market into rural areas was excruciatingly slow. Thanks to the fact that *bacalao* was an imported and new commodity, its march from the coast to the interior towns and rural hamlets could be described relatively well. Understanding what the slow and intermittent path of market integration seen above looked like in locally or regionally produced everyday goods is correspondingly much harder because historians have even more problems estimating availability on the supply side and tracing the demand side (who consumed what and how much).

However, there is a growing historiography about the expansion of consumption possibilities in Spain in the early modern period more generally, which would seem to coincide well with the analysis undertaken here.[53] Fernando Ramos has studied the demand for textiles, household goods, furniture, books, and religious objects in the northern Castilian province of Palencia as reflected in household inventories, and he observes some interesting shifts. His impressively detailed analysis shows that the overall share of spending on these goods hardly changed between the 1750s and the 1840s, confirming the picture of relatively little change in incomes.

Nevertheless, the upward tendency of agricultural prices compared to other goods led to a moderate increase in wealth that transformed the structure of spending quite fundamentally. He, too, found change not primarily in increasing urbanization but in a steady trend that saw rural consumers becoming more like their urban peers. In the 1750s, urban dwellers spent 180 percent more on durables and semi-durables than country folk did, but by 1785–1800 that advantage had fallen to 123 percent. It would continue to fall until the mid-nineteenth century. The country was becoming more like the town, at least in part because the countryside became more integrated with the larger networks of distribution.[54] At the same time, new goods became old faster, meaning that the discount rate of prices of used items rose.[55] Also, the total number of household goods and textiles owned by each family increased substantially, in part because the relative price of these goods sank.[56]

[53] Ramos Palencia, "Pautas"; Torras, "The Old and the New"; Yun Casalilla and Torras Elias, *Consumo*.

[54] Ramos Palencia, "Pautas," 89–105.

[55] Ibid., 145.

[56] Ibid., 172.

The largest share of non-food consumption remained textiles, but they were increasingly cotton textiles rather than woolen cloth as expected. The small capital town of the province, Palencia, enjoyed supplies of these new goods much earlier. In the last decade of the eighteenth century almost one in five textiles in the town was made of cotton, while in its hinterland the percentage was still negligible.[57] Yet the overwhelming share of all of these goods continued to be the output of local production. There is even a little evidence for the kinds of items that families bought in order to consume some of the new American goods. De Vries has pointed out that one of the driving forces of the new northern European consumption patterns was that families began to purchase "consumption bundles." They would not only consume ever-larger amounts of new colonial drinks, such as tea and coffee, but soon equip their households with the corresponding sets of cheap but fancy household items used to prepare and consume them, such as teapots and coffee mills.[58]

However, yet again the process lagged behind considerably in Spain, despite the fact that the new American consumption goods, tobacco, cocoa, or *bacalao*, had been introduced so early. Arguably, potable chocolate was to Spaniards what tea and coffee were to northern Europeans. In the mid-eighteenth century, three-quarters of all the more affluent families in Palencia had a *chocolatera*, a dish to serve chocolate, but only one-quarter of the middle-income households owned one. By the end of the century, mid-income families had caught up with their social betters.[59] That was progress of the pleasant kind, but, relatively speaking, it was not much. De Vries shows that in the Dutch part of Frisia even farming households in the 1780s owned on average not just a few pieces of ceramics but sixty-four.[60] Another "populux" object de rigeur in northern Europe, the pocket watch, had hardly made inroads in a small provincial town in Castile in 1800.[61]

The agents of change that would push the regional economy of Palencia beyond its confines came late in the eighteenth century. On the one hand, the region's agriculture increasingly specialized in grain for export—particularly to Cuba—via the northern port of Santander. On the other, Catalan merchants arrived on the scene, transforming the cozy local mercantile setting.[62] Shops began replacing weekly markets at the end of the eighteenth century. After all, in Palencia and elsewhere there was increased market integration. However, evidence for a consumer revolution of the type observed in northern Europe is limited. New colonial goods were introduced early in Spain and the per capita consumption of new goods, such as tobacco, cacao, coffee, or *bacalao*, increased, but the process of integrating rural consumers into the

[57] Ibid., 178.
[58] De Vries, *The Industrious Revolution*, 34–36, 177.
[59] Ramos Palencia, "Pautas," 259.
[60] De Vries, *The Industrious Revolution*, 133.
[61] Ramos Palencia, "Pautas," 265.
[62] Ibid., 298.

new distribution networks was painfully slow. In the meantime, jurisdictional obstacles to market integration contributed to slowing down urbanization trends because they limited the size of the market. There was growth, but since it was slower than elsewhere in Europe, Spanish consumers were continuously falling further behind.

The Road Not Taken (or Built, for That Matter)

In markets in which transport costs remained relatively high, the additional costs imposed by jurisdictional fragmentation quickly became prohibitive. Spain's economy was trapped. Weak market integration was only slowly remedied by lower transport costs. At the same time, there was no support for more integrated markets from a political economy that failed to lower the costs imposed by Spain's jurisdictional fragmentation. The continuing fragmentation of authority made it impossible to overcome ubiquitous coordination failures between regional and local bodies invested with their own share of sovereignty. Spain did not take the road that might have overcome these coordination failures. Paradoxically, it did not take it in defense of the same contractual notion of governance that restrained the Spanish Crown so successfully. Spanish-style representation and a centralizing coordinating state were incompatible.

In fact, one area where this coordination failure was quite obvious was once again transport. As we saw, municipalities struggled to fund roads, bridges, and piers while desperately trying to service their debt and even pay off a part of the principal, as Spanish towns did for most of the later seventeenth and entire eighteenth centuries. It is thus interesting that travelers and historians alike single out the Basque Country and more specifically the *señorio de* Vizcaya as a place with exceptionally good internal communications. The structure of financing in the Basque Country was identical to that of the rest of Spain: localities had to provide the funds. However, it stands to reason that the overall lower levels of municipal indebtedness gave the Basque towns more room to maneuver when it came to raising funds.

Indeed, the Basque Provinces and Navarra were able to contract substantial credits on the basis of new taxes on wine and liquors in order to improve their roads.[63] After 1629 the Basque province of Guipúzcoa was, for instance, able to charge provincial rather than urban consumption taxes on wine and salt fish in addition to municipal ones. Some of these duties were earmarked for road works, the costs of which would eventually increase substantially in the late eighteenth century.[64] Though this would require more research, it seems likely that the ability of Guipúzcoa to raise consumption taxes at the

[63] Madrazo, *Comunicaciones*, 167, 342.
[64] Mugártegui Eguia, *Hacienda*, 168–69, 205.

provincial level also improved the efficiency of collection, just as the shift from municipal to provincial taxes had done in Holland in the sixteenth century.[65]

In 1765 work began on the construction of a paved road from Bilbao to Pancorbo through the Basque customs border in the mountains at Orduña. It was finished by 1774 and offered an alternative firm road through the Cantabrian Mountain range to Old Castile that separated Bilbao from the interior. This project was actually financed by Vizcayan institutions, the town and Consulado of Bilbao and the *señorio de* Vizcaya, which in turn tried to recover some of their investment through a high toll. It came close to the concept of a turnpike trust like those so successfully applied in England throughout the eighteenth century.

The comparison is interesting because turnpikes in England responded to a transport problem that was quite similar to the Spanish one. Traditionally English towns and villages were charged with improving infrastructure, but by the eighteenth century they were financially out of their depths. The building of hundreds of turnpikes and toll roads administered by trusts and controlled by the local elites not only resulted in markedly lower travel times and transport costs but created multiplier effects in the local economy.[66] Thus Bogart has recently argued that real land rents increased by as much as 20 percent in places that benefited from access to a turnpike.[67] Why did Spain not choose this path?

There is one element of the turnpike success story that economic historians take for granted. English turnpikes involved grants of power from Parliament, that is, the *national* sovereign, which allowed the turnpike trusts not only to charge tolls but also to draw on the moneys traditionally paid by English towns for the upkeep of the roads. Granting the right to charge tolls was not a problem for the Spanish Crown—as the case of the Orduña pass illustrates—and as long as local users were exempted, as they generally were in Spain and in England. However, neither the Spanish Crown nor its local representatives, the *corregidores*, could have forced the towns through an edict to hand over their resources to a private group of investors, such as a turnpike trust. What set English and Spanish institutions apart was that the central authority, be it a parliament or a monarchy, could unilaterally alter both private and public property rights at the local level in the former but not in the latter. Turnpikes, as well as the better-known case of English enclosures, involved an expropriation of individuals and local authorities on a very large scale at the hands of Parliament.[68] Paradoxically, in Spain both private and public property rights were too strong to let political authorities perform the task of overcoming coordination failures in the economy.

[65] Fritschy, "Efficiency."
[66] Daunton, *Progress*, 297–307.
[67] Bogart, "Turnpike Trusts."
[68] Mokyr, *Enlightened Economy*, 173–74; Allen, *Enclosure and the Yeoman*.

In the absence of coercion and enforcement from the central state, coordination costs among towns were prohibitive. An agreement between neighboring towns to pool resources for road improvements meant that they had to have a fair idea of which town was benefiting by how much, an insurmountable coordination problem at the time. Towns sometimes did agree to combine efforts, but it is obvious that such agreements would have worked only where the benefits were both large and transparent. Without a third-party enforcer able to coerce them, towns were always likely to spend too little on infrastructure that would have had a positive impact beyond their region.[69] Only where the territorial power could impose itself could a system of tolls succeed as it did in the province of Guipúzcoa, where the regional juntas imposed it on the towns in the later eighteenth century.[70]

The premise of this chapter has been that premodern societies were poorer than they had to be. Market inefficiency, meaning the mismatching of resources across geography, caused poor allocation. With this came the paradoxical twin problems of backward societies: shortages and slack. Spain was afflicted by these more than most western European societies. A fragmented state authority could not, and would not, perform as a unifying agent to overcome the existing jurisdictional fragmentation or even to counter the tendency for additional obstacles to trade to appear. The problem was not that a strong state was distorting incentives. The empirical evidence provided by many social, cultural, and political historians of Spain, as well as the quantitative evidence presented in this book, disprove the model of the tyrannical, strong predatory state in early modern Spain. Instead, multiple layers of state, the flat hierarchies that shared power, disintegrated the market, and the establishment of a system of governance with a truly central power remained a distant threat for some, a distant dream for others. In the meantime, Spanish workers had little chance to "take advantage of their climate and situation," as Armstrong had exhorted them to do. Nor did they have many incentives as long as the growth of urban markets was stifled by prohibitive, politically determined transaction costs and the development of rural markets evolved at a painfully slow rate with improving transport links.

[69] The problem was very similar to the one described for irrigation projects in southern France by Rosenthal, "Irrigation."

[70] Mugártegui Eguia, *Hacienda*, 164.

Chapter 8 _____

Center and Peripheries

THE MAGIC OF THE MARKET, dependent as it is on price signals, worked poorly where a multitude of local trade and consumption taxes affected relative prices in unpredictable ways. The persistence of fragmented fiscal systems and economic and political institutions further limited market integration in an economy that was already saddled with relatively high transport costs. Allocative inefficiencies were the consequence. Interregional integration was slowed down and sometimes even reversed, and local markets remained at the mercy of the performance—past and present—of urban finances. Naturally, regional and local outcomes varied greatly; this was precisely the nature of the system. However, the empirical analysis of market and state has gone a long way to explain where the stumbling blocks in Spanish economic and political development were and why they stifled growth so significantly.

There was path dependence in fragmented authority in Spain as elsewhere in Europe, but this was only part of the problem. Between roughly the late Middle Ages and the nineteenth century, overcoming divided authority was the essence of the process of European state-building. However, this process was not a more or less linear development across time where variation simply arose from some polities passing through the "necessary" steps earlier than others. There was no predetermined path, or outcome for that matter, from composite kingdoms to nation-states. In Spain the complex combination of institutional heritage and ideological underpinnings of rule made the process of eliminating at least some degree of divided authority especially slow and cumbersome, and a strong tradition of local autonomy remained part of what the compact between rulers and ruled was understood to be. It was not a "failure" to become a more unified state but a variation in the process of European nation-state building that relied more on negotiation and less on centralization.

In all likelihood, however, at least some of the appeal of the "contractual" governance model was functionalist: that it suited local elites surely helped its survival. In the historic territories it was a useful tool against the loss of "freedoms," that is, special rights. At the town level, it was equally often employed to defend local and corporate privilege. Yet it also had support at the center where many of the legally trained members of the councils never quite stopped believing in governance as an act of delivering justice. How much this ideology of power contributed to the survival of divided authority is hard to gauge. It would require an in-depth intellectual history investigation that goes well beyond this present study.[1] Yet it is worth remembering that those eighteenth-century reforms, which really reinterpreted the relation between the constituent parts of the monarchy and the Madrid government, such as the intendancies, counted almost as many foes in Madrid as they did in the provinces.

More important, the issue was not simply that inefficient institutions were allowed to survive thanks to the opposition to reforms of established forms of administration. New organizational forms that looked just the same were continuously created. Jurisdictional fragmentation thus also applied to entirely new tax projects and fiscal, economic, and political institutions. The nightmarish complexity of *alcabalas* and *millones* were in good part the outcome of past centuries of negotiation. The peculiar structure of the tobacco monopoly was a result of contemporary bargaining.[2] The latter thus illustrates the continuing negotiation among local, territorial, and central haciendas. Hence there was evidently a lot of agency involved in the survival of the unusually large degree and complex structure of jurisdictional fragmentation in Spain.

This final chapter will shift the discussion from the pattern and structural causes of slow market integration to the actors. It offers a reinterpretation of the origins of the center-periphery divide—the most notable feature of poorly integrated markets in Spain and a central theme of Spanish history and present-day politics. It challenges a large historiography that juxtaposes a "conservative core" and "progressive peripheries" on the grounds that this juxtaposition is based on several erroneous assumptions. First, the characterization of the conservative core (read Madrid) still relies on the model of the centralizing, absolutist state that we have found so wanting. It combines this with an implicit and possibly unconscious assumption that the commercial and professional elites failed in their role as investors in economic growth, that is, that the misdirection and/or the lack of investible capital was the main bottleneck in the Spanish economy.

Second, the historiography contrasts this erroneous characterization of the conservative core with an equally problematic view of the progressive peripheries. It collapses the relatively faster economic development of Spain's coastal regions into suppositions about poorly defined "progressive," that is, enlightened, ideas among the local elites and an outward commercial orientation of the coastal regions. Zooming in on one particular issue within the center-periphery cleavage, the granting of legal, direct trade between the Basque ports and Spanish America, suggests that we have to disentangle ideological developments, economic interests, and the effects of the existing system of governance to make events on the ground intelligible.

---

[1] See the very interesting discussion in Clavero, *Razón de estado*.
[2] See the length of the entry on the *alcabalas* in La Ripia, *Práctica*.

Two Spains

By the eighteenth century at the latest, it was increasingly clear that the divergence in regional fortunes was not entirely aleatory. Instead, a trend that had been observed by some since the early seventeenth century had become unmistakable. The center of gravity of the Spanish economy was moving from the Castilian heartland to the coasts. Demographic trends illustrate this. Chapter 7 showed that urbanization remained stagnant. However, this is somewhat misleading. It is not that there was no urban growth across Spain, rather population growth and decline canceled each other out. Cadiz, for example, passed from 40,000 to 70,000 and Barcelona grew significantly over the course of the eighteenth century. Increasing urbanization in the coastal provinces was accompanied by de-urbanization in the interior, with the exception of the growing capital Madrid. As a result, the overall share of population in towns hardly changed at all. A look at the population distribution between the coast, interior, and Madrid between 1700 and 1900 in figure 8.1 illustrates the point.

Rafael Dobado has argued that population density in the late eighteenth century was highly correlated with regional levels of economic well-being in Spain in the later nineteenth century, for which more reliable estimates are available.[3] Population density is therefore one of the better indicators for economic growth in an era in which population statistics are a lot more reliable than estimates of income. In 1787 about 160 people lived in every square kilometer in Spain's coastal regions, but only about 75 in the interior.[4] The difference is strikingly large and as figure 8.1 suggests, it only increased over time. The shift from the interior to the coastal regions and to Madrid was still modest in the eighteenth century, but it accelerated in the nineteenth and continued in the twentieth.

In fact, the trend had begun much earlier. In the late sixteenth century the central Castilian regions, that is, Castille-Leon and Castille-La Mancha, accounted for 46 percent of the population of the Spanish territories, while Catalonia and Valencia accounted for about 10 percent. By the mid-nineteenth century they were home to 27 and 19 percent of the total population, respectively.[5] The question thus remains why within a general pattern of slow market integration some regions patently fared worse than others. In other words, what explains the center-periphery divide in Spain, the economic, political, social, and cultural cleavage that has been the central feature of Spanish history and historiography?

Much of the Spanish historiography of the early modern period has developed around the notion of the "Two Spains." In economic history this has been most elegantly elaborated by Ringrose, who has argued in *Madrid and*

[3] Dobado González, "Legado peculiar," 101.
[4] Ibid., 108–9.
[5] Pérez Moreda, "El Legado demográfico," 131.

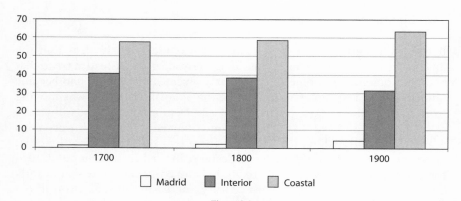

Figure 8.1
Population distribution in Spain: Madrid, interior, and coastal regions,
1700–1900. *Source*: My own elaboration based on Domínguez Martín,
La riqueza, and de Vries, *European Urbanization*. Interior is Castile-La Mancha,
Castile León, Estremadura, La Rioja, Aragon, and Navarra;
coastal is the sum of Andalusia, Asturias, Balearics, Canaries, Cantabria,
Catalonia, Galicia, Murcia, Basque Country, and Valencia.

the Spanish Economy that the rise of the bureaucratic capital of the Crown's making stifled growth elsewhere in central Spain.[6] The consequence was the emergence of two fundamentally different Spains. One Spain comprised Madrid and the Castilian interior, the historic territories of Leon, Old and New Castile, and Estremadura on the Portuguese borders. The other covered much of the coastal regions, in particular the northern Cantabrian coast, including the Basque Provinces and Navarra, the Mediterranean coast with the former reign of Aragon, Murcia, and Andalusia. Essentially the divide was between the "center" and the "periphery."

Ringrose had not invented the idea of Two Spains. It became popular in the second half of the nineteenth century among Spanish commentators from Ramiro de Maeztu y Whitney (1875–1936) to Marcelino Menéndez Pelayo (1856–1912).[7] Since the twentieth century, it has generally been used to describe the conflict between liberal and reactionary forces that opened up after 1808 and persisted throughout the Civil War and dictatorship of the twentieth century. Ringrose simply traced the idea back to what he saw as its regional origins. In this, he was in good company. José Ortega y Gasset, Spain's most influential writer of the early twentieth century, argued in *Invertebrate Spain* (1922) that it would be

[6] "In the case of Madrid and Castile, market oriented commerce developed but only as a consequence of continuous political intervention in the economy." Ringrose, *Madrid*, 2. For a similar argument, cf. Madrazo, *Comunicaciones*, 60–61, and Herr, *Rural Change*.
[7] Juliá, *Historias de las dos Españas*; Alvarez Junco, *Mater Dolorosa*, 383ff.

an insult to historical intelligence to assume that when a superior national unit had been formed out of smaller nuclei, the latter cease to exist as actively differentiated elements. This erroneous idea would, for example, lead to the idea that when Castile reduces to a national Spanish unit Aragon, Catalonia and the Basque Country, these lose their character as distinct peoples [*pueblos*] and become part of the whole.[8]

Not so, Ortega y Gasset exclaimed. While the unification might contain their centrifugal tendencies, it would not break the force of their independence. If the central organ disappeared, the nation would revert to its constituent parts. Disintegration in Spain was thus the corollary of the decadence at the center, in Castile. According to Ringrose, Ortega y Gasset, and many others the decline had started as early as the 1580s and had never ceased.[9] Here were the supposed origins of a division between a conservative, inward-looking interior Spain and an outward-looking, culturally, socially, and economically more advanced coastal Spain.

This narrative mirrors national historiographies in many places. The notion of commercially minded, more tolerant port towns and backward hinterlands has been part of histories written from Hamburg to Boston and from Canton/Guangzhou to Buenos Aires. It appeals as much to cultural historians as to hard-nosed economists, who have argued that Europe's growth in the early modern period was largely "Atlantic," though the latter have a hard time accounting for the poor economic performance of thoroughly Atlantic Spain.[10]

From this point of departure, it was a relatively short step from the Spanish declension narratives of the sixteenth to early eighteenth centuries to the chronologically second half of the Two Spains story, that is, the role of the coastal areas in eventually pulling a recalcitrant hinterland into the modern age. In *Spain, Europe, and the "Spanish Miracle," 1700–1900*, Ringrose took his interpretation into the early nineteenth century and argued that the outward orientation of the coastal regions—exemplified by the early (by Spanish standards) industrialization in Catalonia, the Basque Country, and parts of Andalusia—eventually led Spain out of backwardness.[11] By seeking integration with regions outside the Peninsula, they overcame the nefarious influence of a centralist bureaucracy that, in the later eighteenth century,

---

[8] Ortega y Gasset, *España invertebrada*, 32–33.

[9] There is an endless, self-referential literature on Spanish decline. See, e.g., Elliott, "Decline of Spain," and Kamen, "The Decline of Spain." It is interesting to note that in the 1920s the possible loss of Catalonia or the Basque Country simply looked like a logical continuation of the loss first of the European, then of most of the American territories, and finally of Cuba, Puerto Rico, and the Philippines. For Ortega y Gasset evidently the latter had been just as much part of what he considered Spain as Catalonia; they were all part of the same entity rather than colonies of the Peninsula or even Castile.

[10] Acemoglu, Johnson, and Robinson, "Rise of Europe." Spain's poor economic record is—once more—explained away by its supposed institutional exceptionalism.

[11] Ringrose, *Spanish Miracle*.

contributed only slowly to this drive by opening up the Americas trades, for example. Again Ringrose was building on a long tradition of late nineteenth- and early twentieth-century writers. The young, still liberal Maeztu warned against separatism of the coastal regions. Having spent part of his youth in Havana and returning to Spain just before the U.S. occupation of Cuba, he had witnessed the dismemberment of Spain firsthand. However, he also called for "another" (more modern) Spain that could only be created under the direction of the open- and industriously minded Basques and Catalans.[12]

The Myth of Conservative Cores

The nexus between political economy and market integration in Ringrose's argument is made explicit by contrasting Madrid with London, which experienced massive population growth around the same time. London was a commercial entrepôt and industrial site that benefited its hinterland in multiple ways.[13] By contrast, Madrid's only "industry" was imperial politics, according to Ringrose.[14] It absorbed the resources of its hinterland but "offered to the rural world in exchange little more than a doubtful international policy."[15] Thus, the catalyst of regional divergence was Madrid. The city in the very center of the Peninsula became the capital of Castile in 1561 and, one could argue, of Spain in 1714, when the *foral* institutions of the former *reino* of Aragon had all been abolished. A smallish town in the 1560s, it had become Spain's largest city within less than a century, overtaking Seville.

In the traditional narrative Madrid stood for two exceedingly negative features. First, it became the symbol of a supposedly over-centralizing state. In Ringrose's opinion Madrid should be compared to classical Rome rather than to its contemporaries, London or Paris:

> Both cities [Rome and Madrid] have been described as economic parasites, consuming the wealth of their empires without directly contributing to the creation of wealth. Like imperial Rome, Madrid organized and ran a worldwide political and administrative structure and used that political structure as a framework for controlling, taxing, and shaping a widespread system of commercial activity.[16]

In the words of Stein and Stein: "while Spain was exploiting America, Madrid and its elites were exploiting Spain."[17]

The story of politically driven trade divergence in the interest of imperial *panem et circenses* for the benefit of the capital's population is deeply

---

[12] Maeztu, *Hacia otra España*. See the very interesting discussion of the origins of the concept of the nation in Balfour and Quiroga, *España reinventada*, chapters 1–3.

[13] Ringrose, "El Desarrollo urbano," 41; Wrigley, "London's Importance."

[14] Ringrose, "El Desarrollo urbano," 45. My translation.

[15] Ibid., 49.

[16] Ringrose, *Madrid*, 4.

[17] Stein and Stein, *The Colonial Heritage*.

entrenched in the Spanish historiography. However, it should be abundantly clear by now that these hugely exaggerated positions are backed up neither by the recent historiography on the political process of state-building in Spain nor by the empirical analysis of the development of markets. Ringrose's assertion that Madrid's politically motivated rise destroyed the previously well-integrated urban hierarchy of the interior in the seventeenth century and "undermined older commercial and industrial towns in ways that minimized incentives for rural specialization" is very hard to reconcile with the analysis in chapters 3–6.[18] There is no evidence that Madrid was surrounded by a "desert" of poorly integrated places that suffered from being out-competed by the political capital. That is true in comparison with market integration among the towns in the historic territories, as well as with most of the other Castilian towns. If political power diverted transport and supplies to Madrid by non-market means of coercion, prices in the capital should have begun to diverge from those of towns nearby. Instead, prices between the major towns, Madrid and Toledo, were strongly correlated and converged. The large market at the center of the Peninsula was evidently not a negative influence in the way sometimes posited, quite the opposite. Agglomeration was a good thing. In the case of Madrid, for once the analysis of correlations, volatility, and price convergence all point toward the large capital being a driving force of integration, not disintegration.

Nor should we be too surprised. Llopis Agelan's and García Montero's fascinating recent work on prices and wages in Madrid and Toledo finds strongly integrated markets across goods and factor markets.[19] Both Toledo and Madrid moved—so to speak—slowly but steadily closer to the coast until the late eighteenth-century upheaval threatened to reverse much of the long-term gains. Moreover, we have seen that the twin ideas of strong centralization and extraction, or exploitation as the Steins would have it, are simply untenable. Spain was less centralized than practically all other large contemporary political units in Europe in the seventeenth through early nineteenth centuries. Poland might be the exception, but it also ceased to exist.[20] Empirical evidence for extractive policies vis-à-vis the historic territories in the Peninsula or the other European and American territories is equally thin on the ground, as we saw in chapter 1.

The second criticism leveled against the capital city is more complex. Ringrose's assessment of Madrid continues:

> Madrid was unique, however, since its location kept it from becoming the commercial as well as the political center of its empire. The Spanish political system had a single administrative structure, but it suffered from a pronounced economic

[18] Ringrose, *Madrid*, 15.
[19] Llopis Agelán and García Montero, "Cost of Living."
[20] Some smaller polities, especially the Netherlands, were subject to similar degrees of decentralization. Yet, notwithstanding their economic importance, the Dutch population was even in 1800 less than one-fifth that of Peninsular Spain.

dualism. The imperial trade at Seville and Cádiz and the coastal fringes of the Mediterranean and Basque regions were exposed to the maritime economy of Europe, while interior León and Old and New Castile were physically isolated from the sea.[21]

Madrid was thus not only allegedly powerful and extractive, but its rise also reflected "aristocratic socialization, and conspicuous consumption by elites" and added nothing to its immediate hinterland.[22] This theme has also been a commonplace in Spanish historiography and literature from the nineteenth century onward.[23] Contrasting Madrid with Paris, Ortega y Gasset observed as late as 1927 that it was "boberia," that is, foolishness, to assume that Madrid was a metropolis that benefited its region: "Six kilometers from Madrid the cultural influence of Madrid ends, and, without transition or enlightened hinterland, total backwardness begins abruptly."[24]

Madrid was a peculiar behemoth, not a rising commercial port like Amsterdam or London, not even a traditional economic center like Paris.[25] It was often described as conspicuously void of bourgeois virtues, hardworking craftsmen, and penny-pinching shopkeepers.[26] Madrid instead was meant to be a city full of bureaucrats, nobles, clerics, and vagrants, and its useless elites were thought to specialize in rent-seeking at the expense of the rest of the country and the empire. However, with the increasing realization that there was little extraction, this image, too, becomes problematic. This is not the place to reassess in any detail the role of Madrid in the Spanish economy. Yet maybe one should; and for the time being at least, a few remarks may be permitted.

Undoubtedly Madrid was first and foremost an administrative capital, what Germans used to call a Residenzstadt. Its population was heavily engaged in the service sectors, but that description hides a great diversity of professions engaged in the provision of domestic, religious, legal, political, commercial, and financial services with remarkable success. Part of the prob-

[21] Ringrose, *Madrid*, 4.

[22] Ibid., 15.

[23] Menéndez y Pelayo called around the same time for a cultural development in all regions and towns: "it should be possible to counter this fatal (*funesta*) French-style centralization that wants to cluster all possible literary life in Madrid." Menéndez y Pelayo, *La ciencia española*, 1:80.

[24] Ringrose's translation. Ringrose, *Madrid*, 1. "Madrid nunca ha poseído jamás una cultura creadora. A fuerza de capital de Estado, se ha ido, claro está, cultivando; es decir, ha aprendido del extranjero un mínimum de cosas malamente asimiladas. Esta cultura adquirida . . . le viene muy justa a Madrid para sus necesidades de urbe, para sostener la estricta dignidad de una capital. Pensar en que haya podido nunca irradiar su espíritu es boberia. A seis kilómetros de Madrid, la influencia cultural de Madrid termina, y empieza ya, sin transición ni zona pelúcida, el 'labriego absoluto.'" Ortega y Gasset, *La redención*, 82–83.

[25] Hohenberg and Hollen Lees, "Urban Decline and Regional Economics."

[26] The very old idea that urban bourgeoisies are crucial for economic development has recently been reinvigorated and given a new "rhetorical" twist by Deirdre McCloskey, *The Bourgeois Virtues*.

lem with assessing Madrid's economic role is that economic (and other) historians of all stripes are still spooked by a decidedly Marxian idea. This is that economic development depends on the emergence of a powerful bourgeoisie that accumulated capital, that invested in the "right" kinds of economic activities (manufacturing, possibly long-distance trade), and that favored the "right" kinds of political institutions, that is, parliamentary systems, to boot.[27] These middling sorts allegedly existed in Bilbao, Barcelona and Valencia but not in Madrid.[28] The Madrid bourgeoisie stands accused of being of the treasonous kind in the Braudelian sense of the term; it specialized in the creation of and living off rents.

Alas, recent in-depth research by Sola Corbacho on the investing behavior of Madrid merchants finds little evidence for a retreat from active commerce in the eighteenth century.[29] Mercantile interests diversified their portfolios that included active trade, moneylending, shares, and participations, as well as public debt, whereby the first three in Sola's sample accounted for 83 percent of merchants' activa. Evidently this was not a retreat from the market but an attempt to diversify in a market that was poorly integrated and thus subject to high risks.[30] Not least, the author also found that the size of mercantile fortunes in Madrid has been massively underestimated by most historians who have long argued that the Madrid elite consisted of a close-knit group of aldermen with few interests in active trade.[31]

Given the recent emphasis in the literature on consumption as a driving force of early modern economic growth, the traditional disdain for the large service sector in towns like Madrid seems also completely misplaced. Historians want to have it both ways. In the context of the evidently economically dynamic northern European economies, they have turned to the virtues of a development of an early "consumer society" in order to explain a success that in light of recent research cannot simply be attributed any longer to

[27] Windler has looked at this from a different vantage point. He argues that the dichotomy nobility-bourgeoisie has clearly been abandoned in French Revolution studies and shows convincingly that it should be revised in the Spanish case, too. Windler, *Lokale Eliten*.

[28] Part of the problem is of course the definition of the "middling sorts." Jesus Cruz points out that contemporary Spanish writers considered not just merchants but also bureaucrats, professionals, and property owners very much as *clases medias*. But rather than reflecting on the question as to whether they could have stimulated economic growth, Cruz affirms the obvious difference with Barcelona, namely that the Madrid middle class had hardly any links with the productive sector. Thus he continues to argue that in fact there never was a bourgeoisie in Madrid, in the sense that it transformed society, in an attack on the political narrative of the liberal revolution of 1812 and thereafter. Cruz, *Gentlemen, Bourgeois, and Revolutionaries*, 14ff. For the traditional narrative on Catalonia, see Vilar, *Cataluña en la España moderna*. An alternative description of the difference between commercial elites in the interior and on the coast, which nevertheless also presupposes the "backwardness" of those in the interior, can be found in Molas Ribalta, *La burgesía mercantil*.

[29] Sola Corbacho, "Capital"; Sola Corbacho, "Mercado de crédito."

[30] Sola Corbacho, "Capital," 232.

[31] Sola Corbacho, "Madrid y México," 102–5. He clearly disproves Hernández description of the Madrid elite. Hernández, *Sombra*.

supply side forces, such as increased productivity in either manufacturing or agriculture or both. In the slow-growing southern European societies of the seventeenth and eighteenth centuries, however, the notion of a parasitic and unproductive service sector is being maintained and economic historians still sound like seventeenth-century priests damning conspicuous consumption.

Conservatism, Capital, and Investment

This is particularly surprising given that the "treason of the bourgeoisie" paradigm is at least in part testable. From an economic standpoint, it alleges that investible capital was diverted to non-productive uses thereby creating credit rationing. As in the case of the notion of the extractive state, one way to investigate this issue is through the interest rate. If, as many historians have argued, economic development was held back by low capital accumulation, low savings, and an "attitude" that disfavored commercial investment, then capital should have been expensive, that is, the interest rate should have been high.[32]

Once again this can be put to the test with data from the Cathedral Chapter of Zamora. Not only did it hold *juros*, government annuities, as we saw in chapter 1, but it also lent and borrowed widely through something we might call covered loans. These "mortgages" included well-defined sureties, not always land or other real property but also tax revenues and diverse income streams. The historiography has underplayed the sophistication and development of Spanish credit markets. The wide variety of possible ways to provide surety (land, taxes, government bonds, company shares, livestock, etc.), for example, was instrumental in making credit available even to those with very limited means—and therefore collateral.[33]

While it is dangerous to generalize from this snapshot, the banking operations involved were large enough to allow for a reasonable sample. For comparison the legally determined interest rate on *juros* (the "coupon" rate) from chapter 1 is included once again (see figure 8.2).[34] The schedule for the private mortgage-based bonds (*censos*) is a weighted average of a total of 87 credit transactions recorded by Alvarez Vázquez. These transactions suggest that private interest rates hovered around 4 percent for much of the seventeenth century, falling to 3 percent after the War of the Spanish Succession and as low as 2 percent in the late eighteenth century. The War of Independence drove them up again, and in its aftermath they were still 6 percent.

It should be noted that these (low-risk) private interest rates were at all times lower than the public rates reported in chapter 1 and that the lowering

---

[32] Cf. Stein and Stein, *Silver*, 157.
[33] See, e.g., Sola Corbacho, "Mercado de crédito," 220.
[34] For a discussion of the changes to the legal rate, see chapter 1 footnote 68.

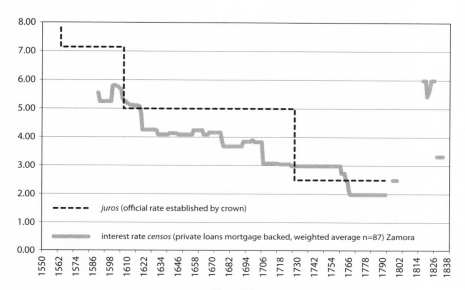

Figure 8.2
Legal interest rates on *juros* and private interest rates (1550–1830).
Source: My own elaboration based on Alvarez Vázquez, *Rentas*.

of the "legal" rate followed market rates rather than leading them. Anecdotal evidence from other places would suggest that these rates reflect, broadly speaking, what was going on elsewhere, including in the capital. The Cinco Gremios de Madrid, an association of the five most important merchant guilds of the capital, which in the eighteenth century also acted as a deposit and exchange bank, would pay about 2.5 to 3.75 percent on the deposits of "widows and orphans" under its management in the 1760s.[35] Private credit contracts in Madrid also seem to have paid around 3 percent, rising to 6 percent during the wars at the end of the century.[36] Similarly, new joint stock companies for trade with Venezuela, Havana, and the Barcelona company raised loans at 2.5 to 4 percent in the second half of the eighteenth century.[37]

Even if credit were cheap it might simply not have been available due to credit rationing caused by usury laws or poor financial intermediation. The former was clearly no issue in Spain. Loan contracts had escaped the restrictions of usury laws early on. From the sixteenth century onward usury laws were circumvented by drawing up *juros* and *censos* in such a way that they represented a contract wherein the lender (*censualista*) acted as a buyer of "proceeds" (*réditos*) sold by the debtor (*censatorio*). This rephrasing converted

[35] Carlos III officially conceded in 1763 the right to operate as an exchange bank to the Cinco Gremios, but they had been operating as such at least since the 1730s. Capella Martínez and Matilla Tascon, *Cinco Gremios*, 42, 260–62, 408–11.

[36] Sola Corbacho, "Mercado de crédito," 215. The author points out, however, that in a large number of contracts the interest rate was not explicit.

[37] Gárate Ojanguren and Blanco Mozos, "Financiación," 194–200.

a potentially usurious credit transaction into a perfectly legitimate sale of a good (the proceeds from the loan), as long as the interest rate stayed within the current market price for such a sale (*precio justo*), that is, what we would think of as the market interest rate.[38] This explains why credit instruments were sold and bought without restrictions, why religious institutions acted as the largest credit intermediaries without any qualms, and why secondary markets in financial instruments were readily available all over Spain (and Spanish America). In any case, private interest rates of 2 to 4 percent were so far below the usury threshold of 5 or 6 percent that usury restrictions and possible credit rationing in their wake were unlikely to be major problems.[39] For most of the seventeenth and the eighteenth centuries these private interest rates also compare favorably with what we know about interest rates in England, France, and the Netherlands.[40] Clark, for example, argues that returns on capital in England as proxied by land rents fell from about 5 to 3 percent over the course of the eighteenth century.[41]

Still, one cannot exclude the possibility that there was credit rationing. That money was cheap is not to say that credit was easy to come by. The development of specialized financial institutions was notably slow in Spain. Ecclesiastical institutions provided vital banking services especially in rural areas, but their lending and borrowing policies were subject to a more complex set of factors than that of banks. The purchase of a new altar piece might thus restrict local credit. The development of formal banking was rudimentary at best. In Madrid the Cinco Gremios served some of the banking needs, as did large commercial houses in some of the important trading towns, such as Seville, Cadiz, or Bilbao.[42] Here, they probably pushed ecclesiastical institutions out of the credit markets in the later eighteenth century.[43] It is also clear that, at least in the second half of the eighteenth century, there was a functioning mechanism in place that allowed religious institutions, the nobility, and private investors to place their funds with the large commercial houses of Madrid that were the recipients of almost half of the loans contracted before notary in the capital.[44] Yet various attempts to create banking institutions, such as the *montes de piedad*, came to little until the creation of the Banco de San Carlos.[45]

---

[38] Alvarez Vázquez, *Rentas*, 256ff. See also Dehouve, "Introducción a la parte histórica."

[39] Alvarez Vázquez, *Rentas*.

[40] Temin and Voth claim that in the early eighteenth century Hoare's Bank still charged close to the usury rate of 5to 6 percent and probably applied credit rationing. Temin and Voth, "Credit Rationing and Crowding Out"; Epstein, *Freedom and Growth*.

[41] Clark, "The Political Foundations."

[42] Capella Martínez and Matilla Tascon, *Cinco Gremios*, 262–63; Bernal, *La financiación*; Gutiérrez Muñoz, *Comercio y banca*.

[43] Sola Corbacho, "Mercado de crédito," 223.

[44] Ibid., 243, table 212.

[45] Cf. Dubet, *Hacienda*; Tedde de Lorca, "San Carlos."

Overall, however, both interest rates and the evidence from regional and local studies suggest that there was too much capital chasing rare investment opportunities.[46] Though this requires a much more thorough study of lending practices than is available at present, it stands to reason that the relaxed capital situation affected the development of banking institutions negatively by lowering the opportunity cost of using non-specialist financing sources. When both Crown and towns markedly reduced the issue of new debt in the eighteenth century, private secondary markets as well as corporations (for example, the *consulados* and the Cinco Gremios) and monasteries catered to those searching for ways to invest.[47] Yet with a relaxed capital constraint there was little pressure for more efficient ways of raising capital and thus institutional development. In the Spanish capital markets the problem was not so different from other markets. The trouble was not shortage but poor allocation, especially outside Madrid and the large ports.

If capital was not the problem another stone falls out of the traditional narrative of the negative role of Madrid's commercial classes and that of Madrid generally. Evidently the problem was not a bourgeoisie that failed to provide the capital for economic development. There is plenty of evidence that Madrid became an important commercial center. Indeed the history of the Cinco Gremios analyzed in great detail more than half a century ago by Capella and Matilla Tascon is testimony to an unusually adaptive strategy of the merchant guilds. Likely unified in 1679, the five mercantile guilds of mercers, goldsmiths, haberdashers, silk, and cloth merchants adopted common ordinances in 1686. By 1731 they had for all practical purposes turned into a mercantile company with interests that ranged from trade to industry, tax farming, banking, and maritime insurance.[48] Given their investment in foreign trade, they opposed much of the protectionist trade policies suggested by eighteenth-century reformers who sought to emulate more mercantilist nations like France and England.[49] Truth be told, their attitude toward political intervention was flexible. In their role as manufacturers of textiles they had little compunction asking for preferential treatment. However, in view of their varied interests, they were hardly the sort of monopolistic guild organization that Julius Klein and Robert Sidney Smith had in mind when they wrote about Spanish guilds in the first half of the twentieth century. The Cinco Gremios were not the type of guild to resist technological change and competition that is often implied in the historiography.

---

[46] Cf. also Fernández de Pinedo, "Deuda."

[47] It is likely that the preponderance of secondary markets for almost every conceivable contract and instrument was a result of capital chasing investment opportunities. This would fit evidence from the Dutch Republic, where primary debt markets developed very early but secondary markets only appeared when increased wealth and lower financing needs of the public purse made investors compete for bonds in the private market. Gelderblom and Jonker, "One System, Seventeen Outcomes."

[48] The guilds were *merceria (especeria y drogueria), joyeria, sederos, lenceros, pañeros.* Capella Martínez and Matilla Tascon, *Cinco Gremios,* 69–87.

[49] Ibid., 87; Grafe, "Mercantilism."

Capella and Matilla Tascon scolded the Cinco Gremios for being the harbingers of conspicuous consumption, as did some of the eighteenth-century reformers.[50] Yet ironically this was precisely where Spain was falling behind. Poorly integrated markets, not the lack of capital, held back the development of a consumer society that did much to foster economic development elsewhere, as we have seen. As Sempere y Guarinos had pointed out in the late eighteenth century: consumption was a good thing.[51] The Marxist inclination of thoroughly neoclassical economists to see potential bottlenecks primarily in the accumulation of capital in merchants' hands has distracted them from another fundamental precondition of growth: integrated markets that could service the consumer. In Spain the bottleneck was on the market side, not the capital side.

The analysis presented in this book has chipped away at the traditional narrative of Spain's failure to achieve faster market growth piece by piece. The notion of absolutist centralism is misplaced in general and in its specific emphasis on the economic role played by Madrid. It simply cannot be seen in the aggregate data on market integration across territories and towns. The explanatory path suggested by Ringrose, that an overpowering Madrid broke the neck of the communication system, is not mirrored in the data either. If, however, it was not the nefarious impact of Madrid as either the center of Hispanic political economy or the home of conspicuous consumers and powerful but rent-seeking mercantile interests that caused the increasing center-periphery divide, what did?

The Myth of Progressive Peripheries

For the traditional story of Spanish economic history, the periphery was what ultimately rescued the Spanish economy from its backward-looking center. Only the eventual devolution of power to the more capitalist-minded elites in the coastal regions and the regional "miracles" they produced since the eighteenth century paved Spain's way toward its final escape from backwardness in the late eighteenth and the nineteenth centuries.[52] Yet a reinterpretation of the function of the center necessarily calls for a revision of the role of the peripheries. More economic integration between periphery and center presented the elites in the periphery with a complex cost-benefit analysis. The cost was almost certainly a loss of power and autonomy. The benefit came in the form of potential returns from larger markets. In the most primitive version of such a calculation one could assume that if the coastal elites had been capable of capturing sufficiently large benefits from more integration with the hinterland they might have been willing to contemplate a loss of

---

[50] Capella Martínez and Matilla Tascon, *Cinco Gremios*, 100.
[51] See chapter 3.
[52] Ringrose, *Spanish Miracle*.

political power. Yet this is obviously too simplistic. At least two additional major factors need to be considered. First, given the strength of a tradition of representation in the remaining historic territories and in most towns, the ideological weight was, as I have argued, stacked heavily against stronger domestic integration. Second, the potential "pull" from more internal market integration needed to be attractive relative to an alternative strategy of closer economic relations with the maritime "hinterland" outside the Peninsula.

It was the nature of the Spanish political economy that the relative costs and benefits of more integration with the interior were hardly the same across peripheral regions. To begin with, the potential loss of autonomy was not the same in the three Basque Provinces and Navarra as it was in the former Crown of Aragon or in Galicia, Murcia, and Andalusia. Furthermore, it should be remembered that Vizcaya, Guipúzcoa, and Alava, as well as Navarra, had extended their autonomy significantly over the later seventeenth and the eighteenth centuries. Catalonia, Aragon, and Valencia had lost much of their formal representation but quite effectively defended their separate, though reformed, fiscal system. On the southern Mediterranean and the northwestern Atlantic coasts, there was no territorial representation but strong municipal governments in the most important ports. In other words, the stakes were vastly different. At the same time, the strength of various commercial interests differed from place to place. Unable to impose reform by either decree or force, Madrid had to try to negotiate time and again for measures that would remove some of the barriers to trade that jurisdictional fragmentation was so obviously creating.

In the late eighteenth century the one bargaining chip for the Crown became direct access to the Spanish American trades. In a polity in which power was as decentralized as in early modern Spain, there were just a handful of economic policy instruments the Crown could control. One of these was to *habilitar* (literally "enable") ports for certain kinds of foreign and long-distance commerce.[53] On the one hand, this was a practical consideration. Foreign customs were one of the few royal sources of rents, even if tariff rates differed from town to town and from historic district to historic district until well into the eighteenth and in some cases nineteenth centuries.[54] Only a port with a royal customs collection point could handle foreign goods.[55] On the other hand, the Crown directly restricted the number of ports "enabled" to participate in a number of trades that were governed by royal charters the Crown had granted to the *consulados*. As I have argued

[53] The *habilitación* implied two things: a royal permit to allow private merchants or a chartered company to conduct foreign or colonial trade through the port and the installation of the necessary administration, such as a customs house and sanitary control.

[54] A degree of unification was achieved with the Arancel de Floridablanca, a new tariff of 1782. Arias de Saavedra Alias, "Rentas generales," 28. The exception here is of course the Basque Provinces since no foreign customs applied.

[55] Though foreign merchandise that landed in a small port could theoretically be taken to the closest customs point. For the location of customs points, see Muñoz Pérez, "Mapa."

elsewhere, these were essentially merchant guilds with the privilege of a regulated company akin to the English Merchant Adventurers of the sixteenth century.[56] In sixteenth-century Spain this applied to the very rich wool trade of the Consulado de Burgos, for instance.

Most famously, however, the Indies trade was governed in this way from roughly the 1520s to 1765.[57] The charter granted to the merchants of the Consulado restricted legal trade to Seville in the Peninsula (after 1717 Cadiz) and to Veracruz (Mexico), Cartagena de Indias (Colombia), and Portobello (Panama) in the Spanish Americas, which were serviced by more or less regular armed convoys.[58] Contemporaries referred to this as the Seville or Cadiz "monopoly," and so do most historians and economists. This is misleading. From a strictly economic point of view the Spanish trade with the Indies was not a monopoly. The royal privilege structured the trade with the Indias through three main provisions. First, it created "staples," single ports of entry and exit. Second, trade was conducted in armed convoys. Third, it granted exclusive license to conduct and administer the trade to a group of private traders organized in the Casa de Contratación and the Consulados in the Peninsula and America. This, however, maintained internal competition in the same way that most guilds relied on internal competition, as well as access to the trade for non-guild members against a "fee" payable to a member for his services of intermediation.

It is well-known that the legal concentration of the Indies commerce on Seville and Cadiz resulted in a trade diversion from other Peninsular ports, but it did not exclude other Spanish merchants from trade with the Spanish Americas. The Catalonian role in the American trade via Andalusia increased substantially in the eighteenth century, while 15 percent of the members of the Consulado de Cádiz between 1743 and 1778 were Basques.[59] Merchants from Bilbao engaged increasingly in the Spanish American trades initially via Cadiz, from the mid-1760s onward via La Coruña (Galicia), and after 1778 via Santander.[60] The power of exclusion of Casa and Consulado, the fundamental feature of a monopoly, was very limited, if compared to real colonial monopolies, such as those exercised by the Dutch or English East India companies. Contemporaries stressed this point incessantly but historians have rarely appreciated it and economists seem to be surprisingly forgetful of their textbooks when it comes to the Carrera de Indias.

[56] Grafe, *Mundo ibérico*. The distinction sometimes made in the historiography between merchant guilds and chartered or regulated companies is completely artificial; they were a variation on a theme. See Gelderblom and Grafe, "Merchant Guilds."

[57] Between 1529 and 1573, Seville had to share the privilege legally with La Coruña, Bayona, Aviles Laredo, Bilbao, San Sebastian, Cartagena, Málaga, and Cadiz for outbound voyages.

[58] For an interesting recent treatment, see Oliva Melgar, *Monopolio de Indias*.

[59] This estimate excludes the Navarrese, who represented another 7 percent. García-Baquero, *Cádiz y el Atlántico*, 470. See also Martínez Shaw, *Cataluña*.

[60] Basurto Larrañaga, *Comercio*, 97–117.

In any case, the system was opened up from various angles from the early eighteenth century onward through both permissions for travel outside the convoys and ironically through the intrusion of geographically limited real monopolies along English lines. On the one hand, individual ships were sent outside the protected fleet system to Buenos Aires under a license to Francisco de Alzáybar, a Basque merchant, since the 1720s.[61] From 1739 to 1755 protected fleets were canceled in favor of the so-called *registros* (single ships).[62] On the other hand, the Crown endorsed the creation of joint stock companies with privileges for particular commodity trades, such as the Real Compañía Guipúzcoana de Caracas (1728) in San Sebastian, which dominated the cocoa trade, the Real Compañía de La Habana (1740), which traded in tobacco and sugar, and the Compañía de Barcelona (1755), which organized the Catalan trade with the Caribbean.[63]

The joint stock companies were proper monopolies that excluded all others from their patch and therefore very controversial in a trade system that had never known such degrees of exclusion. Buenos Aires, for instance, rejected the creation of a Vizcayan joint stock company for trade with the city because such a company would submit the inhabitants of the city to a "barely glossed-over slavery (*esclavitud paliada*)" to the company.[64] Meanwhile, the Guipúzcoana faced a serious rebellion in the cocoa-producing regions in 1752 against its monopoly power, which had pushed producer prices lower.[65] True monopoly needed a willingness and a capacity to enforce it from a centralized ruler, which was not available in Spain. Nor were the subjects of the Spanish Crown suffering a real monopoly gladly and joint-stock monopolies remained a small factor in Spanish trade.

Instead, the Crown extended the privilege of trading between Spain and the Spanish Americas to a larger number of ports in 1765. The impetus to reform came from negotiations between the Cuban elites and the Crown, in which the former had successfully claimed trade concessions in return for an increased fiscal contribution aimed at improving the defenses of the island.[66] Cubans capitalized thus on the Crown's absolute priority for more defense capability after the totally inadequate Spanish military presence in Cuba (and elsewhere in the empire) had been painfully exposed by a British occupation in 1762–63.[67] The Caribbean ports of Cuba, Santo Domingo, Puerto Rico, Margarita, and Trinidad were "habilitated" for free trade with Spain in the Americas, while in the Peninsula, Barcelona, Alicante, Cartagena, Malaga,

[61] Mariluz Urquijo, *Bilbao y Buenos Aires*, 39–41; Lamikiz, "Patrones de Comercio."

[62] Stein and Stein, *Silver*, 191–99.

[63] Gárate Ojanguren, *Comercio ultramarino*; Gárate Ojanguren, *La real compañía*; Oliva Melgar, *Cataluña y el comercio privilegiado*.

[64] *Memorial de Don Domingo de Marcoleta*, reprinted in Mariluz Urquijo, *Bilbao y Buenos Aires*, 138.

[65] The rebellion is generally known by its leader, Juan Francisco de León.

[66] Muñoz Pérez, "Publicación." A postal service that also took goods operated from La Coruña beginning in 1763 with strong Basque participation.

[67] Kuethe and Inglis, "Absolutism." For an attempt to estimate the number of regular troops in Spanish America, see Grafe and Irigoin, "Stakeholder Empire."

Cadiz, Seville, La Coruña, Gijon, and Santander were included. Over the next thirteen years an increasing number of American and Peninsular ports became part of the new trade regime until the Crown issued the "Decreto de Comercio Libre" (free-trade decree) for trade between Spanish and Spanish American ports in 1778.

For understandable reasons, the history of the Comercio Libre has overwhelmingly been written from an American perspective. After all, it opened up legal transatlantic trade in most parts of the continent for the first time.[68] The history of the opening up of the American trades was, however, also that of the opening up of Spanish trade. The first decree of 1765 included practically all of the main Peninsular ports with one conspicuous exception: Bilbao. More notable still, direct trade between the Vizcayan port and Spanish American destinations remained illegal until 1828.[69] In other words, even the "free-trade" regime of the post-1778 era was not universal. The continuing exception of the *señorio de* Vizcaya from the gradual "opening" of the American trade allows for a fascinating view into the complicated center-periphery relations in the late eighteenth century. It illuminates in one particular episode the tensions between reform and status quo. The outcome was not the unintended consequence of tradition and path dependence that simply constrained all actors. Instead, it was the result of the agency of provincial elites that deliberately contested and negotiated with the state in the center.

The contest over Basque exclusion from the Spanish American trade in the eighteenth century also involved some of the central figures and institutions of the Spanish Enlightenment on either side of the divide. The protagonists, such as the *fiscal* (later president) of the Royal Council Pedro Rodriguez (Conde) de Campomanes (1723–1802) and the Real Sociedad Bascongada de Amigos del País (Royal Basque Society of Friends of the Country), left eloquent testimony of their thinking and actions, something that is more difficult to ascertain in other comparable conflicts.[70] This then is not only one of the best-documented episodes of center-periphery conflict, but it also features individuals and organizations that have been identified as key to late eighteenth-century reformism and the supposed late opening of Spain toward the outside world by the enlightened elites from the economically successful peripheries.

A Test Case: Why Were the Basques Excluded from the Comercio Libre?

The behavior of the provincial elite with regard to the opening of the American trades has puzzled intellectual historians. The historiography has tended

---

[68] The quantitative impact of the *libre comercio* is contested. Cf. Fisher, "Imperial 'Free Trade'" versus García-Baquero González, *Comercio colonial*, 187–216.

[69] Rivera Medina, *Burguesía*, 255.

[70] For the centrality of the protagonists within the Spanish Enlightenment, cf. Astigarraga, *Ilustrados Vascos*; de Castro, *Campomanes*; Lluch, *Las Españas Vencidas*.

to stress the dichotomy between the defense of the old order with corporatist freedoms, legal inequality, and special rights of the historical territories on the one hand, and the enlightened freedom of the individual citizen freed from corporatist intervention and religious restrictions of secular life on the other. Within such a framework, however, the Basque elite's response to the conflict over the Spanish American trade is hard to understand. Not surprisingly, the historiographical assessment of this episode has been split between interesting extreme positions. This is particularly true for the evaluation of the role played by the Bascongada, arguably the first economic reform society in the Peninsula, which was legally incorporated in 1763.[71] The society was born out of private initiative beginning in the 1740s with a clear vision of emulating the educational and reforming work of scientific societies that had appeared elsewhere in Europe since the 1660s but had spread particularly since the 1730s.[72]

On the one hand, in the traditional narrative of Spanish Enlightenment, the Bascongada plays the crucial role of catalyst within a Spanish society that had lost contact with developments elsewhere in Europe.[73] In a famous circular published in 1774, the Conde de Campomanes, one of the most active reforming members of the Bourbon political elites and at the time *procurador* of the Royal Council, explicitly encouraged all towns of Spain to create royal economic reform societies mirroring the example of the Bascongada.[74] By 1808 there were seventy to eighty such societies in Spain.[75] And yet the Bascongada stood out from the mass of societies. Most of the smaller municipal societies developed quickly into something that looked more like traditional Spanish confraternities than enlightened reform societies. They were quickly subsumed into traditional forms of association and sociability.[76]

The Basque Real Sociedad de Amigos del País, by contrast, developed an active program of promotion of the Enlightenment among the public; it lobbied for agricultural reform and tried to foster industrial development. It published scientific literature of both Spanish and international origin, undertook educational initiatives, and organized public lectures. Its members made it their business to circulate large numbers of books on the Inquisition's index of forbidden works by obtaining licenses to buy and circulate

---

[71] Agrarian societies had been created around the same time in Lérida (Lleida) and in Galicia, which some historians count as the first ones, but their ambitions were much more limited. Astigarraga, *Ilustrados Vascos*, 46.

[72] McClellan, *Science Reorganized*. McClellan tends to underestimate the Spanish societies because they fit his categorization poorly. The precursor of the society were the *tertulias*, evening discussions, organized by a group of Guipúzcoan nobles in Azcoitia, among them Javier María de Munibe, conde de Peñaflorida, Joaquín de Eguia, marqués de Narros, and Manuel Ignacio de Altuna. For the early history of the society, see Astigarraga, *Ilustrados Vascos*, chapter 1, Portillo Valdés, *Monarquía y Gobierno provincial*, 141–83, and Sarrailh, *España ilustrada*, 230–52.

[73] Cf. Herr, *Eighteenth-Century Revolution*; Sarrailh, *España ilustrada*.

[74] Sarrailh, *España ilustrada*, 236, 252–89.

[75] Windler, *Lokale Eliten*, 187.

[76] Ibid., 357–67.

them.[77] Its annual publication, the *Extractos*, carried contributions that high-lighted the benefits of luxury consumption as an important contribution to economic development, recommended various agricultural improvements, praised Hume's work on the benefits of foreign trade, and, at times, attacked fairly savagely certain sectors of the Catholic establishment and the nobility for their backward attitudes. Although the Inquisition opened its first case against the society in 1776, the Holy Office had little power to influence, much less interrupt, the activities of a body that counted among its members almost the entire provincial elite and quite a few prominent figures from beyond the Basque Provinces.[78]

On the other hand, the traditional narrative of the Bascongada's contribu-tion to popularizing Enlightenment ideas and economic reforms in northern Spain and beyond is contested.[79] The main reason is the society's stance on the question of the *fueros*, that symbol of the old order, which the Bascongada defended vigorously. In a historiography that pitches progressive, "enlight-ened" ideas against those that remained embedded in the old corporate order, the position of the Bascongada was evidently intellectually inconsistent. It has therefore been the object of debate among Spanish historians: while some argue for the enlightened spirit of the institution and the bourgeois and mer-cantile interests in the Basque Provinces (and Navarra) that it represented, others point to its quintessentially conservative stance as a sign of the Spanish Enlightenment's failure to make significant inroads even in these supposedly more open-minded, commercial provinces.

The question of access to the American trades forced the Basque institu-tions, including the Bascongada, to take sides. The conflict over the opening up of the American trades became increasingly important over the course of the eighteenth century and shaped relations between the Basque Provinces and Madrid on the one hand and between various Basque institutions, such as the *juntas generales* (the representative assembly), the *consulados* of Bil-bao and Guipúzcoa, and the Bascongada, on the other. The attempts of the central administration between 1717 and 1721 to abolish the Basque free-trade status and establish royal customs on the coast had failed miserably in the face of sustained and violent resistance, as we have seen. Yet the lack of a unified external customs regime continued to be a major concern for Bourbon reformers. Centralization for the ideological purpose of extending royal power was possibly part of that concern. The experience with mas-sive problems of trade diversion, costly double lines of customs, and loss of revenue due to rampant smuggling in the Basque territories, Navarra, and

---

[77] Though the Inquisition had the same rights to supervision as elsewhere in Spain in Vizcaya, the absence of customs had traditionally meant that indexed books were even more widely available in the Basque Country than in the rest of Spain. Sarrailh, *España ilustrada*, 230–52; Astigarraga, *Ilustrados Vascos*, 61–62.

[78] Astigarraga, *Ilustrados Vascos*, 61.

[79] For a survey of the debates, see ibid., 14–19 and Portillo Valdés, *Monarquía y Gobierno provincial*, 143–69.

the former Kingdom of Aragon (discussed in chapter 5) suggests, however, that there were powerful practical reasons to pursue reform. For the central hacienda, the Basque "customs exemptions," like the Navarrese and surviving Aragonese de facto tax advantages, increased expenditure on enforcement, reduced revenue, and created inequalities in the fiscal system. These, in turn, undermined credibility and tax compliance, thereby increasing tax evasion and avoidance.

For most of the century, the central hacienda could do little to solve this problem and was engaged in damage control; hence its willingness to become the tax farmer of the tobacco monopoly in the service of the Navarrese treasury and to subsidize both the Navarrese and the Alavese treasuries in the case of tobacco. This went hand in hand with increased attempts to enforce the internal customs borders. As the century progressed, the boundaries between the Basque Provinces and Castile became the site of some violent confrontations between customs guards, traders, and smugglers. While locals alleged extortions and abuses of power, smugglers became more professional and violent. Alberto Angulo argues that harsh fines for petty infractions of the tobacco monopoly, in combination with an inability to stop well-organized and heavily armed posses of professional tobacco smugglers, further reduced the legitimacy of the system and stoked general resistance.[80] As we have seen, however, the trend toward more violence was relative. Compared to the French situation, fines and penalties imposed in Spain were very moderate indeed.

The results from the *bacalao* market analysis suggest that the real impact on trade of the surviving internal customs points increased over the eighteenth century as boundaries became less porous and more contested.[81] The pattern of disintegration between towns in the historic territories observed in chapter 5 lends some weight to that argument. Yet this process, too, was not simply a contest between a particularistic Basque territory and a supposedly centralist Crown. It is well-known that competition between the two major ports on the Cantabrian coast, (Basque) Bilbao and (Asturian) Santander, contributed considerably to the conflict. Since at least the late seventeenth century both towns maintained permanent lobbying activities in Madrid in an effort to improve their own set of "freedoms" or at least to reduce those of the rival town.[82]

In order to solve the problem once and for all, the central administration needed a bargaining chip against the historic territories. Over the century, it became increasingly clear that direct access to the American trade was potentially the ace up the Crown's sleeve. Since the 1640s, various projects suggested the creation of a Vizcayan joint stock company for trade with Buenos Aires, but they were resisted in the Rio de la Plata. In 1765 the original project of *comercio libre* had included the Basque ports while the final decree

---

[80] Angulo Morales, *Puertas*, 173–204.
[81] Palacio Atard, *El Comercio de Castilla*, 40.
[82] Ibid., 33–47.

consciously excluded them.[83] The diversion of trade via other "enabled" ports raised transaction costs for Basque merchants substantially, as did the alternative they were increasingly choosing: contraband, that is, illegal direct shipments from Bilbao to American ports, especially Havana and Buenos Aires.[84] In 1775 Campomanes explicitly argued that the opening of American trade should be linked to a general customs reform that ended "unequal treatment" (read Basque exemptions). In 1778 the central administration made a formal offer: the Basque ports would be "enabled" to participate in direct trade with Spanish American ports in return for a transfer of the Basque customs from their inland location to the coast—in effect, the abolition of the customs exempt status that had failed in the 1720s. The first minister, the count of Floridablanca, asked the economic societies to comment on the proposal. This started a remarkable process of consultation that in itself puts paid to the notion of centralist power as the Bascongada in turn drew on its chapters in Vizcaya and Guipúzcoa as well as the *consulados* of San Sebastian and Bilbao for advice.

Basque commercial interests were evidently in favor of opening up direct American trade. The reasons were obvious: new markets and lower transactions costs. The representatives of Basque merchants had long made the case. The question that pitched interests within the Basque Country against one another was, however, what price should be paid. Whatever the merchants would advise, the main obstacle was located in the *juntas generales* of the Basque Provinces, which categorically refused to entertain any proposal that would in the least interfere with the exempt status of the provinces. The historiography has argued that this extraordinarily strong resistance was an outcome of the political representation enshrined in the Basque political system. The pattern of representation in the juntas of both Vizcaya and Guipúzcoa was territorially based. Unusual for Spain, rural interests were dominant while the mercantile sector of the largest ports, San Sebastian and Bilbao, counted barely on one vote for their geographic area. In other words, while the trading sector in these towns accounted for a large share of the provincial economy, it was politically underrepresented.[85]

It is generally argued that rural interests benefited from the "free-trade" regime created by the customs exemptions, which supposedly kept agricultural imports, and thus the cost of living, low. The argument is summed up by Fernández Albaladejo: the provincial nobility enjoyed "good rents and had no necessity to engage in commerce in order to provide a decent living for its families," and this view is endorsed by most historians.[86] The argu-

---

[83] The following discussion of the position of the Bascongada relies mainly on Astigarraga, *Ilustrados Vascos*, 180–204 and Portillo Valdés, *Monarquía y Gobierno provincial*, 461–82.

[84] Rivera Medina, *Burguesía*.

[85] Fernández de Pinedo, *Crecimiento económico*; Portillo Valdés, *Monarquia y gobierno provincial*.

[86] Fernández Albaladejo, "La polémica entre libre comercio y fueros," 239, cited in Astigarraga, *Ilustrados vascos*, 184.

ment, however, has a logical flaw. Rural interests, especially the recipients of agricultural rents, could hardly have an interest in imports free of customs if these imports depressed agricultural prices. Instead, they should have opposed the *foral* regime.

Yet the deliberations of the *juntas generales* show beyond a doubt that rural representatives indeed supported the *fueros* and with them international free trade as well as barriers to market integration vis-à-vis the Castilian and Navarrese hinterland. Logic hence suggests that the argument needs to be turned upside down: evidently the customs exemptions posed no threat to high agricultural prices in the Basque Provinces and thus to rural rents. Instead, it is safe to assume that rural interests feared that pressure from a more integrated internal market might endanger their rents. It is true the Basque Provinces and their juntas defended the free-trade status for centuries with reference to the poor agricultural basis and the need for cheap grain imports to feed the relatively densely populated region. The rhetoric was one of protection of the consumer, an argument that carried weight in Spain. However, a look at trade statistics suggests consumer protection was not what landed interests in the Basque Provinces had in mind.

The provinces had been strongly dependent on imports of the main food grains before the 1630s, but the situation changed thereafter. As I have shown elsewhere, around the mid-seventeenth century previously large imports of grain declined precipitously, most likely as a consequence of the introduction of American maize, which suited the ecological conditions of the Basque Country much better than wheat.[87] Harvest fluctuations notwithstanding, Aingeru Zabala shows that in the last four decades of the eighteenth century, the region was still almost self-sufficient in maize, while around 12 percent of the locally consumed wheat was supplied by imports.[88] Compared to the situation in Valencia, discussed in chapter 5, this constituted hardly a dependence on foreign grain.

The much-quoted "agricultural poverty" of the Basque region was a convenient rhetorical argument rather than an economic reality. It suggested a concurrence of interests between the recipients of rural rents and consumers that did not exist. Instead, this was a period of strong developments in the main grain-producing areas of Castile and Leon. Castilian grain posed a much bigger threat to those living off the rents of an inefficient Basque farming sector that had been sheltered by internal customs than did imports from the Baltic, England, or North America.[89] As in the case of *bacalao* discussed in chapter 5, by the late eighteenth century the Basque exemption from external tariffs hurt consumers because supplies from nearby Castile were held back. The overrepresented rural interests defended the *fueros* not

[87] AFB, CB, Libro 211, nos. 24, 38, 39, 40, 41; Grafe, *Mundo ibérico*, 124ff.

[88] Only in the case of beans (and rice that could not be produced locally) did imports dominate. Zabala Uriarte, *Mundo urbano*, 413–18.

[89] These were the main regions of origin of Basque grain imports in the eighteenth century.

out of sympathy for Basque consumers but as a device that guaranteed their rents at the expense of the consuming masses. Smallholders, who constituted a large sector of the Basque population, and rural nobility were in perfect agreement in this. Landless laborers and urban consumers, however, paid the price. The 1778 proposal to open the American trade in return for an abolition of the internal customs presented all interest groups in the Basque Country with stark choices. The agricultural sector answered unequivocally, rejecting the offer of reduced costs in the American trades at the "expense" of more exposure to competition from the *internal* market.

For the Bascongada, finding a position was more complicated. In its programs to foster industrial development in the region it had repeatedly run into the internal tariffs as a major obstacle. At the same time, it was committed in principle to the persistence of the *fueros*, albeit willing to suggest reforms. This position, which Jesús Astigarraga has aptly labeled "enlightened *foralism*," strove to combine two elements: a principled stance that defended the traditional rights of the historic territories and a willingness to negotiate limited concessions and exceptions from the strict adherence to the customs regime where necessary and convenient.[90] The Bascongada adopted several of the suggestions made by the *consulados*, the merchant guilds, in order to work out a compromise. These included the installation of a tariff regime where royal customs on American products could be levied either by an official in the Basque ports or at the inland posts. The society pointed out, as the *consulados* had done, that there was a precedent for such a limited exception to the free-trade status of the provinces in the wool tax, introduced in 1561.

This was, as Astigarraga explains, an intermediate position that could have been expected to work reasonably well within the existing institutional environment. However, what the Bascongada suggested was the traditional solution to all matter of conflict that arose from jurisdictional fragmentation in Spain: more, not less, fragmentation. A special official to collect the duties from the American commerce to be stationed in Bilbao was a concession, but only in the sense that the Bascongada was willing to make another exception and pay a special duty on a particular trade. It was no concession at all in terms of what eighteenth-century reformers used to call a "rationalization" of public administration. That would have required the mercantile interests to give up autonomy, something they were as unwilling to do as were their rural neighbors.

Little came of the proposals of the Bascongada. Astigarraga points out that the central administration upped the ante at possibly the most sensitive point in the negotiations. In response to the negative attitude from the juntas in 1779, Madrid effectively transformed the Basque Provinces from a giant "free port" into a "foreign" territory by applying external customs to Basque-produced goods. Clearly, the half-hearted compromise of the Bascongada

[90] Astigarraga, *Ilustrados vascos*.

was now not nearly enough to solve the standoff and negotiations broke down. However, the compromise that the mercantile interests of the Basque Country had been willing to concede never went beyond a very traditional strategy. It departed from the point of no change to the existing commercial regime that granted the region a highly beneficial (at least for commercial and rural elites) status akin to a "free port." It seems somewhat naive to suggest that the *consulados* and the Bascongada only insisted on this principle because they knew that the rural interests in the juntas would not discuss this point anyway.[91] The abolition of the commercial *fueros* was not, and could not be, in the interest of Basque merchants, and the opposition of the juntas could easily be instrumentalized in favor of the status quo. The next step then was to offer piecemeal financial benefits to the central hacienda in return for access to the Americas trade. As it turns out, the benefit was not deemed high enough by Madrid.

All of the proposed solutions to this conflict led to more jurisdictional fragmentation, not less. The only alternative was unthinkable as we have seen: a forced abolition of the *foral* regime driven through by the center by force was evidently beyond the reach of Madrid. The position of the juntas, which were happy to allow the opening of American trade but with no concessions on the customs exemption, would have introduced another layer of exception to the American commerce, which the Crown was just trying to rid of exceptions. The Bascongada's proposal would have respected the integrity of the Decreto de Libre Comercio reforms of the American trade but in turn fragmented further the internal and external customs regime in the Basque Provinces. Meanwhile, the decision of Madrid to deal with the problem by declaring the Basque Provinces "foreign" territory in fiscal terms patently deepened the disintegration between the provinces and Castile even further. In a political system based on interterritorial negotiation among very flat hierarchies, it is almost impossible to see a counterfactual outcome short of civil war and territorial disintegration. Here were the seeds of not only poorly integrated markets and more economic hardship but also interregional political conflicts that would turn violent for much of the nineteenth and parts of the twentieth centuries.[92]

Over the past four decades intellectual historians of Spain have challenged the dichotomy between *foral* conservatism and centralizing Enlightenment by claiming that there was not one Enlightenment in Spain but several *regional* Enlightenments in the Basque Provinces and Navarra, in Catalonia and in Valencia in particular. The argument is simple: the Enlightenment stood a chance in Spain wherever it responded to local circumstances.[93] This helps to dissolve some of the intellectual inconsistencies in the position of organizations such as the Bascongada, which could happily claim that the opening of

---

[91] Ibid.

[92] Canal i Morell, *Carlismo*.

[93] Astigarraga, *Ilustrados vascos*, 15; Lluch, *El pensament econòmic*.

the American trade was *not* a *contrafuero* (against the *fueros*), while opening the province toward Castile and Navarra *was* a *contrafuero*.

Yet it is hard to avoid the impression that these regional Enlightenments were less shaped by intellectual disagreements than by the everyday necessities that arose from regionally diverse politico-economic regimes. Hence they are quite easy to understand within the traditional structure of governance in Spain. Basque elites effortlessly combined enlightened free-trade arguments in the international sphere with strong support for maintaining internal customs and differential tax regimes that resulted from the jurisdictional fragmentation in the order of Spain's ancien régime. International and transatlantic integration posed no threat to established regional political power, quite the opposite. By providing a basis for commercial, and later industrial, development it allowed for a significant amount of economic growth within the established order. By contrast, closer integration with the hinterland potentially threatened the strong degree of local power exercised by the same provincial elites and was resisted. The strategy in itself hardly distinguished these regional elites from those in many other countries. The difference was marked by their success. In the medium and long term, it circumscribed both the scale and the scope of the market and seriously depressed economic growth.

The Legacy and the Long Memory of Urbanization

The conflict over Basque access to the American trades was certainly very specific. The distribution of power in the Basque juntas was different from that in the Navarrese estates, which still counted on three chambers. Elsewhere political power was exercised much more through urban institutions. The lesson to be learned from the example is not that the conflict between center and historic territories, or between territories and towns, or between center and towns, opened up the same cleavage everywhere. Quite the opposite. However, what the case illustrates is how the flat hierarchies within the political structure of the Spanish monarchy, even in the eighteenth century, tended to create *more*, not less, jurisdictional fragmentation.

The pattern was not simply one between center and periphery; on the periphery, conflicts between competing urban centers abounded. Ironically, all participants appealed to the Crown and its ministers for mediation. This was true for Bilbao and Santander, Valencia and Alicante, Seville and Cadiz, and so on. The common feature of all these conflicts was that the structure of political governance allowed local elites to defend their position of preeminence. In the Basque Country this took the form of a conflict over the traditional freedoms. Yet Solbes describes a similar process in Navarra, arguing that here, too, the provincial elite instrumentalized the supposed conflict over the territories' historic rights for its own purposes.[94] The historiography

---

[94] Solbes Ferri, *Rentas Reales de Navarra*.

has noted these conflicts for a long time but has failed to offer a convincing interpretive framework that breaks out of the tired notion of the absolutist state that somehow allowed for all these exceptions to occur.

The long-term outcome was the persistence of fragmented authority, which had political as well as economic consequences. The strong reliance of the fiscal system on indirect consumption and trade taxes enshrined the control of urban and regional elites over the sources of power, in spite of serious royal attempts toward administrative reform and notable improvements in the quality of administration. Paradoxically, the lack of a strong center and the relatively large autonomy of towns and historic territories (once again the argument is *relative* not *absolute* autonomy) strengthened the role of the monarchy as the "ultimate arbiter." The political center was crucial because it mediated, not because it mandated. Economically this state of affairs perpetuated a low degree of market integration. Small and shallow markets limited the scope for agglomeration, that is, for the concentration of skills, capital, and people in larger economic regions. Without agglomeration external scale economies in production processes and knowledge creation were limited. The Basque iron industry, for example, fell further behind and would industrialize only later in the nineteenth century, a process that historians have directly linked to the persistence of the *foral* regime.[95]

It is also no accident that Spain experienced no aggregate increase in the rate of urbanization throughout the seventeenth and eighteenth centuries even though economic historians are now quite agreed that economic growth occurred, albeit at a low rate. In the face of political obstacles to more integrated markets, a slow integration of rural consumers into local and regional markets was almost the only way markets could become deeper if not much wider. Thus provincial capitals did relatively well, as did the "capitals" of the historic territories. This explains why the pattern of urbanization in Spain diverges considerably from the European historical norm.[96] The divergence is not the large town at the center, Madrid, but the fact that throughout the early modern period no hierarchy of medium-sized interior places emerged. The lack of a layered urban hierarchy was the mirror image of a fragmented market. On the periphery, regional centers, all of which were either also port towns (Barcelona, Malaga, Cadiz, La Coruña, Santander, Bilbao) and/or capitals of historic territories (Barcelona, Bilbao [de facto], Zaragoza, Pamplona), articulated their direct hinterland and sphere of influence.

Yet powerful political and economic interests sabotaged integration with the interior. At the same time, throughout the eighteenth century maritime trade grew quickly and offered the coastal regions and their ports an alternative growth strategy that did not challenge their traditional freedoms. As we saw in chapter 4, transatlantic trade costs fell much faster than interior trade costs within Spain. For the elites on the coast this added an economic

---

[95] Cf. Fernández de Pinedo, "Bloomery to the Blast-Furnace."
[96] Marrewijk, *International Trade.*

incentive to the political defense of local power and they bet their money and political capital accordingly on transoceanic integration as opposed to stronger domestic markets. Paradoxically, peripheral "regional miracles," as Ringrose calls them, delayed the process of internal integration. The single biggest loser was the Spanish consumer. In the interior, the multitude of political obstacles to more integration increased the final price of goods. Yet consumers in the coastal regions also suffered higher prices for staple goods, as we have seen.

The picture of the Spanish early modern economy suggests that the prime problem of the domestic market was not "poverty." In a highly influential book, Nadal has argued that the "failure" of Catalonia to develop a modern cotton industry in the nineteenth century was due mainly to the poverty of the interior, which stymied demand.[97] However, his thesis has since been qualified from at least two ends. First, the slowly emerging literature on consumer markets in the Peninsula illustrates that Catalan goods were traded deep into the Castilian countryside.[98] Second, Prados has shown that the level of industrial development in Spain throughout the nineteenth century was low at any given level of per capita national income.[99] His results suggest that domestic demand was not the problem, and he concludes that Spain simply failed to develop export markets that could have sustained its manufacturing instead.

If the analysis of one specific consumer market—*bacalao*—presented here is taken as an indicator, however, one should add at least one other factor: per capita national income is a poor guide for effective demand in markets that were persistently marred by jurisdictional obstacles to more integration. The problem was not that Spaniards in the interior or on the periphery were too poor to enjoy some of the new colonial or manufactured consumption goods that became available in the later seventeenth and eighteenth centuries but that inefficient markets did poorly in coordinating between supply and demand. The political choices of elites on the periphery who consciously favored external integration over stronger development of domestic markets perpetuated the existence of large allocative inefficiencies even as income slowly increased. Even worse, the economic benefits from the growth of international markets were sterilized through the lack of domestic market integration. The center could not, and the periphery would not, break the impasse; and as a result the Peninsular economy just kept plodding along, becoming more backward all the time.

[97] Nadal, *El fracaso de la revolución industrial.*
[98] Ramos Palencia, "Pautas."
[99] Prados de la Escosura, *De imperio a nación*, chapter 5.

Conclusions

IN HIS MAGNIFICENT ACCOUNT, *Boundaries: The Making of France and Spain in the Pyrenees*, Sahlins demonstrates how European nation-states were constructed at least as much from the periphery to the center as from the center to the periphery. On the boundaries, allegiances and identities were built in contrast to those on the other side, as well as out of commonality with those on one's own side. The peoples of the peripheries were not the unconscious objects of a process of institutional, ideological, economic, and social-state building imposed from Madrid or Paris but participants in a process that redefined relations across the border, and between the periphery and the center. The preceding pages concur with Sahlins: the people of the peripheries of emerging European nation-states need to be given back their crucial role in shaping the process.

Alas, this book also demonstrates that the kind of nation-state the peripheries constructed could be very distinct on either side of the border. Sahlins focused on the boundaries of the eastern Pyrenees where Catalan-speaking folks became Frenchmen and Spaniards. Had he turned further west, the very different outcomes of this process north and south of the boundary would have been far more obvious. Here he would have had to explain how Basques and Navarrese from north and south of the border became Frenchmen and Spaniards by 1800. He would also have had to discuss why virtually all regional representative institutions had withered away and finally disappeared in Basse Navarra, Labourd, and Soule on the French side, while those in Vizcaya, Guipúzcoa, Alava, and Navarra on the Spanish side had been strengthened throughout the late seventeenth and much of the eighteenth centuries.[1] It is impossible to ignore that the political, economic, social, linguistic, and cultural relations between center and periphery are to this day the single most important issue in Spain while they hardly appear in the political debates north of the Pyrenees. The disdain that French rural folks sometimes express for Paris hardly compares to the constitutional crises, political conflicts, and violence causing hundreds of deaths over the past four decades alone that have characterized center-periphery relations in Spain.

The reason is not that "Spain is different," or at least not that it is different in some existential way that prevents an explanation of its haphazard path to nation-state building and internal market integration within a common comparative European framework. Lest one wishes to agree with

---

[1] Agirreazkuenaga, "Abolition."

Franco's tourism campaigns, the claim that Spain is different is little more than a comfortable exit strategy for a less comfortable problem. The real issue is that important parts of the political economy and historical sociology model world that is used to trace the emergence of early modern European nation-states and nationally integrated markets becomes questionable in light of Spanish early modern history. The first casualty is the lopsided focus of political economy on the predatory state. It is not that the state in all its multilayered appearances never predated on its subjects, thereby affecting incentives and diverting economic resources. Predation was simply the lesser problem. The fundamental unfinished construction site of the creation of the Spanish early modern nation and market was that the state never became autonomous enough.

The second challenge is that the Spanish example shows clearly that early modern European state-building cannot be reduced to the alternatives of tax or perish, that is, of becoming a fiscal-military state that maximizes revenue or else be taken over by a neighbor that did. The simplistic idea that states had to push their revenue-raising capacity to the limit underpins the notion of the predatory state. Alas, we saw that Spain's path diverged. European nation-building was the result of a complex interplay between institutional structures that determined where power was located, an ideology of power that legitimized it and that shaped how it was exercised, and human agency. The dominant model of early modern European state-building had us think- ing teleologically from the end, assuming that the ultimate result had to be a unified fiscal-military state in which power was located at the center and that maximized revenue because it engaged in wars. If we drop that corset Spain is really not that hard to understand.

The historiography has long suggested that Spain never quite transitioned from being a "composite monarchy" to a more "modern" absolutist state, that is, from one where the monarchy was embedded in and shared its powers with territorial and corporate institutions to one that was clearly hierarchical. This is undoubtedly true. Yet this view contains almost as much the notion of a "modernization" process as the political economy model does. Statehood in Spain continued to rely on flat hierarchies, and these shaped the process of both nation- and market-building. Spain was not absolutist in the classic sense of the term, nor was it centralizing or unifying. The main contest over power did not take place between Crown and nobility but between Crown, territories, and urban "republics." The persistence of this multipolar and highly unstable system of governance and its tendency to decentralize power is one of the most fascinating features of Spanish early modern history.

At its urban bases the Spanish composite monarchy was closer to its sixteenth-century nemesis, the northern Netherlands, than its newfound ally of eighteenth-century France. Yet in contrast to the Netherlands, Spain never developed anything akin to the admittedly complex but relatively clearly layered vertical and hierarchical differentiation of competencies that existed between Dutch municipalities, provincial estates, and the Estates General.

In Spain, more often than not, towns, historic territories, or merchant guilds continued to negotiate the exercise of power from a position of hierarchical equality far into the eighteenth and probably nineteenth centuries.

This book has suggested that there were at least two reasons for the system's survival over three centuries. One was an unusually strong ideology of contractual rule that survived in Spain and seems to have stymied the emergence of a notion of divine monarchy that shaped political discourse in countries like France and England. While I have traced its existence and institutional impact, it is beyond the scope of this book to offer an in-depth intellectual history of this phenomenon. The fact is that the institutionalized right to resistance contained in what is sometimes referred to as *pase foral*, but which had meaning far beyond the Basque Provinces, was a unique feature. The fact is also that Spanish archives are full of institutional acts of resistance against attempts at rule from the center.

There is no reason to assume that French mayors were not beaming with civic pride in just the same way Spanish *alcaldes* did; and French writers were adamant that French subjects enjoyed supreme liberty. Alas, as Hoffman has pointed out, they had few institutions that could back them up in their daily interactions with the exercise of power.[2] The veto to the exercise of power in the Spanish composite monarchy mattered because it turned an ideology of contractual power into a legal institution that could be invoked in a court of law. It transformed an act of resistance and evasion of superior power into a perfectly legal challenge to power. It thus substantially lowered the opportunity cost of objection to the implementation of royal policy and slowed down the emergence of a clear hierarchy of corporate entities conspiring against the establishment of an autonomous state. The notion of governance as an ex post act of deliverance of justice rather than an ex ante act of mandating social and economic activities survived even at the supposed center of power, the Royal Council far into the eighteenth century. On the peripheries, it emboldened and protected local and regional elites who needed the center to mediate but loathed the idea that it might mandate. As an economic historian, I am tempted to read opportunism into the support for this ideology of fragmented power. However, intellectual historians will probably prove me wrong.

The second stone in the structure that supported the persistence of shared sovereignty among towns, territories, Crown, and a large number of other corporate bodies was the fiscal system. It is obvious that the early reliance on indirect trade and consumption taxes empowered the towns and the territories. These were quintessentially urban taxes that fell on urban activities and had to be collected by urban authorities. They were also harder to collect, requiring a much more sophisticated administrative structure than the direct land taxes so important in most of the other large European states. In this respect Spain also resembled most closely the Netherlands. No other source of

[2] Hoffman, "France," 248–49.

revenue, not even the Spanish Americas, could match the importance of these trade and consumption taxes that necessarily had to be levied through urban structures. In any case the fiscal powers of the Crown were only marginally larger in the New World, as Irigoin and I have argued elsewhere. In the end, no Spanish king could do without the local indirect taxes. As we saw in chapter 5, strong power in the historic territories made it impossible to increase revenue from the most likely alternative source: external customs. Hence shifting the tax burden away from locally administered trade and consumption taxes was impossible.

The economic effects of this fiscal structure were far-reaching. The *bacalao* market is just one case study for this, but it is arguably well suited for an analysis of the determinants of the slow, regionally diverse, and haphazard process of market integration in Spain. It was a new product that consumers had to learn to like; it is, after all, the ultimate acquired taste. However, it was so successful largely because it became the most important substitute for meat and a crucial source of animal protein. It made sure that Spanish nutritional standards were that much better. Its expansion was breathtaking, and by the mid-seventeenth century it was already a food staple. As a staple it has allowed us to use its prices as a means of understanding market integration. Because it was a new good it also helps us understand how non-local products slowly began to penetrate Spain's rural markets.

The historiography has made much of the claim that Spain suffered the "tyranny of distance" resulting from forbidding geography and poor roads. The analysis of the cod market lends only very limited support to this argument. Transport was slower and more expensive in Spain than in the leading northern European countries. Yet it was improving at a reasonable pace long before the railway age. In fact, transport costs fell faster than the cost of an imported good like cod that necessarily had to be taken from the coast to the final consumer in the interior. In other words, the share of transport costs in final price fell over time. Still, in one respect Spanish domestic transport became *relatively speaking* a larger problem over time. Maritime transport, exemplified by the shipping of cod from North America to Spain, became cheaper faster. This shifted relative prices: internationally produced goods became, ceteris paribus, cheaper than domestically produced goods. For the coastal regions with a choice of external versus internal integration, this clearly increased the attractiveness of the former over the latter in the eighteenth century.

The analysis demonstrates vividly the predominance of political economy factors in explaining the painfully slow path to market integration in Spain. Most of the variation in prices between towns and territories is explained by such factors. Here then was the Achilles' heel of the Spanish system of governance: the reliance on local and regional trade and consumption taxes drastically circumscribed the scope and the scale of the market. The result of low degrees of market integration was misallocation of resources. Spain was undoubtedly poorer than it had to be. The local price of food (and hence wages) depended more on the state of municipal (and territorial) finances than on that of the transport system, or the transatlantic supply lines, or the ability and endeavors of local merchants.

Town finances in turn depended on their contribution to the central treasury but also local management, the amount of real property and other streams of income the town could count on (the *propios*), and their level of debt. All of these together determined how hard the town had to press its consumers. In this way, even the impact of the American trade was largely local. Seville, the richest town in the realm in the sixteenth century and one of the largest contributors (in return for generous privileges) to the central treasury, was so indebted by the late sixteenth century that it had to hold its consumers for ransom. The aldermen had overleveraged the town's finances; that investment strategy turned out to be a disaster when the first cyclical downturn hit the American trades and with it the town's tax take. It took the local governance and tax systems to turn the American trades into price inflation.

Indirect taxation was regressive. Consumers typically paid dearly for meat, wine, oil, and their close substitutes, which rose in price as well. They were also charged so much for the new American consumer goods like cocoa and tobacco that consumption was seriously restricted. Yet the social impact was mitigated by the fact that bread as the most basic staple was not subject to the ubiquitous trade and consumption taxes. This concession to the moral economy made the system more acceptable. The commitment of early modern Spanish towns to provide cheap and plentiful bread, represented by market interventions, grain storages, and other measures, thus becomes also easier to understand.

All institutional development is subject to a tendency toward persistence. However, path dependence describes the political economy of Spain only on the very surface. The increasing center-periphery cleavage illustrates that vividly. The choices made by elites in the peripheries who traded stronger integration with the Spanish hinterland for an outward-looking commercial strategy contributed significantly to the lock-in, as did urban decision makers who fought tooth and nail for their control over tax collection. The loser everywhere was the consumer. As it turns out, the long-held assumption that consumers in the coastal areas did better in part at the expense of those in the interior is incorrect. Elites on the periphery might talk the talk of consumer protection, but, not surprisingly, they walked the walk of producer and mercantile profit.

In April 1808 French troops crossed into Spain, setting off what for Spaniards became the War of Independence, known to Anglophones as the Peninsular War. Napoleon made short shrift of a divided Spanish court, and the abdication of Carlos IV in March was followed by the deposition of his son Fernando VII less than two months later. As they had done in the War of the Spanish Succession a century before, the great powers of Europe, France and England, fought their wars in the Iberian Peninsula. Spain, which had held its own reasonably successfully throughout the eighteenth century in its external wars, once again sank into civil war as a consequence of the implosion at the center. For the French it would remain an inexplicable puzzle why Spaniards from different regions and towns would turn on one another almost as much as on the French. Local juntas sprang up in the Spanish and Spanish American towns as the population reverted to well-known forms of local organization.

Here and there, Spaniards threw themselves valiantly but foolishly in the way of the best-organized and most centralized war machine in Europe. Spanish warfare was guerilla warfare first and foremost, organized and financed at the local level. It would convince the French that Spain was ungovernable. The removal of the king and his government had created a constitutional vacuum that neither the *cortes* of Cadiz, which tried to unify the disparate multitude of political bodies, nor Napoleon's puppet king, Joseph, managed to fill. Without the ultimate arbiter, the location of power reverted to the town level. But the hastily convened *cabildos* and juntas only felt committed to the commonwealth of their urban republic. Historical contingency, a French invasion of unprecedented force, finally caught up with the multipolar governance structure of Spain. Ironically, one of the least centralized countries in Europe simply could not function without its mediator at the center, not because he had ever ruled as an absolutist king but because he had not. For three centuries, however, Spain proved that there were many ways to nation-state building in Europe.

A Note on the Sources _____

THE MAIN DATABASE containing annual prices of *bacalao* that was used throughout this volume is available via http://press.princeton.edu/titles/9625 .html. Prices were derived from unpublished and published sources listed below with a short description of each of the main series. All prices come from the account books of religious or charitable institutions.

Table A. Descriptive Statistics for Price Data

Variable	Obs	Mean Price (gr of silver)	Std. Dev.	Min	Max
year	151			1650	1800
Bilbao	132	3.098	0.903	1.71	5.91
Malaga	9	3.650	0.630	2.58	4.58
Toledo	135	5.195	1.143	3.42	10.04
Madrid	76	5.113	1.597	3.27	10.63
Seville	139	7.010	2.217	3.56	13.59
Pamplona	151	8.536	2.245	3.91	17.03
Albacete	64	3.092	1.453	1.54	8.05
Saha gún	39	3.633	0.893	1.93	5.66
Cadiz	115	2.705	1.208	1.01	7.87
Barcelona	116	3.322	1.163	1.77	11.45
North America	103	1.366	0.225	0.83	2.24
war	151	0.417	0.495	0	1

Sources

Albacete

Franciscanos menores descalzos Nuestra Señora de Llanos, AHN, Clero Libro 37 (1682–1717); 23 (1718–41); 38 (1741–65); 39 (1763–87); 40 (1785–1835).

Note: In Albacete prices were quoted in Valencian and Castilian money depending on purchasing from Valencia or Cartagena. Wherever price equivalents in Castilian *reales* were given these were used directly for the nominal prices. Where prices were quoted in Valencian libras/sueldos/dineros or Valencian pesos these were converted into Castilian *reales* using silver equivalents from Feliu, *Precios y salarios*, vol. 1, tables II.2 and II.4. Occasional references to Castilian silver reales were converted using silver premia by García del Paso, "La estabilización."

Barcelona

Feliu, *Precios y salarios*, vol. 1, 134–35.

Bilbao

Colegiata Santa Maria de Zenarruza, AFB, Eclesiastico, Colegiata Santa Maria de Zenarruza, Libro 32 (1751–1806) and Libro 33 (1806–33) and Convent Santa Isabel de Villaro from: Pedro Maria Legarreta Iragorri, "Precios en Villaro (1627–1879)." Memoria de Licenciatura, Universidad de Deusto, 1974.

Cadiz

Agustinos Calzados Nuestra Señora de Gracia, AHN, Clero Libro 1774 (1757–67); Libro 1782 (1700–1721); Libro 1784 (1721–45); Libro 1787 (1790–98); Libro 1791 (1766–76); Libro 1776 (1793–1806); Libro 1793 (1745–57). Dominicos Nuestra Señora del Rosario, AHN, Clero Libro 1821 (1776–90); Libro 1824–25 (1721–76). Franciscanos Menores Descalzos Reina de los Ángeles, AHN, Clero Libro 1836 (1630–44); Libro 1837 (1686–99); Libro 1850 (1666–78). Jesuitas, AHN, Clero Libro 2195 (1635–46); Libro 2140 (1720–66); Libro 2189 (1668–71); AHN, Clero, Jesuitas, Libro 604.

Madrid

Colegio de Santa Isabel: Archivo del Palacio, Colegio de Santa Isabel, legajos 26–49, libros de cuentas and the Santo Refugio, Colegio de Niñas, Libros de Cuentas 1680-1800. These prices were collected by Enrique Llopis and collaborators and kindly made available to me. I complemented these with additional data from the Casa profesora de San Francisco de Borja AHN, Clero, Jesuitas, Libro 268 (1644–1710).

Malaga

Morilla Critz, *Introducción Al Estudio De Las Fluctuaciones De Precios En Malaga (1787–1829)*, 240.

Pamplona

Fernández Romero, *Gastos*, table 2.

Sahagún

Benedictinos de Sahagún, AHN, Clero Libro 5334 (1701–12), Libro 5315 (1726–38), Libro 5330 (1739–53).

Sevilla

Hospital de la Sangre (o de las Cinco Llagas), del Hospital de Santa Maria and Colegio de San Isidro, Libros de Cuentas. These prices were collected by Enrique Llopis and collaborators and kindly made available to me.

Toledo

Hamilton, *War and Prices*. The cod series is one of the few that is based on prices from one town—Toledo.

Porto

Abreu-Ferreira, "The Cod Trade," 311–12 and table 10.

Newfoundland

Cell, "English in Newfoundland," table 4; Pope, *Fish into Wine*, table 2.

Essex County, Massachusetts

Vickers, "'a Knowen and Staple Commoditie,'" table 1.

Bibliography

Abed al-Hussein, F. H. "Trade and Business Community in Old Castile: Medina Del Campo, 1500–1575." Ph.D. diss., University of East Anglia, 1982.

Abreu-Ferreira, Darlene. "The Cod Trade in Early-Modern Portugal: Deregulation, English Domination and the Decline of Female Cod Merchants." Ph.D. diss., Memorial University Newfoundland, 1995.

Acemoglu, Daron, Simon Johnson, and James Robinson. "The Colonial Origins of Comparative Development: An Empirical Investigation." *American Economic Review* 91, no. 5 (2001): 1369–1401.

———. "Reversal of Fortune: Geography and Institutions in the Making of the Modern World Income Distribution." *Quarterly Journal of Economics* 117, no. 4 (2002): 1231–94.

———. "The Rise of Europe: Atlantic Trade, Institutional Change, and Economic Growth." *American Economic Review* 95, no. 3 (2005): 546–79.

Adelman, Jeremy. "An Age of Imperial Revolutions." *American Historical Review* 113, no. 2 (2008): 319–40.

Ağir, Seven M. "From Welfare to Wealth: Ottoman and Castilian Grain Trade Policies in a Time of Change." Ph.D. diss., Princeton University, 2009.

Agirreazkuenaga, Joseba. "The Abolition of the Representative Assemblies in the Basque Provinces during the Rise of the Liberal Revolution (1789–1876)." *Parliaments, States and Representation* 14, no. 2 (1994): 109–25.

Albareda i Salvadó, Joaquim. *Felipe V y el triunfo del absolutismo: Cataluña en un conflicto europeo, 1700–1714.* Barcelona: Generalitat de Catalunya Entitat Autònoma del Diari Oficial i de Publicacions, 2002.

Allen, Robert C. *The British Industrial Revolution in Global Perspective.* Cambridge: Cambridge University Press, 2009.

———. *Enclosure and the Yeoman.* Oxford: Clarendon Press, 1992.

———. "The Great Divergence in European Wages and Prices from the Middle Ages to the First World War." *Explorations in Economic History* 38, no. 4 (2001): 411–47.

Alonso, Luís "Financing the Empire: The Nature of the Tax System in the Philippines, 1565–1804." *Philippine Studies* 51, no. 1 (2003): 63–95.

Alvarez Junco, José. *Mater Dolorosa: La idea de España en el siglo XIX.* [Madrid]: Taurus, 2001.

Alvarez Nogal, Carlos, and Leandro Prados de la Escosura. "La decadenza spagnola nell'età moderna: Una revisione quantitativa." *Rivista di storia economica* 22, no. 1 (2006): 59–90.

———. "The Rise and Fall of Spain (1270–1850)." *CEPR Discussion Paper 8369,* 2011.

Alvarez Vázquez, José Antonio. *Rentas, precios y crédito en Zamora en el antiguo régimen.* Zamora: Colegio Universitario de Zamora, 1987.

Amelang, James S. *Honored Citizens of Barcelona: Patrician Culture and Class Relations, 1490–1714*. Princeton: Princeton University Press, 1986.

Anderson, Benedict R. *Imagined Communities: Reflections on the Origin and Spread of Nationalism*. Rev. ed. New York: Verso, 2006.

Anderson, Perry. *Lineages of the Absolutist State*. London: N.L.B., 1974.

Andrés Ucendo, José Ignacio. *La fiscalidad en Castilla en el siglo XVII: Los servicios de millones, 1601–1700*. Bilbao: Euskal Herriko Unibertsitatea, Argitalpen zerbitzua, 1999.

———. "Una herencia de los Austrias: Las relaciones entre la fiscalidad municipal y fiscalidad real en Castilla en los siglos XVII y XVIII." Mimeo, 2006.

Andrien, Kenneth J. "The Sale of Juros and the Politics of Reform in the Viceroyalty of Peru, 1608–1695." *Journal of Latin American Studies* 13, no. 1 (1981): 1–19.

Anes, Gonzalo. *Las crisis agrarias en la España moderna*. Madrid: Taurus, 1970.

Angulo Morales, Alberto. "Estanco y contrabando de tabaco en el País Vasco (1684–1876)." In *Tabaco y economía en el siglo XVIII*, ed. Agustín González Enciso and Rafael Torres Sánchez, 191–237. Pamplona: EUNSA, 1999.

———. *Las puertas de la vida y la muerte: La administración aduanera en las Provincias Vascas (1690–1780)*. Bilbao: Servicio Editorial Universidad del País Vasco, 1995.

Aoki, Masahiko. *Toward a Comparative Institutional Analysis*. Cambridge, MA: MIT Press, 2001.

Aparicio, José Inocencio. *Norte fixo y promptuario seguro de monedas*. Madrid: Oficina de Juan de San Martin, Imprenta de la Gaceta, Calle de Alcalá, 1741.

Arias de Saavedra Alias, Inmaculada. "Las rentas generales y los economistas de la segunda mitad del siglo XVIII." In *Estudios de hacienda: De Ensenada a Mon*, ed. Miguel Artola and L. M. Bilbao Bilbao, 17–34. Madrid: Instituto de Estudios Fiscales, 1984.

Armstrong, John. *Letters from Minorca: Describing the Constitution, Government, Produce, Antiquities, and Natural History, of That Island . . .* Dublin: Printed for W. and H. Whitestone, and R. Burton, 1782.

Arriquibar, Nicolás de, and Real Sociedad Vascongada de Amigos del País. *Recreación política: Reflexiones sobre el amigo de los hombres en su tratado de población considerado con respecto á nuestros intereses*. Vitoria: Tomas de Robles y Navarro, 1779.

Artola, Miguel. *La hacienda del antiguo régimen*. Madrid: Alianza, 1982.

———. *La monarquía de España*. Madrid: Alianza Editorial, 1999.

Ashworth, William J. *Customs and Excise: Trade, Production, and Consumption in England, 1640–1845*. New York: Oxford University Press, 2003.

———. "Manufacturing Trust: Public Credit and the Excise in Eighteenth Century Britain." Unpublished paper presented at the conference "Questioning Credible Commitment." Cambridge, 2010.

Astigarraga, Jesús. *Los ilustrados vascos: Ideas, instituciones y reformas económicas en España*. Barcelona: Crítica, 2003.

Atienza Hernández, Ignacio. *Aristocracia, poder y riqueza en la España moderna: La casa de Osuna, siglos XVI–XIX*. Madrid: Siglo XXI, 1987.

Aulnoy, and R. Foulché-Delbosc. *Travels into Spain, Being the Ingenious and Diverting Letters of the Lady*. London: G. Routledge & Sons Ltd., 1930.

Baics, Gergely. "Feeding Gotham: A Social History of Urban Provisioning, 1780–1860." Ph.D. diss., Northwestern University, 2009.

Bailyn, Bernard. *The New England Merchants in the Seventeenth Century*. Cambridge, MA: Harvard University Press, 1955.

Bairoch, Paul, Jean Batou, and Pierre Chèvre. *La population des villes européennes: Banque de données et analyse sommaire des résultats, 800–1850*. Geneva: Droz, 1988.

Baker, Emerson W. "Formerly Machegonne, Dartmouth, York, Stogummo, Casco, and Falmouth: Portland as a Contested Frontier in the Seventeenth Century." In *Creating Portland: History and Place in Northern New England*, ed. Joseph A. Conforti, 1–20. Lebanon: University of New Hampshire Press, 2005.

Balfour, Sebastian, and Alejandro Quiroga. *España reinventada: Nación e identidad desde la transición*. Trans. Ana Escartin. Barcelona: Ediciones Peninsula, 2007.

Barkham, Michael. "French Basque 'New Found Land' Entrepreneurs and the Imports of Codfish and Whale Oil to Northern Spain, c. 1580–1620: The Case of Adam De Chibau, Burgess of Saint-Jean-De-Luz and 'Sieur De St. Julien.'" *Newfoundland Studies* (1994): 1–44.

Barquín Gil, Rafael. "Las elasticidades de la demanda y renta del Trigo: Siglos XIV–XVIII." Mimeo.

———. "The Elasticity of Demand for Wheat in the XIV–XVIII Centuries." *Revista de Historia Económica* 23, no. 1 (2005): 241–67.

———. *Precios del trigo e índices de consumo en España, 1765–1883*. N.d.

———. "Transporte y precio de trigo en el siglo XIX: Creación y reordenación de un mercado nacional." *Revista de Historia Económica* 15, no. 1 (1997): 17–48.

Barrio Gozalo, Maximiliano. "El clero regular en la España del siglo XVIII a través de la 'Encuesta de 1764.'" *Hispania Sacra* 47 (1995): 121–69.

Basurto Larrañaga, Román. *Comercio y burguesía mercantil de Bilbao en la segunda mitad del siglo XVIII*. Bilbao: Universidad del Pais Vasco, 1983.

Bauzon, Leslie E. *Deficit Government: Mexico and the Philippine Situado, 1606–1804*. Tokyo: Centre for East Asian Cultural Studies, 1981.

Bean, R. "War and the Birth of the Nation State." *Journal of Economic History* 33, no. 1 (1973): 203–21.

Beik, William. "The Absolutism of Louis XIV as Social Collaboration." *Past and Present* 188, no. 1 (2005): 195–224.

Bernal, Antonio Miguel. *España, proyecto inacabado: Los costes/beneficios del imperio*. Madrid: Marcial Pons Historia, 2005.

———. *La financiación de la carrera de Indias (1492–1824)*. Seville: Fundación el Monte, 1992.

Bernal Rodríguez, Antonio-Miguel, and Antonio García-Barquero, eds. *Tres siglos del comercio sevillano (1598–1868): Cuestiones y problemas*. Seville: Cámara Oficial de Comercio, Industria y Navegación, 1976.

Bernardos Sanz, José Ubaldo. "El abastecimiento y consumo de pescado en Madrid durante el antiguo régimen." Paper presented at the VII Congreso de la Asociación de Historia Económica, Zaragoza, 2001.

Beveridge, William. *Prices and Wages in England from the Twelfth to the Nineteenth Century*. Vol. 1. London: Longmans, Green, 1939.

Bilbao, Luis María. "La fiscalidad en las provincias exentas de Vizcaya y Guipúzcoa durante el siglo XVIII." In *Estudios de hacienda: De Ensenada a Mon*, ed. Miguel Artola and Luis María Bilbao Bilbao, 67–83. Madrid: Instituto de Estudios Fiscales, 1984.

Bloch, Marc Léopold Benjamin. *The Royal Touch: Sacred Monarchy and Scrofula in England and France*. London: Routledge and Kegan Paul, 1973.

Bogart, Dan. "Turnpike Trusts and Property Income: New Evidence on the Effects of Transport Improvements and Legislation in Eighteenth-Century England." *Economic History Review* 62, no. 1 (2009): 128–52.

Bonney, Richard. *Economic Systems and State Finance: The Origins of the Modern State in Europe*. New York: Oxford University Press, 1995.

———. *The Rise of the Fiscal State in Europe, c. 1200–1815*. New York: Oxford University Press, 1999.

Boserup, Ester. *The Conditions of Agricultural Growth: The Economics of Agrarian Change under Population Pressure*. London: George Allen and Unwin, 1965.

Botero, Giovanni. *Le relationi universali di Giovanni Botero Benese, divise in quattro parti . . . Con le figure in rame, & due copiosissime tavole*. Venetia: Appresso Giorgio Angelieri, 1596.

Braddick, Michael J. *The Nerves of the State: Taxation and the Financing of the English State, 1558–1714*. Manchester: Manchester University Press, 1996.

———. *State Formation in Early Modern England, c. 1550–1700*. Cambridge: Cambridge University Press, 2000.

Braudel, Fernand. *The Mediterranean and the Mediterranean World in the Age of Philip II*. London: Collins, 1972.

Brautaset, Camilla. "Norsk Eksport, 1830–1865: I Perspectiv av historiske Nasjonalregnskaper." Ph.D. diss., Norges Handelshoyskole, 2002.

Brautaset, Camilla, and Regina Grafe. "The Quiet Transport Revolution: Returns to Scale, Scope and Network Density in Norway's 19th Century Sailing Fleet." University of Oxford, Discussion Papers in Economic and Social History 62, 2006.

Brenner, Robert. "The Social Basis of Economic Development." *Journal of Economic History* 32, no. 1 (1972): 361–84.

Brewer, J. *The Sinews of Power: War, Money and the English State, 1688–1783*. London: Unwin Hyman, 1989.

Bringas Gutiérrez, Miguel Ángel. *La productividad de los factores en la agricultura española (1752–1935)*. Madrid: Banco de España Servicio de Estudios, 2000.

Broadberry, Stephen, and Bishnupriya Gupta. "Monetary and Real Aspects of the Great Divergence between Europe and Asia, 1500–1800." Paper presented at GEHN Workshop on Imperialism, Istanbul, 2005.

Brunel, Antoine de, and François van Aerssen. *A Journey into Spain*. London: Printed for Henry Herringman, 1670.

Burguera, Monica, and Christopher Schmidt-Nowara. "Backwardness and Its Discontents." *Social History* 29, no. 4 (2004): 279–83.

Burkholder, Mark A., and D. S. Chandler. *From Impotence to Authority: The Spanish Crown and the American Audiencias, 1687–1808*. Columbia: University of Missouri Press, 1977.

Bustos Rodriguez, Manuel. "La hacienda municipal gaditana en el reinado de Carlos III." *Gades* 9 (1982): 19–57.

Caballero y Estevan, Toribio Tomás. *Las aduanas españolas; Ensayo histórico sobre el orígen y vicisitudes por que ha atravesado la renta de aduanas en España, desde los tiempos más remotos hasta nuestros días por D.T.T. Caballero*. Madrid: Impr. de Antonio Pérez Dubrull, 1882.

Calderón Cuadrado, Reyes. *Empresarios españoles en el proceso de independencia norteamericana: La casa Gardoqui e Hijos de Bilbao*. Madrid: Unión Editorial, 2004.

Canal i Morell, Jordi. *El Carlismo: Dos siglos de contrarrevolución en España*. Madrid: Alianza Editorial, 2000.

Cañeque, A. *The King's Living Image: The Culture and Politics of Viceregal Power in Colonial Mexico*. New York: Routledge, 2004.

Capella Martínez, Miguel, and Antonio Matilla Tascon. *Los Cinco Gremios Mayores de Madrid: Estudio crítico-histórico*. Madrid: Cámara Oficial de Comercio e Industria, 1957.

Casado Soto, José Luís. "Notas sobre la implantación del maíz en Cantabria y la sustitución de otros cultivos." In *Población y sociedad en la España cantábrica durante el siglo XVII*, 159–73. Santander: Institución Cultural de Cantabria, 1985.

Casey, James. *The Kingdom of Valencia in the Seventeenth Century*. Cambridge: Cambridge University Press, 1979.

Cell, Gillian T. "The English in Newfoundland, 1577–1660." Ph.D. diss., University of Liverpool, 1964.

Cervantes Saavedra, Miguel de. *El ingenioso hidalgo Don Qvixote de La Mancha*. Madrid: Por Iuan de la Cuesta vendese en casa de Francisco de Robles librero, 1605.

Chaney, Eric. "Ethnic Cleansing and Long-Term Persistence of Extractive Institutions: Evidence from the Expulsion of the Moriscos." Mimeo, 2008.

Chaunu, Huguette, Pierre Chaunu, and Guy Arbellot. *Séville et l'Atlantique, 1504–1650*. Paris: A. Colin, 1955.

Chiaramonte, José Carlos. "The 'Ancient Constitution' after Independence (1808–1852)." *Hispanic American Historical Review* 90, no. 3 (2010): 455–88.

Chust Calero, Manuel. *1808, La eclosión juntera en el mundo hispano*. Mexico D.F.: Fondo de Cultura Económica, 2007.

Clarence-Smith, William Gervase. *Cocoa and Chocolate, 1765–1914*. New York: Routledge, 2000.

Clark, Gregory. "The Condition of the Working Class in England, 1209–2004." *Journal of Political Economy* 113, no. 6 (2005): 1307–40.

———. "The Political Foundations of Modern Economic Growth: England, 1540–1800." *Journal of Interdisciplinary History* 26, no. 4 (1996): 563–88.

Clarke, Edward. *Letters Concerning the Spanish Nation Written at Madrid during the Years 1760 and 1761. By the Rev. Edward Clarke*. London: Printed for T. Becket and P. A. de Hondt, 1763.

Claverie, Charles. "Voyage D'Antoine de Brunel en Espagne (1655)." *Revue Hispanique* 30 (1914): 119–514.

Clavero, Bartolomé. *Razón de estado, razón de individuo, razón de historia.* Madrid: Centro de Estudios Constitucionales, 1991.

Coase, Ronald H. "The Nature of the Firm." *Economica* 4 (1937): 386–405.

Comín Comín, Francisco, and Bartolomé Yun Casalilla. "Spain: From a Composite Monarchy to a Nation State, 1492–1914. An Exceptional Case?" In *A Global History of the Formation and Efficiency of Fiscal States in Eurasia,* ed. Bartolomé Yun Casalilla and Patrick K. O'Brien, forthcoming.

Comín, Francisco, Mauro Hernández, and Enrique Llopis Agelán. *Historia económica de España: Siglos X–XX.* Barcelona: Crítica, 2002.

Coronas Tejada, Luis. "El abastecimiento de pescado en el Jaen del siglo XVII." *Chronica Nova* 17 (1989): 33–45.

Cremades Griñán, Carmen María. *Borbones, hacienda y súbditos en el siglo XVIII.* Murcia: Universidad de Murcia, Secretariado de Publicaciones, 1993.

Crouzet, François. *La guerre économique Franco-Anglaise au XVIIIe siècle.* Paris: Fayard, 2008.

Cruz, Jesus. *Gentlemen, Bourgeois, and Revolutionaries: Political Change and Cultural Persistence among the Spanish Dominant Groups, 1750–1850.* New York: Cambridge University Press, 1996.

Cubillo de la Puente, Roberto. "Carne y pescado: Su importancia en la alimentación de una ciudad del interior español. León—siglo XVIII." Paper presented at the VII Congreso de la Asociación de Historia Económica, Zaragoza, 2001.

———. *Comer en León: Un siglo de historia, 1700–1800.* Leon: Universidad de León, Secretariado de Publicaciones, 2000.

———. *El pescado en la alimentación de Castilla y León durante los siglos XVIII y XIX, León,* Leon: Universidad de León, Secretariado de Publicaciones, 1998.

Daudin, Guillaume. *Commerce et prospérité: La France au XVIIIe siècle.* Paris: Presses Universitaires de Paris-Sorbonne, 2005.

Daunton, Martin J. *Progress and Poverty: An Economic and Social History of Britain, 1700–1850.* New York: Oxford University Press, 1995.

De Bow, J.D.B. *Encyclopaedia of the Trade and Commerce of the United States: More Particularly of the Southern and Western States: Giving a View of the Commerce, Agriculture, Manufactures, Internal Improvements, Slave and Free Labour, Slavery Institutions, Products, Etc., of the South.* 2nd ed. London: Trübner & Co., 1854.

de Castro, Concepción. *Campomanes: Estado y reformismo ilustrado.* Madrid: Alianza Editorial, 1996.

———. *El pan de Madrid: El abasto de las ciudades españolas del antiguo régimen.* Madrid: Alianza Editorial, 1987.

de Jesus, E. C. *The Tobacco Monopoly in the Philippines: Bureaucratic Enterprise and Social Change, 1766–1880.* Quezon City: Ateneo de Manila University Press, 1980.

de la Sagra, Ramon. *Historia económica, política y estadística de la Isla de Cuba o sea de sus progresos en la población, la agricultura, el comercio y las rentas.* Habana: Imprenta de las Viudas de Arazoza y Soler, impresoras del gobierno y capitanía general, de la Real Hacienda y de la Real Sociedad Patriótica por S.M., 1831.

De Long, Brad, and Andrei Shleifer. "Princes or Merchants: European City Growth before the Industrial Revolution." *Journal of Law and Economics* 36, no. 2 (1993): 671–702.

de Vries, Jan. *European Urbanization, 1500–1800*. Cambridge: Cambridge University Press, 1984.

———. "The Industrial Revolution and the Industrious Revolution." *Journal of Economic History* 54, no. 2 (1994): 249–70.

———. *The Industrious Revolution: Consumer Behavior and the Household Economy, 1650 to the Present*. Cambridge: Cambridge University Press, 2008.

Deans Smith, Susan. "The Money Plant: The Royal Tobacco Monopoly of New Spain, 1765–1821." In *The Economies of Mexico and Peru during the Late Colonial Period, 1760–1810*, ed. N. Jacobsen and H. J. Puhle. Berlin: Colloquium Verlag, 1986.

Dehouve, Daniel. "Introducción a la parte histórica." In *Prestar y pedir prestado: Relaciones sociales y crédito en México del siglo XVI al XX*, ed. M. N. Chamoux, D. Dehouve, C. Guouy Gilbert, and M. Pepin Lehalleur, 19–24. Mexico D.F.: CIESAS, 1993.

Delgado i Ribas, Josep María. "América y el comercio de Indias en la historiografía catalana (1872–1978)." *Boletín Americanista* 28 (1978): 179–87.

Diamond, Jared. *Guns, Germs and Steel*. New York: W. W. Norton, 1997.

Díaz-Plaja, Fernando. *Historia de España en sus documentos: Siglo XVIII*. Madrid: Cátedra, 1986.

Díez Sánchez, Marta. *La hacienda municipal de Alicante en la segunda mitad del XVII: Una aproximación a la organización y gestión económica de los municipios forales*. Alicante: Instituto de Cultura "Juan Gil-Albert," 1999.

Dincecco, Mark. "Fiscal Centralization, Limited Government, and Public Revenues in Europe, 1650–1913." *Journal of Economic History* 69 (2009): 48–103.

Dobado González, Rafael. "Un legado peculiar: La geografía." In *El legado económico del antiguo régimen en España*, ed. Enrique Llopis, 97–119. Barcelona: Crítica, 2004.

Domenech, Jordi. "Working Hours in the European Periphery: The Length of the Working Day in Spain, 1885–1920." *Explorations in Economic History* 44, no. 3 (2007): 469–86.

Domínguez Martín, Rafael. *La riqueza de las regiones: Las desigualdades económica regionales en España, 1700–2000*. Madrid: Alianza Editorial, 2002.

Domínguez Ortiz, Antonio. *Carlos III y la España de la ilustración*. Madrid: Alianza Editorial, 1988.

———. *Orto y ocaso de Sevilla*. 3rd ed. Seville: Universidad, 1981.

Doyle, William. *Venality: The Sale of Offices in Eighteenth-Century France*. New York: Clarendon Press, 1996.

Drelichman, Mauricio. "The Curse of Moctezuma: American Silver and the Dutch Disease." *Explorations in Economic History* 42, no. 3 (2005): 349–80.

———. "Licence to Till: The Privileges of the Spanish Mesta as a Case of Second Best Institutions." *Explorations in Economic History* 46, no. 2 (2009): 220–40.

Drelichman, Mauricio, and Voth, Hans-Joachim. "Lending to the 'Borrower from Hell': Debt and Default in the Age of Philipp II." *Economic Journal* (forthcoming).

————. "Serial Defaults, Serial Profits: Returns to Sovereign Lending in Habsburg Spain, 1566–1600." *Explorations in Economic History*, 48, no. 1 (2011): 1–19.

————. "The Sustainable Debts of Philip II: A Reconstruction of Castile's Fiscal Position, 1566–1596." *Journal of Economic History* 70, no. 4 (2010): 813–42.

Dubet, Anne. *Hacienda, arbitrismo y negociación política: El proyecto de los erarios públicos y montes de piedad en los siglos XVI y XVII*. Valladolid: Secretariado de Publicaciones e Intercambio Editorial, Universidad de Valladolid, 2003.

Dym, Jordana. "Soberanía transitiva y adhesión condicional: Lealtad e insurrección en el reino de Guatemala, 1808–1811." In *1808: La eclosión juntera en el mundo hispano*, ed. Manuel Chust, 105–37. Mexico D.F.: Fondo de Cultura Económica/ Colegio de México, 2007.

Easterly, William, and W. Levine. "Tropics, Germs, and Crops: How Endowments Influence Economic Development." *Journal of Monetary Economics* 50, no. 1 (2003): 3–40.

Ehrenberg, Richard. *Das Zeitalter der Fugger: Geldkapital und Creditverkehr im 16. Jahrhundert*. Jena: G. Fischer, 1896.

Eiras Roel, Antonio, and Juan E. Gelabert. "Contabilidades hospitalarias como fuentes de los transportes internos: Costes de transporte del Real Hospital de Santiago." In *Actas de las I Jornadas de Metodologia Aplicada de las Ciencias Históricas*, 859–61. Santiago: Universidade de Santiago de Compostela, Servicio de Publicaciones, 1975.

Elias, Norbert. *Die höfische Gesellschaft; Untersuchungen zur Soziologie des Königtums und der höfischen Aristokratie*. Neuwied: Luchterhand, 1969.

Elliott, John H. *The Count-Duke of Olivares*. New Haven: Yale University Press, 1986.

————. "The Decline of Spain." *Past and Present* 20, no. 1 (1961): 52–75.

————. "Empire and State in British and Spanish America." In *Le Nouveau Monde, Mondes Nouveaux: L'expérience Américaine*, ed. Serge Gruzinski and Nathan Wachtel. Paris: Éd. recherche sur les civilisations: Éd. de l'école des hautes études en sciences sociales, 1996.

————. "A Europe of Composite Monarchies." *Past and Present* 137 (1992): 48–71.

————. *Imperial Spain*. Reprint. Harmondsworth: Penguin, 1963.

————. *The Revolt of the Catalans: A Study in the Decline of Spain, 1598–1640*. Cambridge: Cambridge University Press, 1963.

Elliott, John H., and José F. de la Peña, eds. *Memoriales y cartas del conde duque de Olivares*. Madrid: Alfaguara, 1978.

Engel, Charles, and John H. Rogers. "How Wide Is the Border?" *American Economic Review* 86, no. 5 (1996): 1112–25.

Engerman, Stanley L., and Kenneth L. Sokoloff. "Colonialism, Inequality, and Long-Run Path of Development." NBER working paper 11057, 2005.

Epstein, Stephan R. "Cities, Regions and the Late Medieval Crisis: Sicily and Tuscany Compared." *Past and Present* 130 (1991): 3–50.

————. "Craft Guilds, Apprenticeship, and Technological Change in Preindustrial Europe." *Journal of Economic History* 58, no. 3 (1998): 684–715.

———. *Freedom and Growth: The Rise of States and Markets in Europe, 1300–1750*. London: Routledge, 2000.

———. "The Rise of the West." In *An Anatomy of Power: The Social Theory of Michael Mann*, ed. John A. Hall and Ralph Schroeder, 233–62. Cambridge: Cambridge University Press, 2006.

Ertman, Thomas. *Birth of the Leviathan: Building States and Regimes in Medieval and Early Modern Europe*. Cambridge: Cambridge University Press, 1997.

Escobar, Jesús Roberto. *The Plaza Mayor and the Shaping of Baroque Madrid*. Cambridge: Cambridge University Press, 2004.

Escobedo Romero, Rafael. *El tabaco del rey: La organización de un monopolio fiscal durante el antiguo régimen*. Baránáin (Pamplona): Ediciones Universidad de Navarra, 2007.

Esdaile, Charles J. *Fighting Napoleon: Guerrillas, Bandits and Adventurers in Spain, 1808–1814*. New Haven: Yale University Press, 2004.

———. *The Peninsular War: A New History*. New York: Palgrave MacMillan, 2003.

España dividida en provincias e intendencia—Nomenclator. Madrid, 1789.

Fagan, Brian M. *Fish on Friday: Feasting, Fasting, and the Discovery of the New World*. New York: Basic Books, 2006.

Feliu, Gaspar. "L'equivalent metàlic d'algunes monedes de compte a l'etat moderna." *Acta numismática* 21–23 (1993): 455–74.

———. *Precios y salarios en la Cataluña moderna*. Vol. 2, *Combustibles, productos manufacturados y salarios*. Madrid: Banco de España, 1991.

Fernández Albaladejo, Pablo. "Algunos textos sobre la polémica entre libre comercio y fueros, hacia 1780." *Boletín de la Real Sociedad Vascongada de Amigos del País* 52 (1976): 229–69.

———. "Cities and State in Spain." In *Cities and the Rise of States in Europe, A.D. 1000 to 1800*, ed. Charles Tilly and Wim P. Blockmans, 168–83. Boulder, CO: Westview Press, 1994.

———. *La crisis del antiguo régimen en Guipúzcoa, 1766–1833: Cambio económico e historia*. Madrid: Akal, 1975.

———. "Monarquía, cortes y 'cuestión constitucional' en Castilla durante la edad moderna." *Revista de las Cortes Generales* 1 (1984): 11–34.

Fernández de Pinedo, Emiliano. *Crecimiento económico y transformaciones sociales en el País Vasco (1100–1850)*. Madrid: Siglo XXI, 1974.

———. "La deuda pública y los juristas laicos (1550–1650)." In *Dinero, moneda y crédito en la monarquía hispánica: Actas del simposio internacional, Madrid 1999*, ed. Antonio-Miguel Bernal Rodriguez, 807–24. Madrid: Marcial Pons, 2000.

———. Fernández de Pinedo, Emiliano. "From the Bloomery to the Blast-Furnace: Technical Change in Spanish Iron-Making (1650–1822)." *Journal of European Economic History* 17, no. 1 (1988): 7–31.

———. "Ingresos de la hacienda catalana en el siglo XVII." In *Haciendas forales y hacienda real: Homenage a D. Miguel Artola y D. Felipe Ruiz Martín*, ed. Emiliano Fernández de Pinedo, 207–24. Bilbao: Servicio Editorial de la Universidad del País Vasco, 1987.

———. "Los ingresos de la hacienda real en Cataluña (1717–1779)." In *Estudios de hacienda: De Ensenada a Mons*, ed. Miguel Artola and Luis María Bilbao, 193–215. Madrid: Instituto de Estudios Fiscales, 1984.

Fernández García, Antonio. *El abastecimiento de Madrid en el reinado de Isabel II*. Madrid: CSIC, 1971.

Fernández Romero, Cayetano. *Gastos, ingresos y ahorro familiar: Navarra, 1561–1820*. Pamplona: Ediciones Universidad de Navarra, 2005.

Figueras Pacheco, Francisco. *El consulado marítimo y terrestre de Alicante y pueblos del obispado de Orihuela*. Alicante: Diputación Provincial de Alicante, 1957.

Fisher, J. "Imperial 'Free Trade' and the Hispanic Economy, 1778–1796." *Journal of Latin American Studies* 13, no. 1 (1981): 21–55.

Fogel, Robert W. "Second Thoughts on the European Escape from Hunger: Famines, Chronic Malnutrition, and Mortality Rates." In *Nutrition and Poverty*, ed. S. R. Osmani, 243–86. Oxford: Clarendon Press, 1991.

Forcione, Alban K. *Majesty and Humanity: Kings and Their Doubles in the Political Drama of the Spanish Golden Age*. New Haven: Yale University Press, 2009.

Fradera, Josep Maria. *Filipinas, la colonia más peculiar: La hacienda pública en la definición de la política colonial, 1762–1868*. Madrid: Consejo Superior de Investigaciones Científicas, 1999.

Fraser, Ronald. *Napoleon's Cursed War: Spanish Popular Resistance in the Peninsular War, 1808–1814*. New York: Verso, 2008.

Fritschy, Wantje. "The Efficiency of Taxation in Holland." In *The Political Economy of the Dutch Republic*, ed. Oscar Gelderblom, 55–84. Farnham: Ashgate, 2009.

———. "Was There a West European Trajectory of State Formation? A Comparison with the Ottoman Empire from a Dutch Perspective." Unpublished paper presented at the AHA Annual Conference, New York, 2009.

Fuchs, Barbara. *Exotic Nation: Maurophilia and the Construction of Early Modern Spain*. Philadelphia: University of Pennsylvania Press, 2009.

Gárate Ojanguren, Montserrat. *Comercio ultramarino e ilustración: La real compañía de La Habana*. Donostia (San Sebastian): Real Sociedad Bascongada de los Amigos del País, 1994.

———. *La real compañía guipuzcoana de Caracas*. San Sebastian: Sociedad Guipuzcoana de Ediciones y Publicaciones, 1990.

Gárate Ojanguren, Montserrat, and Juan Luis Blanco Mozos. "Financiación de las compañias priviligiadas de comercio en la España del siglo XVIII." In *Capitalismo mercantil en la España del siglo XVIII*, ed. Rafael Torres Sánchez, 173–200. Pamplona: EUNSA, 2000.

García-Baquero, Antonio. *Cádiz y el Atlántico (1717–1778)*. Seville: Escuela de Estudios Hispanoamericanos, 1976.

García-Baquero González, Antonio. *El comercio colonial en la época del absolutismo ilustrado: Problemas y debates*. Granada: Universidad de Granada, 2003.

García de Paso, José I. "La estabilización monetaria en Castilla bajo Carlos II." *Revista de Historia Económica* 18, no. 1 (2000): 49–77.

García Espuche, Albert. *Un siglo decisivo: Barcelona y Cataluña, 1550–1640.* Madrid: Alianza Editorial, 1998.

García García, Carmen. *La crisis de las haciendas locales: De la reforma administrativa a la reforma fiscal (1743–1845).* Valladolid: Junta de Castilla y León, 1996.

García Sanz, Angel. "Competitivos en lanas, pero no en paños: Lana para la exportación y lana para los telares nacionales en la España del antiguo régimen." *Revista de Historia Económica* 12, no. 2 (1994): 397–434.

García Zúñiga, Mario. *Hacienda, población y precios (siglos XVI–XVIII): Estadísticas históricas de Navarra.* Pamplona: Departamento de Educación y Cultura, 1996.

García Zúñiga, Mario, Isabel Mugartegui Eguía, and Joseba de la Torre. "Evolución de la carga tributaria en la España del setecientos." In *Homenaje a Don Felipe Ruíz Martín.* Madrid: Instituto de Estudios Fiscales, 1991.

Garzón Pareja, Manuel. *La hacienda de Carlos II.* Madrid: Instituto de Estudios Fiscales, 1980.

Gelabert, Juan E. *La bolsa del rey: Rey, reino y fisco en Castilla (1598–1648).* Barcelona: Crítica, 1997.

Gelderblom, Oscar. "Violence and Growth: The Protection of Long-Distance Trade in the Low Countries, 1250–1650." Working paper, 2005. http://partner.library. uu.nl/vkc/seh/research/Lists/Working%20Papers/Attachments/17/Gelderblom_ ViolenceGrowth_2005.pdf.

Gelderblom, Oscar, and Regina Grafe. "The Rise, Persistence and Decline of Merchant Guilds: Re-Thinking the Comparative Study of Commercial Institutions in Pre-Modern Europe." *Journal of Interdisciplinary History* 40, no. 4 (2010): 477–511.

Gelderblom, Oscar, and Joost Jonker. "One System, Seventeen Outcomes? The Pattern of Public Finance in the Dutch Republic and the Southern Netherlands, 1550–1795." Unpublished paper presented at the conference "Questioning Credible Commitment," Cambridge, 2010.

Gellner, Ernest. *Nationalism.* London: Weidenfeld and Nicolson, 1997.

———. *Nations and Nationalism.* Oxford: Blackwell, 1983.

Giesey, Ralph. *If Not, Not: The Oath of the Aragonese and the Legendary Laws of Sobrabe.* Princeton: Princeton University Press, 1968.

Gil, Xavier. "Republican Politics in Early Modern Spain: The Castilian and Catalano-Aragonese Traditions." In *Republicanism: A Shared European Heritage*, ed. Martin van Gelderen and Quentin Skinner, 263–88. Cambridge: Cambridge University Press, 2002.

Glete, Jan. *War and the State in Early Modern Europe: Spain, the Dutch Republic and Sweden as Fiscal-Military States, 1500–1660.* New York: Routledge, 2002.

Goldstone, J. "Urbanization and Inflation: Lessons from the English Price Revolution of the Sixteenth and Seventeenth Centuries." *American Journal of Sociology* 89, no. 5 (1984): 1122–60.

González de Lara, Yadira, Avner Greif, and Saumithra Jha. "The Administrative Foundations of Self-Enforcing Constitutions." *American Economic Review: Papers and Proceedings* 98, no. 2 (2008): 105–9.

González Enciso, Agustín. "A Moderate and Rational Absolutism: Spanish Fiscal Policy in the First Half of the Eighteenth Century." In *War, State and Development. Fiscal-Military States in the Eighteenth Century*, ed. Rafael Torres Sánchez, 109–32. Pamplona: EUNSA, 2007.

———. *El negocio de la lana en España (1650–1830)*. Pamplona: EUNSA, 2001.

González Fernández, Doria C. "Tabaco y poder: La primera factoría de La Habana." In *Tabaco y economía en el siglo XVIII*, ed. Agustín González Enciso and Rafael Torres Sánchez, 107–22. Pamplona: EUNSA, 1999.

Gorosábel, Pablo de, and Carmelo de Echegaray. *Noticia de las cosas memorables de Guipúzcoa: Descripción de la provincia y de sus habitantes, exposición de las instituciones, fueros, privilegios, ordenanzas y leyes, reseña del gobierno civil, eclesiástico y militar, idea de la administración de justicia, etc.* Tolosa: I. López, 1899.

Grafe, Regina. "Atlantic Trade and Regional Specialisation in Northern Spain, 1550–1650: An Integrated Trade Theory—Institutional Organisation Approach." Working paper, Serie de Historia Económica e Instituciones, Universidad Carlos III de Madrid 01-65(02), 2001.

———. *Entre el mundo ibérico y el Atlántico: Comercio y especialización regional, 1550–1650*. Bilbao: Bizkaiko Foru Aldundia, 2005.

———. "The Globalisation of Codfish and Wool: Spanish-English-North American Triangular Trade in the Early Modern Period." *London School of Economics Working Papers in Economic History* 71, no. 3 (2003).

———. "Guilds, Innovation, and the European Economy, 1400–1800. Edited by S. R. Epstein and Maarten Prak (New York, Cambridge University Press, 2008)." *Journal of Interdisciplinary History* 40, no. 1 (2009): 78–82.

———. "Mercantilism and Representation in a Composite State: The Early Modern Spanish Monarchy." In *Rethinking Mercantilism: New Perspectives on Early Modern Economic Though*, ed. Philip Stern and Carl Wennerlind, forthcoming.

———. "Popish Habits vs. Nutritional Needs: Fasting and Fish Consumption in Iberia in the Early Modern Period." Oxford Discussion Papers in Economic and Social History 55, 2004.

———. *Der spanische Seehandel mit Nordwesteuropa von der Mitte des sechzehnten bis zur Mitte des siebzehnten Jahrhunderts. Ein Forschungsüberblick*. Saarbrücken: VfE, 1998.

———. "The S. R. Epstein Memorial Lecture 2008: Stuck in the Past or Looking Towards the Future? The Deep Historical Roots of Spanish Economic Regionalism." London School of Economics and Political Science, March 2008. http://lse.ac.uk/collections/economicHistory/Epstein%20Memorial%20Conference/GRAFE.pdf.

———. "The Strange Tale of the Decline of Spanish Shipping." In *Shipping and Economic Growth, 1350–1800*, ed. Richard Unger, 81–116. Leiden: Brill, 2011.

Grafe, Regina, and Maria Alejandra Irigoin. "The Spanish Empire and Its Legacy: Fiscal Re-Distribution and Political Conflict in Colonial and Post-Colonial Spanish America." *Journal of Global History* 1, no. 2 (2006): 241–67.

————. "A Stakeholder Empire: The Political Economy of Spanish Imperial Rule in America." *Economic History Review* (forthcoming).

Grafe, Regina, Larry Neal, and Richard W. Unger. "The Service Sector, 1700–1870." In *The Cambridge Economic History of Modern Europe*, ed. Stephen Broadberry and Kevin H. O'Rourke, 187–214. Cambridge: Cambridge University Press, 2010.

Grantham, G. W. "Divisions of Labour: Agricultural Productivity and Occupational Specialization in Pre-Industrial France." *Economic History Review* 46, no. 3 (1993): 478–502.

Greenfeld, Liah. *Nationalism: Five Roads to Modernity.* Cambridge, MA: Harvard University Press, 1992.

Greif, Avner. "Commitment, Coercion, and Markets: The Nature and Dynamics of Institutions Supporting Exchange." In *Handbook of New Institutional Economics*, ed. C. Ménard and M. M. Shirley, 727–86. Springer, 2005.

————. "The Fundamental Problem of Exchange: A Research Agenda in Historical Institutional Analysis." *European Review of Economic History* 4 (2000): 251–84.

————. *Institutions and the Path to the Modern Economy: Lessons from Medieval Trade.* Cambridge: Cambridge University Press, 2006.

Grice-Hutchinson, Marjorie. *Early Economic Thought in Spain, 1177–1740.* London: George Allen and Unwin, 1978.

Grossman, Herschel I. "The Creation of Effective Property Rights." *American Economic Review* 91, no. 2 (2001): 347–52.

Guerra Garrido, Raúl. *Castilla en canal.* Madrid: Alianza, 2005.

Guiard Larrauri, Teofilo. *Historia del consulado de Bilbao y casa de contratación de Bilbao y del comercio de la villa (1511–1699).* Vol. 1. Bilbao: Jose de Astuy, 1913.

Gutiérez Alonso, Adriano. *Estudio sobre la decadencia de Castilla: La ciudad de Valladolid en el siglo XVII.* Valladolid: Universidad de Valladolid, 1989.

Gutiérrez Muñoz, Maria Catalina. *Comercio y banca: Expansión y crisis del capitalismo comercial en Bilbao al final del antiguo régimen.* Bilbao: Servicio Editorial Universidad del País Vasco, 1995.

Halperin Donghi, Tulio. "Backward Looks and Forward Glimpses from a Quincentennial Vantage Point." *Journal of Latin American Studies* (Supplement 1992): 219–34.

Hamilton, Earl J. *American Treasure and the Price Revolution in Spain, 1501–1650.* Cambridge, MA: Harvard University Press, 1934.

————. "Monetary Disorder and Economic Decadence in Spain, 1651–1700." *Journal of Political Economy* 51, no. 6 (1943): 477–93.

————. "The Role of Monopoly in the Overseas Expansion and Colonial Trade of Europe before 1800." *American Economic Review* 38, no. 2 (1948): 33–53.

————. "Spanish Mercantilism before 1700." In *Facts and Factors in Economic History: Articles by Former Students of Edwin Francis Gay*, 214–39. Cambridge, MA: Harvard University Press, 1932.

————. *War and Prices in Spain, 1651–1800.* Cambridge, MA: Harvard University Press, 1947.

Hanney, David. "The Mesta." *Edinburgh Review or Critical Journal* 236 (July–October 1922): 316–32.

Harley, C. Knick. "Ocean Freight Rates and Productivity, 1740–1913: The Primacy of Mechanical Invention Reaffirmed." *Journal of Economic History* 48, no. 4 (1988): 851–76.

Hauser, Henri. *Recherches et documents sur l'histoire des prix en France de 1500 à 1800*. Paris: Les Presses modernes, 1936.

Henshall, Nicolas. *The Myth of Absolutism: Change and Continuity in Early Modern European Monarchy*. London: Longman, 1992.

Hernández, Mauro. *A la sombra de la corona: Poder local y oligarquía urbana, Madrid, 1606–1808*. Historia. Madrid: Siglo Veintiuno Editores, 1995.

Herr, Richard. *The Eighteenth-Century Revolution in Spain*. Princeton: Princeton University Press, 1958.

———. *Rural Change and Royal Finances in Spain at the End of the Old Regime*. Berkeley: University of California Press, 1989.

Herranz-Loncan, Alfonso. "Infrastructure Investment and Spanish Economic Growth, 1850–1935." *Explorations in Economic History* 44, no. 3 (2007): 452–68.

Herzog, Tamar. *Defining Nations: Immigrants and Citizens in Early Modern Spain and Spanish America*. New Haven: Yale University Press, 2003.

Hirschman, Albert O. *Exit, Voice, and Loyalty: Responses to Decline in Firms, Organizations, and States*. Cambridge, MA: Harvard University Press, 1970.

Hobsbawm, Eric J. *Nations and Nationalism since 1780: Programme, Myth, Reality*. 2nd ed. New York: Cambridge University Press, 1992.

Hoffman, Philip T. "Early Modern France, 1450–1700." In *Fiscal Crises, Liberty, and Representative Government, 1450–1789*, ed. Philip T. Hoffman and Kathryn Norberg, 226–52. Stanford: Stanford University Press, 1994.

———. *Growth in a Traditional Society: The French Countryside, 1450–1815*. Princeton: Princeton University Press, 1996.

Hoffman, Philip, and Kathryn Norberg. *Fiscal Crises, Liberty, and Representative Government, 1450–1789*. Stanford: Stanford University Press, 1994.

Hoffman, Philip T., and Jean-Laurent Rosenthal. "The Political Economy of Warfare and Taxation in Early Modern Europe: Historical Lessons for Economic Development." In *The Frontiers of the New Institutional Economics*, ed. John N. Drobak and John V. C. Nye, 31–55. San Diego: Academic Press, 1997.

Hofmann, Christina. *Das spanische Hofzeremoniell von 1500–1700*. New York: P. Lang, 1985.

Hohenberg, Paul, and Lynn Hollen Lees. "Urban Decline and Regional Economics: Brabant, Castile and Lombardy, 1550–1750." *Comparative Studies in Society and History* 31, no. 3 (1989): 439–61.

Hontanilla, Ana. "Images of Barbaric Spain in Eighteenth-Century British Travel Writing." *Studies in Eighteenth Century Culture* 37 (2008): 119–43.

Hosmer, James, ed. *Winthrop's Journal "History of New England," 1630–1649*. 2 vols. New York: C. Scribner's Sons, 1908.

Innis, Harold A. *The Cod Fisheries: The History of an International Economy*. Rev. ed. Toronto: University of Toronto Press, 1954.

Irigoin, Maria Alejandra. "The End of a Silver Era: The Consequences of the Breakdown of the Spanish Peso Standard in China and the United States, 1780s–1850s." *Journal of World History* 20, no. 2 (2009): 207–43.

Irigoin, Maria Alejandra, and Regina Grafe. "Bargaining for Absolutism: A Spanish Path to Empire and Nation Building." *Hispanic American Historical Review* 88, no. 2 (2008): 173–210.

———. "Response to Carlos Marichal and William Summerhill." *Hispanic American Historical Review*, no. 2 (2008): 235–45.

Izquierdo Martín, Jesús, et al. "Así en la corte como en el cielo: Patronato y clientilismo en las comunidades conventuales madrileñas (siglos XVI–XVIII)." *Hispania* 59, no. 1 (1999): 149–69.

Jacks, David S., Kevin H. O'Rourke, and Jeffrey G. Williamson. "Commodity Price Volatility and World Markets Integration since 1700." NBER working paper 14748, 2009.

Jones, Eric L. *The European Miracle*. Cambridge: Cambridge University Press, 1981.

———. *Growth Recurring: Economic Change in World History*. 2nd ed. Oxford: Clarendon Press, 1993.

Jones, Evan T. "Illicit Business: Accounting for Smuggling in Mid-Sixteenth-Century Bristol." *Economic History Review* 54, no. 1 (2001): 17–38.

Jovellanos, Gaspar de. *Informe de la Sociedad Económica de esta Corte al Real y Supremo Consejo de Castilla en el expediente de Ley Agraria*. Madrid: En la imprenta de Sancha, 1795.

Juliá, Santos. *Historias de las dos Españas*. Madrid: Taurus, 2004.

Jurado Sánchez, José. *El gasto de la hacienda española durante el siglo XVIII: Cuantía y estructura de los pagos del estado (1703–1800)*. Madrid: Instituto de Estudios Fiscales, 2006.

Kagan, R. L. *Law Suits and Litigants in Castile, 1500–1700*. Chapel Hill: University of North Carolina Press, 1981.

———. "Prescott's Paradigm: American Historical Scholarship and the Decline of Spain." *American Historical Review* 101 (1996): 423–46.

———. "Universities in Castile, 1500–1700." *Past and Present* 49 (1970): 44–71.

Kamen, Henry. "The Decline of Spain: A Historical Myth?" *Past and Present* 81 (1978): 24–50.

———. "The Establishment of the Intendents in Early Bourbon Spain." In *Crisis and Change in Early Modern Spain*, ed. Henry Kamen. Aldershot, England: VARIORUM, Ashgate, 1993.

———. *Imagining Spain: Historical Myth & National Identity*. New Haven: Yale University Press, 2008.

———. "Melchor de Macanaz and the Foundations of Bourbon Power in Spain." *English Historical Review* 80, no. 317 (1965): 699–716.

———. *Spain, 1469–1714: A Society of Conflict*. New York: Longman, 1991.

———. *Spain in the Later Seventeenth Century, 1665–1700*. New York: Longman, 1980.

———. *The War of Succession in Spain, 1700–15*. Bloomington: Indiana University Press, 1969.

Karaman, Kivanc K., and Sevket Pamuk. "Ottoman State Finances in European Perspective, 1500–1914." *Journal of Economic History* 70, no. 3 (2010): 593–629.

Kasper, Michael. *Baskische Geschichte*. Darmstadt: Primus Verlag, 1997.

Klein, Herbert S. *The American Finances of the Spanish Empire: Royal Income and Expenditures in Colonial Mexico, Peru, and Bolivia, 1680–1809*. Albuquerque: University of New Mexico Press, 1998.

Klein, Julius. *The Mesta: A Study in Spanish Economic History, 1273–1836*. Cambridge, MA: Harvard University Press, 1920.

Knack, Steven, and Philip Keefer. "Institutions and Economic Performance: Cross-Country Tests Using Alternative Measures." *Economics and Politics* 7, no. 3 (1995): 207–27.

Kuethe, Allen J., and G. Douglas Inglis. "Absolutism and Enlightened Reform: Charles III, the Establishment of the Alcabala, and Commercial Reorganization in Cuba." *Past and Present* 109 (1985): 118–43.

Kurlansky, Mark. *Cod: A Biography of the Fish That Changed the World*. London: Jonathan Cape, 1998.

Kwass, Michael. "The First War on Drugs: Tobacco Trafficking and the Fiscal State in Eighteenth-Century France." In *The Hidden History of Crime, Corruption and States*. Berghahn Books, forthcoming.

———. *Privilege and the Politics of Taxation in Eighteenth-Century France: Liberté, Égalité, Fiscalité*. New York: Cambridge University Press, 2000.

La Ripia, Juan. *Práctica de la administración y cobranza de las rentas reales*. Madrid, 1769.

Laborde, Alexandre. *Itinerario descriptivo de las provincias de España, y de sus islas*. Madrid: Imprenta de Ildefonso Mompié, 1816.

Lamikiz, Xavier. "Patrones de comercio y flujo de información comercial entre España y América durante en siglo XVIII." *Revista de Historia Económica* 25, no. 2 (2007): 233–60.

Lapeyre, Henri. "Algunos datos sobre el movimiento del puerto de San Sebastián en tiempos de Felipe II." *Boletin de Estudios Históricos sobre San Sebastián* 5 (1971): 181–91.

———. "El arancel de los Diezmos de la Mar de 1564." *Cuadernos de Investigación Histórica* 7 (1983): 55–77.

———. *El comercio exterior de Castilla a través de las aduanas de Felipe II*. Valladolid: Universidad de Valladolid, 1981.

Larraz López, José. *La época del mercantilismo en Castilla (1500–1700)*. Reprint. Madrid: Asociación Española de Historia Moderna, 2000.

las Casas, Bartolomé de. *De regia potestate*. 1566. Bilingual Critical Edition by Luciano Pereña, J. M. Pérez Prendes, Vidal Abril, and Joaquím Azcárraga. Madrid: Consejo Superior de Investigaciones Científicas, 1969.

Lavrín, Asunción. "The Role of Nunneries in the Economy of New Spain in the Eighteenth Century." *Hispanic American Historical Review* 46, no. 4 (1966): 371–93.

Levi, Giovanni. "Reciprocidad mediterránea." *Hispania* 60, no. 204 (2000): 103–26.

Levi, Margaret. *Of Rule and Revenue*. Berkeley: University of California Press, 1988.

Ling, Richard John. "Long-Term Movements in the Trade of Valencia, Alicante and the Western Mediterranean, 1450–1700." Ph.D. diss., University of California at Berkeley, 1974.

Livi-Bacci, Massimo. *Population and Nutrition: An Essay on European Demographic History*. Cambridge: Cambridge University Press, 1991.

Llopis Agelán, Enrique. "Almacenamientos, volatilidad de los precios de los granos y distribución de la renta: Comentarios a la réplica de Bartolomé Yun." *Revista de Historia Económica* 8, no. 1 (1990): 173–85.

———. "España, la 'revolución de los modernistas' y el legado del antiguo régimen." In *El legado económico del antiguo régimen en España*, ed. Enrique Llopis Agelán, 11–76. Barcelona: Crítica, 2004.

Llopis Agelán, Enrique, and Héctor García Montero. "Cost of Living and Wages in Madrid, 1680–1800." Unpublished paper presented at the Seventh Conference of the European Historical Economics Society, Lund, 2007.

Llopis Agelán, Enrique, and Miguel Jerez Méndez. "El mercado de trigo en Castilla y León, 1671–1788: Arbitraje espacial e intervención." *Historia Agraria* 25 (2001): 13–65.

Llopis, Enrique, et al. "Indices de precios de la zona noroccidental de Castilla y León, 1518–1650." *Revista de Historia Económica* 18, no. 3 (2000): 665–84.

Lluch, Ernest. *Las Españas vencidas del siglo XVIII: Claroscuros de la ilustración*. Barcelona: Crítica, 1999.

———. *El pensament econòmic a Catalunya (1760–1840): Els orígens ideológics del proteccionisme i la presa de consciencia de la burgesia catalana*. Barcelona: Ediciones 62, 1973.

Lockhart, James, and Stuart Schwartz. *Early Latin America: A History of Colonial Spanish America and Brazil*. Cambridge: Cambridge University Press, 1983.

López Losa, Ernesto. "Una aproximación al sector pesquero tradicional vasco (c. 1800–c. 1880)." *Historia Agraria* 28 (2002): 13–44.

Lorenzo Sanz, Eufemio. *Comercio de España con América en la época de Felipe II*. Book 1, *Los mercaderes y el tráfico indiano*. Valladolid: Servicio de Publicaciones de la Diputación Provincial de Valladolid, 1979.

Lovett, A. W. "The Vote of the Millones, (1590)." *Historical Journal* 30, no. 1 (1987): 1–20.

Lydon, James G. "Fish and Flour for Gold: Southern Europe and the Colonial American Balance of Payments." *Business History Review* 39, no. 2 (1965): 171–83.

———. "Fish for Gold: The Massachusetts Fish Trade with Iberia, 1700–1773." *New England Quarterly* 54, no. 4 (1981): 539–82.

Lynch, John. *Bourbon Spain, 1700–1808*. History of Spain. New York: B. Blackwell, 1989.

Macanaz, Melchor Rafael. "Noticias particulares para la historia política de España: Diálogo político entre Rutelio y Clautino, calvinistas. 1744." In *Seminario erudito, que comprehende varias obras inéditas, críticas, morales, instructivas, políticas, satíricas, y jocosas mejores autores antiguos, y modernos. Tomo decimotercero*, ed. Antonio Valladares y Sotomayor. Madrid: Don Blas Roman, 1788.

MacKay, Ruth. *"Lazy, Improvident People": Myth and Reality in the Writing of Spanish History*. Ithaca: Cornell University Press, 2006.

——. *The Limits of Royal Authority: Resistance and Obedience in Seventeenth Century Castile*. Cambridge: Cambridge University Press, 1999.

MacLachlan, Colin M. *Spain's Empire in the New World: The Role of Ideas in Institutional and Social Change*. Berkeley: University of California Press, 1988.

Madrazo, Santos. *El sistema de comunicaciones en España, 1750–1850*. Madrid: Colegio de Ingenieros de Caminos, Canales y Puertos; Ediciones Turner, 1984.

Maeztu, Ramiro de. *Hacia otra España*. Madrid: Ediciones Rialp, S.A., 1899.

Magra, Christopher Paul. *The Fisherman's Cause: Atlantic Commerce and Maritime Dimensions of the American Revolution*. New York: Cambridge University Press, 2009.

Mann, J. L. *The Cloth Industry in the West of England from 1640 to 1880*. Oxford: Oxford University Press, 1971.

Mann, Michael. *The Sources of Social Power I: A History of Power from the Beginning to A.D. 1760*. Cambridge: Cambridge University Press, 1986.

Marañón, Gregorio. *Antonio Pérez (El Hombre, El Drama, La Época)*. Buenos Aires: Espasa-Calpe Argentina, 1947.

Maravall, José Antonio. *Teoría del estado en España en el siglo XVII*. Madrid: Centro de Estudios Constitucionales, 1997.

Mariana, Juan de. *De rege et regis institutione*. Toledo, 1598.

Marichal, Carlos. *Bankruptcy of Empire: Mexican Silver and the Wars between Spain, Britain and France, 1760–1810*. Cambridge: Cambridge University Press, 2007.

Marichal, Carlos, and Matilde Souto Mantecón. "Silver and Situados: New Spain and the Financing of the Spanish Empire in the Caribbean in the Eighteenth Century." *Hispanic American Historical Review* 74, no. 4 (1994): 587–613.

Mariluz Urquijo, José María. *Bilbao y Buenos Aires: Proyectos dieciochescos de compañías de comercio*. Buenos Aires: Universidad de Buenos Aires, 1981.

Marrewijk, Charles van. *International Trade and the World Economy*. New York: Oxford University Press, 2002.

Martínez Ruiz, José Ignacio. "Crédito público y deudas municipales en España (siglos XV–XVIII)." In *Dinero, moneda y crédito en la monarquía hispánica*, ed. Antonio-Miguel Bernal Rodriguez, 865–77. Madrid: Marcial Pons, 2000.

——. *Finanzas municipales y crédito público en la españa moderna*. Seville: Ayuntamiento de Sevilla, 1992.

Martínez Shaw, Carlos. *Cataluña en la carrera de Indias, 1680–1756*. Madrid: Alianza, 1981.

Marx, Karl, and Friedrich Engels. *Revolution in Spain*. London: Lawrence and Wishart, 1939.

Mateos Royo, José Antonio. "The Burden of Tradition: Monetary Circulation, Public Policy and Mercantilist Debate in Seventeenth-Century Aragon." In *Money in the Pre-Industrial World. Bullion, Debasements and Coin Substitutes*, ed. John H. Munro. London: Pickering and Chatto, 2012.

Mathias, Peter, and Patrick Karl O'Brien. "Taxation in England and France, 1715–1810." *Journal of European Economic History* 5, no. 3 (1976): 601–50.

Matilla Tascón, Antonio. *La única contribución y el catastro de Ensenada*. Madrid: Ministerio de Hacienda, 1947.

McClellan, James E. *Science Reorganized: Scientific Societies in the Eighteenth Century*. New York: Columbia University Press, 1985.

McCloskey, Deirdre N. *The Bourgeois Virtues: Ethics for an Age of Commerce*. Chicago: University of Chicago Press, 2006.

McCloskey, Donald N. "The Enclosure of Open Fields: Preface to a Study of Its Impact on the Efficiency of English Agriculture in the Eighteenth Century." *Journal of Economic History* 32, no. 1 (1972): 15–35.

McCusker, John J., and Russell R. Menard. *The Economy of British America, 1607–1789*. Chapel Hill: University of North Carolina Press, 1985.

McGuire, Martin, and Mancur Olson. "The Economics of Autocracy and Majority Rule: The Invisible Hand and the Use of Force." *Journal of Economic Literature* 34, no. 1 (1996): 72–96.

McWilliams, James E. "New England's First Depression: Beyond an Export-Led Interpretation." *Journal of Interdisciplinary History* 33, no. 1 (2002): 1–20.

Meijide Pardo, Antonio. *Economía marítima de la Galicia cantábrica en el siglo XVIII*. Valladolid: Universidad de Valladolid, 1971.

———. *El comercio del bacalao en la Galicia del XVIII*. La Coruña: Diputación Provincial de La Coruña, 1980.

Menard, Russell. "Transport Costs and Long-Range Trade, 1300–1800: Was There a European 'Transport Revolution' in the Early Modern Era?" In *Political Economy of Merchant Empires*, ed. J. D. Tracy, 228–75. Cambridge: Cambridge University Press, 1991.

Menéndez y Pelayo, Marcelino. *La ciencia española*. 2 vols. Madrid: Suárez, 1887.

Mercader Riba, Juan. "Un organismo piloto en la monarquia de Felipe V: La superintendencia de Cataluña (Continuación)." *Hispania* 26, no. 104 (1966): 526–78.

Merino Navarro, José Patricio. *Las cuentas de la administración central española, 1750–1820*. Madrid: Instituto de Estudios Fiscales, 1987.

Miguel López, Isabel. *El mundo del comercio en Castilla y León al final del antiguo régimen*. Valladolid: Varios, 2000.

Mintz, Sidney W. *Sweetness and Power: The Place of Sugar in Modern History*. New York: Elisabeth Sifton Books, Viking, 1985.

Mokyr, Joel. *The Enlightened Economy: An Economic History of Britain, 1700–1850*. New Haven: Yale University Press, 2009.

———. *The Gifts of Athena: Historical Origins of the Knowledge Economy*. Princeton: Princeton University Press, 2002.

Molas Ribalta, Pere. *La burguesía mercantil en la España del antiguo régimen*. Madrid: Cátedra, 1985.

Monod, Paul Kléber. *The Power of Kings: Monarchy and Religion in Europe, 1589–1715*. New Haven: Yale University Press, 1999.

Morilla Critz, José. *Introducción al estudio de las fluctuaciones de precios en Malaga (1787–1829)*. Malaga: Instituto de Cultura de la Diputación Provincial de Malaga, Servicio de Publicaciones, 1972.

Motomura, Akira. "The Best and Worst of Currencies: Seigniorage and Currency Policy in Spain, 1597–1650." *Journal of Economic History* 54, no. 1 (1994): 104–27.

Mousnier, Roland. *The Institutions of France under the Absolute Monarchy, 1598–1789*. 2 vols. Chicago: Chicago University Press, 1974.

Mugartegui Eguía, Isabel. *Estado, provincia y municipio: Estructura y coyuntura de las haciendas municipales vascas: Una visión a largo plazo (1580–1900)*. Oñati: Herri Ardularitzaren Euskal Erakundea, Instituto Vasco de Administración Pública, 1993.

———. *Hacienda y fiscalidad en Guipúzcoa durante el antiguo régimen, 1700–1914*. San Sebastián: Fundación Cultural de la Caja de Guipúzcoa, 1990.

Muñoz Pérez, José. "Mapa aduanero del XVIII español." *Estudios Geográficos* 61 (1955): 747–98.

———. "La publicación del reglamento del comercio libre de Indias." *Anuario de Estudios Americanos* 4 (1947): 615–64.

Munro, John H. "Money, Prices, Wages, and 'Profit Inflation' in Spain, the Southern Netherlands, and England during the Price Revolution Era: c. 1520–c. 1650." University of Toronto, working paper no. 320, 2008.

Nadal, Jordi. *El fracaso de la revolución industrial en España, 1814–1913*. Esplugues de Llobregat: Editorial Ariel, 1975.

Nader, Helen. *Liberty in Absolutist Spain: The Habsburg Sale of Towns, 1516–1700*. Baltimore: Johns Hopkins University Press, 1990.

Nater, Laura. "Cuba and Tobacco in the Spanish Empire in the Seventeenth and Eighteenth Century." Working paper 99021, International Seminar on the History of the Atlantic World. Cambridge, MA, 1999.

Navarra. *Cuadernos de las leyes y agravios reparados por los tres estados des reino de Navarra*. Pamplona: [Diputación Foral de Navarra, Institución Príncipe de Viana], 1964.

Nogues-Marco, Pilar. "Bullionism, Specie-Point Mechanism and Bullion Flows in Early 18th Century Europe." Ph.D. diss., Sciences Po, 2010.

North, Douglass. *Institutions, Institutional Change and Economic Performance*. Cambridge: Cambridge University Press, 1990.

———. "Markets and Other Allocative Systems in History: The Challenge of Karl Polanyi." *Journal of European Economic History* 6, no. 3 (1977): 703–16.

———. "Ocean Freight Rates and Economic Development, 1750–1913." *Journal of Economic History* 18, no. 4 (1958): 537–55.

———. "The Role of Transportation in the Economic Development of North America." In *Les grandes voies maritimes dans le monde, XV–XIX siècles*. Paris, 1965.

———. *Structure and Change in Economic History*. New York: Norton, 1981.

North, Douglass C., and Robert P. Thomas. *The Rise of the Western World: A New Economic History*. Cambridge: Cambridge University Press, 1973.

North, Douglass C., and Barry R. Weingast. "Constitutions and Commitment: The

Evolution of Institutions Governing Public Choice in Seventeenth-Century England." *Journal of Economic History* 49, no. 4 (1989): 803–32.

North, Douglass C., Barry R. Weingast, and W. Summerhill. "Order, Disorder and Economic Change: Latin America versus North America." In *Governing for Prosperity*, ed. B. Bueno de Mesquita and H. L. Root. New Haven: Yale University Press, 2000.

Norton, Marcy. *Sacred Gifts, Profane Pleasures: A History of Tobacco and Chocolate in the Atlantic World*. Ithaca: Cornell University Press, 2008.

Nueva recopilación de los fueros, privilegios, buenos usos, y costumbres, leyes, y orden de la muy noble, y muy leal provincia de Guipúzcoa. Tolosa: B. de Ugarte, 1696.

O'Brien, Patrick K. "European Economic Development: The Contribution of the Periphery." *Economic History Review* 35, no. 1 (1982): 1–18.

———. "The Nature and Historical Evolution of an Exceptional Fiscal State and Its Possible Significance for the Precocious Commercialization and Industrialization of the British Economy from Cromwell to Nelson." *The Economic History Review* 64, no. 2 (2010): 408–446.

———. "The Political Economy of British Taxation, 1660–1815." *Economic History Review*, 41, no. 1 (1988): 1–32.

———. "Taxation for British Mercantilism from the Treaty of Utrecht (1713) to the Peace of Paris (1783)." In *War, State and Development: Fiscal-Military States in the Eighteenth Century*, ed. Rafael Torres Sánchez, 295–355. Pamplona: EUNSA, 2007.

O'Brien, P. K., and P. A. Hunt. "The Rise of the Fiscal State in England, 1485–1815." *Historical Research* 46 (1993): 129–76.

O'Flanagan, Patrick. *Port Cities of Atlantic Iberia, c. 1500–1900*. Aldershot: Ashgate, 2008.

O'Rourke, Kevin H. "The Worldwide Economic Impact of the Revolutionary and Napoleonic Wars." *Journal of Global History* 1 (2006): 123–49.

O'Rourke, Kevin H., and Jeffrey G. Williamson. "Did Vasco Da Gama Matter for European Markets? Testing Frederick Lane's Hypotheses Fifty Years Later." NBER working paper 11884, 2005.

———. *Globalization and History: The Evolution of a Nineteenth-Century Atlantic Economy*. Cambridge, MA: MIT Press, 1999.

———. "Once More: When Did Glob-alisation Begin." *European Review of Economic History* 8, no. 1 (2004): 109–17.

———. "When Did Globalisation Begin?" *European Review of Economic History* 6, no. 1 (2002): 23–50.

Ogilvie, Sheilagh C. "Rehabilitating the Guilds: A Reply." *Economic History Review* 61, no. 1 (2008): 175–82.

Oliva Melgar, José María. *Cataluña y el comercio privilegiado con América: La real compañia de comercio de Barcelona a Indias*. Barcelona: Publ. de la Universitat de Barcelona, 1987.

———. *El monopolio de Indias en el siglo XVII y la economía andaluza: La oportunidad que nunca existió*. Huelva: Servicio de Publicaciones de la Universidad de Huelva, 2004.

Olmeida y León, Joseph de. *Elementos del derecho público de la paz, y de la guerra*. Madrid: Oficina de la viuda de Manuel Fernández, 1771.

Onaindía, Mario. *La construcción de la nación española: Republicanismo y nacionalismo en la ilustración*. Barcelona: Ediciones B Grupo Zeta, 2002.

Ortega y Gasset, José. *España invertebrada: Bosquejo de algunos pensamientos históricos*. 3rd ed. Madrid: Calpe, 1922.

———. *La redención de las provincias y la decencia nacional: Artículos de 1927 y 1930*. Madrid: Revista de Occidente, 1931.

Osterhammel, Jürgen. *Geschichte der Globalisierung: Dimensionen, Prozesse, Epochen*. Munich: C. H. Beck, 2003.

Otazu, Alfonso. *El igualitarismo vasco: Mito y realidad*. [San Sebastián]: Editorial Txertoa, 1973.

Overton, Mark. *Agricultural Revolution in England: The Transformation of the Agrarian Economy, 1500–1850*. Cambridge: Cambridge University Press, 1996.

Palacio Atard, Vicente. *El comercio de Castilla y el puerto de Santander en el siglo XVIII: Notas para su estudio*. Madrid: Consejo Superior de Investigaciones Científicas, Escuela de Historia Moderna, 1960.

Palop Ramos, José-Miguel. *Fluctuaciones de precios y abastecimiento en la Valencia del siglo XVIII*. Valencia: Instituto Valenciano de Estudios Históricos, 1977.

———. *Hambre y lucha antifeudal: Las crisis de subsistencias en Valencia (siglo XVIII)*. Madrid: Siglo Veintiuno Editores, 1977.

Paquette, Gabriel B. *Enlightenment, Governance, and Reform in Spain and Its Empire, 1759–1808*. New York: Palgrave Macmillan, 2008.

Parker, Geoffrey. *The Military Revolution: Military Innovation and the Rise of the West, 1500–1800*. Cambridge: Cambridge University Press, 1988.

Peiró Arroyo, Antonio. *Jornaleros y mancebos: Identidad, organización y conflicto en los trabajadores del antiguo régimen*. Madrid: Crítica, 2002.

Pérez Moreda, Vicente. "El legado demográfico del antiguo régimen." In *El legado económico del antiguo régimen en España*, ed. Enrique Llopis, 121–46. Barcelona: Crítica, 2004.

Persson, Karl Gunnar. *Grain Markets in Europe, 1500–1900: Integration and Deregulation*. Cambridge: Cambridge University Press, 1999.

Phelan, John Leddy. "Authority and Flexibility in the Spanish Imperial Bureaucracy." *Administrative Science Quarterly* 5, no. 1 (1960): 47–65.

———. *The Hispanization of the Philippines: Spanish Aims and Filipino Responses, 1565–1700*. Madison: University of Wisconsin Press, 1959.

Phillips, Carla Rahn, and William D. Phillips, Jr. *Spain's Golden Fleece: Wool Production and the Wool Trade from the Middle Ages to the Nineteenth Century*. Baltimore: Johns Hopkins University Press, 1997.

Pieper, Renate. *Die Preisrevolution in Spanien (1500–1640): Neuere Forschungsergebnisse*. Wiesbaden: Franz Steiner, 1985.

Pitkin, Timothy. *A Statistical View of the Commerce of the United States of America: Including also an Account of Banks, Manufacturers and Internal Trade and Improvements*. New Haven, 1835.

Plaza Prieto, Juan. *Estructura económica de españa en el siglo XVIII*. Madrid: Confederación Española de Cajas de Ahorros, 1976.

Polanyi, Karl. *The Great Transformation: The Political and Economic Origins of Our Times*. 1944. Boston: Beacon Press, 2001.

Pomeranz, Kenneth. *The Great Divergence: China, Europe and the Making of the Modern World Economy*. Princeton: Princeton University Press, 2000.

Pope, Peter Edward. "Adventures in the Sack Trade: London Merchants in the Canada and Newfoundland Trades, 1627–1648." *Northern Mariner* 6 (1996): 1–19.

———. *Fish into Wine: The Newfoundland Plantation in the Seventeenth Century*. Chapel Hill: University of North Carolina Press, 2004.

Porres, Rosario. "De la hermandad a la provincia (siglos XVI–XVIII)." In *Historia de Alava*, ed. Antonio Rivera, 185–306. San Sebastián: Nerea, 2003.

Portillo Valdés, José María. *Crisis atlántica: Autonomía y independencia en la crisis de la monarquía hispánica*. Madrid: Marcial Pons, 2006.

———. *Monarquia y gobierno provincial: Poder y constitución en las provincias vascas (1760–1808)*. Madrid: Centro de Estudios Constitucionales, 1991.

Posthumus, N. W. *Nederlandsche Prijsgeschiedenis*. Leiden: E. J. Brill, 1943.

Pozas Poveda, Lázaro. *Ciudades castellanas y monarquía hispánica: La aportación municipal al gasto del estado*. Cordoba: Servicio de Publicaciones, Universidad de Córdoba, 2001.

Prados de la Escosura, Leandro. *De imperio a nación: Crecimiento y atraso económico en España (1780–1930)*. Madrid: Alianza Editorial, 1988.

Preston, Paul, and Denis Smyth. *Spain, the EEC and NATO*. Boston: Routledge and Kegan Paul, 1984.

Pribram, Alfred Francis, Rudolf Geyer, and Franz Koran. *Materialien zur Geschichte der Preise und Löhne in Österreich*. Vienna: Carl Überreuters Verlag, 1938.

Priotti, Jean-Philippe. *Bilbao y sus mercaderes en el siglo XVI: Génesis de un crecimiento*. Bilbao: Bizkaiko Foru Aldundia, 2005.

Pulido Bueno, Ildefonso. *Consumo y fiscalidad en el reino de Sevilla: El servicio de millones en el siglo XVII*. Seville: Excma. Diputación Provincial de Sevilla, 1984.

Quevedo Villegas, Francisco de. *Obras de Don Francisco de Quevedo Villegas*. A. de Sancha, 1791.

Quijada, Mónica. "El pueblo como actor histórico: Algunas reflexiones sobre el municipalismo y soberanía en los procesos políticos hispánicos." In *El lenguaje de los "ismos": Vocablos vertebradores de la modernidad*, ed. Marta Casaús Arzú. Guatemala: SIC Editores, 2009.

———. "From Spain to New Spain: Revisiting the *Potestas Populi* in Hispanic Political Thought." *Mexican Studies/Estudios Mexicanos* 24, no. 2 (2008): 185–219.

Quiroz, Alfonso W. "Reassessing the Role of Credit in Late Colonial Peru: Censos, Escrituras, and Imposiciones." *Hispanic American Historical Review* 74, no. 2 (1994): 193–230.

Ramos Palencia, Fernando Carlos. "Pautas de consumo familiar y mercado en la Castilla preindustrial: El consumo de bienes duraderos y semi-duraderos en Palencia, 1750–1850." Ph.D. diss., Valladolid, 2001.

Reher, David S. "Producción, precios e integración de los mercados regionales de grano en la España moderna." *Revista de Historia Económica* 19, no. 3 (2001): 539–72.

Reher, David S., and Esmeralda Ballesteros. "Precios y salarios en Castilla la Nueva: La construcción de un índice de salarios reales, 1501–1991." *Revista de Historia Económica* 11, no. 1 (1993): 101–51.

Reinhard, Wolfgang. *Geschichte der Staatsgewalt: Eine vergleichende Verfassungsgeschichte Europas von den Anfängen bis zur Gegenwart.* Munich: Beck, 1999.

Richards, John. *The Unending Frontier: An Environmental History of the Early Modern World.* Berkeley: University of California Press, 2003.

Riley, James C. *International Government Finance and the Amsterdam Capital Market, 1740–1815.* Cambridge: Cambridge University Press, 1980.

Ringrose, David R. "El desarrollo urbano y la decadencia española." *Revista de Historia Económica* 1, no. 1 (1983): 37–57.

———. "The Government and the Carters in Spain, 1476–1700." *Economic History Review* 22 (1969): 45–57.

———. *Madrid and the Spanish Economy, 1560–1850.* Berkeley: University of California Press, 1983.

———. *Spain, Europe, and the "Spanish Miracle," 1700–1900.* New York: Cambridge University Press, 1996.

———. *Transportation and Economic Stagnation in Spain, 1750–1850.* Durham, NC: Duke University Press, 1970.

Rivera Medina, Ana Maria. *La burguesía bilbaína y el comercio colonial.* Unpublished typescript. Bilbao: BBV Comisión "América y los vascos," proyecto I–27, n.d.

Roberts, Michael. *The Military Revolution, 1560–1660: An Inaugural Lecture Delivered before the Queen's University of Belfast.* Belfast: M. Boyd, 1956.

Rodríguez-Salgado, M. J. *The Changing Face of Empire.* Cambridge: Cambridge University Press, 1988.

———. "The Spanish Story of the 1588 Armada Reassessed." *Historical Journal* 33, no. 2 (1990): 461–78.

Rodriguez O, Jaime. "The Origins of Constitutionalism and Liberalism in Mexico." In *The Divine Charter, Constitutionalism and Liberalism in Nineteenth Century Mexico,* ed. Jaime Rodriguez O. Los Angeles: Rowman and Littlefield, 2003.

Rodrik, Dani, Arvind Subramanian, and Francesco Trebbi. "Institutions Rule: The Primacy of Institutions over Geography and Integration in Economic Development." *Journal of Economic Growth* 9, no. 2 (2004): 131–65.

Root, Hilton L. "The Redistributive Role of Government: Economic Regulation in Old Regime France and England." *Comparative Studies in Society and History* 33 (1991): 338–69.

Rosenthal, Jean-Laurent. "The Development of Irrigation in Provence, 1700–1860: The French Revolution and Economic Growth." *Journal of Economic History* 50, no. 3 (1990): 615–38.

———. "The Political Economy of Absolutism Reconsidered." In *Analytic Narratives,* ed. Robert Bates, 64–108. Princeton: Princeton University Press, 1998.

Rosés, Joan R., and Blanca Sánchez-Alonso. "Regional Wage Convergence in Spain, 1850–1930." *Explorations in Economic History* 41, no. 4 (2004): 404–25.

Rowen, Herbert H. *The King's State: Proprietary Dynasticism in Early Modern France*. New Brunswick, NJ: Rutgers University Press, 1980.

Rubio Pérez, Laureano M. *Arrieros maragatos: Poder, negocio, linaje y familia*. [La Robla]: Fundación Hullera Vasco-Leonesa, 1995.

Ruiz Ibáñez, José, and Vicente Montojo Montojo. *Entre el lucro y la defensa: Las relaciones entre la monarquía y la sociedad mercantil cartagena (Comerciantes y Corsarios en el siglo XVII)*. [Murcia]: Real Academia Alfonso X el Sabio, 1998.

Ruiz Martín, Felipe. "Credito y banca, comercio y transportes en la etapa del capitalismo mercantil." In *Actas de las I Jornadas de Metodología Aplicada a Las Ciencias Históricas 1973*, 726–49. Santiago de Compostela: Universidade de Santiago de Compostela, Servicio de Publicaciones, 1975.

Ruiz Martín, Felipe, and Angel García Sanz, eds. *Mesta, trashumancia y lana en la España moderna*. Barcelona: Crítica, 1998.

Ruíz Trapero, María. "La reforma monetaria de Felipe V: Su Importancia Histórica." Mimeo, n.d.

Sahlins, Peter. *Boundaries: The Making of France and Spain in the Pyrenees*. Berkeley: University of California Press, 1989.

Salvio, Alfonso de. "Voltaire and Spain." *Hispania* 7, no. 3 (1924): 157–64.

Sánchez-Albornoz, Claudio. *Despoblación y repoblación del valle del Duero*. Buenos Aires: Instituto de Historia de España, 1966.

Sánchez Belén, Juan A. *La política fiscal en Castilla durante el reinado de Carlos II*. Madrid: Siglo Veintiuno Editores, 1996.

Sánchez León, Pablo. *Absolutismo y comunidad: Los orígenes sociales de la guerra de los comuneros de Castilla*. Madrid: Siglo XXI Editores, 1998.

Sañez Reguart, Antonio. *Diccionario histórico de los artes de la pesca nacional*. 5 vols. Madrid: Impr. de la viuda de Don J. Ibarra, 1791.

Sardá, Juan. *La política monetaria y la fluctuaciones de la economía española en el siglo XIX*. Madrid: CSIC, Instituto de Economía "Sancho de Moncada," 1998.

Sargent, Thomas J., and Francois R Velde. *The Big Problem of Small Change*. Princeton: Princeton University Press, 2002.

Sarrailh, Jean. *La España ilustrada de la segunda mitad del siglo XVIII*. Trans. Antonio Alatorre. Mexico D.F.: Fondo de Cultura Económica, 1979.

Scheel, Fredrik. *Østersjøfart, 1825–1850: Den Norske Sjøfarts Historie*. Oslo: Det Steenske forlag, 1935.

Schofield, R. S. "Taxation and the Political Limits of the Tudor State." In *Law and Government under the Tudors*, ed. C. Cross, D. Loades, and J. J. Scarisbrick, 227–55. Cambridge: Cambridge University Press, 1988.

Scholz, Johannes-Michael. "Amt als Belohnung: Eine spanische Justizkarriere am Ende des Ancien Régime." *Ius Commune: Zeitschrift für Europäische Rechtsgeschichte* 18 (1991): 51–147.

Scott, Hamish M. "'Acts of Time and Power': The Consolidation of Aristocracy in Seventeenth-Century Europe, c. 1580–1720." *German Historical Institute London Bulletin* 30, no. 2 (2008): 3–37.

Sempere y Guarinos, Juan. *Historia del luxo, y de las leyes suntuarias de España*. Madrid: Imprenta Real, 1788.

Serrano Mangas, Fernando. *Vellón y metales preciosos en la corte del rey de España*. Madrid: Banco de España, 1996.

Shepherd, James F., and Gary M. Walton. *Shipping, Maritime Trade, and the Development of Colonial North America*. Cambridge: Cambridge University Press, 1972.

Simpson, James. *Spanish Agriculture: The Long Siesta, 1765–1965*. Cambridge: Cambridge University Press, 1995.

———. "Technological Change, Labour Absorption and Living Standards in Rural Andalucía, 1886–1936." *Agricultural History* 66, no. 3 (1992): 1–24.

Skinner, Quentin. *The Foundations of Modern Political Thought*. 2 vols. Cambridge: Cambridge University Press, 1978.

Smith, Adam. *An Inquiry into the Nature and Causes of the Wealth of Nations*. Reprint. London J. M. Dent and Sons, 1910.

Smith, Robert Sidney. *The Spanish Guild Merchant: A History of the Consulado, 1250–1700*. Durham, NC: Duke University Press, 1940.

Sola Corbacho, Juan Carlos. "Capital y negocios: El comercio agremiado de Madrid a finales del siglo XVIII." *Hispania: Revista española de historia* 60, no. 204 (2000): 225–53.

———. "Madrid y México ante la independencia: Definición y significación de dos centros de poder en vísperas de la descomposición del imperio español." Ph.D. diss., Universidad Complutense de Madrid 1995.

———. "El mercado de crédito en Madrid (1750–1808)." In *Capitalismo Mercantil en la España del siglo XVIII*, ed. Rafael Torres Sánchez, 211–45. Pamplona: EUNSA, 2000.

Solbes Ferri, Sergio. "El proceso de reforma administrativa de la renta del tabaco en Navarra durante el siglo XVIII." *Vegueta* 5 (2000): 193–205.

———. *Rentas Reales de Navarra: Proyectos reformistas y evolución económica (1701–1765)*. Pamplona: Gobierno de Navarra, 1999.

Soranzo, Giovanni. "Ia-Relazione di Spagna di Giovanni Soranzo, 1565." In *Relazioni degli Ambazciatore Veneti al Senato*, ed. Eugenio Albéri. Florence, 1861.

Stasavage, David. *Public Debt and the Birth of the Democratic State*. Cambridge: Cambridge University Press, 2003.

———. *States of Credit: Size, Power, and the Development of European Polities*. Princeton: Princeton University Press, 2011.

Stein, Barbara H., and Stanley J. Stein. *Edge of Crisis: War and Trade in the Spanish Atlantic, 1789–1808*. Baltimore: Johns Hopkins University Press, 2009.

Stein, Stanley J., and Barbara H. Stein. *The Colonial Heritage of Latin America: Essays on Economic Dependence in Perspective*. New York: Oxford University Press, 1970.

———. *Silver, Trade, and War: Spain and America in the Making of Early Modern Europe*. Baltimore: Johns Hopkins University Press, 2000.

Storrs, Christopher, ed. *The Fiscal Military State in the Eighteenth Century*. London: Ashgate, 2009.

———. *The Resilience of the Spanish Monarchy, 1665–1700*. Oxford: Oxford University Press, 2006.

Supple, Barry E. *Commercial Crisis and Change, 1600–1642: A Study in the Instability of a Commercial Economy*. Cambridge: Cambridge University Press, 1959.

Sureda Carrión, José Luis. *La hacienda castellana y los economistas del siglo XVII*. Madrid: Instituto de Economía "Sancho de Moncada," 1949.

Sussman, Nathan, and Yishay Yafeh. "Institutional Reform, Financial Development and Sovereign Debt: Britain 1690–1790." *Journal of Economic History* 66, no. 5 (2006): 906–35.

Swinburne, Henry. *Travels through Spain, 1775–76*. London, 1779.

Tedde de Lorca, Pedro. "El banco de San Carlos y la real hacienda (1794–1828)." In *Estudios de Hacienda: De Ensenada a Mon*, ed. Miguel Artola and L. M. Bilbao Bilbao, 509–28. Madrid: Instituto de Estudios Fiscales, 1984.

Temin, Peter, and Hans-Joachim Voth. "Credit Rationing and Crowding Out during the Industrial Revolution: Evidence from Hoare's Bank, 1702–1862." *Explorations in Economic History* 42, no. 3 (2005): 325–48.

Terreros y Pando, Esteban de. *Diccionario castellano con las voces de ciencias y artes y sus correspondientes en las tres lenguas, francesa, latina é italiana*. 4 vols. Madrid: Viuda de Ibarra, Hijos y Compania, Don Benito Cano, 1786–93.

Thomas, W. *In de Klauwen van de Inquisitie: Europese Protestanten in Spanje, 1517–1648*. Amsterdam: Amsterdam University Press, 2003.

Thompson, E. P. *The Making of the English Working Class*. Harmondsworth: Penguin, 1968.

Thompson, I.A.A. "Absolutism in Castile." In *Absolutism in Seventeenth-Century Europe*, ed. J. Miller, 69–98. Basingstoke: Macmillan, 1990.

———. "Castile: Absolutism." In *Fiscal Crises, Liberty and Representative Government, 1450–1789*, ed. Philip T. Hoffman and Kathryn Norberg, 181–225. Stanford: Stanford University Press, 1994.

———. "Castile: Polity, Fiscality, and Fiscal Crisis." In *Fiscal Crises, Liberty, and Representative Government, 1450–1789*, ed. Philip T. Hoffman and Kathryn Norberg, 140–80. Stanford: Stanford University Press, 1994.

———. "Crown and Cortes in Castile, 1590–1665." *Parliaments, Estates and Representation* 2, no. 1 (1982): 29–45.

———. *War and Government in Habsburg Spain, 1560–1620*. London: Athlone Press, 1976.

Tilly, Charles. *Coercion, Capital and European States, A.D. 990–1990*. Cambridge: Blackwell, 1990.

———. *The Formation of National States in Western Europe*. Princeton: Princeton University Press, 1975.

Toboso Sanchez, Pilar. *La deuda pública castellana durante el antiguo régimen (juros)*. Madrid: Instituto de Estudios Fiscales, 1987.

Tomás y Valiente, Francisco. *Gobierno e instituciones en la España del antiguo régimen*. Madrid: Alianza Universidad, 1982.

———. "Las ventas de oficios de regidores y la formación de oligarquías urbanas en Castilla (siglos XVII y XVIII)." In *actas de las I jornadas de metodología aplicada a las ciencias históricas 1973*, 551–68. Santiago de Compostela: Universidade de Santiago de Compostela, Servicio de Publicaciones, 1975.

Tone, John Lawrence. *The Fatal Knot: The Guerrilla War in Navarre and the Defeat of Napoleon in Spain*. Chapel Hill: University of North Carolina Press, 1994.

Topik, Steven, Carlos Marichal, and Zephyr L. Frank. *From Silver to Cocaine: Latin American Commodity Chains and the Building of the World Economy, 1500–2000*. Durham, NC: Duke University Press, 2006.

Torquemanda Sánchez, María Jesús. "Los puertos secos de Navarra y País Vasco: Su influencia en la problemática foral." *Revista de la Facultad de Derecho de la Universidad Complutense* 75 (1989–90): 1001–64.

Torras, Jaume. "The Old and the New: Marketing Networks and Textile Growth in Eighteenth-Century Spain." In *Markets and Manufacture in Early Industrial Europe*, ed. Maxine Berg, 93–113. New York: Routledge, 1991.

Torres Sánchez, Rafael. "The Failure of the Spanish Crown's Tobacco Tax Monopoly in Catalonia during the XVIIIth Century." *Journal of European Economic History* 35, no. 1 (2006): 721–60.

———. "Possibilities and Limits: Testing the Fiscal Military State in the Anglo-Spanish War of 1779–1783." In *War, State and Development: Fiscal-Military States in the Eighteenth Century*, ed. Rafael Torres Sànchez, 437–60. Pamplona: EUNSA, 2007.

———. "The Triumph of the Fiscal-Military State in the Eighteenth Century: War and Mercantilism." In *War, State and Development: Fiscal-Military States in the Eighteenth Century*, ed. Rafael Torres Sánchez, 13–44. Pamplona: EUNSA, 2007.

Tracy, James D. *Emperor Charles V, Impresario of War: Campaign Strategy, International Finance, and Domestic Politics*. Cambridge: Cambridge University Press, 2002.

———. *Holland under Habsburg Rule, 1506–1566: The Formation of a Body Politic*. Berkeley: University of California Press, 1990.

A Trip to Spain: Or, a True Description of the Comical Humours, Ridiculous Customs, and Foolish Laws of That Lazy Improvident People the Spaniards. In a Letter to a Person of Quality from an Officer in the Royal Navy. London, 1704.

Uebele, Martin. "National and International Market Integration in the 19th Century: Evidence from Comovement." *Explorations in Economic History* 48, no. 2 (2011): 226–42.

Ulloa, Bernardo de. *Restablicimiento de las fábricas, tráfico y comercio marítimo de España*. Madrid, 1740.

Uztáriz, Gerónimo de. *Theorica y práctica de comercio y marina*. 2nd ed. Madrid, 1757.

Valladares, Rafael. *Felipe IV y la restauración de Portugal*. Malaga: Editorial Algazara, 1994.

Vázquez de Menchaca, Fernando. *Controversiarum illustrum usuque frequentium*. Venice: Imprenta de Francisco Rampaceto, 1564.

Velasco Hernández, Francisco. *Auge y estancamiento de un enclave mercantil en la periferia: El nuevo resurgir de Cartagena entre 1540 y 1676*. Cartagena: Excmo. Ayuntamiento de Cartagena, 2001.

Velde, Francois, and David R. Weir. "The Financial Market and Government Debt Policy in France, 1746–1793." *Journal of Economic History* 52, no. 1 (1992): 1–39.

Verbedel, Valero. *El contador moderno, ó, sea practica moderna de contadores en el modo de conocer los generos, diferencias, y extracciones de la cantidad reditu-able, segun el sentido de sus contratos.* Madrid: A. Sanz, 1734.

Vermeesch, Griet. *Oorlog, Steden en Staatsvorming: De Grenssteden Gorinchem en Doesburg tijdens de geboorte-eeuw van de Republiek (1570–1680).* Amsterdam: Amsterdam University Press, 2006.

Vicens Vives, Jaime (with Jorge Nadal Oller). *An Economic History of Spain.* Trans. Frances M. Lopez-Morillas. 3rd ed. Princeton: Princeton University Press, 1969.

Vickers, Daniel. *Farmers & Fishermen: Two Centuries of Work in Essex County, Massachusetts, 1630–1850.* Chapel Hill: University of North Carolina Press, 1994.

———. "'a Knowen and Staple Commoditie': Codfish Prices in Essex County, Massachusetts, 1640–1775." Essex Institute, *Historical Collections* 124 (1988): 186–203.

Vilar, Pierre. *Cataluña en la España moderna: Investigaciones sobre los fundamentos económicos de las estructuras nacionales.* 3rd ed. Barcelona: Editorial Crítica, 1987.

———. *Crecimiento y desarrollo.* 2nd ed. Barcelona: Ariel, 1974.

———. *Oro y moneda en la historia.* Barcelona: Ariel, 1969.

Voltaire. *Oeuvres complètes.* Ed. Louis Moland. Paris: Garnier, 1883.

Voth, Hans-Joachim. "The Longest Years: New Estimates of Labor Input in England, 1760–1830." *Journal of Economic History* 61, no. 4 (2001): 1065–82.

———. "Physical Exertion and Stature in the Habsburg Monarchy, 1730–1800." *Journal of Interdisciplinary History* 27, no. 2 (1996): 263–75.

Wadsworth, James. *The European Mercury: Describing the Highwayes and Stages from Place to Place, through the Most Remarkable Parts of Christendome. With a Catalogue of the Principall Fairs, Marts, and Markets, Thorowout the Same. By J.W. Gent. Usefull for All Gentlemen, Who Delight in Seeing Forraign Countries; and Instructing Merchants Where to Meet with Their Conveniences for Trade.* London: Printed by John Raworth for H. Twyford, 1641.

Ward, Bernardo. *Proyecto económico: Edición y estudio preliminar por Juan Luis Castellano Castellano.* 1777. Madrid: Instituto de Estudios Fiscales, 1982.

Wattley Ames, Helen. *Spain Is Different.* Yarmouth, ME: Intercultural Press, 1992.

Weber, Max. *Wirtschaft und Gesellschaft, Grundriss der Socialökonomik; III. Abt.* Tübingen: J.C.B. Mohr (P. Siebeck), 1922.

Weir, David R. "Tontines, Public Finances and Revolution in France and England, 1688–1789." *Journal of Economic History* 49, no. 1 (1989): 85–124.

White, Eugene. "Was There a Solution to the Ancien Regime's Financial Dilemma." *Journal of Economic History* 49, no. 3 (1989): 545–68.

Wilson, Charles. "Treasury and Trade Balances: The Mercantilist Problem." *Economic History Review* (1949): 152–61.

Windler, Christian. *Lokale Eliten, seigneurialer Adel und Reformabsolutismus in Spanien (1760–1808): Das Beispiel Niederandalusien.* Stuttgart: F. Steiner, 1992.

Winkelbauer, Thomas. *Ständefreiheit und Fürstenmacht: Länder und Untertanen des Hauses Habsburg im Konfessionellen Zeitalter.* 2 vols. Vienna: Überreuter, 2003.

Wrigley, Edward Anthony. "A Simple Model of London's Importance in Changing English Society and Economy, 1650–1750." *Past and Present* 37 (1967): 44–70.

Yanguas y Miranda, José. *Diccionario de antigüedades del reino de Navarra.* Vol. 2. Pamplona: Imprenta de Francisco Erasun, 1840.

Yun Casalilla, Bartolomé. "The American Empire and the Spanish Economy: An Institutional and Regional Perspective." *Revista de Historia Económica* 16, no. 1 (1998): 123–57.

———. *Marte Contra Minerva: El precio del imperio español, c. 1450–1600.* Barcelona: Crítica, 2004.

———. "De Molinos a Gigantes (a propósito de los comentarios de E. Llopis a Sobre La Transición al Capitalismo en Castilla: Economia y Sociedad en la Tierra De Campos, 1580–1830)." *Revista de Historia Económica* 7, no. 2 (1989): 461–77.

———. *Sobre la transición al capitalismo en Castilla: Economía y sociedad en Tierra de Campos (1500–1830).* Valladolid: Junta de Castilla y León, Consejería de Educación y Cultura, 1987.

Yun Casalilla, Bartolomé, and Francisco Comín. "Spain: From a Composite Monarchy to a National State, 1500–1900." Forthcoming.

Yun Casalilla, Bartolomé, and Jaume Torras Elias, eds. *Consumo, condiciones de vida y comercialización: Cataluña y Castilla siglos XVII–XIX.* Madrid: Marcial Pons, 1999.

Zabala Uriarte, Aingeru. *Mundo urbano y actividad mercantil: Bilbao, 1700–1810.* Bilbao: Bilbao Bizkaia Kutxa, 1994.

Zabala y Auñon, Miguel de, and Martin de Loynaz. *Miscelanea economico-politica, ó, discursos varios sobre el modo de aliviar los vasallos con aumento del real erario.* Madrid: En la imprenta y libreria de A. Ulloa, 1787.

Index

THE PRINCETON ECONOMIC HISTORY
OF THE WESTERN WORLD

Joel Mokyr, Series Editor

Unsettled Account: The Evolution of Banking in the Industrialized World since 1800,
by Richard S. Grossman

States of Credit: Size, Power, and the Development of European Polities,
by David Stasavage

Creating Wine: The Emergence of a World Industry, 1840–1914,
by James Simpson

The Evolution of a Nation: How Geography and Law Shaped the American States,
by Daniel Berkowitz and Karen B. Clay

Distant Tyranny: Markets, Power, and Backwardness in Spain, 1650–1800,
by Regina Grafe